Sport in the city

Sport has become a major industry as well as a major cultural preoccupation in the contemporary world. Cities are increasingly using major sporting events and activities to re-image themselves, promote urban development and fund economic growth and regeneration.

Including international case studies from the Sydney Olympics to urban school sports, this book looks closely at how sport has been used in contemporary cities across the world, and evaluates policies, strategies and management. Key areas examined are:

- sport and urban economic regeneration
- sports events bidding
- planning and organisation
- urban sports tourism
- sport and urban community development
- urban politics and sports policy.

Sport in the City is an invaluable guide to the political, cultural and economic role of sport and represents an essential resource for urban policy makers and the sports policy community. It will also be invaluable reading for sports studies students and urban geographers.

Chris Gratton is a Director of the Leisure Industries Research Centre at Sheffield Hallam University. **Ian Henry** is a Director of the Institute of Sport and Leisure Policy at Loughborough University.

Sport in the city

The role of sport in economic and
social regeneration

**Edited by Chris Gratton and
Ian Henry**

Routledge
Taylor & Francis Group

LONDON AND NEW YORK

First published 2001
by Routledge
2 Park Square, Milton Park, Abingdon, Oxfordshire OX14 4RN

Simultaneously published in the USA and Canada
by Routledge
711 Third Avenue, New York, NY 10017

First issued in hardback 2016

Routledge is an imprint of the Taylor and Francis Group, an informa business

© 2001 Chris Gratton and Ian Henry

Typeset in Times by
HWA Text and Data Management, Tunbridge Wells

British Library Cataloguing in Publication Data
A catalogue record for this book is available from the British Library

Library of Congress Cataloging in Publication Data
Sport in the city : the role of sport in economic and social regeneration /
edited by Chris Gratton and Ian P. Henry.
    p. cm.
  Includes bibliographical references and index.
    1. Sports–Economic aspects. 2. Sports–Social aspects.
  3. Community development, Urban. 4. Urban renewal.
  I. Gratton, Chris, 1948– II. Henry, Ian P., 1951–

GV706.8 .S6585 2001
796–dc21   00-047053

ISBN 13: 978-1-138-14396-8 (hbk)
ISBN 13: 978-0-415-24349-0 (pbk)

Contents

Tables

Figures

Contributors

Jenny Anderson, Southampton Institute, East Park Terrace, Southampton, SO14 0YN

Peter Bramham, School of Leisure and Sports Studies, Leeds Metropolitan University, Beckett Park, Leeds, LS6 3QS

John L. Crompton, Department of Recreation, Park, and Tourism Sciences, Texas A&M University, Room 106, Francis Hall, College Station, Texas, 77843-2261, USA

Nigel Dobson, UK Sports Council, 40 Bernard Street, London, WC1N 1BR

Chris Edwards, Southampton Institute, East Park Terrace, Southampton, SO14 0YN

P. R. Emery, University of Northumbria at Newcastle, Division of Sport & Recreation Wynne-Jones Centre, Newcastle Upon Tyne, NE1 8ST

Chris Gratton, Leisure Industries Research Centre, Sheffield Hallam University, Unit 1, Sheffield Science Park, Howard Street, Sheffield, S1 2LX

C. Michael Hall, Tourism and Services Management, Faculty of Commerce and Administration, Victoria University of Wellington, PO Box 600, Wellington, New Zealand

Ian Henry, Institute of Sport and Leisure Policy, Dept. of Physical Education, Sports Science and Recreation Management, Loughborough University, Loughborough, LE11 3TU

Lynley Ingerson, Deakin University, Faculty of Business and Law, Burwood Campus, 221 Burwood Highway, Burwood Victoria, 3125 Australia

Sam Johnstone, Department of Economic and Social History, University of Liverpool, 11 Abercromby Square, Liverpool, L69 3BX

Paul De Knop, Free University of Brussels (VUB), Faculty of Physical Education and Kinestherapy, Pleinlaan 2 (L405), B-1050 Brussels, Belgium

Jonathan Long, School of Leisure and Sports Studies, Leeds Metropolitan University, Beckett Park, Leeds, LS6 3QS

Nicola Matthews, Cheltenham and Gloucester College of Higher Education, GL50 4AZ

Rex Nash, Department of Economic and Social History, University of Liverpool, 11 Abercromby Square, Liverpool, L69 3BX

Ian Sanderson, School of Leisure and Sports Studies, Leeds Metropolitan University, Beckett Park, Leeds, LS6 3QS

Kimberly S. Schimmel, School of Exercise, Leisure and Sport, Kent State University, 263 Macc Annex, Kent, OH-44242, USA

Simon Shibli, Leisure Industries Research Centre, Sheffield Hallam University, Unit 1, Sheffield Science Park, Howard Street, Sheffield, S1 2LX

Roslyn Sinnamon, Cable & Wireless plc, 76 Hammersmith Road, London, W14 8UD

Andrew Smith, Leisure Industries Research Centre, Unit 1, Sheffield Science Park, Howard Street, Sheffield, S1 2LX

Peter Taylor, The Management School, 9 Mappin Street, 2nd Floor, Room 217, Sheffield University

Tracy Taylor, University of Technology, School of Leisure and Tourism Studies, Sydney, PO Box 222, Lindfield, NSW 2070, Australia

Marc Theeboom, Free University of Brussels (VUB), Faculty of Physical Education and Kinestherapy, Pleinlaan 2 (L405), B-1050 Brussels, Belgium

Eleni Theodoraki, Loughborough University, Institute of Sport and Leisure Policy, Dept. of Physical Education, Sports Science and Recreation Management, Loughborough, LE11 3TU

Kristine Toohey, University of Technology, School of Leisure and Tourism Studies, Sydney, PO Box 222, Lindfield, NSW 2070, Australia

Part I

Introduction

1 Sport in the city

Research issues

Ian Henry and Chris Gratton

Although until relatively recently sport might have been described as a neglected topic in social analysis, the significance of sport in contemporary societies seems undeniable. In economic terms sport is estimated to represent 3 per cent of GDP in the OECD countries. In cultural terms more than two-thirds of the world's population saw some part of the 1996 Atlanta Olympic Games via television (LIRC, 1998). In political terms sport has been employed as a policy tool by nation states, as for example in the struggle against apartheid in South Africa, and in the Olympic Games' boycotts of the 1980s, or more recently in promoting the new or reviving nationalism of the post-communist Central and Eastern European states.

However at the same time that sport has come to be recognised as being of considerable significance for the nation state as a social, economic and cultural concern, ironically, the role and significance of the nation state as the primary policy influence has been subject to pressures (della Sala, 1997). Developments in economic policy such as the advent of the Euro, and associated harmonised economic planning, have de facto reduced national powers, while globalising trends have also impacted considerably on social policy (Wilding, 1997) and cultural life (Featherstone, 1995; Negus, 1993).

Globalisation is of course not a unidirectional phenomenon, nor are its effects uncontested at the local level (Hirst and Thompson, 1995; Keil, 1998). Nevertheless recognition of its significance does imply the need to move beyond state-centric approaches to analysis, and to incorporate a recognition of both transnational and sub-national elements of governance. The city in particular is considered to play a key role in the evolving system of governance (Andrew and Goldsmith, 1998; Wilheim, 1996). As cities compete with one another for inward investment and struggle to deal with problems of social and economic disruption, increasingly cultural policy, including policy for sport, is developed to address the twin aims of economic development and social inclusion (Mayer, 1994).

A concern related to the diminution of the role of the nation state is that of the 'hollowing out of the state' (Patterson and Pinch, 1995; Rhodes, 1994). This phenomenon relates both to the movement of policy concerns upwards to the transnational level and downwards to the sub-national level, as well as to the growing trend in privatisation and contract culture, and the involvement of the commercial and voluntary sectors that is evident in policy areas previously considered to be the province of government. Ironically, while one might expect sport to be one area of policy in which the principles of vertical and horizontal subsidiarity would most effectively be applied, in the past decade in the European context, some far reaching policy developments have been initiated by transnational bodies, particularly by the European Union. The Bosman ruling effectively imposed on professional sport a requirement to allow free access for employment to any national market within the EU for any citizen of a member state, while sporting bodies themselves lobbied for sport to become a competence of the European Union. Although the revision of the Treaty on European Union which was signed in 1997 by member states in Amsterdam, did not incorporate a treaty article on sport, it did incorporate a declaration on sport for the first time (Henry and Matthews, 1998).

In the British context, sports funding on the part of the state declined, as local government budgets were effectively squeezed, with only partial compensation attained by the introduction of National Lottery funding for sport (Henry, 1999), and sporting investment by the state as a social service has thus declined. Competitive tendering for the management of public sector sports facilities, as a means to generate efficiencies and save on public sector budgets, and privatisation in the sports sector have become popular strategies in developed economies. However, mindful of the potential costs of social exclusion, cities have continued to focus some sporting investment on targeting disadvantaged groups and communities with programmes such as *opérations d'été* and *équipements de proximité* in France (Henry, 1997), or schemes targeted at the unemployed in Britain and Spain (Glyptis and Pack, 1989; González Ferreras and Urkiola, 1989) or at ethnic minorities (Arnaud, 1999; Augustin, 1996; Rijpma and Meiburg, 1989) in Britain, France and the Netherlands. However, such programmes tend to be marginal rather than mainstream.

In addition to the decline in sport as social investment, the nature of sporting provision made by local government has also been greatly affected by the changing nature of local governance and local economic development concerns. Sport as a welfare service may be in decline, but as an element in city marketing, an attractor of the tourist market or of inward investment, sport has grown in significance for local government and in particular for cities. Sports facilities may be seen as triggers to further growth (Page, 1990). A classic strategy of inter-urban competition has been the bidding for the staging of major events (Cochrane, Peck, and Tickell, 1996; House of Commons, 1995) very often linked to a reimaging process (Dobson and Gratton, 1996). Such a process of urban competition through sport may be conceptualised as occurring on the global, continental, national, or regional/local level.

In a quasi central place theory approach, one might develop a hierarchy of sports places at each of these levels. At the global level there are perhaps only three major sporting events, the Olympics, the soccer World Cup, and the World Athletics Championships, which carry with them the potential to establish global place recognition. Of these only the Olympics and the Athletics Championships are 'city-located' rather than staged in multi-urban centres, and while the Olympics carry instant global recognition, the World Athletic Championships are less effective. Most sports fans could cite the location of the last six or eight summer

Olympic Games, while many would have difficulty in identifying the last four locations for the World Athletics Championships. The World Cup is of course not city-based and while providing income and some recognition for host cities, is also not of the same order as the Olympics. Thus while Barcelona, Seoul, or Los Angeles may be instantly recognisable as world sporting cities, the same may not be true for example of Stuttgart (host to the 1993 World Athletics Championships).

The Commonwealth Games does generate interest across the globe though only in respect of those associated with Commonwealth activities, in a sense raising identity in a global sub-set of locations. There are in addition some 'location bound' world sporting events or facilities which promote strong identities though these are not always city-based. The establishment of the Royal and Ancient, Golf's governing body at St Andrews, or the All England Club and the tennis championships at Wimbledon are cases in point, while the world's major soccer stadia (for example the Nou Camp, Maracanna, Wembley, or even Old Trafford) are also symbols with global currency.

At the continental level, for example, one might identify European cities of sport as those which host major athletics competitions (European Athletics Championships, the Europa Cup, or Grand Prix meetings), soccer finals (European Championship, European Champions League, UEFA Cup), other major championships such as the European Swimming Championships, or even 'national' events of international significance (for example those cities that host a stage of the Tour de France). At this level in particular, cities are often second cities, or at least those which lie in the shadow of the dominant (usually capital) city. Lyon for example, and Stuttgart, have both sought to establish themselves beyond the shadow of Paris, and Berlin/Munich/Hamburg respectively (Henry, 1997). At the national level support of some local authorities for local professional clubs is commonplace and the system of inter-urban competition evident in the North American scramble to host sports franchises represents this level of competition (Leone, 1997; Shropshire and Dunn, 1996). How the hierarchy of identities from global to local is developed is not of course restricted to place promotion through sport, but sport has come to play an increasingly significant role in such processes.

Given the above range of issues, social, symbolic, economic and political, how has commentary on sport and the city developed? What are the key themes and perspectives in the literature, and how does this book contribute to the literature? There are perhaps five broad areas of literature on sport and the city which we might identify as follows.

Sport and economic regeneration

Perhaps the largest set of studies in relation to recent literature on sport and the city has focused on economic impacts, and broader evaluations of economic costs and benefits of sport-led development. The role of sport in urban economies is one which has begun to be recognised, particularly in the context of deindustrialisation and the growing importance of the service sector in such circumstances. There is also a literature relating to the costs and benefits of stadium development, particularly in the US (Baade and Dye, 1988a; Baade and Dye, 1988b; Pelissero,

1991; Shropshire and Dunn, 1996), but with some more recent contributions relating to Britain (Black and Lloyd, 1994; Churchman, 1995; Page, 1990; see also Williams, 1997 for a detailed discussion of related material).

The role of sports events in urban regeneration

A particular sub-set of the literature on sport and economic regeneration is about the promotion of urban sporting events. A number of authors have addressed the role of the promotion of single large-scale events in economic development (for example Foley, 1991; Kidd, 1979; Roche, 1992), while others have focused on the economic impact of programmes of significant sporting events (Baade and Dye, 1990; Crompton, 1995; House of Commons, 1995; Law, 1994; Turco and Kelsey, 1992) or on the social impact (Hall, 1992; York, 1991). Thus there is a mix of positive prescription (KPMG Management Consulting, 1993) and critical analysis (Bramwell, 1997; Hall, 1992; Law, 1994). Within this literature, there is also some critical material on the application of economic impact analysis (Crompton, 1995; Turco and Kelsey, 1992).

Urban sports tourism

In addition to the social scientific analysis of sport in urban areas, there is a growing literature on urban sports tourism and on sport and city marketing. This literature has a predominantly managerialist set of concerns (Kotler, Haider, and Rein, 1993; Law, 1996; Smyth, 1994), though with some more critical approaches (Hall, 1992; Hall, 1997).

Sport, social division and the development of urban communities

The notion of the two tier city has grown in the literature (Jones, 1998; Lash and Urry, 1994), particularly as the result of the marketisation of services (Lorrain and Stoker, 1997). Thus the impact on ethnic, gender, and class groups of development decisions and the marketisation of public sector sports services are treated more or less directly by a number of authors (Pitter and Andrews, 1997; Tatz, 1995; Verma and Darby, 1994; Yule, 1997). The pervasive growth of the individualistic philosophy of neo-liberalism is seen by many to ignore and (thereby) reinforce the growth of such cleavages (McKay, 1994). As market freedom is prioritised over welfare provision, so access to sport as a welfare service is likely to decline, fuelling the differences between those who can afford to avail themselves of market provision and those who cannot.

Politics and urban sports policy

The urban politics literature has recently burgeoned with studies of the development of the city as a growth machine (Logan and Molotch, 1996), or the development of urban coalitions and partnerships (Jonas, 1992), or of urban regimes which may promote or inhibit growth or may seek socially progressive goals (Stone, 1989). Nevertheless, despite this recent growth, there has been a dearth of materials which specifically address the role of sport in regime or coalition construction and the role of regimes and or coalitions in the development of sports strategies. There are some exceptions, such as Cochrane, Peck and Tickell's (1996) account of the role of public-private partnership in the generation of Manchester's bid for the 2000 Olympics, which they describe as, in effect, a 'grants coalition' formed to maximise the opportunities to access government monies, rather than a growth coalition seeking to foster urban growth by maximising exchange values of urban resources (for further discussion of the Manchester case see Hill, 1994; Law, 1994; Leatham, 1993). Henry and Paramio Salcines (1999) provide an account of attempts to construct a symbolic regime around sport in Sheffield to recast the image of the city which goes beyond earlier accounts that focus only partially on regime analysis (Rosentraub, Swindell, Przybylski, and Mullins, 1994; Schaffer, Jaffee, and Davidson, 1993), while Pelissero (1991) seeks to locate an account of the construction of a sports stadium in the context of regime activities, and Sack and Johnson (1996) provide an account of the role of urban regime analysis in explaining the attraction and retention of a major tennis event to New Haven.

A relatively neglected area of political activity in the regime literature is the symbolic construction of shared meanings and values, which is particularly significant in the reimaging, or 'reimagining', of the city (Bianchini, 1990; Bianchini and Schwengel, 1991). The significance for postmodern politics in the urban context of sport and reimaging is related to Bourdieu's (1989) account of distinction, taste and lifestyle. Just as new social groups (particularly the emerging new service class) seek to distinguish themselves through new cultural configurations and to undermine traditional cultural hierarchies, so new forms of politics move away from the class-based system of the old social structure. Restructuring of the global economy implies not just restructuring of class structures and cultural hierarchies, it also implies the restructuring of urban hierarchies. Just as individuals and new groups seek to redefine their identity, so too places, particularly deindustrialised cities (or groups of actors within them), seek to reimagine the identity of place. Thus sport, as a popular cultural form, not directly associated with the old industrial politics of class (unlike, for example, the public-private schisms in traditional service areas such as education, housing, or transport) tends to lend itself to postmodern politics of the urban in such redefinition processes. As with individuals the cultural capital of place will be either immediately or ultimately convertible into economic capital: thus sport provides opportunities for direct profit generation, or as part of an attractive infrastructure attracting inward investment does so indirectly. Material which deals with sport and urban symbolism is, however, still relatively rare, with Harvey (1987) and Henry (1997) among the few exceptions.

These then are the five major areas that can be identified in the literature on sport and the city. The perspectives evident in this literature range from classic positive economics, through radical perspectives (predominantly neo-Weberian, neo-Marxist, and/or feminist and anti-racist in origin), to critiques (and celebrations) of the postmodern city, and post-Fordist accounts of urban social regulation. The structure of this book reflects the range of concerns and to a large extent the perspectives highlighted here. The intention of the book is to bring together in one place, and to extend, this wide ranging set of arguments as a resource to researchers and practitioners working in this area of urban cultural, economic and political activity.

References

Andrew, C. and Goldsmith, M. (1998). 'From Local Government to Local Governance – and Beyond?' *International Political Science Review*, Vol. 19(2), 101–117.

Arnaud, L. (1999). *Politiques Sportives et Minorités Ethniques*. Paris: L'Harmattan.

Augustin, J.P. (1996). 'Sport Used as a Means of Integrating Immigrants' Children', 'L'intégration par le sport des enfants d'immigrés'. *Espace populations sociétés* Vol. 2–3), 467–474.

Baade, R. and Dye, R. (1988a). 'An Analysis of the Economic Rationale for Public Subsidisation of Sports Stadiums'. *Annals of Regional Science*, Vol. 22(2), 37–47.

Baade, R. and Dye, R. (1988b). 'Sports Stadiums and Area Development: a Critical Review'. *Economic Development Quarterly*, Vol. 2(3), 265–275.

Baade, R. and Dye, R. (1990). 'The Impact of Stadiums and Professional Sports on Metropolitan Area Development'. *Growth and Change*, Vol. 21(2), 1–14.

Bianchini, F. (1990). *Urban Renaissance? The Arts and the Urban Regeneration Process*, Liverpool: University of Liverpool.

Bianchini, F. and Schwengel, H. (1991). 'Re-imagining the City', in Corner, J. and Harvey, S. (eds) *Enterprise and Heritage: Crosscurrents of National Culture*, London: Routledge.

Black, J.S. and Lloyd, M.G. (1994). 'Football Stadia Developments: Land-Use Policy and Planning Controls'. *Town Planning Review*, Vol. 65(1), 1–20.

Bourdieu, P. (1989). *Distinction: a Social Critique of the Judgement of Taste*. London: Routledge.

Bramwell, B. (1997). 'Strategic Planning Before and After a Mega-Event'. *Tourism Management*, Vol. 18(3), 167–176.

Churchman, C. (1995). 'Sports Stadia and the Landscape: a Review of the Impacts and Opportunities Arising as a Result of the Current Development of Football Grounds'. *Built Environment*, Vol. 21(1), 6–24.

Cochrane, A., Peck, J. and Tickell, A. (1996). 'Manchester Playing Games: Exploring the Local Politics of Globalisation'. *Urban Studies*, Vol. 33(8), 1319–1336.

Crompton, J. (1995). 'Economic Impact Analysis of Sports Facilities and Events: Eleven Sources of Misapplication'. *Journal of Sports Management*, Vol. 9, 14–35.

della Sala, V. (1997). 'Hollowing Out and Hardening the State: European Integration and the Italian Economy'. *West European Politics*, Vol. 20(1), 14–33.

Dobson, N. and Gratton, C. (1996). 'From City of Steel to City of Sport: Evaluation of Sheffield's Attempt to Use Sport as a Vehicle of Urban Regeneration'. *Higher Degrees of Pleasure, World Leisure and Recreation Association Conference, Cardiff, July*.

Featherstone, M. (1995). *Undoing Culture: Globalization, Postmodernism and Identity*. London: Sage.

Foley, P. (1991). 'The Impact of the World Student Games On Sheffield'. *Environment and Planning C-Government and Policy*, Vol. 9(1), 65–78.

Glyptis, S. and Pack, C. (1989). *Developing Sport and Leisure: Good Practice in Urban Regeneration*. London: Department of Environment, HMSO.

González Ferreras, J. and Urkiola, A. (1989). 'Leisure Policy in Spain'. In Bramham P., Henry, I., Mommaas, H. and van der Poel, H. (eds), *Leisure Policy in Europe*. Wallingford: CAB International.

Hall, C.M. (1992). *Hallmark Tourist Events: Impact, Management and Planning*. London: Belhaven.

Hall, C.M. (1997). 'Geography, Marketing and the Selling of Places'. *Journal of Marketing Management*, Vol. 97, 61–84.

Harvey, D. (1987). 'Flexible Accumulation through Urbanization: Reflections on "Postmodernism" in the American City'. *Antipode*, Vol. 19(3), 260–86.

Henry, I. (1997). 'The Politics of Sport and Symbolism in the City'. *Managing Leisure: an International Journal*, Vol. 3(2), 1–19.

Henry, I. (1999). Globalisation and the Governance of Leisure: the Roles of the Nation-State, the European Union and the City in Leisure Policy in Britain. *Loisir et Société/ Society and Leisure*, Vol. 22(2), 355–379.

Henry, I. and Matthews, N. (1998). 'Sport Policy and the European Union: the Post-Maastricht Agenda'. *Managing Leisure: an International Journal*, Vol. 4(1), 1–19.

Henry, I. and Paramio Salcines, J. (1999). 'Sport and the Analysis of Symbolic Regimes: an Illustrative Case Study of the City of Sheffield'. *Urban Affairs Review*, Vol. 34(5), 641–666.

Hill, C. R. (1994). 'The Politics of Manchester Olympic Bid'. *Parliamentary Affairs*, Vol. 47(3), 338–354.

Hirst, P., and Thompson, G. (1995). 'Globalization and the Future of the Nation-State'. *Economy and Society*, Vol. 24(3), 408–442.

House of Commons. (1995). *Bids to Stage International Sporting Events, Fifth Report*. London: HMSO.

Jonas, A.E.G. (1992). 'A Place For Politics in Urban Theory – the Organization and Strategies of Urban Coalitions'. *Urban Geography*, Vol. 13(3), 280–290.

Jones, M. (1998). 'Restructuring the Local State: Economic Governance or Social Regulation?' *Political Geography*, Vol. 17(8), 959–988.

Keil, R. (1998). 'Globalization Makes States: Perspectives of Local Governance in the Age of the World City'. *Review of International Political Economy*, Vol. 5(4), 616–646.

Kidd, B. (1979). *The Political Economy of Sport*. Ottowa: Canadian Association of Health, Physical Education and Recreation.

Kotler, P., Haider, D. and Rein, I. (1993). *Marketing Places*. New York: Free Press.

KPMG Management Consulting. (1993). *Manchester 2000: Economic Benefits and Opportunities of the Olympic Games*. London: KPMG Management Consulting.

Lash, S. and Urry, J. (1994). *Economies of Signs and Space*. London: Sage.

Law, C. (1994). 'Manchester Bid For the Millennium Olympic Games'. *Geography*, Vol. 79(344 Pt3), 222–231.

Law, C.M. (1996). *Tourism in Major Cities*. London: Routledge.

Leatham, A. (1993). 'Going for Gold'. *Leisure Opportunities, 107*, 32–3.

Leone, K.C. (1997). 'No Team, No Peace: Franchise Free Agency in the National Football League'. *Columbia Law Review*, Vol. 97(2), 473–523.

LIRC. (1998). *Leisure Forecasts: Leisure Away from Home 1998–2002*. Sheffield: Leisure Industries Research Centre.

Logan, J. and Molotch, H. (1996). 'The City as a Growth Machine'. In S. Fainstein and S. Campbell (eds), *Readings in Urban Theory*. Oxford: Blackwell.

Lorrain, D. and Stoker, G. (1997) (eds), *The Privatization of Urban Services in Europe*. London: Cassell.

Mayer, M. (1994). 'Post-Fordist City Politics'. In A. Amin (ed.), *Post-Fordism: A Reader*. Oxford: Blackwell.

McKay, J. (1994). 'Masculine Hegemony, the State and the Incorporation of Gender Equity Discourse – the Case of Australian Sport'. *Australian Journal of Political Science*, Vol. 29(1), 82–95.

Negus, K. (1993). Global Harmonies and Local Discords – Transnational Policies and Practices in the European Recording Industry. *European Journal of Communication*, Vol. 8(3), 295–316.

Page, S. (1990). 'Sport Arena Development in the UK: Its Role in Urban Regeneration in London Docklands'. *Sport Place*, Vol. 4(1), 3–15.

Patterson, A. and Pinch, P.L. (1995). 'Hollowing Out the Local State – Compulsory Competitive Tendering and the Restructuring of British Public-Sector Services'. *Environment and Planning a*, Vol. 27(9), 1437–1461.

Pelissero, J.P. (1991). 'Urban Regimes, Sports Stadiums, and the Politics of Economic Development Agendas in Chicago'. *Policy Studies Review*, Vol. 10(2/3), 117–129.

Pitter, R. and Andrews, D. L. (1997). 'Serving America's Underserved Youth: Reflections on Sport and Recreation in an Emerging Social Problems Industry'. *Quest*, Vol. 49(1), 85–99.

Rhodes, R. (1994). 'The Hollowing Out of the State: the Changing Nature of the Public Service in Britain'. *The Political Quarterly, 65*(2), 138–151.

Rijpma, S. and Meiburg, H. (1989) 'Sports Policy Initiatives in Rotterdam: Targeting Disadvantaged Groups', in Bramham, P., Henry, I., Mommaas, H. and van der Poel, H. (eds), *Leisure and Urban Processes: Critical Studies of Leisure Policy in Western European Cities*, London: Routledge.

Roche, M. (1992). *Problems of Rationality and Democracy in Mega-Event Planning: a Study of Sheffield's World Student Games 1991*. Paper presented at the Leisure and New Citizenship, the VIIIth European Leisure and Recreation Association Congress, Bilbao, Spain.

Rosentraub, M.S., Swindell, D., Przybylski, M. and Mullins, D.R. (1994). 'Sport and Downtown Development Strategy – If You Build It, Will Jobs Come'. *Journal of Urban Affairs*, Vol. 16(3), 221–239.

Sack, A.L. and Johnson, A.T. (1996). 'Politics, Economic-Development, and the Volvo-International-Tennis-Tournament'. *Journal of Sport Management*, Vol. 10(1), 1–14.

Schaffer, W., Jaffee, B. and Davidson, L. (1993). *Beyond the Games: the Economic Impact of Amateur Sports*. Indianapolis: Chamber of Commerce.

Shropshire, K., and Dunn, R. (1996). 'The Sports Franchise Game: Cities in Pursuit of Sports Franchises, Events, Stadiums, and Arenas [review]'. *Journal of the American Planning Association*, Vol. 62(3), 407.

Smyth, H. (1994). *Marketing the City: the Role of Flagship Projects*. London: Routledge.

Stone, C. (1989). *Regime Politics: Governing Atlanta, 1946–1988*. Lawrence: University Press of Kansas.

Tatz, C. (1995). 'Racism and Sport in Australia'. *Race and Class, 36*(4 SI), 43–54.

Turco, D. and Kelsey, C. (1992). *Conducting Economic Impact Studies of Recreation and Parks Special Events*. Arlington, VA: National Recreation and Park Association.

Verma, G.K. and Darby, D.S. (1994). *Winners and Losers: Ethnic Minorities in Sport and Recreation*. London: Falmer Press.

Wilding, P. (1997). Globalization, Regionalism and Social Policy. *Social Policy and Administration*, Vol. 31(4), 410–428.

Wilheim, J. (1996). 'Introduction: Urban challenges of a transitional period'. *International Social Science Journal*, Vol. 48(1), 9 (7 pages).

Williams, C. (1997). *Consumer Services and Economic Development*. London: Routledge.

York, K. (1991). 'Sport and Community Identity: the Case of Bath Rugby Football Club'. *South Hampshire Geographer*, Vol. 20, 12–23.

Yule, J. (1997). 'Engendered Ideologies and Leisure Policy in the UK. Part 1: Gender Ideologies'. *Leisure Studies*, Vol. 16(2), 61–84.

Part II

Sport and economic regeneration

2 Public subsidies to professional team sport facilities in the USA

John L. Crompton

Cities do not use public money to build skyscrapers and then hand them over gratis to IBM or Telecom, even though such businesses are likely to have a positive economic impact on a community. However, in the US they do use public money to build stadia for professional football and baseball teams, and arenas for professional hockey and baseball teams, and then give them to the millionaire owners of those teams. This largesse is particularly remarkable given the conditions of financial crises and infrastructure deterioration that prevail in major cities. A letter writer to the *Baltimore Sun* captured the apparent absurdity of this state of affairs:

> The city is full of ruined houses, the jails are overcrowded, the dome is falling off City Hall, there are potholes in the streets, crippled children can't get to school, taxes are up and services are going down – but we're going to have a sports complex.
>
> (Cited in Richmond 1993, p. 50)

This Baltimore scenario is not unusual, it is the norm. In 1997 there were 113 major league professional franchises in the four sports listed above. Between 1989 and 1997, thirty-one of them had a new stadium or arena built; and in 1997 an additional thirty-nine teams were actively seeking new facilities, finalising a deal to build one, or waiting to move into one (Noll and Zimbalist, 1997). All of these were built with public money and leased to the owners for either no rental fee or nominal sums which do not approach the amount needed to cover the debt charges involved. These facilities are not cheap. The typical arena cost for hockey and basketball is around $150 million while for football and baseball stadia the typical cost increases to approximately $250 million.

While it is the major league buildings that capture the headlines, the scenario is repeated among the approximately 200 professional minor league teams, especially those in baseball. To attract and retain these franchises, small cities use public funds to build their new stadia which are leased to team owners for nominal rents. The cities' financial subsidy to their major league franchises was estimated in 1992 to be $500 million per year (Quirk and Fort 1992). Given the extensive number of new stadia and arenas constructed since that time, and including the minor league structures that were excluded from that estimate, it seems likely that the current cities' public subsidy may be close to $1 billion per year.

This chapter analyses the sources of momentum which have been widely used to generate support for these major investments of public funds in the construction of major sports facilities and events. In the US, all capital expenditures by local government for any purpose generally have to be authorised by a public referendum of voters in the jurisdiction. This contrasts with the UK, where elected officials are usually entrusted to make such decisions on behalf of their constituents. The need for an affirmative vote at the polls before a project can be constructed, means that extensive emotional public debate invariably surrounds these decisions. The author's analysis of these debates suggests that advocates use five lines of argument to support their case: (1) economic impact from the spending of visitors to the community; (2) increased community visibility; (3) enhanced community image; (4) stimulation of other development; and (5) psychic income. The chapter discusses the legitimacy of these arguments.

Economic impact

Sports teams and events are business investments both for the organisations that sponsor them and for the communities which subsidise and host them. Communities often invest public tax dollars because they anticipate that the sports event will attract visitors from outside the community, whose expenditures while they are there represent an infusion of new wealth into the community. While the organisation has a directly measurable bottom line that evaluates its private economic performance, a community needs to assess benefits in a broader public context.

Figure 2.1 illustrates the conceptual thinking that underlies the investment of public funds in sporting events and facilities for economic purposes. *Residents* of a community 'give' funds to their city council in the form of taxes. The *city council* uses a proportion of these funds to subsidise the production of an event or the development of a facility. The *facility* or *event* attracts out-of-town *visitors*, who *spend money in the local community* both inside and outside the facility they visit. This 'new money' from outside the community creates *income and jobs* in the community for *residents*. This completes the cycle: community residents are responsible for creating the funds, and they receive a return on their investment in the form of new jobs and more household income.

Thus, commissioning an economic impact study to demonstrate the economic returns to a community will exceed its investment is de rigueur, because economic impact has been the primary, and in some cases the only, justification proposed by advocates. Typically, external consultants are hired to conduct a study. They have the appearance of being both expert and neutral but unfortunately many times they are more concerned with telling their clients what they want to hear, since this is the key to future repeat business. Even the most honorable consultants with impeccable integrity will produce numbers that are challengeable, because the methodology of economic impact analysis is inexact. Discrepancies occur because economic impact analysis can be conducted using different assumptions and

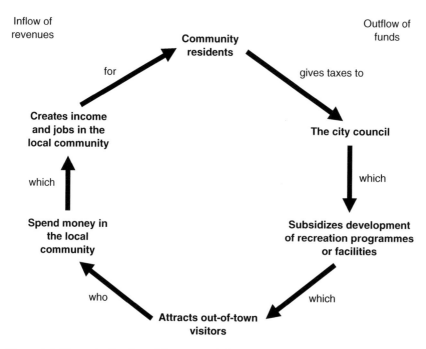

Figure 2.1 Conceptualisation of the economic investment and returns made by residents in communities that subsidise sports events or facilities

procedures, many of which are erroneous, which leads to dramatically different impacts being identified. Sometimes the errors result from a genuine lack of understanding of the economic impact concept and procedures used to measure it, but on other occasions they are undertaken mischievously to deliberately mislead and generate large numbers.

These erroneous procedures have been reviewed by the author elsewhere (Crompton 1995) so discussion here is limited to the four most egregious errors: the use of sales rather than income multipliers; the misrepresentation of employment multipliers; the inclusion of local participants/spectators; and failure to exclude 'time-switchers' and 'casuals'. Their misuse is illustrated with data taken from a study by the author of the economic impact of a sports festival on a major Texas city.

Use of sales rather than income multipliers

A *transactions or sales multiplier* measures the direct, indirect and induced effect of an extra unit of visitor spending on economic activity within a host community. It relates visitor expenditures to the increase in business turnover which it creates. It may be of some interest to business proprietors interested in sales impacts, or to officials in governmental entities who are interested in approximating sales revenues which may accrue. In contrast, an *income multiplier* measures the direct, indirect and induced effect of an extra unit of visitor spending on the changes which result in level of household incomes in the host community. It is operationalised as the *ratio of change in income to the initial autonomous change in expenditure that brings it about*. It most clearly demonstrates the economic impact on residents of the host community.

Table 2.1 reports the multiplier coefficients derived by the author using the IMPLAN model, for the economic impact study in city X. The table illustrates two points that are crucial to properly interpreting and communicating the impact of a multiplier. First, the coefficients are different for each category of expenditure that is listed. Thus, in city X, a $1 expenditure by visitors on gasoline (private auto) yielded substantially less household income than a similar $1 expenditure on food and beverages (69 cents compared to $1.26).

The second notable point illustrated in Table 2.1 is that the values of sales coefficients are substantially higher than those of personal income coefficients. For example, the table indicates that, on average, each $1 expenditure by visitors on accommodation will generate $1.05 in income for residents of the city, but business activity in the city should rise by about $2.51. Since both of these multipliers are measured in dollars they are often confused. If it is not clearly defined which multiplier is being discussed, then there is a danger that inaccurate, spurious inferences will be drawn from the data.

In an economic impact analysis of a sports facility or event, sales multipliers are likely to be of little interest to most local residents. The point of most interest is likely to be the impact of those sales on household income. Most residents are likely to be interested in knowing how much extra income they will receive from the injection of funds from visitors. Their interest in value of sales per se is likely to be limited since it does not directly impact their standard of living. Further, the high sales multipliers may give a false impression of the true impacts of visitor spending, because the highest income effects are not necessarily generated from the highest increases in sales. Nevertheless, because sales multipliers are substantially larger than income multipliers they tend to be attractive political tools for advocates to use in attempting to further the cause of their facility or event.

The income multipliers shown in Table 2.1 are high, because city X was a large urbanised community and thus the impact on a three county area was measured, rather than the single county in which the guidelines were based. The magnitude of a multiplier varies according to the structure of the host community: that is, the extent to which businesses where visitors spend their money proceed to trade with other businesses within the host economy. A smaller community tends not to have the sectoral interdependencies which facilitate retention of monies spent during the first round of expenditures. Hence, much of the expenditure would leak outside the immediate region leading to a lower local economic multiplier. Typically, the larger the defined area's economic base, the smaller is the leakage that is likely to occur and the larger is the value added from the original expenditures. In the author's experience, income multipliers in most communities are within the range of 0.4 to 0.7.

Table 2.1 A comparison of the sales and personal income coefficients for a sports festival in city X

Item	Sales coefficients				Personal income coefficients			
	Direct	Indirect	Induced	Total	Direct	Indirect	Induced	Total
Food and beverages	1	0.18	1.68	2.86	.58	.06	.62	1.26
Admission fees	1	0.22	1.72	2.94	.37	.07	.63	1.07
Night clubs, lounges and bars	1	0.31	0.92	2.23	.61	.13	.34	1.08
Retail shopping	1	0.18	1.48	2.66	.51	.07	.54	1.12
Lodging expenses	1	0.27	1.24	2.51	.49	.10	.46	1.05
Private auto expenses	1	0.25	0.71	1.96	.33	.10	.26	.69
Commercial transport	1	0.30	0.68	1.98	.45	.11	.25	.81
Other expenses	1	0.18	1.48	2.66	.51	.07	.54	1.12

Misrepresentation of employment multipliers

An *employment multiplier* measures the direct, indirect and induced effect of an extra unit of visitor spending on employment in the host community. It shows how many *full-time equivalent* job opportunities are supported in the community as a result of the visitor expenditure. Table 2.2 shows the employment multipliers derived by the author in the sports festival impact study for city X. It indicates that for every $1 million spent on food and beverages by visitors from outside the area, *81 full-time equivalent jobs* would be created.

Table 2.2 Employment coefficients for a sports festival in city X

Item	Employment coefficients			
	Direct	Indirect	Induced	Total
Food and beverages	46.65	2.81	32.06	81.52
Admission fees	46.93	3.39	32.81	83.13
Night clubs, lounges and bars	21.09	5.95	17.52	44.56
Retail shopping	40.59	2.87	28.18	71.64
Lodging expenses	32.23	4.30	23.68	60.21
Private auto expenses	16.46	4.45	13.55	34.47
Commercial transportation	15.78	4.37	13.06	33.21
Other expenses	40.59	2.87	28.18	71.64

The employment multiplier assumes that all existing employees are fully occupied, so an increase in external visitor spending will require an increase in level of employment within the region. However, its use in the context of sports facilities and events may give decision-makers a misleading impression, because local businesses are likely to respond to additional demand by greater utilisation of their existing labour force. It is unlikely that businesses would hire additional employees as a result of a sports event, because the extra business demand only lasts for a short time period. Rather, existing employees are likely to be released from other duties to accommodate this temporary peak demand or requested to work overtime. At best, only a few very short-term additional employees may be hired. Thus, the 'full-time' jobs which decision-makers may be anticipating (not understanding the significance of the word 'equivalent') as a result of the multiplier, do not come to fruition.

Some empirical confirmation of these types of employment adjustments was reported by Arnold (1986) and Bishop and Hatch (1986) after their interviews with managers of transportation and restaurant businesses immediately after the Adelaide Grand Prix. They found that companies in both types of businesses increased their labour requirements by increasing the hours of existing employees, although some restaurant establishments indicated they hired 'casuals' to supplement this action. Arnold (1986) concluded:

> There were virtually no new permanent jobs in the transport area generated as a result of the Grand Prix. In fact several companies had organised the increased work load in such a way that they did not pay overtime although this was not possible for all the extra work (p. 81).

Inclusion of local spectators

Economic impact attributable to a sports facility or event relates only to new money injected into an economy by visitors, media, external government entities, or banks and investors from outside the community. Only visitors who reside outside the jurisdiction and whose primary motivation for visiting is to attend the event, or who stay longer and spend more because of it, should be included. Expenditures by those who reside in the community do not represent the circulation of new money. Rather, they represent only a recycling of money that already existed there. It is probable that if local residents had not spent this money at the sports festival, then they would have disposed of it either now or later by purchasing other goods and services in the community. Twenty dollars spent by a local family at a sports event is likely to be twenty less dollars spent on movie tickets elsewhere in the community. Thus, expenditures associated with the event by local residents are merely likely to be switched spending which offers no net economic stimulus to the community. Hence, it should not be included when estimating economic impact.

The difference in impact when local residents are included in an analysis and when they are omitted is illustrated by the sales and personal income values in Tables 2.3 and 2.4. When residents from within the local area were included, sales

Table 2.3 Economic surge in the city X area created by residents and non-residents who attended the sports festival events

Item	Sales output	Personal income	Full time equivalent jobs created
Food and beverages	109,196,634	48,238,234	3,110
Admission fees	38,691,412	14,200,095	1,095
Night clubs, lounges and bars	20,163,133	10,987,611	402
Retail shopping	66,934,134	28,159,101	1,805
Lodging expenses	47,872,258	19,922,456	1,148
Private auto expenses	14,727,339	5,123,586	259
Commercial transportation	22,146,640	9,126,217	370
Other expenses	1,874,950	1,076,825	69
Total	321,606,498	136,834,125	8,258

Table 2.4 Economic impact in the city X area created by non-residents who attended the sports festival events

Item	Sales output	Personal income	Full time equivalent jobs created
Food and beverages	37,859,887	16,737,554	1,078
Admission fees	7,837,688	2,875,055	222
Night clubs, lounges and bars	4,555,057	2,478,865	91
Retail shopping	23,545,491	9,909,880	635
Lodging expenses	35,124,109	14,637,961	843
Private auto expenses	4,744,930	1,653,118	84
Commercial transportation	10,710,664	4,340,311	179
Other expenses	1,088,768	458,243	29
Total	125,466,594	53,090,987	3,161

and personal income impacts associated with the sports festival were $322 million and $137 million, respectively (Table 2.3). However, when only expenditures by visitors from outside the area were included, these impacts were reduced to $125 million and $53 million, respectively (Table 2.4).

These substantially different economic impact estimates illustrate why the widespread admonition from economists to disregard locals' expenditures is frequently ignored by sports event organisers; that is, when expenditures by locals are omitted, the economic impact numbers become too small to be politically acceptable. To rectify this, two disconcerting new terms are emerging in the economic impact vocabulary. First, some sponsors now report their sports event contributed $X million 'to local economic activity'. The second term is 'economic surge' and it has been incorporated in the title of Table 2.3. Both of these terms are used to describe all expenditures associated with the event, irrespective of whether they derive from residents or non-residents. This generates the high numbers that study sponsors seek, but the surge or economic activity figure is meaningless. Its only purpose is to enable advocates to obfuscate and deliberately mislead decision-makers and the public for the purpose of boosting their political advocacy position.

Failure to exclude 'time switchers' and 'casuals'

Visitor expenditures should be net of 'time-switchers' and 'casuals'. Some non-local spectators at a sports event may have been planning a visit to the community for a long time, but changed the timing of their visit to coincide with the event. Their spending cannot be attributed to the event since the expenditure would have been made if it had not occurred, albeit at a different time of the year. Other visitors already may have been in the community, attracted by other features, and elected to go to the sports event instead of doing something else. These two groups may be termed 'time-switchers' and 'casuals'. Expenditures by these visitors would have occurred without the sports event, so income generated by their expenditures should not be attributed to it. In these cases, it is necessary to distinguish between gross visitor expenditures and the net increment of those expenditures, which is the spending attributable to increased length of stay because of the event.

In the city X study, respondents were asked questions which enabled the author to conclude that 27 per cent were 'time-switchers' who would have visited the city without the event, but the event was a reason that influenced their decision to come at that time. Another 43 per cent were 'casuals' who would have come to the city at that time, irrespective of the event. They went to the sports festival because it was an attractive entertainment option while they were in the community. Table 2.5 shows the impact on the city when these two groups were discarded, because their expenditures would have entered the city's economy even if the event had not been held. The survey failed to include a question which asked if the 'casuals' had extended their stay because of the event. If they did, then that increment of their expenditures should be included in those totals. To that extent, the economic impacts shown in Table 2.5 may be underestimates.

The advocacy conundrum

The sports festival case described here demonstrates the wide range of numbers which purport to measure economic impact that could be presented by the advocates or organisers from the same set of primary data. If a press conference was held in city X to report the sports festival's economic impact, the organisers could, at one extreme, announce that the sales output from the economic surge associated with the festival was almost $322 million (Table 2.3). At the other extreme, they could announce that the economic impact of the festival on personal income was

Table 2.5 Economic impact in the city X area created by non-residents (excluding casuals and time switchers) who attended the sports festival events

Item	Sales output	Personal income	Full time equivalent jobs created
Food and beverages	7,371,629	5,088,151	328
Admission fees	1,550,953	874,005	67
Night clubs, lounges and bars	606,780	753,562	28
Retail shopping	4,943,987	3,012,571	193
Lodging expenses	6,655,528	4,449,879	256
Private auto expenses	824,220	502,541	25
Commercial transportation	1,897,734	1,319,433	54
Other expenses	213,126	139,305	9
Total	24,063,957	16,139,447	960

approximately $16 million (Table 2.5). It is clear to the author that the latter figure is the more appropriate measure of economic impact, but unfortunately a review of almost twenty studies sponsored by sports facility advocacy groups revealed that none of them opted to report economic impact with this measure.

In the case of sports events, rather than facilities, there is a real dilemma for sponsors. If the correct $16 million figure for city X is presented, the festival's economic contribution is likely to appear relatively insignificant compared to other events the city sponsors, when those events announce the equivalent of the $322 million figure as their estimated economic impact. In this situation, the relatively small impact of the festival is likely to translate into commensurately less political and resource support for it from decision-makers, and perhaps, ultimately, even withdrawal of revenues from it.

Acting ethically, when others do not, could critically damage the event's standing. Alternatively, it could be rationalised that it is equitable to use the same set of measures to compare the economic contributions of sports facilities and events, even though the results of all of them are grossly misleading. Hence, abuses incorporated into an economic impact analysis are contagious because when precedent has been established in one study, some advocates are likely to feel compelled to knowingly perpetuate the abuse by incorporating the misleading procedures into their own analyses.

Increased community visibility

A major professional sports event is likely to attract a significant amount of media coverage for the city in which it is located. The importance of this exposure was recognised by an official in Washington, DC when the Washington Redskins football team was considering a move from that city to Arlington, Virginia (Corliss, 1992):

Officials in Washington could only fear that getting Skinned meant the town would be rubbed off the map. 'Brooklyn has never been the same since the Dodgers left', said the D.C. council chairman whose own city lost two baseball clubs in the 1950s. 'You don't even think about Brooklyn' (p. 51).

Efforts are sometimes made to attribute an economic value to this exposure. For example, a study undertaken by Chicago's Department of Economic Development reported 'that the championship-winning 1985–86 Chicago Bears football team produced publicity for Chicago equivalent to a \$30 to \$40 million promotion campaign' (cited in Baade and Dye, 1988, p. 46). The study does not describe the procedures used to derive this value, but a widely used method of obtaining a crude dollar value measure of media exposure is to use prevailing advertising rates in the media in which it appears. This approach is frequently used by companies to measure economic value of their sponsorship.

The city of Green Bay in Wisconsin is an outstanding example of the visibility brought by a professional team. The Green Bay Packers NFL team has a long and distinguished heritage. Unlike other professional franchises in the US, it is essentially owned by the city. Green Bay would have remained anonymous and unknown to most of America but for the exploits of its football team.

The effectiveness of a sports event in raising awareness of a city was measured by Ritchie and Smith (1991). Their context was the Winter Olympics held in Calgary in 1988. They used samples taken from a number of locations drawn both from Europe and the United States and traced changes in the awareness of Calgary during a three year period from 1986–1989. The changes were dramatic. The nearby city of Edmonton served as a control location against which the magnitude of changes in Calgary's level of awareness could be measured. Among the European sample in 1986 and 1987, Calgary obtained unaided-recall percentages of 10 per cent and 12 per cent, respectively, whereas comparable figures for Edmonton were 5 per cent and 5 per cent. The main impact of the Games was shown in the 1988 figures where Calgary's unaided recognition level jumped to 40 per cent, while Edmonton's remained at just over 6 per cent. In 1989, Calgary's was at 33 per cent and Edmonton's at 5 per cent. Similar impacts were observed among the US samples, although the growth in awareness of approximately 23 points was not quite so dramatic as the 28 point gain recorded by the European samples.

The instrumental purpose and value of high exposure has been articulated in the following terms in relation to the city of Adelaide's investment in its Grand Prix event (Van der Lee and Williams 1986):

This is the first step in marketing Adelaide to international markets. Any promotion to create market knowledge of what Adelaide has to offer as an international visitor destination can only be effective after potential visitors know it exists and where it is. Achieving this prerequisite awareness is a considerable hurdle to be overcome. The cost and effort in doing so for a new long haul destination is quite high. Therefore the Grand Prix influence (of which the first year is only part of a cumulative process) is quite valuable in that it would be difficult to achieve by alternative means (p. 54).

Enhanced community image

Increased exposure offers opportunities for more sharply defining or changing a city's image. The Mayor of Jacksonville, for example, perceived that a major league team in his city would provide 'a real signature of the community' (Fulton, 1988, p. 34). It has been suggested that major sports events and teams are the new 'image builders' for communities (Burns and Mules, 1986). In the construction years after World War II, this role was performed by tall building tower skylines, large-span bridges, or manufacturing industries (for example, 'Motor City' or 'Steel City'). In the 1980s, festival market places and shopping malls were the downtown attractions. Today, as the economy has switched to a service orientation, major sports events and teams capture the imagination and help establish a city's image in people's minds.

This type of image change was documented by Ritchie and Smith (1991) in their study of the impact of the Winter Olympics on Calgary. In their 1987 surveys, the Calgary Stampede was the dominant image associated with the city, being mentioned by 26 per cent of respondents, and the Olympics were second most frequently mentioned with 17 per cent. In the 1988 surveys, the Olympics were mentioned by 77 per cent of respondents, with the Stampede falling to a mention of only 11 per cent.

During the debate over construction of the Herbert H. Humphrey Metrodome in Minneapolis, the late Vice-President was asked if he thought keeping the Vikings and Twins in Minneapolis was important. 'Yes', he retorted. 'What do you want to become a cold Omaha?' (Business Week, 1983, p. 110).

In Sheffield, England, the city's high public investment in facilities and in-kind assistance to host the World Student Games was justified on the basis of image improvement. The games were intended to be the 'flagship' that management consultants had recommended the city seek to help scrub away Sheffield's 'steel and grime' image (Economist, 1991). The city's chief planner stated:

> Sheffield has an image problem – Sheffield's smokey image acquired during the heydays of the steel industry, is proving difficult to shake off – Sheffield's image is obviously important if the city is to attract footloose industry. In a period when every town and city is extolling its local virtues Sheffield has something that is different. The World Student Games should raise the city's profile throughout the United Kingdom and hopefully much of the world. Indeed, some of those associated with the games have suggested that the attraction of footloose industry may be one of the most significant effects of the games. The legacy of excellent sporting facilities after the games should enable Sheffield to stand out from the clamour of towns and cities claiming to be different.
>
> (Cited in Foley, 1991, p. 73)

The following description of the Adelaide Grand Prix is another example of how a city used a sports event to change its image:

Promotion of the Grand Prix by both the organisers and the sponsors focuses on the action and the glamour aspects which dominate the image of the event. The event becomes recognised as part of the Adelaide tourism product and hence strongly associated with the City's image. The Grand Prix has made an immediate impact on the State's tourism image. People now associate the Grand Prix with South Australia and South Australia with the Grand Prix. Recent market research conducted in Melbourne supports this. Among Melbourne residents who said it was either extremely or highly likely that they would visit Adelaide during the next 12 months, 22 per cent said the Grand Prix was a very important factor in their decision to visit South Australia. The perceived excitement and action of the Grand Prix, aptly captured in the Grand Prix marketing slogan 'Adelaide Alive' contrasts markedly with Adelaide's longstanding image in interstate markets as being 'boring', 'quiet', 'City of Churches', etc. The existing image has acted to inhibit consideration of Adelaide as a travel destination for many would-be visitors. The Grand Prix influence in changing that image thus creates a greater market receptiveness to promotion of Adelaide as a travel destination.

The resources required to achieve such an impact on Adelaide's image by alternative means would be substantial, and hence the value of this tourism benefit is considerable. However, this is only a potential tourism benefit since if the opportunity is not effectively exploited then no tourism benefit is gained.

(Van der Lee and Williams, 1986)

The Grand Prix motor race was used to spearhead the 'Adelaide Alive' image which was intended to replace Adelaide's traditional rather unexciting image. Expectations at both the Sheffield and Adelaide events were that a change in image would lead to increases in tourism and in businesses relocating from elsewhere. After the America's Cup races were held in Freemantle, Western Australia, it was observed: 'based on the crowds which continue to come to Freemantle day and night, the town has become a major destination for tourists and local visitors in the year since it was "discovered" by the Cup' (Newman, 1989, p. 55).

The image of prominent 'first-tier' cities is molded by a host of symbols, events, people, and behaviours; thus, the incremental contribution of a sports event, facility, or team to the image of those cities is likely to be relatively small. Los Angeles has lost two NFL teams, but it is still Los Angeles. The contribution of sports events to the image of 'second-tier' cities is likely to be proportionately more substantial (Fulton, 1988, p. 36):

While the largest cities viewed sports teams as an important piece of their overall cultural package, in many less populous cities the teams have become inextricably linked with the city's image. Cities such as Oakland, St Louis, Kansas City and Cincinnati – none of them among the top 25 cities in population – all have proved to be great sports towns; in many cases, their sports franchises constitute validation that these cities were in the 'big leagues'.

'Sports means more to Oakland' says the former city manager. It makes less of a difference to New York, San Francisco, or Chicago.

Many believe the adage that 'No place really can be considered to be a "big town" if it doesn't have a professional team'. This type of thinking was espoused by the mayor of San Jose when she was trying to persuade the San Francisco Giants to move to her city (Fimrite, 1992):

> She asserts that the Giants will also bring her city the recognition she feels it has earned as a big league metropolis. 'The best kept secret in the country', says the mayor 'is that San Jose, with a 1992 population of 803,000, not only is larger than San Francisco by 75,000 people, but also is the third largest city in the nation's largest state – behind only Los Angeles and San Diego – and the eleventh largest in the country' (p. 51).

When the San Jose Sharks National Hockey League team commenced play in the city in the early 1990s, the city built a new arena for them in 1993. One commentator reported that it 'transformed' the city:

> In eight months of operation the new downtown arena has brought San Jose into the big leagues of sports and entertainment. This, combined with a revitalised downtown and a lively arts scene, has given its citizens something to brag about.

People frequently make judgments about the competence of a city's administration and its quality of life by extrapolating from snippets of information or from symbols. A sports team is a highly visible symbol. Thus, another dimension of the image issue relates to perceptions of the level of competency of a community's governance. A sports franchise may be considered by some as a symbolic embodiment of the city as a whole (Euchner, 1993). If a city successfully negotiates and implements a major sports event or facility, then the inherent complexity of the task and the wide publicity these actions generate are likely to convey an aura of high competency upon the city's leadership. In contrast, if cities lose a sports facility, team or event, it may create the impression that local officials and politicians are incompetent. Those in leadership roles, for example, in cities that lost the Oakland Raiders, Indianapolis Colts, and St Louis Cardinals may be forever stigmatised in the eyes of many, irrespective of the intrinsic merits of their decisions. Further, those cities may be perceived as 'declining', 'losers', or 'lacking in civic pride' because of the high profile loss. Baade and Dye (1988) note:

> A mayor's political stock rises substantially if the mayor secures a professional sports presence and falls just as rapidly if his or her name is associated with the loss of a team. During Chicago's most recent mayoral campaign there was much speculation about what a White Sox move would do to Mayor Harold Washington's chances for reelection. Perhaps no one has stated as succinctly what underlies the fear of a franchise loss than the individual who headed Minnesota Governor Rudy Perpich's task force of revitalising the state's economy. He commented: 'It's almost worse for a city's image to lose a major league team than to have never had one at all' (p. 37).

Given the potential positive impact of a sports team, facility or event on a city's image, those cities with most to gain from it are those that are in decline. They are most desperate to communicate signs of economic and social rejuvenation. Unfortunately, these struggling cities also are least able to make major investments.

Stimulation of other development

The notion that a sports event or facility will stimulate additional development and thus contribute to expansion of a city's tax base is at least in part a consequence of the increased visibility and enhanced image cities believe will accrue from their investment. The types of development envisaged by proponents of this notion can be classified under three headings: complementary development, proximate development, and general development.

Complementary development refers to the upgrading or initiation of businesses as a result of the demand for their services that is directly created by the sport facility or event. For example, it was reported that the Adelaide Grand Prix 'played a catalytic role in motivating some existing tourism operators to upgrade their business in terms of facilities and/or services' (Van der Lee and Williams, 1986, p. 55). Demand for the event itself was concentrated on a week-long time period which makes it unlikely that such upgrading would be cost-efficient, but 'the event raised expectations of higher tourism growth for the future' (Van der Lee and Williams, 1986, p. 55). The event provided a psychological boost and created an atmosphere of optimism that, in themselves, are sometimes sufficient to become a self-fulfilling prophecy. That is, the upgrading of amenities in the area may be a central factor in attracting increased visitation during the remainder of the year.

The America's Cup Challenge when it was held in Freemantle, Western Australia, had the effect on the city of boosting development of both new marine-related industries and non-marine related high-technology businesses, such as computer systems, advanced metals technology, and synthetic fibres. These products were prominently publicised in the Australian media in the period of many months during which the media were preoccupied with the America's Cup. The frequent references to high technology products and Freemantle created a nexus in many people's minds (Newman, 1989).

Publicly subsidised professional sports facilities are increasingly conceptualised as being part of a total package incorporating *proximate development* that may include retailing, property development, and general leisure provision. The sports facilities are used to attract other businesses to the area. Thus, when the America West Arena opened in downtown Phoenix as home to the Phoenix Suns NBA team, it spurred a 13 per cent increase in tax revenues from associated downtown development (Gross, 1994). This also was the thinking underlying development of Joe Robbie Stadium (now renamed the Pro Player Stadium), the home of the Miami Dolphins NFL team, which is the only private sector stadium developed in the past two decades. The stadium is on a 160-acre site that is part of a 430-acre parcel owned by developers. They gave a long-term lease on the stadium site for a rental of $1 per year believing that the stadium would greatly enhance the value of the remaining property. The lease was given to Dade County which then offered it on a similar lease to the team owner. Because it was now on city property, the team received major benefits, including substantial rebates on sales taxes. The developer observed: 'The stadium is the catalyst. The business potential is fantastic' (cited in Lowenstein 1985, p. 33). Although plans for development around the stadium were slow to materialise because of a downturn in the economy and lawsuits brought by opponents of the development (Baker, 1992), the value of the remaining property was trebled as a result of the stadium's presence.

At the minor league level, Port St Lucie, located north of Fort Lauderdale on Florida's southeast coast, appears to offer an example of successful development facilitated by baseball (Johnson, 1993):

> In 1988, the New York Mets' spring training activities and minor league team were lured from St Petersburg by a new $10 million state-of-the-art stadium and training facility. The land for the stadium was provided by the city and funded through the county's tourist-tax revenues. The stadium developer, Thomas J. White Development Company of St Louis, also was building a $2 billion residential and commercial project adjacent to the stadium. Mets team members were involved in the project's marketing strategy.
>
> Port St Lucie viewed this as a winning policy. The city nearly quadrupled its population, from 14,000 in 1980 to 55,866 by 1990. It has expanded its tax base, and baseball provides an amenity package to attract residents. The developer has a stadium located next to his development, which draws prospective buyers. The team uses a new premiere facility, subsidised by local government, for spring training and its minor league team (p. 158).

An element of a Virginia legislature study that investigated the case of subsidising a new stadium for the Washington Redskins in Alexandria, Virginia, was a survey of the other 27 NFL stadiums. It concluded that seven of them had served as magnets for development, but five of them were part of a convention centre, were domed stadiums, or were part of multipurpose facilities (Baker, 1992). One of the stadiums where proximate development occurred was the Superdome in New Orleans. Its construction led to a revival of downtown with office buildings, hotels, and a shopping centre being developed nearby. However, the Superdome's greatest attraction to other developers was its vast and inexpensive parking garage (Fulton, 1988).

In contrast to the Superdome situation, some large parking lots that surround many stadiums are 'dead' space for most of the year, which mitigates against social and economic integration with other commercial entities. If a stadium is intended to stimulate other development, then fans should be channelled to it through carefully planned corridors to maximise secondary economic activity (Baade and Dye, 1988). It has been noted that:

> Many sports facilities constructed in the post-World War II era, beginning with County Stadium in Milwaukee and Memorial Stadium in Baltimore, accommodated the preference for automobile transportation and population shifts within an urban area from the central city to the suburbs. Surrounding

a stadium with a sea of asphalt or concrete eases entry and egress of automotive traffic, but mitigates the spillover of stadium pedestrian traffic into other commercial sites in the city, particularly in the stadium's environs. New sports facilities in downtown Cleveland, Baltimore, and Denver have departed from automobile-inspired designs and locations. The early evidence indicates that these more synergistic urban stadium plans may promote neighborhood economic development beyond that experienced by facilities shaped by automotive imperatives.

(Baade and Sanderson, 1997, p. 95)

The antithetical goals of team owners and public officials who are seeking to use a new stadium to stimulate redevelopment of downtown areas are noted by Johnson (1991):

From the team's perspective the ideal location will be a site that is easily accessible, has visibility from major highways, and is compatible with the direction of existing and future population growth. It should not be a surprise that the community goals of local officials, often do not match the location criteria and business interests of team owners. As one interviewer commented, team owners are not in the urban redevelopment business (p. 319).

In Indianapolis, the Hoosier Dome sparked the redevelopment of Union Station and was a major anchor for downtown development; therefore, it had a proximate development impact. An official also observed: 'the best advertising this city has is that the dome exists – You never know who is watching an NFL game. Often viewers include promotion and convention planners. So the team really has proven to be a benefit for us'. This type of optimistic statement exemplifies the belief that the 'big-league' image will serve as a magnet and attract *general development*, which is neither complementary nor proximate, to the city.

The rising fortune of Newcastle United in the English soccer league is believed to have been influential in the revitalisation of that city. Newcastle has shed the image of poverty, crime and unemployment and the heart of the city has been rebuilt:

Newcastle United's success is more than just a symbol of the city's new confidence. A trip to St James's Park, Newcastle's stadium, helped to persuade Samsung's directors to site their £450 million complex in the English northeast.

(Hinde, 1994)

When the team qualified for a European competition and flew to Spain to play against Bilbao, 20 local industrialists trying to win Spanish investment went with them. One of them stated: 'The trade mission will help to sell this region, and the club's participation is crucial' (Hinde, 1994, p. 12).

In Atlanta, Operation Legacy was developed by state officials and local business executives to use the 1996 Olympic Games in a strategy to recruit up to twenty major companies or facilities to Georgia. In the preceding years, every couple of months, about forty top executives from a single industry, such as auto parts, communications, and agribusiness, were invited with their spouses to spend several days in the city and state. They were entertained, encouraged to use the Olympic facilities, exposed to those organising the Atlanta Games, and to discussions about economic development. About 200 of those considered good prospects for the city, were invited back with their spouses to the Games (Ruffenach,1995). The event was used as a strategic tool to secure long-term economic development for the area.

Psychic income

Frequently, benefits accrue to the collective morale of residents from a sports event or team, especially if it is successful, and these benefits may be termed 'psychic income'. Those involved in successfully organising a major sports event are likely to grow in confidence and feel a sense of pride in their accomplishment. More generically, however, psychic income refers to benefits received by many community residents who are not involved in organising and who do not physically attend the event, but nevertheless, strongly identify with it. Lipsky (1979) writes that sports involvement can be:

> a counterpoint to the decline of political effect and the widespread nostalgia for community in America ... The language of sports is the symbolic glue that holds the entire social lifeworld. It is the common idiom that links (hereto-fore male) Americans in the taverns, the living rooms, car pools and offices ... The team acts in many ways as the symbolic community that unites belief systems and authority structures with people's everyday lives (pp. 67–68).

Elsewhere, Lipsky (1981) eloquently observed: 'Sport is the magic elixir that feeds personal identity while it nourishes the bonds of communal solidarity' (p. 5). A substantial proportion of a community emotionally identifies with 'its' team or event and feels elation, anxiety, despondency, optimism, and an array of other emotions according to how the team performs. Some of these people may not understand the nature of the event or how the activity is performed. Nevertheless, the team constitutes 'a common identification symbol, something that brings the citizens of the city together, especially during those exhilarating times when the city has a World Series champion, or a Super Bowl winner' (Quirk and Fort, 1992, p. 176).

This joyous reaction is a physiological reaction. For those who identify with teams winning and losing have a direct effort on the chemical composition of the brain, particularly on levels of a neuro-transmitter called serotonin. Winning raises levels, losing lowers them. One commentator observed: 'On Thursday the male population of England had an experience not unlike taking the rave drug Ecstasy. England's cricketers annihilated Australia, the best team in the world' (James 1997, p. 16). Even though they are not present at a sports event, millions may gain benefits of this nature from it.

The value of this type of psychic income to an individual fan is illustrated by the following statement: 'I'm a Lakers fan and pay nothing for it. If someone said, "Give me $100 or the Lakers will fold," I'd pay it' (Korman, 1989, p. 32).

The Cleveland Indians NFL team is making available 4 million shares of stock in the team, at a price of $15 per share. In documents filed with the offering, the team make it clear that it does not expect to pay a dividend. Nor do the new shareholders have any influence in running the club, because the owner's existing stock has 10,000 times the voting rights of the new stock. Despite the poor prospects of any return on their investment, the stock was purchased by fans who could gain substantial psychic income from bragging to their friends that they 'own' a piece of the team (Nocera, 1998).

It has been suggested that the subsidies sports event or team managers negotiate from public sector officials through the political process can be conceptualised as a measure of the value of psychic income received by a community:

> Team owners deal with us collectively at the city level in selling major league status to cities. We're better off paying it than not having the team.
> (Korman, 1989, p. 32)

An indication of the 'extensity' of the psychic income emerged from studies undertaken at the Adelaide Grand Prix. Researchers reported (Burns and Mules, 1986): 'The most interesting result from the studies on traffic congestion, travel time lost, noise and property damage was the number of people who, while being affected by these problems, were nevertheless strongly in favour of the Grand Prix' (p. 26). The researchers went on to speculate about what could have generated the psychic income:

> For many, of course, there was the general air of excitement and the feeling that South Australians were participating in a world event. Perhaps for a while we secured for ourselves some of the glamour often associated with other Grand Prix venues such as Monza, Monaco and Brand's Hatch. Certainly it seems to be the case that people felt good about themselves. This feeling was increased with the winning of the award for the 1985 Grand Prix.
> (Burns and Mules, 1986, p. 27)

Building offices, factories or distribution outlets create economic development, but they do not have sport's capacity for creating personal joy and community pride and solidarity. Psychic income may be the major justification for public sector subsidisation of private sports teams and events.

Conclusion

Out of the five sources of momentum which have been used to generate support for major investment of public funds in the construction of major sports facilities and the hosting of major events, the one that has had most research effort and funding targeted at it has been the economic impact argument. Although this is the benefit most easily measured, it has proved to be the area where often the benefit has been susbtantially exaggerated. This chapter has argued that the other four benefits of investing in major sports facilities or hosting major sports events may in the long run be greater than the immediate economic impact generated by the spending of visitors to these facilities and events. The problem for economists is to devise adequate research tools for the effective measurement of such benefits.

References

Arnold, A. (1986). The Impact of the Grand Prix on the Transport Sector', in J.P.A. Burns, J.H. Hatch, and T.J. Mules (eds), *The Adelaide Grand Prix: The Impact of a Special Event*, 58–81. Adelaide: The Centre for South Australian Economic Studies.

Baade, R.A. (1987). 'Is There an Economic Rationale for Subsidizing Sports Stadiums?' *Heartland Policy Study No. 13*. Chicago: The Heartland Institute.

Baade, R.A. and Dye, R.F. (1988). 'An Analysis of the Economic Rationale for Public Subsidization of Sports Stadiums'. *The Annals of Regional Science*, Vol. 22(2), 37–47.

Baade, R.A. and Sanderson, A.R. (1997). 'The Employment Effect of Teams and Sports Facilities', in R.G. Noll and A. Zimbalist (eds), *Sports, Jobs and Taxes*. Washington, DC: The Brookings Institution, pp. 92–118.

Baker, D.P. (1992). 'Cooke would get good deal after he pays for stadium'. *The Washington Post*, August 22, pp. C1, C3.

Bishop, G. and Hatch, J. (1986). 'The impact of the Grand Prix on the Accommodation Sector', in J.P.A. Burns, J.H. Hatch, and T.J. Mules (eds), *The Adelaide Grand Prix: The Impact of a Special Event*, pp. 82–94. Adelaide: The Centre for South Australian Economic Studies.

Burns, J.A. and Mules, T.J. (1986). 'A Framework for the Analysis of Major Special Events'. In J.A. Burns, J.H. Hatch and T.J. Mules (eds), *The Adelaide Grand Prix*, pp. 5–36. Adelaide: The Centre for South Australian Economic Studies.

Business Week (1983), 'Suddenly everyone wants to build a superdome', December 5, pp. 110–112.

Corliss, R. (1992). 'Build it and they might come'. *Time*, August 24, pp. 50–52.

Crompton, J.L. (1995). 'Economic Impact Analysis of Sports Facilities and Events: Eleven Sources of Misapplication'. *Journal of Sport Management*, Vol. 9(1):14–35.

Euchner, C.C. (1993). *Playing the Field: Why Sports Teams Move and Cities Fight to Keep Them*. Baltimore: The Johns Hopkins University Press.

Fimrite, R. (1992, June 1). 'Oh give me a home…'. *Sports Illustrated*, pp. 50–52.

Foley, P. (1991). 'The impact of the World Student Games on Sheffield'. *Environment and Planning C: Government and Policy*, Vol. 9, 65–78.

Fulton, W. (1988, March). 'Politicians Who Chase After Sports Franchises May Get Less Than They Pay For'. *Governing*, pp. 34–40.

The Economist (1981), 'Games people shouldn't play'. April 6, p. 58.

Gross, J. (1994). '"Big League" ambition transforms San Jose'. *The New York Times*, May 6, Section A, p. 10.

Hinde, S. (1994). 'City of gloom flourishes in northern bloom'. *The Sunday Times*, October 30, p. 12.

James, O. (1997). 'The Serotonin Society'. *The Observer*, June 8, p. 16.

Johnson, A.T. (1991). 'Local Government, Minor League Baseball, and Economic Development Strategies'. *Economic Development Quarterly*, Vol. 5(4), pp. 313–324.

Johnson, A.T. (1993). *Minor League Baseball and Local Economic Development*. Urbana, IL: University of Illinois Press.

Korman, R. (1989). A Matter of Pride. *Sports Inc.*, February 20, pp. 32–37.

Lipsky, R. (1979). 'Political Implications of Sports Team Symbolism'. *Politics Soc.*, Vol. 9, 61–88.

Lipsky, R. (1981). *How We Play the Game: Why Sports Dominate American Life.* Boston: Beacon.

Lowenstein, R. (1985). 'Miami Dolphins owner builds a stadium with private financing and fancy seating'. *Wall Street Journal*, November 15, Section 2, p. 33.

Newman, P.G. (1989). 'The Impact of the America's Cup on Freemantle – An Insider's View', in G.S. Syme, B.J. Shaw, D.M. Fenton and W.S. Mueller (eds), *The Planning and Evaluation of Hallmark Events*, pp. 46–58. Aldershot, England: Avebury.

Noll, G. and Zimbalist, A. (1997). 'Build the stadium – Create the jobs', in Roger G.Noll and Andrew Zimbalist (eds), *Sports, Jobs and Taxes*. Washington, DC: The Brookings Institution, pp. 1–54.

Quirk, J.P. and Fort, R.D. (1992). *Pay dirt: The Business of Professional Team Sports.* Princeton, NJ: Princeton University Press.

Richmond, P. (1993). *Ballpark: Camden Yards and the building of an American dream.* New York: Simon and Schuster.

Ritchie, J.R.B. and Smith, B.H. (1991). 'The impact of a mega event on host region awareness: a longitudinal study'. *Journal of Travel Research*, Vol. 30(1): pp.3–10.

Ruffenach, G. (1995). 'The outlook: Atlanta hopes games yield lasting benefits'. *The Wall Street Journal*, October 30, Section A., p. 1.

Van der Lee, P. and Williams, J. (1986). 'The Grand Prix and Tourism', in J.P.A. Burns, J.H. Hatch and T.J. Mules (eds), *The Adelaide Grand Prix*, pp. 39–57. Adelaide: The Centre for South Australian Economic Studies.

3 The role of major sports events in the economic regeneration of cities

Lessons from six World or European Championships

Chris Gratton, Nigel Dobson and Simon Shibli

Introduction

Up until the 1980s, hosting major sporting events such as the Olympics were thought of as a financial and administrative burden to the organising city and country. This view was confirmed by the loss of £692 million made by Montreal in the staging of the 1976 summer Olympics. The previous summer Olympics in Munich in 1972 made a loss of £178 million.

Following these escalating losses, it seemed as if any host city would have to accept such a financial burden if it were to stage the Olympic Games or any other major sports event. However, the 1984 Los Angeles Olympics changed the economics of major sports events. These games made a surplus of £215 million. The financial success of the Los Angeles Olympics changed the way cities and governments regarded the hosting of major sports events. Partly as a result of this, but also because there developed a greater understanding of the broader economic benefits to a city and country that could result from the staging of a major sports event, cities started to compete fiercely to host major World and European championships across a wide range of sports.

This chapter concentrates on the economic importance of major sports events using data from six major sports events, all either World or European Championships, staged in England and Scotland between1996 and 1999. All six were held in Britain's 'National Cities of Sport', Sheffield, Birmingham, and Glasgow. These six events were part of a study carried out for the UK, English, and Scottish Sports Councils. This chapter attempts to draw some general conclusions for the economic benefits of sports events to the hosting cities and therefore puts these six events in the context of other studies that have been carried out over recent years. Before we move on to consider the details of the six events, we first of all review the developing literature on major sports events.

The economic importance of major events

The study of hallmark events or mega-events became an important area of the tourism and leisure literature in the 1980s. The economic benefits of such events has been the main focus of such literature, although broader based multidisciplinary approaches have been suggested (Hall, 1992; Getz, 1991). Within the area of mega-events, sports events have attracted a significant amount of attention.

One of the first major studies in this area was the study of the impact of the 1985 Adelaide Grand Prix (Burns, Hatch and Mules, 1986). This was followed by an in-depth study of the 1988 Calgary Winter Olympics (Ritchie, 1984; Ritchie and Aitken, 1984,1985; Ritchie and Lyons 1987, 1990; Ritchie and Smith, 1991).

Mules and Faulkner (1996) point out that even with such mega-events as F1 Grand Prix races and the Olympics, it is not always an unequivocal economic benefit to the cities that host the event. They emphasise that, in general, staging major sports events often results in the city authorities losing money even though the city itself benefits greatly in terms of additional spending in the city. Table 3.1 shows the losses made by Australian cities hosting major sporting events, at the same time as indicating the increase in Gross State Product (GSP) generated as a direct result of the event. Thus the 1994 Brisbane World Masters Games cost A$2.8 million to put on but generated a massive A$50.6 million of additional economic activity in the State economy. Mules and Faulkner's basic point is that it normally requires the public sector to be in the role of staging the event and incurring these losses in order to generate the benefits to the local economy:

> This financial structure is common to many special events, and results in the losses alluded to above. It seems unlikely that private operators would be willing to take on the running of such events because of their low chance of breaking even let alone turning a profit. The reason why governments host such events and lose taxpayers' money in the process lies in spillover effects or externalities.

It is not a straightforward job, however, to establish a profit and loss account for a specific event. Major sports events require investment in new sports facilities and often this is paid for in part by central government or even international sports bodies. Thus some of this investment expenditure represents a net addition to the local economy since the money comes in from outside. Also such facilities remain after the event has finished acting as a platform for future activities that can generate additional tourist expenditure (Mules and Faulkner, 1996).

Increasingly sports events are part of a broader strategy aimed at raising the profile of a city and therefore success cannot be judged on simply a profit and loss basis.

Often the attraction of events is linked to a re-imaging process, and in the case of many UK cities, is invariably linked to strategies of urban regeneration and tourism development (Bianchini and Swengel, 1991; Bramwell 1995; Loftman and Spirou 1996; Roche 1992a). Major events, if successful, have the ability to project a new image and identity for a city. The hosting of major sports events is often justified by the host city in terms of long-term economic and social consequences, directly or indirectly resulting from the staging of the event (Mules and

Table 3.1 Financial costs and economic impact of various events

Event	Financial loss (A$ million)	Impact on GSP (A$ million)
1985 Adelaide Grand Prix	2.6	23.6
1992 Adelaide Grand Prix	4.0	37.4
1991 Eastern Creek Motor Cycle Grand Prix	4.8	13.6
1994 Brisbane World Masters Games	2.8	50.6

Source: Mules and Faulkner (1996)

Faulkner 1996). These effects are primarily justified in economic terms, by estimating the additional expenditure generated in the local economy as the result of the event, in terms of the benefits injected from tourism related activity and the subsequent re-imaging of the city following the success of the event (Roche 1992b).

Cities staging major sports events have a unique opportunity to market themselves to the world. Increasing competition between broadcasters to secure broadcasting rights to major sports events has led to a massive escalation in fees for such rights, which in turn means broadcasters give blanket coverage at peak times for such events, enhancing the marketing benefits to the cities that stage them.

Measuring the economic impact of major sports events

The economic impact of major sports events is normally assessed using multiplier analysis as discussed by John Crompton in the previous chapter. Multiplier analysis converts the total amount of additional expenditure in the host city to a net amount of income retained within the city after allowing for 'leakages' from the local economy.

The ultimate purpose of multiplier calculations is that they can be used as the basis for further economic analysis such as making estimates of job creation attributable to a given inflow of income into a local economy. Sustained additional income into a local economy will lead to the creation of additional jobs within that economy. As the previous chapter indicates, many such multiplier studies have in the past been flawed. We believe we have avoided such mistakes in our study and the details of our approach appear in Chapter 6 where we look in detail at a similar methodological approach applied to two other events. Here we concentrate on the comparison between these six major events in order to make some general conclusions about the role of sports events in the economic regeneration of cities.

Although the formal multiplier study approach to the calculation of economic impact was used in this study, for comparison across the six events it is useful to compare the additional expenditure generated in the host city by the event and the source of that additional expenditure. This will be the approach taken when discussing the results.

Major sports events in the UK

In the UK there has been a recent acknowledgement of the economic and social benefits that major events can have upon the host city, region or country. The setting up of the Major Events Support Group, now the Major Events Steering Group (MESG), in 1994, by the Sports Council was an attempt to assist governing bodies and local authorities in bidding for, and staging, major sports events. A report by the former National Heritage Committee (1995) entitled 'Bids to Stage International Sports Events' provided a framework for a co-ordinated approach to attracting events. The report indicated that the UK had started to fall behind other countries in its approach to attracting major sports events and that the UK had lacked a consistent approach for bidding for events. One of the principal objectives in setting up the UK Sports Council was to rationalise the system. The UK Sports Council has since adopted a Policy and Strategy for Major Events and funding is now available from the National Lottery to support major sports events.

The National Heritage Committee (1995) report stated:

> It is clear that bids to stage major sporting events … can operate as a catalyst to stimulate economic regeneration even if they do not ultimately prove successful.

The report used the case of Sheffield and Manchester to highlight the regenerative impact of sports events in the UK:

> … once the initial redevelopment has taken place, the existence of high quality facilities means that the cities concerned are able to attract other sports events. The impact however does not stop there. Many of the facilities are suitable for other uses such as conferences and concerts. In addition the favourable publicity which can follow from a successful event may increase the attractiveness of a city, raise its profile overseas, and enable it to attract an increasing number of tourists.

The economic importance of major sports events became an increasingly important issue in Britain following the economic success of the Euro 96 football championships. Euro 96 was the largest sports event to be held in Britain since the 1966 World Cup. It was an economic success story for the host cities and the British tourism industry, attracting 280,000 overseas visits, spending around £120 million in the eight host cities (Dobson, Gratton and Holliday, 1997). The Euro 96 matches held in one of these host cities, Sheffield, is one of the events in this study.

The success of Euro 96 has also led to an increased demand for more major sports events to be staged in Britain in the future, most notably the bids to stage the 2006 soccer World Cup Finals and the 2012 Olympic Games. The UK also hosted the 1999 Rugby Union and Cricket World Cups, and will host the 2002 Commonwealth Games.

However, every year in the UK there is a rolling programme of major sports events, some of which are of global significance. The Sports Council's 'Calendar of Major Sporting Events' lists 291 major sports events that took place in Great Britain in 1997. Out of the 291 events listed, 46 would attract major television coverage outside, as well as inside, Britain. These would include the Six Nations Rugby Tournament, Wimbledon, the Open Golf Championship, the FA Cup Final, the Boat Race, and the Grand National. Britain probably has the broadest portfolio of annual major sports events in relation to its population size of any country in the world. This gives an expertise and experience that represents a competitive advantage in this rapidly growing global market. It also signals a need to more fully understand how sport events can generate benefits to the cities that host them.

In the UK, three cities, Sheffield, Glasgow, and Birmingham, have adopted an economic strategy based on attracting major sports events to their area as a catalyst to stimulate economic regeneration. These three cities have been designated 'National Cities of Sport' and two of these, Sheffield and Birmingham, were also host cities in Euro 96. All of the six events that are the focus of this study took place in these 'National Cities of Sport'.

The economic importance of major sports events: a study of six events

This section reports the results of a study of six major sports events held in the United Kingdom between June 1996 and December 1999. The research was carried out on behalf of the UK, English and Scottish Sports Councils by the Leisure Industries Research Centre. The study aimed to evaluate the economic impact of these events on the local economies of host cities and towns as well as to investigate the complicated economics of staging major sports events.

The six events studied were:

1	9 – 20 June 1996	Group D Matches, Euro 96, Hillsborough Stadium, Sheffield
2	22 June – 3 July 1996	World Masters Swimming Championships, Ponds Forge International Sports Centre, Sheffield
3	19 May – 1 June 1997	World Badminton Championships and Sudirman Cup, Scotstoun Leisure Centre, Glasgow
4	11 – 13 December 1998	European Short Course Swimming Champion-ships, Ponds Forge International Sports Centre, Sheffield
5	7 – 10 October 1999	World Judo Championships, Indoor Arena, Birmingham
6	3 – 5 December 1999	World Indoor Climbing Championships, Indoor Arena, Birmingham

Figure 3.1 shows the wide variety in the economic impact generated by the six events. The Euro 96 matches in Sheffield generated by far the highest additional

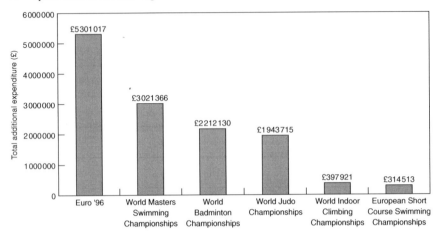

Figure 3.1 The economic impact of major sports events

expenditure in the host city, even though this event involved only three football matches. Euro 96 was also the highest profile event with the widest media coverage. The next in economic impact terms was the World Masters Swimming Champion-ships also taking place in Sheffield just a few days after the Euro 96 event had finished in the city. Although there was very little media coverage of this event, it involved over 4,000 competitors from all over the world staying for a considerable period in the city. These competitors also brought along friends and family who were the main spectators of the event. Given the large number of competitors there was also a considerable number of coaches and officials making a total of 6,500 visitors to the city as a result of the event. In contrast, Euro 96 attracted 61,000 visitors to the city but the majority of these were day-visitors not overnight stays. However, given the large number of visitors the economic impact was still considerable.

Table 3.2 shows that when the number of event days is taken into account the dominance of Euro 96 over the World Masters swimming becomes greater since there were 12 event days for the Masters but only three for Euro 96. The spend per event day of £1.77 million for Euro 96 is way ahead of any of the other events, again establishing this event as the third largest in the world in economic terms.

The World Masters Swimming and Euro 96 both illustrate that certain events are more attractive economically than others because of the number and type of 'sports tourists' they attract. The types of 'sports tourist' associated with the Masters event were typically from the more affluent sections of society, more likely to stay overnight in the city (an average stay in the city of 5.82 nights for all visitors), with greater disposable income and with an increased ability to inject money into the local economy. £100,000 was generated through the sale of merchandise to visitors related to the event. Their impact stretched beyond the days of competition, as a result of a further vacation in Sheffield, its surrounding region or other parts of the UK. This type of event is an ideal type of sporting event upon which to base

Table 3.2 Average additional visitor expenditure per event day

	Average additional expenditure per event day
Badminton	£158,091
Climbing	£132,640
Euro 96	£1,767,006
Judo	£485,928
Masters swimming	£251,781
Short course swimming	£104,838

sporting regenerative strategies. Unfortunately, like all similar sports events there is fierce competition to secure such events.

Figure 3.1 shows that the World Badminton Championships and the World Judo Championships were similar in overall impact with the badminton generating just over £2 million in additional expenditure and the judo just less than £2 million. However, the badminton lasted much longer and hence Table 3.2 shows that judo generated over three times as much on a per event day basis than badminton.

The World Indoor Climbing and the European Short Course Swimming Championships were the events generating the smallest impacts with the former generating nearly one third more additional expenditure than the latter. Since the number of event days is identical at three, the relationship is also identical in Table 3.2. The additional expenditure in Sheffield generated by Euro 96 is nearly seventeen times greater than that generated in the same city by the European Short Course Swimming Championships, even though both events consisted of three event days. This illustrates the considerable variation in the contribution major sports events make to economic regeneration.

Figure 3.2 shows the relative contribution to economic impact of spectators on the one hand and competitors, officials and media representatives on the other. Euro 96 is at one end of the spectrum with 84 per cent of additional expenditure generated by spectators. At the other end is the European Short Course Swimming Championships with 91 per cent of additional expenditure in the city generated by competitors, officials and media. This is the typical picture for a major swimming championship, and the World Masters proportions confirm this. What is perhaps more surprising is that the World Indoor Climbing Championships is at the Euro 96 end of the spectrum whereas the World Badminton Championships is closer to the picture for swimming. The World Judo Championships have almost a 50:50 split between additional expenditure generated by spectators and competitors, officials and media.

The level of additional expenditure generated by competitors, officials, and media should be relatively easy to forecast in advance since it depends on the numbers of competitors and officials visiting and the number of event days. Hence, forecasting the economic impact of competitor-driven events is not a major problem. In Sheffield, for the European Short Course Swimming Champioships, it was possible to build up a profile of expenditure on the main items of accom-

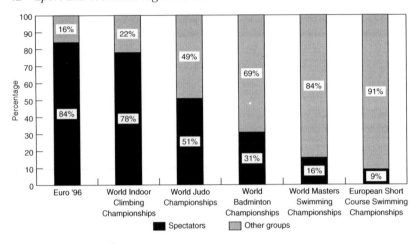

Figure 3.2 The continuum from spectator to competitor driven events

modation and food by investigating the terms offered by the hotels to the visiting teams and officials. There was little additional expenditure in addition to that on accommodation and food. In such circumstances it is possible to build up a very accurate forecast of the economic impact of the event prior to bidding for the event by investigating the number of competitors, officials and media present at previous stagings of the same championships and the number of days for which the championships ran.

Predicting the impact of spectators is much more difficult. In general, those cities bidding for events such as World or European Championships tend to overestimate the number of spectators that will attend. For instance, the predicted attendance for the World Badminton Championships in Glasgow was 35–40,000 whereas the actual attendance was 21,642. This illustrates the danger of staging special 'one-off' events. Projected attendances have a high error margin and mistakes can have a dramatic effect on the final budget out-turn as well as on the economic impact of the event in the local economy.

Implications for the economic importance of sports events in the UK

All the six events studied in this project were special 'one-off' events that would not normally take place in Britain on a regular basis. They are all World or European Championships that cities from different countries bid to host. It is just this type of event that cities target as part of their economic regeneration strategy.

The present authors (Gratton, Shibli, and Dobson, 2000) have developed a typology of major sports events as indicated below:

Type A: Irregular, one-off, major international spectator events generating significant economic activity and media interest (e.g. Olympics, Football World Cup, European Football Championship).

Type B: Major spectator events, generating significant economic activity, media interest and part of an annual domestic cycle of sports events (e.g. FA Cup Final, Six Nations Rugby Union Internationals, Test Match Cricket, Open Golf, Wimbledon).

Type C: Irregular, one-off, major international spectator/competitor events generating uncertain economic activity (e.g. World and European Championships in all sports).

Type D: Major competitor events generating limited economic activity and part of an annual cycle of sports events (e.g. National Championships in most sports).

Use of the word 'major' in each of these categories is to signify the importance of sporting outcomes of such events (e.g. national, European, or World Championships) rather than the economic importance. The typology is relevant to indicate that not all events that are 'major' in sporting terms are important in economic terms.

The majority of sports events in any one year are of Types B, C and D. Five of the events studied here are Type C. However, in terms of economic impact it is the Type A and B events that will dominate the contribution to economic impact in any one year.

Type D events, though of limited economic significance, also have limited additional costs of staging, since they are annual events and the governing bodies have long-term experience in terms of putting on such events.

Type C, however, are special events that take place on a one-off or irregular basis. Even if they take place regularly, from any one country's point of view they will be irregular since they move from country to country. Such events have to be planned and managed from scratch, and potentially pose a major organisational problem for the governing bodies and the cities in which they take place, since they will not have had the experience in hosting that particular event. Mega-events such as the Olympics and the World Cup (Type A), which also pose a similar problem, have proved that the costs of staging such events are easily matched by the economic benefits generated. However, for smaller events such as the World Badminton Championships the true costs of the organisation and staging of the event are probably greater than or equivalent to the economic benefits. In addition, it is very difficult to predict the level of spectator interest in such an event. Whereas the World Badminton Championships attract huge interest in Asia, it would have been difficult to forecast the level of spectator demand in Glasgow. The more competitor-driven the event then the easier it is to forecast the economic impact, but also the less the impact is likely to be.

For Type D events, the benefits do not cover the costs in economic terms and the rationale for bidding for such events must lie outside the purely economic domain.

Type A and B events will generate the largest economic benefits to the cities that host them. This is already well-known for Type A events, hence the fierce competition between cities to host them. The majority of Type B events either do not move venues for year to year (e.g. Wimbledon) or if they do, cities are not able to bid to host them. What is not generally realised, however, is that Britain is unusual in having a very high number of such events. This means that the sports event business is a significant industry in Britain and Britain has a competitive advantage over most other nations in having considerable expertise and experience in staging major sports events.

Type B events are a low-risk investment for any hosting city since spectator demand is relatively easy to predict. However, for cities trying to follow an event-led tourism strategy, such events are not normally 'on the market'. The result is that cities compete to stage Type C events, which is the most uncertain category in terms of economic impact. The results of this study, together with previous event impact studies, allow us to make certain generalisations about Type C events:

- the economic impact of competitor-driven events is relatively easy to forecast in advance;
- the more senior the event and the longer the event, then the larger the economic impact, with World Masters events, in particular, generating significant impacts as large numbers of relatively affluent competitors stay in the host city for several weeks;
- spectator forecasts for Type C events are subject to large error margins and the tendency is to make highly optimistic forecasts that rarely materialise, with the result that higher than expected losses are made on the event.

As more and more economic impact studies of sports events are carried out it will be possible to identify with more certainty the parameters of events that categorise their economic significance. Twenty years ago little was known about the economic significance of Type A and B events. The challenge for the next 10 years is that we understand more about the economics of Type C events. This study is hopefully one step along the path to meeting that challenge.

Conclusions

Major sports events are now a significant part of Britain's tourism industry. Britain has, partly by historical accident rather than by design, become the global market leader in the staging of major sports events because many of our annual domestic sporting competitions such as the FA Cup Final and Wimbledon attract a large number of overseas visitors and a global television audience. Major sports events held in Britain are a crucial ingredient in the creation of the tourist image of Britain. The evidence presented above indicates that some major sports events also have the potential to generate significant economic impact in the local economy of the host city. This is most recognised in the USA and Australia, but has been less so in Britain. The Australian Tourist Commission estimates that major events contribute 5 per cent of Australia's total tourism income each year.

This chapter has shown that there is a wide variation across sports events in their ability to generate economic impact in the host city. Just because the event is a World or European Championship does not guarantee that it will be important in economic terms. We are only just beginning to understand the parameters of the economics of staging major sports events. We hope that the evidence presented in this chapter enhances that understanding.

References

Bianchini, F. and Schwengel, H. (1991) 'Re-imagining the City'. In: Comer, J. and Harvey, S. (eds), *Enterprise and Heritage: Crosscurrents of National Culture.* Routledge: London, pp. 214–234.

Bramwell, B. (1991) 'Sheffield. Tourism Planning in an Industrial City'. *Insights*, March 23–28.

Bramwell, B. (1995) 'Event Tourism in Sheffield: A Sustainable Approach to Urban Development?' Unpublished paper. *Centre for Tourism.* Sheffield Hallam University.

Burns, J.P.A., Hatch, J.H. and Mules, F.J. (1986) (eds), *The Adelaide Grand Prix: the Impact of a Special Event.* Adelaide: The Centre for South Australian Economic Studies.

Dobson, N., Gratton, C. and Holliday, S. (1997) *Football Came Home: The Economic Impact of Euro 96.* Sheffield: Leisure Industries Research Centre.

Getz, D. (1991) *Festivals, Special Events, and Tourism.* New York: Van Nostrand Reinhold.

Gratton C., Shibli, S. and Dobson, N. (2000) 'The Economic Importance of Major Sports Events'. *Managing Leisure*, Vol. 5(1), January, pp. 17–28.

Hall, C.M. (1992) *Hallmark Tourist Events: Impacts, Management and Planning.* London: Belhaven Press.

Loftman, P. and Spirou, C.S. (1996) *Tourism & Culture: Towards the 21st Century.* Conference; Centre for Travel & Tourism. Durham.

Mules, T. and Faulkner, B. (1996) 'An Economic Perspective on Major Events'. *Tourism Economics*, Vol. 12(2).

National Heritage Committee (1995) Bids to Stage International Sporting Events. *Fifth Report. House of Commons.* London: HMSO.

Ritchie, J.R.B. (1984) 'Assessing the Impact of Hallmark Event: Conceptual and Research Issues'. *Journal of Travel Research*, Vol. 23(1), pp. 2–11.

Ritchie, J.R.B. and Aitken, C.E. (1984) 'Assessing the Impacts of the 1988 Olympic Winter Games: the Research Program and initial results'. *Journal of Travel Research*, Vol. 22(3), pp. 17–25.

Ritchie J.R.B. and Aitken, C.E. (1985) 'OLYMPULSE II – Evolving Resident Attitudes Towards the 1988 Olympics'. *Journal of Travel Research*, Vol. 23(Winter), pp. 28–33.

Ritchie, J.R.B. and Lyons, M.M. (1987) 'OLYMPULSE III/IV: a Mid Term Report on Resident Attitudes Concerning the 1988 Olympic Winter Games'. *Journal of Travel Research*, Vol. 26(Summer), pp. 18–26.

Ritchie, J.R.B. and Lyons, M.M. (1990) 'OLYMPULSE vi: a Post-event Assessment of Resident Reaction to the XV Olympic Winter Games'. *Journal of Travel Research*, Vol. 28(3), pp. 14–23.

Ritchie, J.R.B. and Smith, B.H. (1991) 'The Impact of a Mega-Event on Host Region Awareness: a Longitudinal Study'. *Journal of Travel Research*, Vol. 30(1), pp. 3–10.

Roche, M. (1992a) 'Mega-Events and Urban Policy'. *Annals of Tourism Research* Vol. 21(1).

Roche, M. (1992b) 'Mega-Event Planning and Citizenship: Problems of Rationality and Democracy in Sheffield's Universiade 1991'. *Vrijetijd en Samenleving*, Vol. 10(4), pp. 47–67.

4 A comparison of the economic contribution of hallmark sporting and performing arts events

Lynley Ingerson

Introduction

The staging of major events is emerging as a major strategy used by governments in an attempt to attract non-residential individuals to a particular destination. The use of event tourism to boost national and regional development tends to make government and tourism authorities sensitive to the impact of tourism. Given the increasing competition between nations and regions for generating incomes, the hosting of major events can make a significant economic contribution. Event tourism aims to create 'tourist attractions capable of generating travel demand or satisfying visitor needs' (Getz, 1991, p. 45). In Australia, the state government of Victoria is at the forefront of generating economic growth by the hosting of hallmark sporting events which also contributes to raising its profile nationally and internationally.

Economic analysis by government and independent organisations is occurring more frequently as a justification for the spending of public money on major events. It can provide the framework for identifying a number of issues related to resource allocation and public sector support in policy decisions and fund injections for events. In the context of sport and performing arts events, economic impact can be defined as the 'net economic change in the host community that results from spending attributed to the event or facility' (Crompton, 1995). Within Australia, Victoria maintains a clear leadership position in hosting sporting events. Examples include the Spring Racing Carnival, Formula One Grand Prix and the Australian Tennis Open each showing substantial economic worth (A$174 million, A$96 million and A$70 million respectively) for the state. Under the Arts 21 strategy a number of successful performing arts initiatives such as *Beauty and the Beast*, *Phantom of the Opera* and the Three Tenors have also had a substantial impact on the Victorian economy.

Much economic analysis research undertaken in the sport and arts fields looks at a number of different estimation mechanisms (Throsby and Withers, 1979; Myerscough, 1988; Richardson, 1996; Howard and Crompton, 1996) which arguably exaggerate positive benefits and ignore negative effects. In particular, cost-benefit, input-out analysis, econometric models and the multiplier effect are the major economic measurement tools used. For example, in determining the direct and indirect impact of several hallmark events staged in Victoria the National Institute of Economic Impact Research (NIEIR) utilise input-output analysis and the IMP model, a Keynesian style model specifically devised for estimating economic impacts of events in Australia. However, in measuring performing arts activity, Throsby and Withers (1979) reasoned that it was difficult to accurately quantify output because performing arts is part of the service industry which invariably has many qualitative components.

The first part of this paper identifies the competition that exists between state governments in Australia when applying tourism strategies to differentiate one region from another. In particular, it will focus on the use of sport and performing arts activities for event tourism purposes. The use of economic measurement techniques to estimate the impact of events on the economy has been the subject of much debate in recent times and while the paper does not discuss in detail the capacities of economic measurement tools it does describe examples of measurement tools utilised in Victorian economic impact studies. There has been an increasing number of economic impact studies undertaken both prior to and following the holding of major events with many of the studies being carried out by and on behalf of government authorities to justify public spending.

The second part of this paper discusses the use of economic measurement tools in relation to hallmark events staged in Victoria. The discussion reveals that there is reasonable economic worth for staging hallmark events in Victoria as part of a tourism strategy. However, much of the information available to the public highlights positive benefits and largely ignores the associated costs. The paper points out a number of issues that could be included in the analysis which assist in providing a more objective and realistic account of the contribution arts and sports events make to the Victorian economy.

Economic competition for tourism between Australian states

Much rivalry exists between the states in Australia for economic opportunity. Australia is a country whose primary export commodities include agriculture, petroleum and mining products. For some Australian states, given their richness in these resources, there has been little need to diversify economic activity. Other states have recognised that to remain economically competitive there is a need to develop strategies in other areas. Tourism, and in particular the use of major events, is a relatively new phenomena which emerges as an innovative economic possibility. The degree of event tourism undertaken by each Australian state depends upon a number of factors such as geography, climate, accessibility to non-residential participants, facilities, infrastructure and financial support. However, as Richardson (1996) identified: 'all (states and Territories) are involved in international and domestic tourism … and most are involved in one way or another in the development of tourism' (p. 210). Competitive advantage for a state lies in its ability to produce a tourism strategy that attracts the most visitors, enhances its image worldwide and does not strain the region's resources (financial and physical).

The tourism industry in Australia has a unique base as an industry as it comprises a wide range of organisations which serve a broad cross section of consumers. For example, the tourism industry in Australia includes man-made facilities (such as the Sydney Opera House), natural physical attractions (Kakadu National Park), exhibitions (Madame Tussaud's Wax Works Tour), conferences, events and festivals (Gay and Lesbian Mardi Gras) which all utilise a number of different organisations, people from government agencies and the goods and services industries to effectively promote and deliver the attractiveness of the destination. Tourism in Australia has an annual growth rate of around 10 per cent which equated to over 3 million visitors in 1995. This represents approximately 0.5 per cent of the world market (Tourism Forecasting Council, 1995). The economic worthiness for developing tourism in an area is of considerable importance for many governments and corporate organisations. For the injection of funding and resources into tourism activities, such as major events, there needs to be some recognisable benefits to help justify the investments made.

Tourism is largely a decentralised industry which is carried out regionally throughout Australia. Thus the benefits gained can impact at both the regional and national level simultaneously. For example, the Mardi Gras Festival was initially a local parade based in Sydney but, for twenty years, has produced such extraordinary support from interstate and international participants, that it now generates significant economic benefits for the nation as well as for Sydney itself and has gained the recognition as a premier festival of international status.

Objectives for tourism development at state level generally resemble those at national level. However, each state has a different focus for the direction and implementation of its development of tourism. For instance, the Australian Bureau of Statistics identified that New South Wales, which has the greatest volume of tourism (43 per cent of total in-bound tourism), considers its greatest tourism assets to be man-made structures such as the Opera House and Darling Harbour. Given its ideal climate, Queensland tourist authorities focus on resort tourism (29 per cent in-bound tourists). In response to these, the Victorian tourism authorities (13 per cent in-bound tourists) have adjusted their product strategy to focus on attracting major national and international events to the state (ABS, 1997a). It is clear that Victorian tourism strategies are intended to have commercial orientations which arguably help the state's economic profile.

The use of events to stimulate economic growth

Events draw people to destinations because of what is happening there rather than because of what is there (French, Craig-Smith and Collier, 1995). A visitor's initial experience of a region may be due to a cultural event rather than a desire to visit a specific location. Events such as the Olympic Games or the Oberamagau Festival are good examples of events attracting visitors to a city. The involvement of government in supporting events is therefore important for economic, social and cultural reasons.

All three levels of government in Australia support the securing of events both indirectly by providing the necessary infrastructure and directly through the provision of capital. There is concern by some observers that government involvement is not appropriate given the significant levels of public money allocated to events. However, the use of events has become one means by which governments can promote themselves for political purposes and to stimulate new industry activity. Supporters of government involvement see event tourism as being essential to the economic advancement of a region, city or state. The level of state government involvement is dependent upon the size of the government, its stage of development and the state's political philosophy.

There is no clearer example of effective involvement by government in the attraction of major events to the state than in Victoria. The current state government was quick to recognise the economic value of attracting events to the state for marketing and business investment purposes. The importance of event tourism for Victoria is evident by the variety of major international events the government actively pursues. Table 4.1 indicates the list of hallmark events staged in Victoria in 1996/7 and their contribution to the state economy.

Funding for major events is provided through the government offices of Sport and Recreation, Arts Victoria and Tourism Victoria. A recent study undertaken by the Industry Commission estimated that the states spent a total of $2.5 billion in 1994/95 on various forms of support for industry in an effort to attract businesses and special events to their particular state. Victoria accounted for about 25.5 per cent ($637.5m) of this figure (Colebatch, 1998). In 1995 a total of $534 million was spent by the Victorian government in support of industry. Of that, over 26 per cent was spent on a number of selective industry areas including major projects ($9m), tourism ($28m), the Motor Cycle Grand Prix ($31m), museums, arts and film ($74m). This has caused some concern to the Commission as to the discriminatory way the Victorian Government is allocating funds (Colebatch, 1998). The need for the Victorian government to justify its event-related investments has brought about an increase in the number of economic impact studies produced for major sport and performing arts events.

Economic impact studies

Howard and Crompton (1995) identified that because of a scarcity of tax dollars in today's society, there is a need to justify the spending of taxpayers' money on certain activities. Australia, and in particular the people of Victoria, have a reputation of being sport and theatre enthusiasts. Some of the data collected for economic impact studies attempts to identify those intrinsic benefits which satisfy specifically, sport and theatre taxpayers. Other components identified in economic analysis, such as job creation and generation of revenues, are important concerns for all taxpayers. Increasingly, the need for government accountability and the necessity for control mechanisms, such as performance indicators, has led to economic measurement tools being applied to government operations.

Table 4.1 International events staged in Victoria in 1996/7 and their economic contribution

Event type Sport	Economic contribution $m	Event type Arts	Economic contribution $m
Rip Curl and Pro Surf Classic	$2.5	International Flower and	$2.4
Masters Golf	$4	Garden Show	
World Cup tie (soccer)	$34.9	Melbourne Festival	$13
Bledisloe Cup (Rugby Union)	$61	International Comedy	$17
Motor Cycle Grand Prix	$63	Festival	
Australian Tennis Open	$70	The Three Tenors	$38
Formula One Grand Prix	$96	Avalon Airshow	$63
(Motor Racing)		Beauty and the Beast	$100
Spring Racing Carnival	$174		
(inc. Melbourne Cup)			

Sources: State Development, Annual Report, 1996/97; Sport and Recreation Victoria, 1997; Tourism Victoria, 1997; Richardson & Coffey, 1998

Given that in today's environment there is a wide range of leisure options from which consumers may choose, investment into specific arts and sport events may only be of importance to a very small section of the community. However, economic impact studies can provide descriptive information and a financial account of an event which may have an impact on the wider community and ultimately influence them to also support such activities.

In recent years the Victorian government has undertaken, both internally and by independent organisations, a number of economic impact studies for major events. In accordance with its Strategic Plan (1997–2001), those departments responsible for major events such as Tourism Victoria, evaluate their performance by using a 'weight of evidence' approach (Tourism Victoria, 1997). Tourism Victoria argued that no one indicator can fully measure impact given the wide range of variables related to an event. To obtain information on the worthiness of sport and performing arts events, it uses a combination of syndicated research, tailored research, internal data and commissioned independent research agencies such as NIEIR.

When evaluating economic impact, both estimation measurement tools and expenditure areas need to be discussed. The factors to measure and the most appropriate economic model to apply has generated considerable discussion in recent times. The use of economic analysis can provide the structure and framework for identifying a number of tourism issues. These include areas such as resource allocation problems, forecasting trends and when there is a need for public sector support for tourism activities (such as major sport and arts events) in policy making and the injection of funds. The four most common measures for economic impact studies are input-output, econometric model, cost-benefit analysis and the multiplier effect.

There are a variety of authors and researchers (Throsby and Withers, 1979; Myerscough, 1988; Richardson, 1996; Crompton, 1995; Howard and Crompton, 1995) who have contributed to the capabilities and practicalities of these mechanisms in great detail but it is not the intent of this paper to discuss their work. The economic impact studies carried out in Victoria primarily use cost-benefit analysis, input-output analysis, the multiplier effect and the NIEIR IMP model. With the use of the IMP model, NIEIR studies are able to include measures of aggregate economic activity, over an extended period of time. This enables the inter-relationship between activities in different sections (primary, manufacturing and tertiary industries) and different levels of the economy to work themselves through, to show what the final effect would have been (Brain and Manolakos, 1991). The application of the IMP model in determining whether hallmark events such as the Australian Tennis Open are beneficial, includes elements such as direct operating expenditure, direct revenues, foreign funding and earnings induced from international tourism. Brain and Manolakos (1991) reasoned that 'the economy is not boosted by an increase in government (spending) ... because that wealth is already held in the economy, and is simply diverted from other uses. Any real increase in the wealth of the country (or region) occurs when additional funds flow in from outside the economy' (p. 16).

In the context of event tourism, the economic impact can be defined as the 'net economic change in the host community that results from spending attributed to the event or facility' (Crompton, 1995, p. 15). It is the quality and accuracy of data input which ultimately determines the quality and precision of the estimates. As identified previously, much economic analysis for events has been to justify the spending of public money on events or facilities specific to arts and sports (Crompton, 1995; Eadington and Redman, 1991). Crompton (1995) argued that the 'motives of those commissioning the economic impact analysis appear to lead to adoption of procedures and underlying assumptions that bias the resultant analysis so the numbers support their advocacy position' (p. 15).

Economic impact studies carried out on Victoria arts and sports events apply some of the measurement tools identified in this paper. However, there are a number of issues emerging from economic impact analysis which need to be discussed in relation to hallmark events held in Victoria.

Discussion

As pointed out much of the economic analysis undertaken for Victorian hallmark events has been carried out by and on behalf of the Victorian government. It could be argued that in applying a variety of economic measurement techniques and the misuse of the multiplier, distortions may occur leading to a false indication of the productiveness of the event. It is beyond the scope of this paper to critically review the measurement tools in economic impact studies undertaken for hallmark events in Victoria. However, the focus of the discussion will highlight some of the mechanisms applied to Victorian performing arts and sporting events as well as consider other issues of importance in economic analysis.

Organisations which undertake events in the performing arts sector are largely non-profit based and given the high costs to produce performing arts events, require substantial assistance from both government (Victorian and Federal) and private sectors to support their activities. Lingle (1992) argued that there is a growing acceptance of government support for the arts. Arts are perceived as 'merit goods' and that without society being exposed to arts activities there may be a detrimental effect on society members. This may 'spill over' into other areas such as education. By and large, arts audiences are reluctant to bear the full costs of producing arts events and thus government and private organisations provide financial support, so that they may be offered to the community at an affordable price (Lingle, 1992). For example, *Beauty and the Beast* was reported at conservatively costing $12 million to produce. It required an extended season and corporate support to ensure it was accessible to price sensitive patrons. The latest figures from the Bureau of Statistics recorded that Australians spend $25.59 per week on cultural activities. Live theatre admission accounts for $1.29 (5 per cent) of weekly spending (ABS, 1997b). With such a small amount of household expenditure allocated to theatre activity it is clear that there is a need for government and corporate support for the arts.

When staging arts events there are a number of input sources which contribute to the economic analysis. Inputs may include labour, capital, the number of performances, tickets available for sale and actual ticket sales, and the number of separate productions mounted. Labour itself is a complex input as it can be separated into a number of areas including artisitc performance, technical and administration, making it difficult to accurately measure inputs. In support of input analysis it is important to note performing arts activity is part of the service industry which invariably has many qualitative components. The diversity of inputs and the difficulty in measuring qualitative inputs, makes it hard to quantify output and provide an accurate representation of staging the event.

Throsby and Withers (1979) proposed that there are a number of influences which impact on the value of economic analysis, including price, availability of substitutes, income levels, available leisure time and product differentiation. For example, product differentiation at the Melbourne Festival may include the variety in performance standards, location of the various activities, diverse promotional and advertising mechanisms and the offering of ancillary services such as food and drink, theatre comfort, and social ambience. It could be suggested that to produce accurate results each area requires specific measurement tools which may not be practically or financially feasible.

From the impact studies analysed it appears that the size of the event is a contributing factor in determining whether economic analysis is managed internally. Figure 4.1 indicates a comparison of spectators attending hallmark sports and arts events.

Given that the analysis of most performing arts events in Victoria is carried out by Tourism Victoria, the real economic value of the event can be questioned. Crompton (1995) supported this assumption by stating that: 'too often, the motives of those commissioning an economic impact analysis appear to lead to adoption

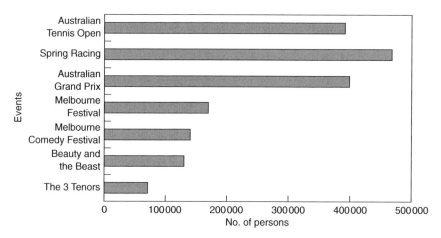

Figure 4.1 Attendances at hallmark events

of procedures and underlying assumptions that bias the resultant analysis so the numbers support their advocacy position' (pp. 15–16).

Tourism Victoria identified, through cost-benefit analysis, that the economic value of *Phantom of the Opera* clearly exceeded the face value of tickets sold and the associated benefits to various other industry sectors such as venue, hospitality and transport. Cost-benefit analysis should identify the true economic value of the event. However, there is little evidence in the documentation available as to who received the profits from the event and who bore the losses. Often the economic importance of arts activity is overestimated. This can amplify the impact on other economic sectors like tourism (Brosio, 1994). The analysis undertaken for the *Phantom of the Opera* event included interstate visitors as well as international visitors. The implications for this is that overall benefits to Victoria would in fact be less positive as it is only spending by overseas visitors which has any real impact. Interstate visitors have only shifted their spending from one area to another and the spending occurred by interstate visitors is substantially less than that of overseas visitors.

The contribution of festivals for Victoria involved the analysis of expenditure by attendees of the festival and the direct and indirect flow-on benefits. A difficulty in measuring economic benefits of festivals is determining which tourists were visiting Victoria specifically to attend the festival and which tourists were there anyway (and may have also attended the festival). The complication is in determining a visitor's actual festival related expenditures. Often the timing of the research can affect the results. That is, expenditure information may be incomplete if gathered during a festival (where spending by the participant has not stopped) or after a festival (where some expenditure items are forgotten). Other expenditure that has occurred in the festival region should be separated from festival spending.

When identifying total ticket sales as a means of determining the number of spectators at an event further problems arise. In the case of festivals or multiple performance events, the total ticket sales may overstate the total number of visitors as some patrons may attend more than one performance. An effective methodology is needed to overcome the problem of double counting. Even combined art sector events like opera and orchestra make it difficult to determine who receives the benefits (such as government funding) for staging the event, and the distribution of costs between the two segments. That is, if production costs for opera are greater than orchestra production costs, we lose the possibility of control over the effectiveness of government funding.

It could be argued that the economic assumptions applied to performing arts events differ from other activities, such as sport. Myerscough (1988) suggested that the economic analysis of the arts sector in the past has 'grossly exaggerated positive economic benefits, ignored negative effects and used "second hand" multipliers, measuring displacement effects rather than the real gains' (p.5). The application of economic analysis to the arts should not be restricted to a (narrow) economic, material or monetary aspect because of its many qualitative features and high production costs.

Economic analysis methods for sports events differ from arts events because most hallmark sports events in Victoria are 'one-off' occurrences. The performing arts events often take place over an extended period of time and are reproductions of existing creations. This can make performing arts events less attractive to international visitors. However, economic studies of hallmark sporting events in Victoria are generally carried out by independent organisations. It would be expected that an external organisation, with no direct association with the government, undertaking economic analysis should produce objective cost and benefit outcomes associated with the event. Hallmark sporting events in Victoria attract more patrons and therefore it is more difficult for government authorities, given their limited resources, to undertake data collection for a large volume of patrons, over a short time period.

The economic analysis of hallmark sporting events takes into consideration the rate of economic activity generated by spectators and participants of the event. The hosting of hallmark events can have continuous benefits for some regions. Infrastructure and facility development specifically created for an event can provide opportunities for the region to host other events and festivals of similar size and importance. For example, the National Tennis Centre (Melbourne Park) is a facility which was primarily designed to host the Australian Tennis Open (ATO) but has the capacity to host a wide variety of sport and entertainment activities, including sporting events, concerts, conferences and exhibitions. As evidence for this its major hiring revenues, excluding the ATO, has increased by over 75 per cent in the past five years (Melbourne and Olympic Parks Trust Annual Reports, 1992–1997).

Generally, the economic impact studies undertaken on sporting events in Victoria have involved the analysis of two key elements – costs and revenues to the event organisers and the impact of the event on the area. However, the general measures for an event fail to include direct expenditures on facilities, indirect expenditures on infrastructure, transport and accommodation and operating costs of the event.

Frey (1994) found that economic analysis does not take into account externalities such as constraints on individuals. For example, non-participation at an event may be due to income restraints (inability to purchase a ticket), time (when the event is scheduled), social constraint (unable to find or afford baby sitters) or physical issues (unable to get to Melbourne to attend). Forgone opportunity costs may increase the net loss. Other negative externalities to consider include the inconvenience of the event such as road closures, crime, vandalism, noise and air pollution to non-event Victorian taxpayers. On the other hand, positive externalities which may benefit the community include provision of much needed amenities, city clean-up and international exposure through event telecast. When externalities are included in the analysis the net benefit results could be quite different.

An area which is generally not researched is the respondents' intention to return to Victoria. Estimations are carried out on the likelihood of a return visit. However, there is no indication in the existing documentation that follow-up research has been carried out to identify return visitations to the region. For tourism strategy purposes it would be of value to know the long-term benefits events have on tourism through repeat visitations. When international visitors pay for goods and services related to the event, there is a net benefit. But as Dwyer and Forsyth (1993) pointed out, additional tourist expenditure on government subsidised goods and services such as public transport may actually impose additional costs on the host city.

Corporate entertainment by government is a cost not generally included in cost-benefit analysis. For example, the Victorian Government spent $270,000 on corporate entertainment at the 1997 Australian Grand Prix (Richardson and Coffey, February 19, 1998). This is a further cost to event production. A further expense not included in economic analysis is government funding allocated to hosting international event delegations who visit Victoria to inspect competition and venues for new events, such as has been allocated by the Victorian Government for Melbourne's 2006 Commonwealth Games bid.

For the Australian Tennis Open, inclusion of foreign participation at pre-ATO events, induced tourism from ATO foreign publicity and world-wide television exposure of Victoria as a potential tourist destination is worth further examination. Table 4.2 indicates the estimated exposure arts and sports events have received through television. Results of impact studies invariably include the level of inter-national and interstate media exposure obtained through staging an event. Dwyer and Forsyth (1993) found that there has been little research carried out which identifies the costs and benefits of tourism promotion. Thus the real costs and benefits of television and advertising exposure are largely ignored.

Employment opportunities that the performing arts and sports event offer provides another area for discussion. The majority of events conducted rarely accommodate permanent long-term employment. Both the arts and sports industries generally have a high level of volunteer workers and with events and festivals held over a number of days, the use of volunteers is economically beneficial for the event organisers. For large scale sports events in particular, much of the employment involves some full time staff in the planning and delivery stages, limited short-term employment for staff in the delivery and wind up periods of the event and

Table 4.2 International television exposure for selected hallmark events

Event	Estimated television audience
The Three Tenors	1.2 billion
Spring Racing Carnival	300 million
Australian Grand Prix	500 million
Australian Tennis Open	600 million

volunteer staff accounting for a significant proportion of the 'hands on' activities. In this situation economic analysis would take into consideration the effects of an employment multiplier. To date there has been no data collected from the Population Census on employment associated with events.

Black and Pape (1995) argued the need for caution when considering additional employment for hallmark events. State governments consistently use the generation of 'equivalent permanent jobs' in seeking taxpayer support. However, the figures produced are often misleading as government funding allocated for events could have been redirected to other areas of interest for non-event taxpayers (such as education or health services) which could also create job opportunities. In fact, the employment figures are just a shift in employment which has little or no effect on the total unemployment (Black and Pape, 1996).

Another consideration is to determine who is the primary beneficiary of an event. By and large it is the event promoter, especially those who hold monopoly rights over the supply of the event. Moreover the promoter is often located away from Australia so that profits are not even part of the national income (Gans, 1996). The London-based Formula One Construction Authority as event promoter of the Australia Formula One Grand Prix is an illustration of this. The Grand Prix Corporation identified Victorian government appropriations for the 1995 and 1996 events to be in excess of $60 million which included nearly $1 million for protester-related costs and $5 million to cover the operating deficit for both years.

There are problems in estimating the contribution cultural activities make to the economy. Much of the discussion held centres around the underlying motives of those who have economic studies carried out. 'The quality and accuracy of data input ultimately determines the quality of the estimated figures and levels of precision that are associated with any estimates' (Uysal and Gitelson, 1994, p. 4). Areas of information collection are easily defined but difficulty lies in the diversity of the multiple sources from which data is collected. A carefully designed data collection method needs to be applied with built-in monitoring mechanisms for attitude changes over time.

It has been difficult to obtain reliable information on arts activity from government and public agencies because there are no precise rules in adopting the institutional decisions. Also there are no codified criteria in the selection of recipients for support or in setting quantity and timing of public financial support. More importantly, there appears to be no political or social pressure to identify the government's objectives and range of actions. The community is usually concerned to see a broad distribution of government funds, but this research indicates a major weakness as being the lack of a competitive selection process for funding recipients. Those who support arts and sports events are generally 'lovers' of that activity and therefore there is an increased risk that there are emotions that bias the economic outcomes rather than a rational or academic approach (Frey, 1994). It could be argued that when government strategies and performance indicators are applied there is a greater expectation to ensure goals are met.

Given that government involvement in events is mostly a capital expenditure outlay there appears little evidence available, other than economic impact to support outlay decisions. Other management processes included identification of alternative investment proposals, evaluation criteria for selected projects and public input to review government investment for events.

Conclusion

The Victorian government hosts hallmark sport and arts events as part of its tourism strategy. Economic impact studies are frequently applied as a tool for identifying the benefits of staging hallmark events. Cost-benefit analysis, input-out analysis, the multiplier and the IMP model are the most frequently applied economic measurement tools in impact studies. However, it has been found that economic impact studies have invariably concentrated on the positive impacts such as increased tourism, exposure, spending and employment with little quantitative evidence on externalities such as vandalism, environmental costs, construction costs and service fees.

Economic impact studies are produced as part of the government's responsibility for accountability and become a performance measurement tool. However, the level and quality of information undertaken for an economic impact analysis is often limited due to budget constraints.

From the research it was found that it is difficult to apply the same economic models of measurement for arts and sport. Performing arts, by and large, generally generate more psychic than pecuniary income and therefore operate under different economic assumptions. Given the dependence for significant government subsidy, private funding and individual contribution, benefits for performing arts events may be only marginally different from costs.

The research further revealed that sports events generate a greater economic contribution than performing arts events but given the costs such as facility pro-vision, service fees to private event organisations and other hidden government costs it is unlikely that the true impact of staging hallmark sports events has been recognised. For less distorted results on the impact of performing arts and sports events a number of management procedures should be adopted such as the selection criteria for government funding, follow up research for repeat visits by event tourists and Victorian taxpayer input in the hallmark event review process.

References

Australian Bureau of Statistics (1997a) *The Victorian Yearbook*, No. 109. Melbourne: Australian Government Printing.

Australian Bureau of Statistics (1997b) *Cultural Trends: A Statistical Overview*, No. 4172.0. Melbourne: Australian Government Printing.

Australian Bureau of Statistics (1994) *The Arts Industry in Victoria: A Statistical Overview*. Melbourne: Australian Government Printing.

Black, T. and Pape, S. (1996) 'Special Events – Are They Beneficial?'. *Policy*, Summer 1995–96, pp. 34–38.

Brain, P. (1986) *The Microeconomic Structure of the Australian Economy*. Melbourne: Longman Cheshire.

Brain, P. and Manolakos, J. (1991) '1996 Melbourne Olympics: an Economic Evaluation', *National Economic Review*, National Institute of Economic and Industry Research, Melbourne, No. 14, January, pp. 14–21.

Brosio, G. (1994) 'The Arts Industry; Problems of Measurement', in *Cultural Economic and Cultural Policies*. The Netherlands: Kluwer Academic Publishers, pp. 17–22.

Colebatch, T. (1998) 'States Must Ban Incentives to Firms, Report Urges'. *The Age*, Monday, February 23, p. A5.

Crompton, J. (1995) 'Economic Impact Analysis of Sports Facilities and Events: Eleven Sources of Misapplication'. *Journal of Sport Management*, Vol. 9(1), pp. 14–35.

Department of State Development, *Annual Report*, 1995/96 and 1996/97, Victorian Government, Melbourne.

Dwyer, L. and Forsyth, P. (1993) 'Government Support for Inbound Tourism Promotion: Some Neglected Issues'. *Australian Economic Papers*, December, pp. 355–374.

Eadington, W. and Redman, M. (1991) 'Economic and Tourism'. *Annals of Tourism Research*, Vol. 18(1), pp. 41–56.

French, C., Craig-Smith, S. and Collier, A. (1995) *Principles of Tourism*. Australia: Longman Group.

Frey, B. (1994) 'Art: The Economic Point of View', in Peacock, A. and Rizzo, I. (1994) (eds), *Cultural Economic and Cultural Policies*. The Netherlands: Kluwer Academic Publishers, pp. 3–16.

Gans, J. (1996) 'Of Grand Prix and Circuses'. *The Australian Economic Review*, 3rd Quarter, pp. 299–307.

Getz, D. (1991) *Festivals, Special Events and Tourism*. New York: Van Nostrand Reinhold.

Howard, D. and Crompton, J. (1995) *Financing Sport*. Morgantown, USA: Fitness Information Technology.

Lingle, C. (1992) 'Public Choice and Public Funding of the Arts', in Trowse, R. and Khakee, A. (eds), *Cultural Economics*. Heidleberg, Germany: Springer-Verlag, pp. 21–30.

Melbourne and Olympic Parks Trust, *Annual Reports, 1991/92–1996/97*. Melbourne, Victoria.

Myerscough, J. (1988) *The Economic Importance of the Arts in Britain*. London: PSI Publications.

Peacock, A. and Rizzo, I. (1994) (eds), *Cultural Economic and Cultural Policies*. The Netherlands: Kluwer Academic Publishers.

Richardson, J. (1996) *Marketing Australian Travel and Tourism: Principles and Practice*. Melbourne: Hospitality Press.

Richardson, N. and Coffey, M. (1998) 'On a Winner in any Event'. *Herald-Sun*, Thursday February 19, 1998, pp. 14–15

Sport and Recreation Victoria (1997) *The Business of Sport*. Melbourne: Victorian Government.

Throsby, C. and Withers, G. (1979) *The Economics of Performing Arts*. Port Melbourne: Edward Arnold (Aust).

Tourism Forecasting Council (1995) *Forecast: The second report of the Tourism Forecasting Council*, Vol.1(2). Canberra: Commonwealth Department of Tourism.

Tourism Victoria (1997) *Strategic Business Plan 1997–2001: Building Partnerships*. Melbourne: Victorian Government.

Uysal, M. and Gitelson, R. (1994) 'Assessment of Economic Impact: Festivals and Special Events'. *Festival Management and Event Tourism*, Vol. 2, pp.3–9.

Part III

Sports events

Bidding, planning and organisation

5 A critical analysis of the organisation of major sports events

Nigel Dobson and Roslyn Sinnamon

'The Olympics is like a hurricane; it's coming, we're not ready for it and we can't stop it.'

(Citizen of Atlanta: *The Times*, 1996)

Introduction

The world of major sports events is a dynamic, evolving and growing industry (like the business of sport itself), with an increasing number of major world events, of increasing size, taking place with increasing regularity, with increasing technological advancement, spiralling broadcasting rights and cut throat competition to be the host. This fierce competition to host events sets nations against each other in the race to reach the golden prize. The tension between England and Germany for the European nomination to host the 2006 World Cup illustrates the importance placed upon the benefits associated with major events, not least because of the estimated 5 billion DM in additional income predicted over 15 years in Germany if it secures the tournament. There is a need therefore to get all aspects of delivering the event right, particularly the bidding stage in the first instance. The host nation, region or city is on show to the whole world. Failure to organise a successful event is not just unacceptable, it is now potentially catastrophic and can have long lasting effects.

This chapter will examine the critical organisational factors that are faced by host cities and Organising Committees within the sphere of major events. In particular, it will use the engineering modelling techniques that have been applied to other industries to prevent system failures.

It is evident that system reliability demands extend to the sports world, where the smooth running of major sports events, such as the Olympic Games, is critical for the cities involved, the huge sponsorship giants, the broadcasters, the high-profile athletes competing and last but not least the millions of spectators. Take the Atlanta 1996 Olympic Games, described by many as both the best and worst ever to have been held. Organisational difficulties affected a number of key players at the event. IBM was just one of the casualties, receiving bad publicity due to their computer system taking 10 days to get up and running smoothly (during which time a French fencer had been credited with the 400 m record). The world's press poured scorn with headlines such as 'Atlanta wins for Chaos' (*The Times*, 1996) splashed across their front pages, all united in condemning the organisation of the Games.

There were obviously a number of associated problems within the Atlanta Olympic socio-technical organisation system, these included the chaos fuelled by friendly volunteers being ill-informed and ill-prepared about their role and responsibilities; for instance officially appointed bus drivers had to ask visiting journalists for directions. This chapter, through an appraisal of several major events, attempts to identify the types of chaos often associated with major events, and focuses on whether these failures could have been avoided by having adequate redundancy and contingency plans in place, within the system as a whole, in the event of a crisis or failure of a sub-system to function. The negative effects of bad publicity resulting from chaos affect not only the image of the event and the city, but also the revenue of sponsoring companies and the reputation of the International Organising Committees themselves.

This chapter also attempts to conceptualise the organisation of a sports event as a system comprised of modular or functional sub-systems whose reliability is essential for the smooth running of the event, whether this is at the scale of a major world championship or just a regionally significant event. Each sub-system identified (for example transport, technology or sports equipment) can then be subjected to an engineering technique such as a type of failure modes effects and criticality analysis, the results of which will highlight those effects which are unacceptable or catastrophic to the system. Where appropriate, these 'hazardous' conditions can be quantitatively analysed thereby ascertaining the probability and frequency of occurrence of the hazardous event. If the probabilities or frequencies are too high then either redundancy will have to be introduced or the system design/ organisation altered, which could prove very cost effective in preventing undesirable consequences.

A definition of major sports events

What, therefore, do we understand and mean by the term major or hallmark events? Hopefully a definition of events, offered by a number of academics illustrates the parameters of the concept being appraised. The major theoretical problem with attempting to conceptualise a definition for major events is the scale (Davidson and Schaffer, 1980). Ritchie (1984) suggested the use of the term 'hallmark events'. These, he suggests are major events which have an ability to focus national and international attention to a destination.

Hallmark events have assumed a key role in international, national and regional economic development and tourism marketing strategies (Hall, 1992). The primary reason for fostering events and associated tourism are economic, based on the facts that events can be used like export industries to generate income and jobs and to act as catalysts for other forms of development (Getz, 1991).

It is the short time frame in which events operate that distinguishes the 'hallmark'/major events from other tourist attractions (Hall, 1992). Ritchie (1984) attempted to define the concept as

> major one-time recurring events of limited duration, developed primarily to enhance awareness, appeal and profitability of a tourism destination in the short and long term. Such events rely for their success on uniqueness, status or timely significance to create interest and attract attention.

Burgan and Mules (1992) and Mules and Faulkner (1996) suggest that major/hallmark events are events that are expected to generate large external benefits, or where the external benefits are so widely distributed and the event costs are so substantial that they are funded, either partially or wholly with public monies.

However, while far less academic, the opinion of Mr. Gouillou of the French World Cup Organising Committee (McGookin, 1998), illustrates what one understands by a major one time sports event and the subsequent demands and expectations on the organisation: *'We are a company with no past and a company with no future'.*

The basis of the definition offered by Hall (1992) is, however, appraised by Elvin and Emery (1997) as too involved in the principles of project management rather than operational management. There is therefore great pressure on 'Event Organisers' to get the organisation and operation right as the event is finite, of short-term temporary duration, with the limited availability of sport event specialists. Elvin and Emery (1997) suggest one further point. The authors illustrate that the world of major events does not store information or appraise the successes or failures of events so that it might learn from mistakes in the future:

> Despite general reporting of past Olympic Games very little attention has been paid to research which systematically evaluates the many impacts of events.... From an academic perspective virtually no effort has been made to accumulate a comprehensive body of knowledge concerning either the impacts of Olympic events or the research methods appropriate to study the impacts.
>
> (Elvin and Emery, 1997)

The importance of major sports events

The appeal of events such as the Olympic Games is their ability to attract those whose viewing is light and never entails sport. Research illustrates (*Sports Business*, no. 4) that families with an income of at least $60,000 were 41 per cent more likely to watch the Atlanta Games, i.e. those families with a higher expendable income, which is precisely why sponsoring companies are prepared to invest large sums of money in the event. Adidas experienced a 56 per cent rise in profits in 1996, the year of Atlanta Olympics, compared to 1995. As a sponsoring company they were fortunate to have more than 200 Olympic medals won by Adidasequipped athletes (*Sports Business*, no. 4). It is therefore obvious that it is in the interests of these sponsoring companies that their particular athletes arrive on time and that there preparation is not disrupted.

The value of major sports events to cities, countries, athletes and sponsors is enormous. This is supported by studies of the economic impact of events around the world (Yardley *et al.,* 1990; Frisby and Getz, 1988; Mules and Faulkner, 1996; Crompton, 1995; Turco and Kelsy, 1992; Dobson, Holliday and Gratton, 1997). Delivering the right product is essential and often ultimately upon which the event is judged. The media will judge the event in terms of an increase in sales or viewing/ listening figures. Sponsors examine the event in the light of the increase in sales before, during, and immediately after the period of the event, while the civic leaders will attempt to appraise the event in terms of the increased exposure of their city as a result of the event and the subsequent economic impact associated with the influx of visitors before, during and after the event (Elvin and Emery, 1997).

People have a tendency to remember the things that go wrong and that is why it is essential for cities and countries to get the organisation right. Due to the high profile of the Olympics (Atlanta having a gross audience of 19.6 billion viewers (*Sports Business*, no. 4)), any adverse publicity has an immediate and huge impact throughout the world. Those who did not even watch the Olympics will remember the Centennial Park bomb. Many in the UK will remember Linford Christie getting disqualified in the 100m final, but few, except the avid enthusiasts, will remember without hesitation the winner of the men's 100 m, or who won Britain's only gold medal.

The growth of technology at major sports events

One of the biggest advancements in the deliverance of the event system has been the increasing role and sophistication of event and computer technology. The Nagano Winter Olympics 1998 utilised eye recognition systems for rifle release in the biathlon, microphones embedded into the ice for speed skating and traffic control systems around the city. The World Cup 1998 illustrates the enormous reliance upon IT networks and infrastructure that have taken nearly six years to develop. Major sports events have become the largest short-term socio-technical systems in the world, with almost twenty-four hour exposure to a global audience, organised by a creature with no past, the shortest possible life-cycle and no future.

Given the demands placed upon these systems to deliver, it is extremely surprising that a critical appraisal of the organisational and technical aspects of major sport events has not been the subject of more rigorous academic research. This is even more surprising if one stops to consider the fact that major events have the ability to re-image cities and involve expenditure of billions of pounds from sponsors, the media, civic authorities and local tax payers themselves, both the sponsors and clients at these events (St Onge, 1991).

The application of risk, safety and reliability techniques to sports events

For each of the individual sets of groups involved; the organisers, the athletes, coaches, officials, sponsors and the spectators, the successful and smooth operation of any major sports event is critical. Montreal, the host of the 1976 Olympics can bare testimony to this, but even more harrowing is the failure of the Hillsborough Stadium event system in 1989. This organisational failure resulted in the ultimate price, the loss of 95 lives (Taylor Report, 1990).

Poor or insufficient organisation, together with inadequate emergency planning procedures and crisis management techniques, can lead to disastrous consequences for all involved, as the Hillsborough disaster tragically illustrates (Taylor Report, 1990). Assessing the safety and reliability of these systems is therefore critical, and it is important that sports management utilises the techniques developed within the world of industrial engineering, where these techniques have proved vital to the successful operation of potentially lethal systems.

The organisation of major sports events

An overview of the key players and agencies

Too often in the past, as the continued media attention on the 1996 Olympics in Atlanta illustrates, civic authorities have become too embroiled in the organisation of major events and have failed the citizens of the host city as a consequence (Miller, 1996). Political expediency has often impinged upon the role and influence of professional management and as a consequence the cities themselves have suffered. With the power of the world's media looking in at every aspect of the event the need to 'get it right' is vital. Added pressure is often exerted upon the civic authorities by the International Federations or International Organising Committees themselves.

Critics of the organisation of major sports events are quick to dismiss those entrusted with the task of putting on the event on behalf of the city, region or country. As Brodie (1997) comments, 'a sardonic joke heard in Atlanta nowadays is that the only amateurs left in the Olympic Games are unfortunate civic leaders forced with organising them'. While this simplifies the argument, it is obvious that the modern demands placed upon organising committees are enormous, the resignation of two SOCOG chairmen (the Sydney 2000 Olympic Organising Committee), bares testimony to the demands placed by the Olympic Games.

The 'no past ... no future' argument (McGookin, 1998) also encourages the expediency of the local political hierarchy to continue their involvement, with obvious escape routes out of public life provided by the numerous commercial organisations vying for the high profile associated with such men and women after the event, as they appear to champion the city and have a global presence and appeal.

The growth of the socio-technical sports system

A close examination of the complexity of events and the associated organisational problems with events such as the modern Olympics, highlights the need to re-appraise all aspects of major event organisation, to ensure that the probabilities of chaos and disaster are limited.

Together with an evaluation of the critical technological demands and require-ments of major events, this reliability requirement introduces the fundamental argument put forward by this chapter. It can be seen that the experience of modelling reliability, safety and system design in the process, gas, nuclear, water, waste management and transport industries has a fundamental application in the arena of major events. Further, the application of these techniques to the issue of crowd control following the Hillsborough disaster, prove how fundamental the principles of safety and reliability are to particular aspects of major event organisation.

Within industry there is a large overlap between those techniques which assess the reliability of a system (i.e. the probability that it will run without any failures) and those techniques which assess safety. The consequences of a system failure often jeopardise the safety of the system (Sinnamon, 1996; Andrews and Moss, 1993).

It is apparent that there is increasing use of these techniques outlined above. Several British companies assisted Sydney with skills and specialist knowledge in the areas of transport modelling, water and environmental management, ticketing, security and hospitality. Likewise, the organisers of the Kuala Lumpa Common-wealth Games 1998 utilised the services of recognised specialists.

Organisational and technical complexity

The Olympic Games is an obvious example where efficient and reliable operation of the event management systems is critical for the overall success of the Games. However, during such a mammoth sporting event as the Olympics, it is inevitable that things will go wrong. The sheer volume of organisation required at Atlanta for the 30,000 accredited personnel, 10,000 competitors, 271 events, 100,000 organising staff, 46,000 volunteers and 10 million ticket-holders (Miller, 1996) is a large scale logistical nightmare.

A brief evaluation of the challenge facing the Organising Committee of the Sydney Olympics highlights the complexity of the organisational arrangements required and hence the justification for utilising these techniques. The logistical problems for the athletes village alone are quite staggering. Around 200,000 people need to be transported in and out of the Olympic sites twice a day during the 17-day event, and with no private transport allowed into the area, the organisers plan to lay on a fleet of 240 buses, as well as a train service capable of carrying 50,000 persons per hour (*Sports Business*, no. 1). This assessment takes no account of the crowd safety issues associated with each of the Olympic events and their crowd movements.

Similarly, the growth of technology has given way to the need to have faster more efficient systems, capable of handling data faster and in more complex manners. The experience of IBM at Atlanta has illustrated the need to get it right and the necessity for dry run testing of the event. Similarly the demands upon the technology associated with the World Cup '98 were huge, and the systems took nearly six years to develop and are described as a 24 hours a day,7 days a week operation for the five weeks of the World Cup (McGookin, 1998). This operation will utilise about 12,000 workstations and 100 servers across 100 local area networks. The complexity of all the organisational aspects of France '98 necessitated a dry run of the event through Le Tournoi, the previous year (in similar fashion to athletics at the Atlanta Olympics).

An illustration of the organisation and personnel required for Wimbledon fortnight each year, illustrates the complexity and sheer numbers involved in this type of high profile Grand Slam tennis event (*The Guardian*, 1998). Getting the organisation correct involves satisfying the expectations of over 430,000 tennis fans over the two weeks, let alone the millions of television viewers, radio listeners, the media and players and coaches themselves. In fact, planning for the next tournament begins the moment the previous one is over. In total there are 1,400 jobs, in what is said to be the single biggest catering operation for a single sports event in Europe, to serve over 27,000 kilos of strawberries, 190,000 sandwiches, 285,000 cups of tea and coffee, 90,000 pints of beer and 12,500 bottles of champagne.

The ferrying of players and officials to and from the courts requires 230 drivers, helping spectators around the 42 acres and 20 courts involves 130 members of the association of Wimbledon Honorary Stewards, with help from the Corps of Commissioners and a group totalling some 500 made up from members of the armed services, all volunteers. Some 300 security guards control the entrance gates.

Ensuring the condition of the courts is up to scratch requires 45 ground staff, some 330 court officials and 15 members of the referees office oversee fair play. A total of 125 staff are taken on to cover the courts and about 70 people operate scoreboards and the latest computer technology to provide ball-by-ball coverage. More than 750 journalists from 50 countries get press passes and 182 ball boys and girls train for the event from February of each year.

Planning for and managing crisis

As the chapter so far has attempted to suggest, the organisational complexity of events requires that planning for the worst case scenario is essential (Weir, 1991). The recent PruTour Cycle race (Tour of Britain) is a prime example of where innocuous problems can occur (*The Times*, 1998). The peleton were directed the wrong way when chasing the lead group and this nearly lead to their disqualification, leaving potentially only five cyclists in the event from a started field of nearly 100. For the sponsors and organisers this had potentially enormous consequences for this new event, as did the killing of a police motor cycle escort at a road junction the following day (*The Times*, 1998b).

The pressure that is created at these events by the expectation of the media and worldwide audience is enormous and a contingency plan for every aspect of the event is vital. Disasters such as Kings Cross, Piper Alpha, Clapham, Zeebrugge and Hillsborough (Richardson, 1993; Weir, 1991; Androff, 1984; Perrow, 1984; Mitroff, 1984) illustrate how devastating mismanagement of organisational and procedural tasks can be and emphasises the need for safety and reliability techniques applied across all aspects of the organisation.

In similar fashion to the potential hazards of a nuclear power station, each particular event will have its own individual requirements and thus potential problems. Often these problems occur at the human-techno interface (Weir, 1991). The techniques utilised in the industrial world will also therefore assist with highlighting the probability of certain critical aspects of the organisation and technology going wrong and assisting with ordering, prioritising and developing hierarchies that will identify the critical cut off points required to avoid the 'big bang'. A review of the recent World Athletic Championships in 1997 in Athens and the potential problems facing France '98 provided below illustrate this point.

Identifying potential problems and critical pathways

The average number of spectators for the first four days at the World Athletic Championships in Athens 1997, was fewer than 24,000, in a stadium with a capacity of 85,000 (*The Times*, 1997a). At this stage in the competition the media were making a big play on this issue and questioning the ability of Athens to host the 2004 Olympic Games, prior to the decision being made by the International Olympic Committee (IOC). The pressure on the organisers to get bodies into the stadium was immense and all efforts had to be put into attracting the citizens of Athens to attend the event.

The organiser of the World Cup '98 were faced with the opposite problem. The potential of dealing with excess demand for tickets to the matches and hence associated problems with the black market and supporters travelling with no hope of getting into the stadia has created a number of security related problems. Contingency and crisis management plans (Weir, 1991) have therefore been critical and involved the co-ordination of intelligence and police forces throughout the world. These security forces acted before the tournament to minimise associated risks and potential terrorist attacks, but application of further techniques is essential as illustrated by the hooliganism that has dogged the tournament.

There are also other unforeseen problems that knowingly create chaos, such as striking pilots, railway workers and lorry drivers. All placed a potential organisational threat that required negotiation, crisis management techniques and planning.

Applicability of techniques to smaller sports events

While this chapter has so far considered the application of the techniques used in the industrial world to the organisation of major sports events such as the World Cup and Olympics, it is obvious that their application also applies to smaller local and regional events. The authors recently experienced a twenty-minute delay at the start of the English Amateur Athletics Association half-marathon in Wilmslow, Cheshire, owing to the blocking of emergency vehicular access along routes close to Manchester Airport. With over 3,500 runners in the field the potential to worsen an aeronautical crisis at the airport was self-evident, but received inadequate attention before the event.

In similar fashion the Welsh Games in 1996 experienced unpredictable failures with two photocopiers and several telephone and ISDN lines, as the British media clambered around the Cardiff Stadium expecting Linford Christie to announce his retirement. Confusion and irritation reigned, creating ill feeling and lack of confidence in the ability of the event organisers.

In this sense the need for organisational and professionalism in the delivery of all events is critical. Elvin and Emery (1997) suggest there is a need for the sports world to accept that major investments in sport requires trained and competent professionals to plan, manage and evaluate sports events using skills and techniques that are often used in other industrial and commercial sectors. The rapid development in sport and event specific information technology and technical wizardry that accompanies each new major event demands a professional approach and a reliable and critically safe approach, with management plans, dry testing, crisis management and disaster recovery plans.

Sports management is plagued with a representation that it is over-academic in its application and needs to pay closer attention to the requirements of the real sports world. This chapter, whilst acknowledging that the subject is still in its embryonic stage, has attempted to contextualise the area for further research and raise the question of whether it is possible for the practical application of specific management techniques utilised in the industrial sectors to be applied to the organisation of major sports events. The need for these techniques for a sporting perspective appears to be self-evident as the above examples illustrate and are acknowledged as an imperative part of event management according to this quote by the Elvin and Emery (1997):

> … expensive mistakes are therefore bound to be made in an environment where too many sports events practitioners are literally working in the dark, basing decisions upon limited or insufficient information.

Organisational requirements

While the previous sections have provided an overview of some of the organisational difficulties experienced at major sports events, this section will outline in more specific detail the range of tasks required for major events. Prior to discussing the further applicability of these industrial techniques, the section will provide a number of examples of the complexity of the requirements of major sports event by evaluating the role of the 1999 Rugby World Cup Local Organising Committee in Cardiff and by highlighting some of the critical factors associated with the organisation of the 1998 Commonwealth Games in Kuala Lumpur.

The requirement for this type of evaluation at all levels of sport event organisation is evident and the demands identified by Elvin and Emery (1997) in their appraisal of the XXIII Snickers World Cross Country Championships illustrate the need to apply industrial techniques to the world of major sports events:

Establishing specific plans for the crowd control for totally unknown numbers at a free event, with unknown demands for branded merchandise (possessing a very short perishable life cycle), at a major outdoor sports event greatly influenced by the weather, all under the global media spotlight, must be the event organisers worst nightmare.

Organisation of the Rugby World Cup

The Rugby World Cup 1999 is the fourth largest sports event in the world and the biggest sports event ever to be held in Wales. The tournament is likely to have a major impact on the UK economy in general, with some estimates suggesting an overall economic impact in excess of £800 million. Therefore the need for a coordinated approach across all areas of the organisation of the event is critical. At the local level, there was a range of groups participating in the Cardiff Steering Committee. This illustrates the need to co-ordinate the input of a number of different departments into a number of different sub-groups. These include departments responsible for Policy, Environmental Protection, Property, Planning, Sports and Leisure, Planning, Education, Economic Development, Social Services, Financial Services and Highways and Transportation.

1998 Kuala Lumpur Commonwealth Games

The organisation and integration of all information systems vital to the successful staging of the event in Kuala Lumpur is outlined below, however this does not take account of the problem of forest fires raging around Kuala Lumpur prior to the event, which is an additional environmental factor, adding to the political and economic frailties putting the staging of the event in jeopardy. The following items below are critical components essential for the smooth running of the Commonwealth Games and illustrate the areas to which the techniques might be applied (Source: Sema Group, 1998).

The games management system

- Accreditation
- VIP management
- Games staffing and volunteer management
- Materials planning
- Transport and medical supply tracking
- Village accommodation planning

The results management systems and services

- Competition schedules
- Start lists
- Official results

- Other Games statistics to the media, the Games family, television viewers and the general public (including commentators information system)

The information system

- Enabling all media personnel, the Games family, the general public and Internet surfers to access general and historical information about the event, including real-time results, medal standing, press updates etc.

The application of industrial and engineering techniques

Safety and Reliability engineers are often called upon in industry to identify any potential hazards that could lead to undesirable consequences. Formal techniques, such as HAZOPs (Hazard and Operability Studies) and FMEA's (Failure Mode and Effects Analyses), have been widely adopted in the process, gas, nuclear and transport sectors, where the aim is to understand the integrated functionality of the system and weed out the failures or deviations from normal operation that pose serious problems both in terms of safety and reliability.

The reliability of the Olympic event, as a system, over the two-week duration could be considered as important, in monetary terms, as that of a nuclear power plant supplying energy to the UK year in, year out. Sponsors paid $40 million each to be associated with the Atlanta Olympics and $600 million came from the public purse towards the organisation.

Typically a nuclear power station would have a turnover of approximately, £150 million per year. Both systems create a huge number of full-time equivalent job years for the economy and both systems require safe and reliable running to achieve a successful end product. It is the long-term benefits that a city or a sponsoring company can accrue from hosting the Games that drives the Olympic bid (*Sports Business*, no. 1).

This chapter considers the application of a reliability analysis technique, namely a Failure Mode and Effects Analysis (FMEA), to identify the problem areas or 'hazards' in a major sporting event. An undesirable potential hazard of a nuclear power station is the release of radioactivity to the environment, whereas in a sporting event the hazard could range from stadia collapse, to traffic congestion, to a sponsor experiencing a huge loss in sales as a result of negative marketing or even more damaging, a terrorist threat producing a global 'own goal' for the city itself. Failure mode and effects analysis is a procedure by which each potential failure mode in a system is analysed to determine its effect on the system and to classify it according to its severity. The objective is to identify the reliability and critical areas in a system where modifications to the design are required to reduce the probability of failure (Andrews and Moss, 1993).

Identifying problem areas/asking the right questions

Identifying the problem areas in an industrial system and providing remedial actions is just one of the core tasks of a reliability engineer.

One approach to a FMEA is the 'functional approach' where sub-assemblies are treated as 'black boxes' providing some required function in the system (Andrews and Moss, 1993). In this approach the reliability engineer considers the effect of loss of inputs and internal failures on each component or sub-system.

Crisis identification and management

The FMEA technique can successfully identify those potential 'failures' of the sporting event which may result in crisis. The next stage in the remedial process is to determine the crisis management procedures to be undertaken. There must be a proper concern that there is attention paid to the aetiology of the event in order to assess the potential problems and to assist with the identification of the factors that led to the problem. Weir (1991) highlights the need to identify both causal and consequential factors and the procedures implemented must attempt to rectify the problems identified in the most efficient and cost effective manner.

The FMEA technique can further aid the consequential procedure by actually calculating which crisis is most likely to occur (i.e. the probability of the cause being realised). This eliminates those events which are deemed highly improbable and have negligible probabilities of occurring.

After the event it is always worth critically appraising the organisational aspects so that lessons can be learned and effective techniques put into place. The changes in the delivery of IT systems between Atlanta and Nagano by IBM justify this investment. As with many socio-technical system, sports events have a mixture of 'soft' and 'hard' technology . The hard technology often guides the soft aspects of events organisation (such as checking accreditation), but as mistakes in the past have illustrated, often the 'softer' elements (often human error) cause critical failures in the system. The accreditation system at the last Olympics proved technologically sound, however the failure of security guards to scan the passes properly resulted in unaccredited persons entering the village (Rushman, 1998).

FMEA application to a sports event

Every sporting event has a 'hit list' of elements or functions that are required to run the event. The Organising Committees for sports events such as Wimbledon, which occur annually and in the same location, will be well aware of what is required for the event, simply through experience and hopefully learning from any mistakes that have occurred in the past. However, an event which moves to a new global capital every four years or one that is run in a city or region for the first time will have location specific issues or potential problems which cannot be dealt with by a generic 'hit list'. Identifying these issues or potential problems requires a structured thought-invoking approach, one which can identify any critical areas of concern within the system. A failure mode and effects analysis is one such approach. The units within the system can be refined into their own individual hit lists, the items of which can then be subjected to a FMEA. The objective of the FMEA is to identify items within the hit lists whose failure to function as required will have an undesirable or unacceptable consequence to the system.

The most prestigious event of the Olympic Games is the men's 100 m final, the title of 'The Fastest Man in the World' is the ultimate goal of any sprinter. The immense popularity of this event therefore breeds competition among the sponsors to compete for valuable 'air time', during and prior to the event. The 100 m final has been selected as an understandable and simplified case study for the application of a FMEA.

An important part of the preparation for a FMEA is the consideration and recording of the assumptions that will be made in the study. These assumptions will include definitions of the boundaries of the system and each sub-system, down to the expected level of analysis of the system (Andrews and Moss, 1993). This preparation can be made by the person undertaking the FMEA in conjunction with the Organising Committee and relevant technical experts of the 100 m event.

The consequences of a failure mode are defined by a severity index related to the degree of damage that could ultimately occur. These severity ranks can be defined at four levels:

1 Catastrophic – complete loss of system.
2 Critical – severe reduction of functional performance resulting in a change in operational state.
3 Major – degradation of item functional output.
4 Minor – no effect on performance.

Two of the most obvious items of the 'hit list' for the 100 m final are the competitor and the starter gun. Each item of the hit list can be fully analysed in this way.

Conclusions

The world of major sports events is a rapidly expanding market. There are key lessons for event organisers, sponsors, the media and for sports management as an emerging discipline. Collaboration in applied research will enrich events, encourage the development and transferability of skills and relevant objectives of all groups involved.

Employing such a technique to the whole Olympic system may have prevented the transport problems and the enormous difficulties with the results system in the Atlanta Games. The British rowers Steven Redgrave and Matthew Pinsent experienced enormous transport problems in Atlanta. They were appalled that their four year preparation for the event was put in jeopardy by the transport system. In the end they elected to make their own transport arrangements after several hours of delays to and from training (*The Times*, 1996). If a FMEA had been applied to the transport system then perhaps this would not have occurred. The potential thought of Britain not gaining its one and only medal because its two star athletes did not turn up because of traffic congestion would have demoralised British sport even further.

The International Olympic Committee (IOC) and the Organising Committee for the Sydney Games in the year 2000 have learnt from the problems experienced in Atlanta and have upgraded Sydney's road and rail networks. The question is what will the IOC and the Athens Organising Committee learn from the Sydney Olympics that can be passed to Athens in 2004. Certainly FIFA must take stock after the problems of France '98 and the potential for hosting problems between Japan and Korea in 2002.

References

Andrews, J.D. and Moss, T.R. (1993), *Reliability and Risk Assessment*. Longman Scientific and Technical.

Androff, H.S. (1984). *Implanting Strategic Management*. Englewood Cliffs: Prentice Hall.

Brodie, J. (1997). 'Bitter Atlanta still licks its wounds'. *The Times*, 1 August 1997.

Burgan, B. and Mules, T. (1992). 'Economic Impacts of Sports Events'. *Annals of Tourism Research*.

Crompton, J.L (1995). 'Economic Impact Analysis of Sports Facilities and Events: Eleven Sources of Mis-application'. *Journal of Sports Management*, Vol. 9(1).

Davidson, L.S. and Schaffer, W.A. (1980). 'A Discussion of Methods Employed in Analysing the Impact of Short-Term Entertainment Events'. *Journal of Travel Research*, Vol. 18(3).

Dobson, N, Gratton, C. and Holliday, S. (1997). *Football Came Home. The Economic Impact of Euro '96*. Sheffield: Leisure Industries Research Centre.

Elvin, I.T. and Emery, P. (1997). 'The Role of Professional Sports Management: The XXIII Snickers World Cross Country Championships'. *European Journal of Sports Management*, Vol. 4(1).

Frisby, W. and Getz, D. (1988). 'Festival Management : A Case Study Perspective'. *Journal of Travel Research*, Vol. 28(1).

Getz, D. (1991). *Festivals, Special Events and Tourism*. New Jersey: Van Nostrand Reinhold.

Glickman, N.J. (1977). *Econometric Analysis of Regional Systems: Explorations in Model Building and Policy Analysis*. London: Academic Press.

Goeldner, C. and Long, P. (1987). 'The Role and Impact of Mega-Events and Attractions on Tourism Development in North America', in Getz, D. (1991), *Festivals, Special Events and Tourism*. New Jersey: Van Nostrand Reinhold.

Hall, C.M. (1992). *Hallmark Tourist Events: Impacts, Management and Planning*. London: Belhaven Press.

Law, C.M. (1994). *Urban Tourism: Attracting Visitors to Large Cities*. England: Mansell.

Long, P.J. and Perdue, R.R. (1990). 'The Economic Impact of Rural Festivals and Special Events: Assessing the Spatial Distribution of Expenditures'. *Journal of Travel Research*, Vol. 28(4).

Lord Justice Taylor (1990). Report into the Hillsborough Disaster.

McGookin, S. (1998). 'On Side for Soccer IT', *The Financial Times* (1997).

Miller, D. (1996). 'The Greatest Show on Earth', *The Times Olympics*, July 15.

Mintroff. S.S. (1988). *Normal Accidents: Living with High Risk Technologies*. New York: Basic Books.

Mules, T. and Faulkner, B. (1996). 'An Economic Perspective on Major Events'. *Tourism Economics*, Vol. 12(2).

Perrow, C. (1984). 'Crisis Management. Cutting through the confusion'. *Sloan Management Review*, Vol. 29(2).

Ritchie, J.R.B. (1984). 'Assessing the Impacts of Hallmark Events: Conceptual and Research Issues'. *Journal of Travel Research*, Vol. 23(1).

Roche, M. (1992a). 'Mega-Events and Urban Policy'. *Annals of Tourism Research*, Vol. 21(1), pp. 1–19.

Rushman, N. (1998). Event Services Web Page.

Sinnamon, R. (1996). *Fault Tree Analysis for Binary Decision Diagram*. Loughborough: Loughborough University of Technology.

St Onge, T. (1991) Canada's 125th Anniversary: An Example of Public Participation'. *Journal of Applied Recreation Research*, Vol. 16(1), pp. 53–60.

Sport Business, July 1996, No. 01.

Sport Business, September 1996, No. 03.

Sport Business, October 1996, No. 04.

Sport Business, March 1997, No. 08.

The Guardian (1998). 'Service Ace on the Line'– Wimbledon. 30 May 1998.

The Times (1997). World Athletic Championships. 'Show time is right for the Greeks'.

The Times (1998b). 'Excuse me, which way to Blackpool?' – Pru Tour Cycle Race of Great Britain.

Wier, D.T.H. (1991). 'Communication Factors in System Failure or Why Big Planes Crash and Big Businesses Fail'. *Disaster Prevention Management*, Vol. 2(2).

Wilson, A.G. (1974). *Urban and Regional Models in Geography and Planning*. Chichester: J. Wiley.

Whitson, P. and McIntosh, D. (1993). 'Becoming a World Class City: Hallmark Events and Sports Franchises in the Growth Strategies of Western Canadian Cities'. *Sociology of Sport Journal*, Vol. 10.

Yardley, J.K., MacDonald, J.H. and Clarke, B.D. (1990). 'The Economic Impact of a Small Short-term Recreation Event on a Local Economy'. *Journal of Park Recreation Administration*, Vol. 8.

6 The economic impact of two major sporting events in two of the UK's 'national cities of sport'

Simon Shibli and Chris Gratton

Introduction

The relatively few economic impact studies carried out at major sporting events in the UK are characterised by not being in the public domain and having objectives that were unique to the event under investigation. Consequently, there is little publicly available data for promoters of events to use to evaluate, and even less data that are directly comparable between two or more events. The shortage of research into the impacts of major sporting events was noted by Elvin and Emery (1997) who state:

> With so many major sports competitions taking place world-wide and on a regular basis, and with rivalry to host these events keener than ever, it is perhaps surprising that there has been only limited applied research which has examined the impact of the wide variety of sports events on local, regional or national economies.

This chapter compares the economic impact of two major sports events on the cities of Sheffield and Glasgow. Using an identical research instrument and methodology at each event, the economic impact of a one-day high profile athletics meeting is compared with a four-day relatively lower profile swimming championships. Although the events had broadly similar economic impacts, the means by which they were generated were considerably different. The main body of the paper contains a detailed analysis of the characteristics of the economic impact in each city and also offers some explanations as to the causes of the variations identified between each city. Using primary data, the difference between 'competitor driven' and 'spectator driven' is demonstrated, as is the difference between accommodation and shopping driven events. The cost of hosting major events is linked with the subsequent economic impact derived from the events in order to derive simple performance benchmarks. The chapter concluded by suggesting that local authorities wishing to use major sporting events as vehicles for urban regeneration should do so from an informed position. In practice this means integrating the economic impact objectives into the overall objectives for an event. Use of the growing volume of data in the public domain regarding the typology of events and the likely economic impacts associated with them, may assist local authorities make more informed decisions regarding the type of events to bid for and underwrite.

The events

The two events discussed in this paper are: first, the International Amateur Athletics Federation (IAAF) Grand Prix 1 held at the Don Valley Stadium in Sheffield on 29th June 1997; and second, the European Junior Swimming Championships held in Glasgow from 31st July – 3rd August 1997.

IAAF Grand Prix 1

The event was promoted jointly by Sheffield City Council's Events Unit and the British Athletics Federation (BAF). It was the first time that Sheffield had hosted an IAAF Grand Prix event and the event had been secured via a competitive bid against two other cities. The organisers regarded the event as an ideal opportunity to forge a positive relationship with BAF with the intention of attracting more high profile athletics meetings to Sheffield in the future. A secondary objective was the potential for the positive place marketing of Sheffield via television coverage. Staging the event for its direct financial impact (for example making a surplus) or its economic impact were not explicit objectives.

The European Junior Swimming Championships

The event was promoted jointly by Glasgow City Council and the Scottish Amateur Swimming Association (SASA). It was the fourth occasion on which the UK had hosted the event with the three previous occasions being in Leeds. Glasgow was awarded the event after a competitive bid against Leeds. The ingredients of the successful bid were financial support of £80,000 from Glasgow City Council and a £47,000 guarantee against loss from the Scottish Sports Council's National Lottery Major Events fund. The event attracted a record number of entrants from nations affiliated to the European governing body for swimming, Ligue Européen de Natation (LEN), with 39 nations present out of a total 50 affiliates. The objectives of the event were to demonstrate Glasgow City Council's commitment to regeneration through sport and the SASA's organisational ability. As in the case of the Sheffield event, financial and economic impacts were not explicit objectives.

The Sheffield event took place on one day, a Sunday afternoon, with the first event starting at 4pm and the final event concluding at 8.45pm. The Glasgow event, by contrast, took place over four consecutive days of heats and finals. The difference in the scale and nature of the events, using the same research methodology, has produced results that give unique insight into the economic impacts of different types of major sporting events.

Methodology

The principal research instrument was a self completion questionnaire which had been used 4,500 times at events in Sheffield in 1996 and had been approved by the research sponsors and event promoters. In order to obtain accurate results, the key challenge is to survey a representative sample of people from those competing, spectating, officiating or carrying out media work at the event. In practice, this can only be done with the full support and co-operation of the organisers in arranging access to key groups of people for data collection. The co-promoters of the events in both Sheffield and Glasgow enabled, and in some cases arranged, unlimited access to the various respondent types. The size of the respondent type sub-sets and the number of interviews conducted is shown in Table 6.1.

Table 6.1 shows that respectable samples for each type of respondent group were obtained in both the Sheffield and the Glasgow studies. The group most difficult to sample was competitors. The main reason for this was the cycle of training and resting which athletes adopt in competition.

Post-research evaluation suggests that the best time to survey competitors is at accreditation or other pre-tournament gatherings such as team meetings. However, the main economic impact of competitors can often be assessed from desk research and follow up interviews after the event. At both events, the promoting governing body was responsible for booking and paying for the competitors' hotel accommodation. It was therefore easier and more accurate to assess the additional expenditure on hotels in the cities concerned from the primary documentation of the hotel bills, than it would have been from questioning the competitors directly. Thus although the sample sizes of competitors in both studies are relatively low, the major components of their economic impact – accommodation and food – were quantified accurately via post-event desk research and follow up interviews with key personnel from the relevant governing body

The results

A full summary and discussion of the results for each event is available in the respective final report produced by the Leisure Industries Research Centre and available from the UK, English, and Scottish Sports Councils. The purpose of this section is to examine some of the more significant issues arising from the results by making comparisons between the two events.

Before looking at the results in detail it is worth explaining what is meant by the economic impact of an event in this context. For the purposes of this chapter, economic impact is defined as the additional expenditure generated in a local economy by visitors from outside the local economy which can be legitimately attributed to an event taking place. Thus for expenditure made at an event to be eligible for inclusion as economic impact it must meet two criteria:

1 the expenditure must be made by a non-resident of the local economy as it is assumed that spending by locals would have taken place on other products regardless of an event taking place;

Table 6.1 Respondents by group, population and sample size in the Sheffield and Glasgow studies

Sheffield	Population	Sample	Glasgow	Population	Sample
Spectators	16025	1268	Spectators	65	65
Officials	69	69	Officials	72	72
Media	60	59	Media	5	5
Athletes/BAF	190	21	Swimmers/coaches	582	137
Total	16344	1417	Total	724	279

2 the main reason for visitors being in the local economy must be because of the event and not some other reason such as being on holiday, otherwise the expenditure is not directly attributable to the event.

All of the additional expenditure figures reported in this chapter have passed the two 'filters' detailed above. We now consider the results in detail.

Table 6.2 shows an overview of the additional expenditure in each city that was directly attributable to the event. Although the total spend in each city was broadly similar – £176,937 v £257,802 – the manner in which these sums were generated was radically different. Some of the key explanations for the differences are explained below.

The timing, duration and scale of the events

The Sheffield event generated approximately 800 commercial bed-nights, whilst the Glasgow event generated 4,287 commercial bed-nights. Much of the disparity between the two sums can be attributed to the duration of the events i.e. one day (Sheffield) compared with four days (Glasgow). In Sheffield, the event took place, in effect, over a half day, a Sunday evening from 4pm to 8.45pm. The event was in school term time and did not coincide with a Bank Holiday or other holiday period. Consequently, children attending school and adults going to work would not have

Table 6.2 Summary of the additional spending in Sheffield and Glasgow

Spending estimates	Sheffield	Glasgow
A. Accommodation	£31,714	£210,370
B. Other expenditure by overnight visitors to city	£19,117	£47,432
C. Sub total overnight visitors i.e. (A+B)	£50,831	£250,802
D. Expenditure by day visitors to city	£100,106	£0
E. Overnight and day visitors' spend in city (C+D)	£150,937	£250,802
F. Organisational spend	£27,000	£7,000
I. Total spend in city attributable to event	£176,937	£257,802

been inclined to stop overnight in Sheffield on the night of the event. Thus it was not surprising to discover that only a small minority (1.4 per cent) of the 11,050 non-Sheffield attenders actually spent the night in the city. Of the commercial bed-nights generated in Sheffield, the athletes and the governing body were the greatest contributors (Table 6.3). Many of the athletes arrived in Sheffield after a midweek athletics meeting in Germany and stayed in the city up to and including the night of the event, thereby generating an average of 2.4 bed-nights each, despite the event itself taking place for only a half-day. Although the Glasgow event lasted for four days, the average stay in the city for competitors was 6.6 nights. The reason for this relatively long average duration can be explained by the need for accreditation, participation in team meetings, the organisation of training times in the pools, and the need for pre-competition rest. Because the event finished on a Sunday evening, most countries were unable to catch connecting flights out of Glasgow until the next day. Unlike the Sheffield event, the Glasgow event took place during pan-European school holidays. Therefore, there were no pressing reasons for competitors to truncate their stays in order to get back to school or work.

The key differences between the events can be summarised as follows.

- In Sheffield 18 per cent of the additional expenditure was spent on accommodation and more than half of this expenditure (57 per cent) was attributable to the competitors and the governing body.
- In Glasgow, 82 per cent of the additional expenditure was spent on accommodation and 88 per cent of it was attributable to the competitors and their team managers.

One operational factor that explains why the accommodation expenditure in Glasgow was such a large proportion of the total expenditure, is that all competitors were on full board tariffs. Thus there is a significant element of catering expenditure included within the accommodation category.

Furthermore, because the food for competitors was provided by either hotels, or a local university, the amount spent by the competitors themselves on food and drink elsewhere in Glasgow was almost negligible. A similar pattern was found in Sheffield albeit on a much smaller scale. All of the competitors and governing body officials (who contributed most of the accommodation expenditure) were on

Table 6.3 Bed-nights generated by respondent types in Sheffield and Glasgow

Respondent type	Sheffield		Glasgow	
	Bed-nights	% of total	Bed-nights	% of total
Spectators	200	25	283	7
Officials	23	3	182	4
Media	118	15	28	1
Competitors/team management	456	57	3,794	88
Total	797	100	4,287	100

a half-board tariff. The nature of these inclusive tariffs is that it is not possible to itemise an accommodation and a catering component separately with any degree or reliability. However, for future studies, this finding raises the issue that money spent in hotels is not necessarily spent on accommodation only.

The considerable disparity in the role played by accommodation at the two events resulted in considerable disparities in the distribution of spending in other expenditure categories. In particular, Glasgow fared relatively poorly from expenditure on areas such as shopping and catering, whilst Sheffield fared relatively well. The evidence and suggested explanations for this are discussed in the next section.

The principal 'drivers' of additional expenditure at an event

It has long been recognised that major events tend to be either 'spectator driven', or 'competitor driven' in terms of creating an economic impact in a host city. In Sheffield, Euro '96 and the World Masters' Swimming Championships (LIRC, 1996) are classic examples of how similar amounts of money (circa £5m per event) can be generated using spectators or competitors as the principal contributors of additional expenditure. The different nature of the events in this research reveals that the drivers of the associated economic impact were different, i.e. Sheffield was spectator driven whilst Glasgow was competitor driven.

However, in addition to examining the broad nature of expenditure drivers, it is also possible to examine the types of expenditure on which the principal drivers spent their money. In this case, the Sheffield event was predominantly spectator driven on non-accommodation expenditure, whilst the Glasgow event was competitor driven almost exclusively by accommodation expenditure. The results of analysing the Sheffield and Glasgow events by category of expenditure are shown below in Table 6.4.

The variations in additional expenditure by category of expenditure shown in Table 6.4 suggests that not only were the events themselves different, but also the

Table 6.4 The categories of additional expenditure in Sheffield and Glasgow

Category	Sheffield		Glasgow		Difference
	Total	%	Total	%	Sheffield – Glasgow
Accommodation/ hotel catering	31,714	18	210,370	82	(178,656)
Food and drink	34,536	20	18,452	7	16,084
Entertainment	7,362	4	4,380	2	2,982
Programmes and merchandise	18,409	10	2,963	1	15,446
Shopping/souvenirs	27,049	15	16,563	6	10,486
Travel	21,344	12	2,480	1	18,864
Other	36,523	21	2,594	1	33,929
Total	176,937	100	257,802	100	(80,865)

expenditure patterns of those present were also different. Some of the possible explanations for the magnitude of the variances are explained below.

ACCOMMODATION/HOTEL CATERING

In addition to the earlier explanation of this discrepancy there is a financial consideration which is contrary to the rationale for using events to generate economic impact. Junior swimmers are likely to be economically inactive and dependent on their parents. Furthermore, governing bodies are not in a position to underwrite fully the costs of participation. Therefore, swimming championships of this nature have to be organised on a tight budget that is often supplemented by families. In Glasgow, in return for high occupancy rates per room in hotels, it was possible to obtain full board tariffs for £48 per person per night. In Sheffield, the governing body had negotiated a half board tariff of £50 per person per night. This reveals an interesting tension in the nature of organising events. Local authority promoters have a financial accounting responsibility to operate within the resources allocated to them or even to make a surplus. This may well mean having to negotiate discounts and minimise payments locally. However, there exists the conflicting objective of maximising the economic impact of an event.

An additional finding which reinforces the importance of accommodation as an important component of economic impacts on host cities was that those who tended to stay overnight also tended to spend more on the other categories of expenditure monitored by the survey. This is consistent with a classic principle of retailing, that the longer people's 'dwell time' the greater their propensity to spend. An analysis of the spending habits of day visitors and overnight visitors to Sheffield is shown in Table 6.5.

Table 6.5 shows that in addition to their expenditure on accommodation in Sheffield, overnight visitors spent 4.6 times as much as day visitors on other categories of expenditure. No comparable data are available for Glasgow as all of the relevant expenditure was made by overnight visitors. However, the Sheffield finding was replicated in the four other studies included in the overall research project.

Table 6.5 The spending patterns of day and overnight visitors to Sheffield

Expenditure category	Day visitors	Overnight visitors	Difference	Factor[1]
Food and drink	£2.73	£14.95	£12.22	5.5
Entertainment	£0.61	£3.71	£3.10	6.1
Programmes/merchandise	£1.60	£5.16	£3.56	3.2
Shopping/souvenirs	£1.37	£9.62	£8.25	7.0
Travel	£1.85	£3.53	£1.68	1.9
Other	£0.86	£4.67	£3.81	5.4
Total	£9.02	£41.64	£32.62	4.6

1 Factor = the number of times expenditure by overnight visitors exceeds that of day visitors e.g. 14.95/2.73 = 5.5 times

FOOD AND DRINK

It is not surprising that relatively little was spent on additional food and drink in Glasgow because competitors received three meals a day on a full-board tariff. Thus additional expenditure was limited to £2.53 per day (mainly canned drinks) per competitor. As there was little public interest in the event (65 visiting parents/ families) there were few spin-offs for local suppliers in Glasgow. By contrast the Sheffield event achieved average food and drink sales of £2.87 per head, but there were 11,050 non-Sheffield spectators making this average purchase value.

ENTERTAINMENT

At first glance it may be surprising that in Glasgow, where the average stay was for one week, the amount spent on entertainment was only £4,380 when £7,362 was spent in Sheffield in an afternoon. Aside from the low economic status of junior competitors, a key reason for this finding is the regime of elite athletes at major championships. A typical day for competitors at the European Junior Swimming Championships involved early morning training, resting, taking part in heats, resting and competing in 'A' or 'B' finals. Consequently, outside of competition there was little time for entertainment. On average competitors spent a total of £6.19 per day of which £2.53 was spent on food and drink. Thus even if time had been available for entertainment, their contributions would not have caused noticeable injections into the Glasgow economy. The average expenditure of £0.13p per competitor over a week is, therefore, not surprising. In Sheffield expenditure on entertainment averaged £0.65 per head for spectators. This may at first seem low, but the nature of the event was such that most expenditure took place in or around the stadium and thus a limiting factor was the availability of entertainment for money to be spent on. The only real entertainment expenditure opportunity at the Sheffield event was the purchase of prize draw tickets.

PROGRAMMES, MERCHANDISE AND SHOPPING

Three key factors explain the considerable differences in programme and merchandise sales at the two events. First, programmes in Sheffield were priced at £3 each and were bought by one in four spectators, whilst programmes in Glasgow were distributed free. Second, the availability of merchandise was an important factor. At the Sheffield event a large number of merchandise stalls were present selling souvenirs and sportswear, whilst in Glasgow there was only a sole trader selling swimwear in the foyer. There was no merchandise sold in Glasgow such as event T-shirts, sweatshirts or other event-specific memorabilia. Finally, the resources of the principal drivers were radically different.

TRAVEL

In Glasgow the main travel usage was the transporting of competitors from their accommodation to the competition venue and back again. This service was provided as part of the city council's support for the event, thereby not requiring additional expenditure by the competitors themselves. In Sheffield, the principal drivers of the economic impact were spectators who typically arrived by car or public transport. The expenditure on petrol or public transport fares generated an average spend of £1.85 per head on travel in Sheffield.

The rationale for outlining the differences between the Sheffield and Glasgow events is not to identify their diversity. Rather it is to enable local authorities and promoters of major events to be more proactive in their analysis of events. It is significant that the basic demand assessment before each event was significantly more optimistic than the reality. In Sheffield a crowd of 20,000 was expected and a total of 16,025 actually watched the event. In Glasgow, 1,400 admissions were expected over the four days and the 65 parents and families of the competitors generated just over 500 admissions by attending two sessions per day for four days. Therefore, if demand is lower than forecast, then this puts downward pressure on both the direct financial performance of an event and the wider economic impact benefit of an event. Thus a key objective of this paper is to suggest some simple evaluation techniques which may help promoters of events to make more informed decisions about which events or types of events to support. These recommendations are covered in the final section of this paper.

Towards evaluating the economic impact of events

Two common reasons cited for local authorities promoting major sporting events and making a direct loss on them are 'spillover' effects and externalities (Mules and Faulkner, 1996). This paper is not concerned with the measurement of externalities, rather it focuses on the spillover effects of the increased expenditure in a host city as a result of hosting a major sporting event. The first performance measure we suggest is to make a comparison between the net cost of an event and the additional direct expenditure the event generated in a given city. For the Sheffield and Glasgow events the results of this analysis are shown in Table 6.6.

Table 6.6 demonstrates that for each £1 of cost incurred by Sheffield City Council's Events Unit £2.96 of additional expenditure was generated within the city, which was 46 per cent more than the Glasgow event (£2.03 per £1 of cost). In the case of both events, the economic impact associated with each event was not a stated objective. Using an analysis such as that shown in Table 6.6, event promoters can quantify and justify their net expenditure on events. Furthermore, funders of such events have the chance to assess the opportunity cost of funding an event relative to other projects competing for the same resources. Estimating the economic impact of a major sporting event in advance of it taking place has always been fraught with difficulty because of a lack of data in the public domain from which to make comparisons. However, the data from the six events evaluated for the UK, English, and Scottish Sports Councils, of which this paper covers but two, means that there is now in the public domain comparable data sets from which events promoters can derive some parameters by which to estimate the impacts of future events.

Table 6.6 The costs of events compared with the non-local expenditure

Cost v expenditure analysis	Sheffield	Glasgow
Net cost of promoting event	£59,726	£127,000
Extra expenditure generated	£176,937	£257,802
Impact per £1 of cost	£2.96	£2.03

The use of the comparison between the cost of staging an event and its subsequent economic impact is already in use in Australia. Cities or local authorities competing for the right to stage have adopted a 'rule of thumb' constant of A$8 of additional spending to A$1 of event net cost as a benchmark target for justifying investment in events. Clearly the Sheffield and Glasgow events featured in this chapter, with cost to additional spending ratios of £3 to £1 and £2 to £1 respectively, fall considerably short of what is considered to be worthwhile (in economic terms) in Australia.

While the cost to non-local spending ratios are approximations, they are nonetheless useful in making outline estimates. For example, when staging a spectator-driven one-day event during school term time, only a tiny minority of people are likely to stay overnight in the host city. When promoting junior events, any economic impact is likely to be limited to being competitor driven and characterised by relatively low expenditures per visitor. The use of such parameters when trying to predict the impact of an event will help to offset some of the over-optimistic, non-empirically based estimates that have been used by some promoters in the past.

Table 6.7 illustrates some other measures of performance from the Sheffield and Glasgow events which could be used to assess the likely impact of comparable events in other cities.

In addition to assisting with the pre-planning of an event and the creation of a culture of 'realism' among events promoters, attempts to structure the potential economic impact of an event serves two additional purposes. First, a transparent analysis of data enables the results to be used for advocacy purposes. In making a comparison with the performing arts venues in Sheffield, the athletics event compared favourably in attracting people from outside the region. At the IAAF Grand Prix athletics meeting, 74 per cent of all visitors were from outside the Sheffield area, while it has been shown consistently that audiences at Sheffield's

Table 6.7 Simple measures of assessing the economic impact of events

Measure	Sheffield	Glasgow
Main cause of impact	Spectators (57%)	Competitors (81%)
Overall effect on hotels	800 commercial bed-nights	4,287 commercial bed-nights
Revenue per bed-night	£39.64	£49.07
Revenue in hotels sector	£31,714	£210, 370
Non-hotel expenditure	£145,223 (1 day of event)	£47,432 (4 days of event)
Non-hotel expenditure per day	£145,223	£11,858

theatres are predominantly local with only a 15 per cent regional or national audience. While we are not suggesting that potential economic impact is a primary reason for funding sport or the arts, the use of the results of economic impact studies can help to make the case for funding or to justify existing funding. Second, economic impact data has a valuable role to play in public accountability and value for money exercises. In many cases only the bottom line financial performance of an event is publicised – largely because no economic impact study has been conducted – and therefore only a partial and often uncomplimentary view of an event is presented to the public, for example the 1991 World Student Games held in Sheffield.

The additional expenditure generated in cities, in particular the impacts on hotels, can help to present a more balanced perspective on how any evaluation of an event is presented to the public. Allied to the requirement to demonstrate public accountability for the direct financial performance of an event, is the wider concept of providing value for money for any losses made or subsidy used. In isolation, the finding that each £1 of cost in Sheffield led to an additional expenditure of nearly £3 in the city does not provide a meaningful evaluation of the event. The missing ingredient needs to be a comparison with what the expenditure concerned was planned to achieve with other events that an authority has promoted; or even external comparison with the results achieved by other promoters in other local authorities.

Conclusion

It is arguable that if authorities wish to use major sporting events as vehicles by which to regenerate cities, then measurement of how policies are working in practice is essential to evaluate their performance. By committing to such measurement, authorities will in effect be integrating economic impact objectives into their overall event appraisal, rather than looking upon them as being desirable but unmeasurable intangibles. Furthermore, there is considerable economic and political logic to comparing the additional resources flowing into a city as a result of an event with the resources used to generate such inflows. The results of both the Sheffield and Glasgow studies are positive statements of how events can boost local economies and have been welcomed by both the governing bodies and city councils. The expense of conducting such studies, often an explanation for not doing them, is not necessarily prohibitive. The cost of the Sheffield and Glasgow research projects was approximately £5,000 each. It would therefore appear that there are several reasons for conducting economic impact studies at major sports events and very few reasons for not doing so.

References

Elvin, I.T. and Emery, P. (1997) 'Running on Empty: What Do We Really Know About a Sports Event?' *Recreation*, December 1997, pp. 19–26

Mules, T. and Faulkner, B. (1996) 'An Economic Perspective on Special Events'. *Tourism Economics*, Vol. 2(2), pp. 107–117.

Leisure Industries Research Centre (1997) *The Economic Impact of Major Sporting Events: Grand Prix 1, Don Valley Stadium, Sheffield, June 30th 1997*. Sheffield: LIRC.

Leisure Industries Research Centre (1997) *The Economic Impact of Major Sporting Events: European Junior Swimming Championships, Tolcross Park Leisure Centre, Glasgow*. Sheffield: LIRC.

Leisure Industries Research Centre (1997) *The Economic Impact of Major Sporting Events: Final Report*. Sheffield: LIRC.

Leisure Industries Research Centre (1997) *The Economic Impact of Major Sporting Events: Guidance Document*. Sheffield: LIRC.

Leisure Industries Research Centre (1996) *The Economic Impact of Major Sporting Events: Euro '96 and the World Masters' Swimming Championships*. Sheffield: LIRC.

7 Bidding to host a major sports event

Strategic investment or complete lottery

P. R. Emery

Introduction

Robert Scott (1992), Chairman of the Manchester 2000 British Olympic bid, once commented:

> It is a commonly held view that the toughest Olympic event is the marathon….
> [But by comparison] there is another Olympic event which makes the marathon
> look gentle. It has only a handful of competitors, lasts many years, is fought
> out in every continent of the world, and ends with the presentation of just one
> medal.

He was of course, specifically referring to the highly competitive global contest to host the world's largest sporting event, namely the Summer Olympic Games. Indeed, Smales (1996) elaborates that for the ambitious, upwardly mobile city, this represents the ultimate marketing initiative, where charismatic leaders pursue their own dreams to enter the premier division of a global urban hierarchy.

Sport, and more specifically, the hosting of major sports events is a recent global phenomena, where cities utilise the medium as an economic development tool for urban regeneration. Harvey (1988) even goes so far as to suggest that such prestige projects have become common, and perceived by civic leaders and officials as essential features of city revitalisation schemes within developed western nations. Likewise, Hall (1993) argues that cities unwilling to embrace such policies and participate in this global competition, are actually deemed to be contributing to their own demise.

Perhaps this is not entirely true, but more cities than ever before are now trying to use sports events to achieve strategic corporate objectives (Loftman and Spirou, 1996). No more is this apparent than in the United States of America (Atlanta, Baltimore, Chicago, Cleveland and Denver) and Great Britain (Birmingham, Glasgow, Manchester and Sheffield), where emerging academic study has given rise to the concepts of 'place marketing' and 'civic boosterism' (Law, 1993; Smyth, 1994; Duffy, 1995; Bunce, 1995; Loftman and Spirou, 1996; Hamilton, 1997). The rationale behind acceptance of such concepts is that sport and/or sports events are capable of providing unique opportunities for significant economic, social and/or political benefits for the host nation, region and city (Hall, 1992; Elvin and Emery, 1995; Gratton *et al.*, 1996; Davies, 1997; Dobson, Gratton and Holliday, 1997; Hamilton, 1997).

Such dramatic effects are clearly evident when one refers to the recent euphoria created by England hosting just one major sports event, namely the Euro '96 Football Championship (*The Times*, 1996). The results and performances of England's five football matches dominated every national UK media source over the three week duration of the championship. Adopting the nostalgic theme 'football's coming home', the event created a 'sense of national purpose, national unity and national pride' (Blair, 1996), and was instrumental in developing the feel-good factor, cherished by all governments. As Joseph (1996) makes the point:

> In 90 minutes, and four goals, football had done what a thousand speeches by government ... has all failed to do. England feels great about itself, almost invincible – not just on the football field, but in business, the Olympic Games, politics, you name it.

However, the significant benefits of hosting major sports events, must be appraised in the light of the unenviable record of incidents (fatalities, riots, financial mismanagement, unethical practices etc.). Specific examples include, the near bankruptcy of the City of Montreal (1976 Olympic Games), the Heysel (1985) and Hillsborough football disasters (1989), the £10.4 million debt of Sheffield City Council (1991 World Student Games), the Grand National cancellation/postponement (1993/ 1997), and the description attributed to the 1996 Atlanta Olympic Games – 'complete chaos' (the *Observer*, 1996), and 'the worst organised event ever known' (Redgrave, 1996). Against this background, sports event management despite its long history and meteoric growth, is clearly still in its infancy. Before further disasters result, there appears to be an urgent need to systematically appraise what is known, as well as what is not, about successfully managing major sports events. A wider investigation than the present study was therefore initiated, with the primary objective being to establish how major sports events from around the world, are managed. Reviewing the fundamental management processes as identified by Chelladurai (1985), planning, organising, leading and evaluating, the ultimate aim was to identify examples of good practice to improve future practice.

This particular study is just one component of the wider brief, and focusses upon the actual management processes and practices used in the bidding process from the perspective of the practitioner at the local organising committee level. It aims to address the following research questions:

- Why do cities bid to host major sports events?
- What is the selection and sanctioning process of a city wishing to host a major sports event?
- What planning techniques are utilised in the pre-event management process?
- What lessons can cities learn for the future, to improve their chances of successful bidding?

Drawing upon a diverse range of sports events from around the world, the findings aim to elucidate the practitioner actions and perceptions of bidding to host major sports events so that cities in the future are better informed to decide whether this may be considered a strategic option or, at best, desperate optimism as experienced in any lottery.

Background

Major sports event concept

In targeting this type of event, it begs the question, what specifically are major sports events, and how are they distinctly different from other events? In first addressing the nature of scale, a review of event literature reveals that the terms 'Hallmark events' and 'mega-events' have both been used to describe major events (Richards, 1994). These have been classified by reference to their volume of visitors, cost, image or economic effect (Marris, 1987). However, Getz (1991) concludes that

> *Hallmark event* is now a widely used term, but, like mega-event, it also resists precise definition. Some use it as a synonym for special event, while others suggest it is a particular class of event that has a unique image or appeal.

However, the validity of this study is bound by the definition of a 'major' sports event, despite its subjective interpretation. In an attempt to encapsulate the typical usage of the above terms, and to apply a similar meaningful definition upon which future comparisons can be made, this study will adopt the following definition of a 'major' sports event as

Either – a sporting championship recognised by the appropriate governing body
          of the sport *and* attracting a minimum of 1,000 spectators (e.g. Euro'96),
Or   – a sports event that receives national or international media coverage as
          a result of the calibre of competition, *and* one in which a minimum of
          1,000 spectators are present at the event (e.g. Le Tour de France).

Major sports event management environment

Given the temporal and unique characteristics of an event (Torkildsen, 1994), this study can directly draw upon the relatively well developed management discipline of project management (Morris and Hough, 1993). From such a classification, sports event management can be considered a subset of project management, and therefore can be diagrammatically represented as in Figure 7.1.

However, this does not convey the full complexity of the situation encountered by the manager of major sports events, as highlighted in Figure 7.2.

This model provides a basic summary of the typical relationships found between, and within the key organisations involved in most major international sports events. In particular, it recognises that a minimum of three organisational levels are involved

Figure 7.1 Project management environment

Adapted from Briner, Geddes and Hasting (1990), and Kerzner (1995).

– at the international, national and local levels. However, further analysis reveals that each level is usually much more complicated than this, as was reported by Murray (1995). In referring specifically to the Atlantic Olympic Committee, he suggested that this vertical and horizontal involvement included relationships with more than 1,000 different organisations!

In summary, cities who enter the contest to host major sports events are likely to experience all categories of Maylor's (1996) project complexity:

- *organisational complexity* – the number of people, departments, organisations and nations involved,
- *resource complexity* – the volume of resources involved, time, capital, processes,
- *technical complexity* – the level of innovation in the product or the project process.

Management of major sports events, are therefore some of the most complex projects imaginable, and it is upon this premise that they are being investigated as a separate identity in their own right.

The bidding process

Against this background, it is apparent that even the most basic process of bidding to host a World or European Sports Championship involves considerable risk and commitment. For example, such a bidding process is likely to entail:

1 Organisational approval
2 Competitive bid to the national sports governing body

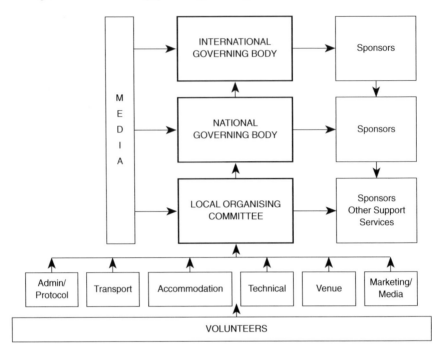

Figure 7.2 Basic summary of major sports event organisation relationships and structures

3 Acceptance as the winning bid by the national governing body
4 National competitive bid to the international sports governing body
5 Acceptance as the winning bid by the international sports governing body

Each stage experiences further resource commitment, more bureaucracy, and the nature of the outcome even if they do win, means that they ultimately face the role of a low level contractor, accepting responsibility for nearly all of the project's major risks.

According to project management and event management theory, the project (to host the event) is initiated from an internally or externally generated idea. This is developed into one or more projects, which need to strategically fit both present and future organisational and environmental requirements (Johnson and Scholes, 1993). The feasibility of each project then needs to be considered against organisational selection and sanctioning criteria/procedures (Durham MBA, 1993). Wearne (1989) suggests that such a process ensures:

> that sufficient work is carried out to reduce the uncertainties to acceptable levels. Within the procedure, expenditure is sanctioned in one or more stages to produce increasingly more reliable statements of viability. Thus the decision-making authority has the opportunity of reviewing the proposal as it progresses through defined stages before taking a final commitment decision.

However, all this assumes that the appropriate information is readily available, and that rational planning and decision making are the norm, either as a potential candidate, or as an international/national governing body. In an ideal world, this may be very much the case, but in the selection process, complexity and uncertainty remain throughout the project. This often means that it is quite possible that a decision not to proceed will be taken before the bidding phase begins or in extreme cases the day before presentation, as was the case with Sheffield City Council in its national bid to host the 2002 Commonwealth Games (Waple, 1994).

Given that the hosting of a specific major event may literally be a once in a lifetime organisation experience, uncertainty and risk are likely to be experienced throughout the life cycle of the project. But does this mean that the Garbage Can Model of organisational decision-making (Aguilar-Manjarrez, Thwaites and Maule, 1997), is the most appropriate to the environment encountered? Or indeed, is it the case, as reported by Lynch and Jenson (1984), that the desirability of cities to host major sports events is still based more on personal and political conviction than that of careful appraisal of merits?

Whatever the driving force behind the bidding process, or the model of organisational decision making utilised by the candidate city, the core management process of planning must be considered essential if the national or international governing body and city wish to maintain any present/future credibility. As highlighted by Watt (1994):

> It is always a little dangerous to select one management function rather than another, but in terms of event organization, it would appear quite legitimate to select planning as the prime factor of success ... Planning is so valuable because it reduces uncertainty; focuses attention on goals and produces unity of purpose; makes for efficient operation; and ensures appropriate control systems are established.

The old adage 'if you fail to plan, then you plan to fail', seems to apply equally to the bidding process as to the whole project. Furthermore, the processes of planning and control must be considered as interrelated processes, where one is identifying the route, and the other checking to see that the most effective/efficient usage of resources are being utilised to access this destination point. But this is all theory, what happens in practice, in the major sports event environment? Are event managers even aware of systematic planning techniques, and if they are, do they use them, and under what circumstances? These questions and many more, need addressing, and are the main purpose behind this research.

Methodology

Design overview

Given the broader remit of the wider investigation, nearly 400 major sports event organisers (Table 7.1) were invited to provide retrospective data on the management practices and contextual detail, of their most recently managed major sports event.

Table 7.1 Sample frame

England	Nos.	Non-England	Nos.
1 Sports national governing bodies (23 priority sports)	33	1 Sports international/Pan European governing bodies (23 sports and additional bodies)	40
2 Public authorities			
– Metropolitan Borough Councils	36	2 European Association for Sport Management contacts	71
– London Borough Councils	33		
– Known County/Local Councils	20	3 Known commercial organisers	7
3 Known commercial organisers	25	4 Major international events/venues omitted from 1–3 above	81
4 Major events/venues omitted from 1–3 above	31	5 Other Associations	9
5 Other Associations	8		
Total	186	Total	208

In summary, the data collection utilised a piloted two-stage approach, was entirely in English, and entailed:

- a self-administered postal questionnaire, with covering letter and pre-paid self addressed envelope. This was sent to the Chief Executive Officer or equivalent position from the above sample frame.
- this was followed up by indepth semi-structured interviews, involving a convenience sample of three public authority case studies in England. Their selection was based upon them returning the previous questionnaire, and being successful within the last five years, at both national and international bidding stages in the process to host a major sports event.

Research tools

Given the need to gain access to both a widely dispersed geographical population and a large volume of data, a postal questionnaire was deemed to be the most appropriate research tool (Labovitz and Hagedorn, 1976). Whereas the questionnaire focused on general event management detail, such as contextual information, resource utilisation, functional procedures and methods, the interviews provided a richer data source of bidding procedures. For example, questions pertaining to explanations of specific successful and unsuccessful bidding processes were explored, along with the rationale behind specific actions.

Data analysis

All quantitative data in this study was analysed utilising the SPSS for Windows (Version 7) statistical package. To describe, differentiate and highlight the significance of such data, both descriptive and inferential statistics were used on the

Table 7.2 Respondent frame

England	Nos.	Non-England	Nos.
1 National governing bodies	7	1 Sports international/Pan	3
2 Public authorities		European governing	
– Metropolitan/London B.C.	6	bodies	
– County/Local Councils	5	2 EASM contacts	10
3 Commercial organisers	2	3 Commercial organisers	2
4 Major events/venues	3	4 Major international	5
5 Other Associations	1	events/venues	
		5 Other Associations	2
Total	24	Total	22

data. Given the sheer volume of data collected, and the word limit of this paper, only statistically significant findings ($p<0.05$) are reported in this text. Qualitative data, on the other hand, was analysed manually and key remarks are used to further substantiate the quantitative findings.

Results

After introducing a brief profile of the respondents, this section is presented according to the fundamental questions that this research set out to achieve, with both quantitive and qualitative data included under each of these headings.

Respondent profile

Taking into account spoilt responses and those organisations that did not meet the qualifying criteria, the final usable sample constituted 46 organisations (13 per cent response rate). Despite this relatively low response rate, the sample, as seen in Table 7.2, appears to be representative of the planned sample frame.

More specifically, 25 different sports and two multi-sport events were represented, of which fourteen were classified as world championship events. Of the public sector respondents, only 16 respondents constituted the sample frame (11 England; 5 non-England). However, the majority of these cities possessed a wealth of event management experience, with cities such as Sheffield, Edinburgh, Glasgow, Gateshead and Sunderland each reporting that they had hosted at least three world championship events/international competitions within the last five years.

Why do cities bid to host major sports events?

Adopting Bunce's (1995) categorisation of motives behind public sector involvement, Figure 7.3 illustrates a diversity of reasons/benefits for hosting such events.

At first glance, it is apparent that sport promotion (mean of 6.9) and then economic development (4.7) appear to be the major reasons behind organisational involvement. However, such findings may well be attributed to the specialist needs of individual stakeholders, for example national governing bodies being involved

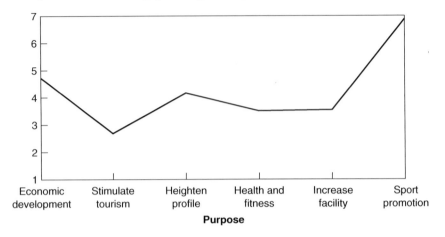

Figure 7.3 Event purpose means (1 = not important – 7 = very important)

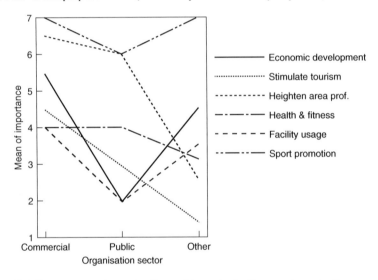

Figure 7.4 Event purpose by sector (1 = not important – 7 = very important)

specifically in sport development. Further analysis (Figure 7.4) reveals that all sectors (excluding the voluntary sector, due to insufficient data being available), value the importance of sport promotion (minimally valued at 6.0).

More specifically, the public sector equally values the importance of sport promotion (6.0) and heightening area profile (6.0), but at present places minimal importance to increase facility usage (2.0) and economic development (2.0). Such findings concur with Bunce (1995), who similarly identified that the prime motive behind hosting events, regardless of public sector political divide, was to heighten the profile of the area. This in turn, he suggests, facilitates inward investment from business and tourists, which consequently leads to satisfying the demands of the resident population.

Table 7.3 Case study: corporate strategic aims

Organisation	Strategic aim
City of Sunderland Council	• To promote the changing face/profile of the locality as an emerging 'new' city
City of Durham Council	• To promote awareness and investment opportunities and to extend the tourism season to a city/region decimated by the collapse of the coal mining and steel industries
Gateshead Metropolitan Borough Council	• To extend the depth of the event portfolio of a focused sport and to celebrate the millennium significance

However, further statistical analysis between event purpose and organisation sector, via Kruskal-Wallis and Jonckheere trend tests, reveals that public sector organisations value sport promotion (p<0.023) and economic development (p<0.047) less significantly than commercial sector and 'other' organisations. Referring to the former, the relatively low value apportioned to sport promotion can be explained by corporate objectives dominating leisure policy objectives. However, extending this argument to economic development motives, it does not explain why public sector organisations value economic development less than other sectors. Perhaps, economic development was perceived narrowly and interpreted as 'profitable development'. In this sense, it may be considered to be related to organisational survival. The global recession of the 1990s has obviously impacted all sectors, but by comparison, this may affect more the very existence of many commercial and voluntary sector organisations, unlike the relatively safe environment of the public sector. In the former case, financial mismanagement may be the complete demise of the organisation, whereas in the latter case, the public sector organisation and officers are likely to still have a future, albeit it may be under the direction of different councillors.

The public sector event organisers stressed the prioritised importance of raising the area profile/image. Illustrated in Table 7.3, all reflected corporate strategic aims, which as highlighted later, provided a specific context for the organisational selection of the choice of sport and/or event.

In essence, a global sports event was perceived to be the medium by which the city could develop both its national and international profile, which in turn could lead to sustainable local growth via economic development, inward investment and tourism stimulation. As succinctly summarised by one interviewee:

The councillors required a plan that would first and foremost involve a short-term investment with minimum risk, but long term, would stimulate economic growth and provide a healthy future. The medium of sport appeared the ideal vehicle to meet such criteria.

What is the selection and sanctioning process of a city wishing to host a major sports event?

Given the diversity of sports and/or events available to a city, how is the choice made and why? In all cases, belief in the resource capability, in terms of finance, facilities and experienced staff, are obviously fundamental to any project being initiated, as is the image synergy between the prospective host organisation and the sport and/or event.

This is clearly evident, in considering the City of Durham Council's bid to host the World Cross Country Championships. According to Elvin and Emery (1997), the unique selling features and synergistic image of this particular event, from Durham's perspective were:

1   a sport that offered a traditional, competitive and demanding image – a positive attribute to any organisation and region
2   an event that involved few capital costs (i.e. specialist facilities or infrastructure), hence limited financial risk
3   a short duration event that appealed to the medium of television, and had more nations participating in a single day, than any other event in the world
4   a very experienced team who had previously been involved in other national and international events in the sport of athletics.

Synergy is important, but a number of events could meet such need. So how do organisations differentiate between investments and/or sports events? The study revealed that a proactive selection process based upon rational decision-making, was nigh on impossible due to the limited nature and accuracy of information available. As explained by one case study respondent:

> On the one hand, international and national governing bodies typically provide a framework for the bidding process and operational management of the event, but the practical reality is that very few sports and or events offer factual detail on event profiles and/or cost/benefit analyses of previous events.

If this is the case, and comparisons are not possible, where does the selection process start, and how does it progress? The initial impetus/idea behind all the events reviewed, was borne from a Leisure Officer of the respective councils. Normally in the course of his/her informal socialisations at a sports event, the idea originates. In some cases, large local authorities with a strong portfolio of event management experience, may be proactive in declaring their interest in hosting major events. In many others, it is quite literally a reactive comment, often in the presence of a personally known national governing body representative.

Further internal and external informal discussions ensue, until eventually the chief executive and/or prominent councillors are involved. Only when considerable personal support is established, will the proposal become an agenda item on any formalised council committee structure. However, in many cases the bidding time scale and established council practices dictate that informal approvals are given before the relevant committee sits.

This may partially explain why formalised selection criteria were not evident in any of the public sector organisations included in the sample. Assuming project synergy to strategic direction and organisation competence, particularly technical competence, the investment appeared to progress to the sanctioning stage, based upon the primary concern of the worst case scenario, meaning bottom line cost. Additional selection included personal politics, media profile (particularly television), and the potential for community involvement. For any chance of success, it was argued that the chief executive and/or a charismatic councillor(s) needed to drive the project. As revealed from the case studies, such interest and commitment appeared to be primarily derived from either the personal ambition of the status/ kudos associated with the event and/or a direct personal interest in sport in general.

In summary, there existed a formal process of internal selection and sanctioning, but this did not include absolute and immutable selection criteria, nor was it based entirely upon financial information. Key decisions were commonly made via informal processes, and rational arguments relating to specific decisions, if used at all, were often formalised a considerable time after decisions were made. For example, and as will be seen later, few organisations possessed aims and objectives for their events, and many were established after the event, principally being used for evaluative rather then directional purposes. The main exception to this was financial considerations, which meant that a multi-stage sanctioning procedure as highlighted by Wearne (1989) was in operation, with the key milestones being the bidding stage and the event implementation stage.

Similarly, the importance of networking/political lobbying was clearly evident in the external selection and sanctioning processes. For example, one scenario was presented whereby a national governing body approached a specific local authority detailing a financial arrangement to host the event, before the formalised bidding process had begun. Another respondent also revealed that an international governing body agreed to award a world event to an organising committee, not even for the year that they were bidding for!

What planning techniques are utilised in the pre-event management process?

Planning – aims/objectives

Despite 64 per cent of the respondents suggesting that they used aims/objectives, only 10 provided them. On further analysis, the findings reveal that most constituted a single very general aim and only three were remotely detailed. Of these, all focused upon task outcomes, as distinct from team and individual aims (Adair, 1988), and only one could be considered SMART (Randolph and Posner, 1988). Unsuccessful event management is supposedly characterised by 'vague aims and hopes and no clear objectivity' (Torkildsen, 1994), but the findings reveal that few organisations formalise event aims/objectives, which is suggested to be a basic necessity by most event management texts (Hall, 1992; Richards, 1994; Torkildsen,

1994; Watt, 1994). Furthermore, given the fact that all the events provided retrospective data, it is not even as if directional planning (Chelladurai, 1985) was utilised by the majority. Of the aims that were considered detailed, in at least two cases of the three, directional planning was evident with clarity and specificity of objectives being incrementally developed (Morris and Hough, 1993) across the event life-cycle. In contrast, organisational aims/objectives were found to exist, but rarely evident. Why this was the case is unclear. Is it because such events involve too much uncertainty, or that targets could become political yardsticks for evaluation? Or is it in fact, just an impossible task, due to the diversity of stakeholder aims/objectives that need to be reconciled? Further research is required in this area.

Planning techniques

One further explanation why terms of reference were barely utilised, is perhaps due to reasons of complacency. For example, 13 per cent of respondents as well as reporting that they did not use aims/objectives, refrained from answering the questions on planning techniques. Instead, typical comments put forward included:

- We are talking here of an organisation that has been evolved for 80 years.
- We do a budget. We then follow what we do each year without written or formal plans. Most key members have been with the event 11–14 years
- This makes the event look terribly disorganised – unplanned and ad-hoc. The truth is all the systems, formal and informal have developed over 16 years, and with one exception, the management team is the same as 1981. As director, I enjoy the luxury of TOTALLY trusting my team of managers.

The majority of respondents, on the other hand, suggested that they did use a variety of plans, usually formalised (minimally 88 per cent). The financial plans (90 per cent usage) and marketing plans (80 per cent usage) were the most commonly used, with the feasibility and bidding plans being most infrequently used (less than 45 per cent usage). This is quite surprising given the external environment previously identified, where it was hypothesised that the numerous risks and complexities need to be identified at the outset of the project selection. Without a feasibility study and/or bidding plan, major resource investments do perhaps appear to be initiated more on personal and political conviction than of careful appraisal (Lynch and Jensen, 1984). Of even greater surprise, given their electorate accountabilities, was the statistically significant finding that public sector organisations were less likely to use a bidding plan than any other organisation type (Kruskal-Wallis/Jonckheere trend – 8.478; $p<0.04$). As previously explained, this may be attributed to the finding that the bidding process appears to be driven by politics rather than formalised criterion referencing. However, despite this recognition by candidates, the formalised process adopted by national and international governing bodies, typically a thirty minute presentation that includes questions, is taken very seriously by the majority of candidate cities. Case study respondents highlighted that they often employed specialist agencies to advise them on production/presentation tactics, and most presentations were very carefully scripted, including detailed dress rehearsals. Successful applicants minimally used a colour brochure, a promotional video, and a sporting personality, that would be instantly known to the panel.

In summary, event managers reported that their pre-event planning in general, was 'over planned'. No one reported anything less than average planning, but in reality, would anyone report his or her inadequacies in such a public forum? However, from an external, independent perspective, complacency and vague terms of reference provide evidence of Wearne's (1989) under-planning characteristics.

With specific reference to the bidding planning process, no respondent used theoretical techniques such as capital investment appraisals, risk/sensitivity analyses, competitor analyses, despite the fact that each city was likely to incur a minimum cost of £20,000.

What lessons can cities learn for the future, to improve their chances of successful bidding?

In summary, case study respondents suggested that the key lessons for entering the major sports event arena, are as follows:

1 Develop relevant professional credibility.
2 Fully understand the brief and the formal/informal decision-making processes.
3 Do not assume that decision-makers are experts, nor that they use rational criteria for selection.
4 Customise professional (in)tangible products/services and give them more than they ask for.
5 Know your strengths and weaknesses relative to your competition.

In systematically reviewing each of these key lessons in turn, it is first and foremost apparent that relevant and recent experience/competence are fundamental to any successful application. A portfolio of different national and international events is obviously ideal, but this can be overcome by carefully selecting key personnel, and inviting them to join the organising team. However, it is the operational event manager that will make or break any event. He/she has the unenviable role of being everything to all people – in other words, a superb planner, skilled administrator, brass-knuckled fighter, sensitive psychiatrist, experienced negotiator, enthusiastic leader, creative communicator, unshakable optimist and a miser .

Furthermore, successful city applications are dependent upon in-depth knowledge of networks, processes and people. Formal processes must clearly be understood, but equally the informal process and protocol must never be underestimated. As expressed by one respondent:

> Politics in sport, makes politics in government look like mere play. Unilateral decision making by numerous stakeholders is the name of the game, and this gets faster and infinitesimally more complicated, as the sports event gets closer.

The importance of politics was similarly attributed to many unsuccessful bids, with comments including:

- We simply did not know the panel members well enough.
- We were out politicked.
- We were too naive. We thought that it was a level playing field.

Such comments further illustrate the misconceived assumptions that decision-makers on the various panels were experts, and that rational decision making was the norm. In briefly reviewing the former, it became apparent that it was in fact the full-time council officers (professionals) who are more likely to be the experts, with councillors and governing body representatives being the part-time non-experts (amateurs). Despite such persons being very committed volunteers, it was they that possessed the power. This might also explain why the formal selection process still typically utilises just a thirty-minute interview, which epitomises employment practices of more than a decade ago. Within this time frame, it really is impossible to review the depth of any bid and the consequence of this is that information presented is generally accepted at face value. This should really be unacceptable if rationality is to prevail, as very large discrepancies between proposal and outcome are frequently experienced. As evident in the 1992 Winter Olympics in Albertville, the initial proposal calculated that the event would quite literally break-even. In reality, it left the French town with debts of £20 million (Lewis, 1998). Unsubstantiated claims were therefore reported to be common throughout the bidding process, which led to some respondents questioning the fairness of the selection process as well as the rationality of some of the decisions. Successful and unsuccessful candidates concluded, that the most professional presentation, addressing all publicly declared criteria, did not necessarily mean that it would win. For example, specific comments included:

- As soon as we arrived, we realised that the selection process had already been agreed, before the formal presentations had even begun.
- The attractiveness of the location, to the panel members and their wives, clearly determined the final outcome.
- It was actually their turn to win.

This latter comment, perhaps further supports the work of Lawson (1996), who argues that the candidates need to initially learn the unwritten rules of the selection process. In this sense, the initial bid may be used as a pre-requisite to the establishment of cultivating networks for a more serious challenge in the future.

Central to all of the key lessons are the underlying principles of marketing. Relationship marketing, via the identification and satisfaction of a plethora of stakeholder needs, above that of the competition, appear to be the main criteria for success. This entails focusing clearly upon the formal and informal client needs of the powerful decision-makers, at each stage of the bidding process. Effective bids were therefore not necessarily the most efficient, but they were fundamentally based upon a personalised approach which aimed to exceed individual stakeholder expectations. Such comments that reveal this approach include:

- A known figurehead to spearhead the bid is essential for inside knowledge of the key decision-makers.
- Our presentation was aimed at their requirements, with very much a technical customised video, unlike one of our competitors who just provided a tourism video.

Additionally, given the present market place of increased demand from cities wishing to host major sports events (Smales, 1996), respondents suggested that there is likely to be a growing importance placed upon establishing competitive advantage. The implication of this is that weaknesses need to be reviewed against competitors. Conversely, strengths relative to competition, need to be fully appraised, and then the unique selling features need to be communicated via strategic and tactical promotions for maximum effect. For example, one respondent identified that no candidate was prepared to underwrite the risks and costs of the event. He proposed that his city would, which immediately killed off the competition, despite the fact that at this stage, he had not the authority to make such a decision, nor had the team calculated the consequence of such a statement. A further respondent illustrated this haphazard bidding environment, suggesting that:

> In reality, bidders do not really know what they have let themselves in for at this stage of the process. But they have to make promises to beat off the competition ... Having gone through the whole process, the plan suggested at the bidding phase actually bares little resemblance to the final implementation.

Conclusions

In summary, the evidence provided from this study, appears to support the notion that the present bidding process is characterised by personal ambition rather than rational management. One explanation may be attributed to the fact that major sports events are characterised by a complex interdependency of national and international organisational relationships that have evolved over many years. Within this context, there exist diverse personal and cultural needs involving opportunities for considerable autonomy and power. This environment has developed against a background of little professional and/or academic sport management training and/ or education, with the outcome, as cited by Keegan (1997) specifically referring to the administration of professional football, being;

> As good as these people are in giving up their time to the game, the sport and the clubs have overtaken them, and that is a problem given that they enjoy a position of power.

In major sports events, those in power are likely to be committed amateurs who possess limited technical and operational knowledge, but considerable political influence and experience. It is little surprise then, that the present formalised antiquated selection process, that typifies most international bidding frameworks, appears to operate more on hidden agendas and informal processes, than on the application of systematic techniques and principles. This seems to occur within and between councils, national governing bodies and international governing bodies.

However, it is envisaged that in the future, there will be more major sports events and more competition. The consequence of this is that bidding is likely to become even more extravagant and expensive. Despite the fact that the National Lottery have now provided independent funds available for bidding and staging World Class Events, the risks and costs faced by individual cities are likely to escalate. With increased levels of accountability being experienced around the world, no city can continually face the consequences of hosting major sports events as experienced at the most recent Winter Olympics in Nagano:

> The millions spent putting together these Olympics, which were popular with the city's 347,000 population, will now have a reverse effect … Shocked ratepayers face debts of up to £20,000 a household to balance the city's books after hosting the greatest sports show on earth.
>
> (Lewis, 1998)

To reduce such levels of financial debt, innovative bidding partnerships are likely to prevail, as witnessed in the present race to host the Football World Cup. The downside of this, is that it is likely to involve more stakeholders, which potentially means more politics, more uncertainty and less rational management. Is bidding to host a major sports event seriously becoming a strategic corporate option, or does it appear vaguely familiar to a civic leader pursuing his/her dream, and purchasing a national lottery ticket on a Saturday night?

References

Adair, J. (1988) *The Action Centred Leader*. Gower.

Aguilar-Manjarrez, R., Thwaites, D. and Maule, J. (1997) *The Application of Organisational Buyer Behaviour Theory to Sport Sponsorship Selection Decisions*. 5th European Congress on Sport Management – Glasgow.

Blair, T. (1996) 'We're Now a More United Kingdom'. Article in the *Daily Mirror* on 28th June.

Briner, W., Geddes, M. and Hasting, C. (1990) *Project Leadership*. Gower.

Bryman, A. and Cramer, D. (1990) *Quantitative Data Analysis for Social Scientists*. Routledge.

Bunce, D. (1995) *Major Sporting Events and Local Authorities: Who Benefits?* Unpublished MSc. Strategy and Resource Management Dissertation – University of Northumbria.

Chelladurai, P. (1985) *Sport Management: Macro Perspectives*. Sport Dynamics.

Davies, L. (1997) *The Economic Impact of Sport in the City: A Case Study of Sheffield*. 5th European Congress on Sport Management – Glasgow.

Dobson, N., Gratton, C. and Holliday, S. (1997) *Football Came Home: The Economic Impact of Euro '96*. 5th European Congress on Sport Management – Glasgow.

Durham, M.B.A. (1993) *Project Management* – University of Durham Business School.

Elvin, I.T. and Emery, P.R. (1995) *The Impact of the XXIII IAAF/SNICKERS World Cross Country Event*. Unpublished Consultancy Report.

Elvin, I.T. and Emery, P.R. (1997) 'A Role for Professional Sports Management: The XXIII Snickers World Cross Country Championships'. *European Journal of Sport Management*, Vol. 4(1), 6–25.

Getz, D. (1991) *Festivals, Special Events and Tourism*. Van Nostrand Reinhold.

Gratton, C., Dobson, N., Holliday, S. and Davies, L. (1996) *The Economic Impact of Sports Events: Euro'96 and the VI FINA World Masters Swimming Championships in Sheffield*. Proceedings of the 1996 Regional Studies Association Annual Conference.

Hall, C.M. (1992) *Hallmark Tourist Events: Impacts, Management & Planning*. Belhaven Press.

Hall, P. (1993) 'Forces Shaping Urban Europe'. *Urban Studies*, Vol. 30(6), 883–898.

Hamilton, L. (1997) *Sports Events & Place Marketing: A Means for Generating Tourism in Victoria, Australia*. 5th European Congress on Sport Management – Glasgow.

Harvey, D. (1988) 'Voodoo Cities'. *New Statesman and Society*, 30 September, 33–35.

Johnson, G. and Scholes, K. (1993) *Exploring Corporate Strategy: Text and Cases*, 3rd Edition. Prentice Hall.

Joseph, J. (1996) 'So This Is The Feel-Good Factor At Last'. Article in *The Times* on 20th June.

Judd, D.R. (1995) 'Promoting Tourism in US Cities'. *Tourism Management*, Vol. 16(3), 175–187.

Keegan, K. (1997) *Kevin Keegan: My Autobiography*. Little, Brown & Company.

Kerzner, H. (1995) *Project Management: A Systems Approach to Planning, Scheduling, and Controlling*, 5th Edition. Van Nostrand Reinhold.

Labovitz, C. and Hagedorn, R. (1976) *Introduction to Social Research*, 2nd Edition. McGraw Hill.

Law, C. (1993) *Urban Tourism: Attracting Visitors to Large Cities*. Mansell.

Lawson, T. (1996) 'After It's All Over'. *The Geographical Magazine*, July, Vol. LXVIII, No. 7, 20–23.

Lewis, R. (1998) 'Nagona Counts Cost'. Article in *Express Sport* on 24th February.

Loftman, P. and Nevin, B. (1992) *Urban Regeneration and Social Equity: A Case Study of Birmingham 1986–1992*. University of Central England in Birmingham.

Loftman, P. and Spirou, C.S. (1996) *Sports, Stadiums & Urban Regeneration: The British and United States Experience*. Paper presented at the Tourism and Culture: Towards the 21st Century Conference – Morpeth.

Lynch, P.G. and Jenson, R.C. (1984) 'The Economic Impact of the XII Commonwealth Games on the Brisbane Region'. *Urban Policy and Research*, Vol. 2(3).

Marris, T. (1987) 'The Role and Impact of Mega-Events and Attractions on Regional and National Tourism Development: Resolutions'. *Revue de Tourisme*, Vol. 4, 3–10.

Maylor, H. (1996) *Project Management*. Pitman Publishing.

Morris, P.W.G. and Hough, G.H. (1993) *The Anatomy of Major Projects – A Study of Reality of Project Management*. J.Wiley & Sons.

Murray, M. (1995) 'How Atlanta Plans To Win Gold'. *Event Organiser*, Vol. 23, 16–17.

Randolph, W.A. and Posner, B.Z. (1988) *Effective Project Planning and Management*. Prentice Hall.

Redgrave, S. (1996) Cited in Sports Section of *The Guardian* on 21st July.

Reilly, K, and Gysin, C. (1996) 'We Won by £300 Million'. Article in the *Daily Mirror* on 28th June.

Richards, B. (1994) *How to Market Tourist Attractions, Festivals and Special Events*. Longman.

Scott, R. (1992) 'Is it the Dollar or the Spirit that Inspires Cities to Bid to Host the Olympic Games?' Paper presented at the International Olympic Academy – 32nd Session for Young Participants. Ancient Olympia – Greece.

Smales, L. (1996) 'Bidding for the 2004 Olympic Games as a Catalyst for Urban Regeneration'. Proceedings of the Regional Studies Association Annual Conference.

Smyth, H. (1994) *Marketing the City: Flagship Developments in Urban Regeneration*. Spon.

Sports Council (1992) *Sport in the Nineties: New Horizons – Part One and Two*. The Sports Council.

Sports Council (1996) *A Directory for Northern Sport and Recreation*. Northern Region Sports Council.

The Times (1996) Article in the Sports Section on 17th June.

Torkildsen, G. (1994) *Torkildsen's Guide to Leisure Management*. Longman.

Walpe, A. (1994) 'All Played Out'. Article in the *Sheffield Telegraph* on 4th February.

Watt, D.C. (1994) *Leisure & Tourism Events Management and Organisation Manual*. Longman.

Watt, D. (1995) 'Wise Before the Event'. *The Leisure Manager*, October/November, 31–32. ILAM.

Wearne, S. (1989) *Engineering Management – Control of Engineering Projects*. Thomas Telford Ltd.

8   The case of Euro96

Where did the party go?

Rex Nash and Sam Johnstone

Sports tournaments, cultural programmes and the sponsorship system

As is well known, since the 1984 Olympics (which generated a surplus of over $200m), sport tournaments can be enormously big business, and are increasingly designed with the needs of sponsors and other major corporate interests in mind. At their most successful, major tournaments like the Olympics or the World Cup can enormously improve the economic status and tourist appeal of a city or region. Investment floods into the area, infrastructural redevelopment is carried out, and local populations can witness increased trade, repeat tourism, and the creation of a whole new image for a city or region within the global economy (Brunet, 1996), although as Critcher (1992) argues, this is by no means guaranteed. Whitson and Macintosh (1993) argue that tournaments can be a useful, if difficult, way of recreating the entire image of a region in a de-localised global economy with the capacity to locate its operations anywhere in the world. De Moragas Spa, Rivenburgh and Garcia (1996) meanwhile have demonstrated how the globalising, homogenising tendencies of events like the Olympics can be resisted, and the technology behind homogenisation subverted and put to work in support of local, specific and diverse cultures.

Behind the World Cup and the Olympics, the European Championship in football is the third biggest sporting event in the world and, as such, has the potential to impact on regions and cities in similar ways. The 1996 European Championship was held in England, branded as Euro96, and was widely deemed a success. Dobson, Holliday and Gratton (1997) estimated that the total extra expenditure arising out of Euro96 at some £195m, including £75m extra spending by UK citizens, and although the Football Association (FA) managed the seemingly impossible (to lose money on a major sports tournament), the England team performed well and an estimated 250,000 overseas visitors passed through the eight host cities in a friendly atmosphere. Glen Kirton (then the FA's Euro96 Tournament Director, now working for UEFA's marketing rights partner ISL) estimated the event made £500m in revenue and exposure. Many of the fixtures did not sell out, far from it in some cases, leading to serious criticisms of the entire ticketing system, but the FA was sufficiently satisfied with its performance that it reneged on promises made to Germany's Football Federation and announced it would bid for the 2006 World Cup.

Increasingly, cities and regions seek to ensure that major sporting tournaments have not just external or economic impacts, seeking through the staging of cultural programmes to create a carnival atmosphere around the tournament and a sense of genuine inclusion for the local community. For Euro96, programmes of events were planned in each of the eight host cities for both the travelling European fans and the local population. It is to these cultural events that this chapter is addressed, specifically how the programmes were affected by the operation of the sponsorship system within the context of the overall funding regime of the tournament and the interests of global capital.

As suggested above, cities commonly lay on cultural events to create a carnival spirit and draw in the local population, offering those not directly interested in the sport some way to participate. Liverpool City Council for instance suggested that: 'major sporting events can be greatly enhanced by staging a series of cultural events' (Connor, 1996), while the Football Supporters Association (FSA) saw the cultural programme as a way of avoiding potential violence, by creating a good atmosphere and peaceful links between fans (*Guardian*, 1995). With councils in each of the host cities generally short of money, it was clear they would essentially perform a co-ordinating role in regard to the events. Each incurred secondary costs from the tournament (security, transport, cleaning, police), but the burden of staging cultural events was expected to be met by private finance: Nottingham City Council forecast in their strategy that the events programme would be funded very largely by 'sponsorship and monies from activities run jointly with the FA' (Nottingham City Council, 1995), who advised councils and local event organisers to approach the family of sponsors (discussed below) for funding for such programmes. Given current demands on limited local council funds and the spending restrictions put in place by Conservative Governments during the 1980s, it would be strange indeed had councils found considerable funds for these events. Previous instances of councils spending millions of pounds on sports and arts events have caused considerable controversy, as in Sheffield or Glasgow in the early 1990s. The arguments advanced here are not a 'public good, private bad' mantra, but concern the type of private finance, and the impacts of the Euro96 sponsorship system on the scope for expressions of local diversity and distinctiveness, and for community participation. Indeed, two host cities (Newcastle and Manchester) created successful partnerships with local capital and used private promotions companies in their own planning, so this is not a knee-jerk rejection of the private sector.

UEFA, through ISL, created a 'family' of sponsors whose logo would appear on all Euro96 material. Canon, Carlsberg, Mastercard, McDonald's, Philips, Coca-Cola, Snickers, Fujifilm, JVC, Umbro and Vauxhall/Opel each paid £3.5m for exclusive rights of association with Euro96, and any events claiming a connection to it. The deal also included the right of first refusal on sponsoring events connected to Euro96, and the right to prevent the involvement of any non-family sponsor. This is the central context for this analysis, and preliminary research into Liverpool's experience of Euro96 (Nash and Johnstone, 1997) suggests the cultural programmes encountered problems as a result. The aim here is to identify whether host cities experienced these problems more widely as a result of this system, focusing on events in Nottingham, Liverpool and Leeds, and drawing upon interviews with key personnel in each council and event organisers, plus an interview with Glen Kirton, now of ISL but previously FA Euro96 tournament director. The analysis also draws upon council strategy and debriefing documents, and reports produced for the UK Sports Council.

The Nottingham experience

Nottingham clearly did encounter problems with its cultural programme that can be squarely attributed to the sponsorship system: council tourism manager Kevin Liepins concluded that it failed Nottingham, and nearly all the family sponsors either showed no interest in local events, or already had other funding priorities. The council certainly had started with the intention of putting on an extensive programme, which one council official (who preferred to remain anonymous) felt would help local people feel part of the tournament, especially under-privileged and minority groups. The involvement of such groups within the tournament was also a second-level FA objective for Euro96. The council's 'Original Euro96 Strategy' suggested the 'programme of events will … help to create a "feel good" factor with local residents' (Nottingham City Council, 1995), and that Euro96 'can also involve local people by focusing and enhancing the events programme'. This emphasis on the local community (including for instance events like an International Festival for the Disabled) sits uncomfortably with the commodified culture that is the likeliest focus of most family sponsors. Council officials described their original plans as 'quite extravagant', including laser shows, street theatre and music programmes, and the Original Strategy expressed optimism that family sponsors would help fund the programme, noting their 'significant budgets to spend on activities associated with Euro96'. As with other cities, Nottingham City council did not intend to fund events: it put £80,000 into Euro96 overall, but planned to facilitate rather than fund cultural programme. In reality, the anticipated funds from family sponsors failed to materialise, and the programme had to be drastically cut back. Only £30,000 was ultimately drawn down from family sponsors.

Liepins reported that the only sponsor who became involved was Coca-Cola, who sponsored a five-a-side football tournament in the city centre, but Nottingham's decision to respect the rights of family sponsors meant the flow of funds to local organisers was very limited. Generally, there was a simple lack of contact from most global sponsors: apart from Coca-Cola and Snickers, only Mastercard got involved in Nottingham, at the planning stage for a street theatre, dance and music festival, and discussing funding of between £20,000 and £25,000, though this did not ultimately materialise. There was one instance where a breakdown in communications meant Nottingham potentially lost a sponsorship deal from Snickers, but Liepins noted how structural delays in accessing family sponsors caused by the attitude of ISL and the FA generally meant sponsors' promotional budgets had already been allocated before they had even considered the options in

Nottingham. Putting the whole official Euro96 sponsorship onus on a few companies clearly failed to deliver the funds to meet the full potential of the cultural events, and so therefore of the tournament in Nottingham overall.

The other elements of the system clearly restricted other funds that could be raised: predictably, local companies were unable or unwilling to become a City Host (and so sponsor the city, rather than single events) given its high costs and limited benefits, but Liepins reported there were local companies who would have contributed if only 'they didn't feel so tied to the rules and regulations [of] the ISL sponsorship deals'. The council official noted interest from local companies (like Diamond Cable and Boots), but their inability under the sponsorship system to exploit the official Euro96 logo or name, or directly associate themselves with it, made them reluctant to support events. While there were legal loopholes (success-fully exploited by other cities), Nottingham suffered in this regard, as global sponsors were uninterested in local events, and the scale of permissible involvement would have been excessive for local sponsors or the benefits unclear. Liepins suggested becoming a City Host would generally have been cost-prohibitive for most local companies.

The net effect was to scale down the cultural programme Nottingham could stage. The co-ordinator noted how the street festival proposal, costing around £80,000, was cut to £15,000 and just a fraction of its original scale: instead of a major laser lights show, the city could only afford to stage two laser and two firework displays, while the city centre street festival was cut from a daily schedule (to run into each evening), to just four hours per day and two evenings. The optimism of the council was thus misplaced, as global capital took no interest in Nottingham, or wanted too much for their investment: Liepins noted how Master-card wanted to take over the city centre and expected 'excessive' control. Indeed, the expectation that family sponsors would contribute actually cost the city money (in lost rent), after the council had given them prime advertising sites for free. The event organiser also noted one significant occasion when exclusivity clauses worked directly against the city, as Mastercard were prepared to fund events but only to the exclusion of all other sponsors, which the council felt would have netted little revenue and damaged long-term relations with other companies.

Thus, the sponsorship system, which Liepins called 'a real disappointment and a lesson learnt', failed the city in a number of ways. Glen Kirton claimed there were sufficient funds within the system to support the cultural programmes, but this was clearly not the case in Nottingham. He also suggested some councils had been politically motivated (specifically a Labour campaign against the central Conservative government), but there is no evidence of this in Nottingham. The city made significant efforts to attract private funding, and minimise the cost of events (producing what Liepins called 'a very base programme', which could be increased if extra funding was raised), yet still failed to attract any significant backing for its programme. Crucially, the matching of the agenda of global capital and local managers, that the system fundamentally depended upon, failed to materialise. The one global sponsor who did fund events in Nottingham, Coca-Cola, was sufficiently determined to profit from Euro96 that they sponsored all eight host cities, so even their contribution was not due to Nottingham's specific plans for the tournament. None of the other sponsors contributed to Nottingham at all, which itself suggests the system failed.

There was particularly little that highlighted or celebrated Nottingham's history or identity. The limited nature of the funding available in the end meant that Nottingham, like other host cities, could do little more than organise existing annual events around Euro96 (like the Lord Mayor's show, or the BBC Radio One Roadshow), and the fact that many local people were reportedly unable to afford the ticket prices immediately reduced the impact of the tournament anyway, without cuts in the cultural programme adding to that. No doubt overseas visitors (one of the Council's target groups) enjoyed their stay in Nottingham, but whether the local population got as much from Euro96 as was possible is debatable.

The Liverpool experience

Liverpool experienced very similar problems. Once more, the council hoped to put on a programme of events, which they would co-ordinate and facilitate, but not directly fund, that, according to council officer Rob Connor, would seek to involve all elements of the community. Very early in the process, the council suggested that visitors to the city 'would prefer events/activity which emphasise Liverpool's culture' (Liverpool City Council, 1995a), that Liverpool should respond to that, and that the programme would help include sections of the population who had been excluded from the matches, like the young.

But Liverpool ran into the same difficulties with family sponsors as Nottingham. Connor (1996) reported that the contribution of family sponsors 'was very minor, nothing like the amount we had hoped, and for that reason, our programme was scaled down to quite a significant degree'. As early as May 1995, council officials were noting the lack of interest from sponsors, and complaining that the FA were reluctant to invest sufficiently in Euro96 (Liverpool City Council, 1995b). Most global sponsors ultimately did very little in Liverpool: with less than a month to go before the event, the council reported that 'the response [of sponsors] in general has been slow and disappointing' (Liverpool City Council, 1996a), and were forced to try to raise additional funding right up to the last few weeks before the tournament. Liverpool clearly tried to attract sponsorship, employing a consultant and event management company for the purpose, but the council reported in February 1996 that 'sponsors have not come forward to support our planned events' (Liverpool City Council, 1996b), despite being sent promotional material four months previously. This is not to say Liverpool failed to attract any commercial backing, as the FA's City Dressing programme was well supported: however, since this involved minimal expense (and particularly no ongoing costs) and purely consisted of placing 16,000 FA-supplied tournament banners (featuring family sponsor names) in city centres and on major roads in and out of host cities, the programme in no way represents a cultural event. The fact that the cultural programme struggled to secure funding, while the City Dressing programme was popular, perhaps indicates the priorities of the global sponsors. This is also highlighted by the fact that sponsors were happy to pay for maps of Liverpool, took out visibility sites around the city, set up receptions, and in the case of Carlsberg, renovated their pubs and distributed free beer around the city: these are all examples of promotional activity designed to meet sponsor advertising and brand awareness objectives, and not of events that in any way actively involved the community, except as consumers, or expressed Merseyside's rich, diverse and, in many ways, unique history and culture. Even Persil, who agreed to become the City Host for Liverpool (contributing £14,000 to the cultural programme) preferred to focus mainly on increased media advertising.

One or two family sponsors did show some interest in the cultural events in Liverpool, but their suggestions reveal their totally different conceptualisation of Euro96 and their role within it. Snickers planned a one-day Roadshow for the Chevasse Park area of Liverpool, to feature Gladiators-style games and football target shooting (which was ultimately dropped), while Philips created a Roadshow to feature games based on their computer products. Both events could have been held anywhere, as their commodified family entertainment ethos lacked any connection whatsoever to Liverpool, Merseyside or even Euro96. Out of a total of £30,000 drawn down from family sponsors by Liverpool, Carlsberg contributed £20,000 to existing events in return for staging their own promotional events, and Snickers held a 'family' street festival, but otherwise there was very little interest, and those who did get involved, predominately preferred their own promotional events or high visibility advertising.

A case in point was the Stanley Festival. Organised and staged annually by local community volunteer Bob Croxton, the Festival's centre-piece is a football tournament for children in one of Liverpool's most deprived areas: essentially an annual community event organised by the community, it has totally different objectives and ethos from the family sponsors. Croxton was persuaded by the council to move the Festival into the ambit of Euro96 and reshape it, and approached four family sponsors as a consequence. Only Coca-Cola showed any interest, but their involvement would have redesigned the Festival beyond all recognition, turning it into what Croxton called an 'advertising campaign', so the deal was dropped, and Coca-Cola instead created their own roadshow in Wavertree Park. Interest in the Stanley Festival was however shown by Barclays in Liverpool, freezer group Iceland and local 'philanthropists' Littlewoods, and a deal with Barclays worth between £20,000 and £25,000 was drawn up, before the council advised that ISL regulations made it illegal, and it was dropped. Croxton was already aware of ISL's outstanding lawsuits against unofficial USA94 sponsors, and expressed his reluctance to go to jail for the Festival.

Croxton secured £2,000 from the council for the event, and by drawing on existing reserves of £5,000, the event escaped unscathed and was officially the most popular 'Euro96' event in Liverpool. But had Croxton given credence to the predictions of serious sponsor interest and redrawn the Festival with this in mind, in his view, in reality, it would have 'fallen apart'. He found the attitude of family sponsor Umbro particularly galling and indicative of the whole approach of the family sponsors: Umbro declined to become involved with the Festival, and instead staged a promotional football match between the foreign journalists based in Liverpool. While clearly an excellent public relations move for Umbro, this highlights the family sponsors' attitude towards genuine cultural or community events. Global sponsors clearly found little in the Liverpool events programme that suited their ethos or promotional strategy, and with local sponsors systemically prevented from becoming actively involved, event organisers, local distinctiveness and the community were left in the middle. Connor noted how other contributions (from the Department of National Heritage) arrived very late in the planning process, and how funds the host cities had been advised to approach (Sportsmatch, and the Foundation for Sport and the Arts) treated their submissions like any other, such that they did not seek to compensate for the lack of interest from family sponsors, who 'by and large ... did not want to get involved'. Another council official, Colin Moneypenny, noted that 'the whole thing was geared to the needs of huge multi-national sponsors', but the system was unable to compensate for the possibility (or the fact) that they might not actually be interested.

As with Nottingham, Liverpool also had to compress annually-staged events into a short timeframe around Euro96: of the fifteen cultural events the council planned to hold in the summer, nine are staged annually anyway, and of the other six, one was heavily scaled down and two were only designed to last two days. This minimal additional input, compared to the average Liverpool summer, indicates how problems created by the funding system fundamentally affected the ability of organisers to create a genuine cultural programme.

The Leeds experience

Eight months before Euro96, Leeds City Council's Leisure Services Directorate decided to create 'More than a Game ...?', an exhibition charting the social history of English football, with a particular emphasis on supporters, and the nations based in Leeds for Euro96 (Spain, Romania, France and Bulgaria). The contract was awarded to Richard Fowler Associates and a budget of £430,000 agreed. Exhibition material was to be curated by the Museums and Galleries Division of Leeds City Council, directed by senior curator Maggie Pedley.

Initial calculations suggested an extra 30 per cent would be raised from family sponsors in addition to the funds from the council, and the design team created plans on that basis. In reality, however, the expected funding from the sponsors proved as elusive for 'More than a Game' as it had in Liverpool and Nottingham. Family sponsors would require some exposure through the exhibition but they would not fund it, and the expected 30 per cent extra was spent on the banner outside the site, leading to a serious shortfall in the finances for the exhibition. Other sponsors outside the family circle were however interested: Portakabin, who were providing premises for the event, were willing to meet some costs, but were once more put off by ISL's regulations, which the event organisers felt was an unfair obstacle. The company felt they would not benefit from sponsoring a non-'Euro96' event. Fowler noted 'other sponsors, for instance Portakabin, didn't want to put money in ... partly because they were mean, and partly because they didn't want to be dominated by these major sponsors who they thought should be putting in money for the exhibition.' He also noted the general lack of help from the FA's Euro96 committee and ISL:

> The impression I got from the Euro96 people I met was 'thanks a lot for putting the exhibition on for our tournament, it's very kind of you, but don't expect any money for it', and that was actually said at a meeting I had with Euro96.

The local authority also complicated the issue, by refusing to name a site for the exhibition during the tendering process: an obvious site was council-owned Elland Road, home of Leeds United and host to three Euro96 matches.

The emphasis on family sponsors in the planning of events and their subsequent reluctance to become involved thus caused a financial crisis for the exhibition just months before opening. With local companies clearly loathe to involve themselves in a tournament dominated by family sponsors, the expected local sponsor windfall did not materialise: other events in Leeds were also affected, but with the largest budget, the exhibition was the hardest hit as £150,000 worth of cuts were made, leaving the whole event in jeopardy. Leeds City Council's refusal to use Elland Road as a venue for the event meant alternative accommodation had to be found quickly: three months before opening, it was decided to build a permanent structure in the stadium grounds (representing therefore a long-term legacy from the tournament for the future), but as the finances disappeared, so did that plan. Instead a labyrinthine configuration of ten inter-linked mobile units was constructed (which created new problems and costs for the exhibition like insurance for theft, fire and vandalism), to be dismantled after the event, reducing further the long-term community benefit arising from Euro96.

Both Fowler and Pedley criticised the lack of positive involvement from ISL, who they had been led to believe would supply contacts and expertise that the council and the exhibition specifically could draw upon. Fowler said that he:

> felt sorry for Leeds council, there were problems everywhere, and the backing from the organisers was pathetic; the advice was terribly misguided, and if Leeds had any inkling of the lack of sponsors, and of the fact that nobody would hang around after a game [at Elland Road], then they would not have gone ahead with the exhibition.

Other event organisers noted the 'bad advice' passed on by the Euro96 committee and ISL: more than one city reported that official intelligence suggested that large numbers of overseas fans would stay at stadia for significant periods of time before and after matches, and made specific arrangements on that basis (such as organising on-site cultural events, catering, campsites and security), and were then dismayed to find that the actual numbers of fans fell so far short of official estimates as to make the contingency plans a total waste of resources. Kirton's suggestion that problems were caused by the political affiliations of the council was again dismissed as not relevant to Leeds. Pedley suggested instead:

Leeds is quite an enlightened authority, and has a very good set of relationships with local businesses etc, [but] the whole feasibility of it, from a marketing point of view, was poor. They had said yes to the exhibition without consulting anyone from Museums and Galleries, which is crazy. There was a huge amount of enthusiasm ... but it needed channelling through the right people and departments.

Fowler equally noted problems with the council:

The planning wasn't great. We initially pitched for the work eight months before we were appointed, which is eight months lost. It all became very tight at the end. We had no location ... four separate sites were mooted, none of which were ideal. When I suggested that it should be within the stadium ... as a permanent museum, and the stadium was owned by Leeds City Council ... it didn't happen, as the relationship between Leeds United and Leeds City Council wasn't terrific ... all of this was in the hands of the council, and it highlighted the dreadful planning.

The exhibition ultimately ran for four months (attracting good visitor numbers compared to many Euro96 events), and Fowler and Pedley would still contemplate staging such events during future tournaments, but only within a different sponsorship system. Fowler argued that it:

would have to change, less naiveté ... the organisation behind location, funding, longer lead time into curation etc. It would have been nice if the exhibition had been able to have a second life, for schools ... the exhibition was worthy, but it was just the wrong stage in terms of finance, location, organisation ... it was a miracle that we pulled it off.

More generally, the familiar problems of unclear relationships with sponsors, the FA's limited and unhelpful role, and low levels of funding from family sponsors affected the programme in Leeds. ISL were reported to have generally caused problems, in that they appeared to have given family sponsors the impression that they were buying control of all arrangements in Leeds, while flawed FA intelligence on fan numbers led to the creation of a campsite at Temple Newsam, that was completely under-utilised in the event and a waste of time and resources. A senior council official concluded that 'endless meetings [with the FA and sponsors] resulted in very little in the way of support or funds due largely ... to the total lack of understanding on their part of the Council's role' (Tourism Research and Marketing, 1996).

Summing up Euro96

It can be plausibly argued that the sponsorship system was most effective in circumstances where it contributed to expressions of homogenised global capitalism, the foregrounding of images of commodified capitalism, and not local cultures, identities, or indeed genuine participation. Glen Kirton thought the system suitable for future tournaments, and felt that the emphasis on global sponsors served the host cities well; the only change he suggested was a greater partnership to ensure that the cities did not indulge in 'a lot of activity that is out of control'. But clearly there were problems: by the end of Euro96, only 0.2 per cent of the estimated £100m promotional budget spent by the family sponsors had reached the cultural programme (Tourism Research and Marketing, 1996).

Many of the cities' experiences of Euro96, and their complaints, were very similar, with their programmes involving similar events, and regional and local diversity visibly lacking. There was very little in Liverpool, Nottingham or Leeds that expressed or represented the culture of the city or region, despite their respective uniqueness, and very little that distinguished events in one city from another. Despite their best efforts, the planning that each city could engage in proved problematic, and too liable to being damaged by decisions of family sponsors. The FSA concluded that 'many events happening under the umbrella of Euro96 were happening anyway and merely padded out what, in some places, seemed fairly threadbare programmes (FSA, 1997).

All the host cities were able to 'attract' the global sponsors' promotional road-shows, but as general Euro96 debriefing reports suggested, those cities who stayed strictly within the letter of the law as laid down by ISL found great difficulties obtaining funding for grass-roots or community driven events that did not fore-ground the promotional interests of global capital or allow them to dictate the nature of the event (Tourism Research and Marketing, 1996). In this sense, the sponsorship system primarily served the interests of international capital, and contributed to expressions of their homogenised commercial culture. This seems an instance of globalising forces creating cultural homogeneity not so much by destroying or replacing local culture, but simply by preventing its expression. Events like Euro96 represent a substantial opportunity for cities to mark out the distinct images and identities needed to compete in the global economy, yet with the current system, they are unable to fully take it.

The three successful Euro96 cities, Newcastle, Manchester and Sheffield, require further analysis before the sponsorship system can be completely written off as a failure. Their strategies, though successful and admired by other cities, came close to breaking ISL rules, and so maybe are not plausible long-term options. Newcastle and Manchester re-branded all their events, Newcastle as 'Eurofest' and Manchester as 'SoccerCity', a calculated risk since, while neither city used the Euro96 logo and so could claim they were respecting family sponsors' rights, each was clearly promoting its events around Euro96, and so did run the risk of legal action. ISL did not take action against either city, nor against an apparently more blatant breach, Sheffield's sponsorship by local firm Morrison's. But this is not always the case, and it has been suggested that an action against Sheffield would have succeeded, and that the numerous USA94 sponsorship infringement actions brought by ISL instilled caution into cities and local companies. Even if the models used by Manchester, Newcastle and Sheffield were actually within the rules, uncertainty about their status made both local sponsors and event organisers wary of creating arrangements that could be seen as infringing ISL's jealously protected rights. Even though three cities secured funding, the fact that they were operating outside, or close to outside, the rules does not alter. Liepins suggested that Morrison's involvement was central to Sheffield's ability to produce a successful programme, highlighting how bending the rules (however justifiably) was central to the city's experience of Euro96.

The significance of the cultural programme may not be obvious, yet all the cities recognised how these events can contribute to the overall, long-term success of an event. Swiss and Dutch supporters were impressed by the atmosphere in Birmingham (Birmingham City Council, 1996), and research into images of Birmingham found that the city centre established itself as a place to visit: 74 per cent of respondents found it a 'very good' or 'fairly good' attraction. 60 per cent of those foreign visitors who had negative views of Liverpool on arrival changed that to a positive view afterwards, and 40 per cent of all visitors indicated they were 'definite' or 'likely' to return (Cunnigham and Taylor, 1996). While the approval rate for the cultural events programme in Liverpool was relatively low compared to approval for the provision of information for fans, for instance, nonetheless 53 per cent of visiting fans were impressed by the events (Cunningham and Taylor, 1996). The potential role of cultural and social events in creating positive long-term images is clear. Brunet argues that the atmosphere in Barcelona around the 1992 Olympics helped create a lively, dynamic image attractive to global capital and tourists alike (Brunet, 1996). The question of creating and funding a well-organised events programme is thus significant, even without considering the local inclusiveness it can generate, the impact on civic pride and the sense of community participation. Crichter (1992) notes for instance the genuine sense of energy felt throughout Sheffield during 1991

All this may seem little more than a debate about marketing at major sports events, but in fact it highlights much more significant issues, notably who such tournaments are designed for? This question is at the centre of the sponsorship system, since it directs the tournament in certain directions and away from others: the current sponsorship arrangements exemplify a tournament structured for global sponsors and the needs of international capital (including of course UEFA), and as a result, host cities and their communities usually operated as little more than Euro96 staging posts. Local populations had little role to play within the official discourses of Euro96, except to consume and attend matches. Homogenisation of the tournament away from the football was the result in those cities that operated within the sponsorship system, a system that actively suppressed local cultures or distinctions by denying them a public space for expression, submerged beneath a commodified homogenous capitalism. Yet, lest this be seen as somehow inevitable, there are examples of tournaments where host cities have successfully combined commercial considerations with a community focus and expressions of a regional culture, without harming either. Crucially however this depends on an altogether different conceptualisation of the tournament. There is also some (limited) evidence to suggest that community-rooted events can be more popular than the socially disconnected commercial events created for and by sponsors: Bob Croxton noted how Coca-Cola's roadshow in Liverpool (set up in direct competition with the Stanley Festival) was a complete failure by comparison. This example clearly requires further investigation, but it is maybe evidence of the diverse aspirations of the populations of host cities, and hence the need for the sponsorship system to pay far more attention to the specific features of individual cities.

Alternative sponsorship systems

It is of course easy to assert the need for change, to allow local interests and regional distinctiveness some space for expression round major sporting tournaments, and allow at the least the opportunity for genuine local participation (aside from consumption), but obviously some concrete measures for achieving this need to be identified. The first change is in the logic underpinning the sponsorship system. As operated at Euro96, the system clearly relied on global capital having an understanding of, and interest in, local conditions and needs, which seems rather unlikely given their multi-national nature, and the significance they attach to TV promotions around the fixtures. Cities whose economies depend on attracting international capital often struggle to impart to it a genuine sense of local needs, as the city becomes simply one more remote cog in the multi-national wheel: Parkinson and Bianchini (1993) contend for instance that Liverpool has suffered in the last two decades because of its dependence on 'absentee' international capital, so it is maybe inevitable that the global family sponsors lack the perspective to recognise the local context and community when taking funding decisions. Local companies are much more likely (as genuine community stakeholders) to have at least a direct commercial imperative to become involved and a greater awareness of local conditions, distinctions and needs. As Liepins suggested, 'you have all these people [as major sponsors] sitting in London or America, and they don't really know what is happening in Liverpool or Manchester'.

The sponsors' conceptualisation of the tournament and their role within it has direct consequences for the programmes of events that create the festival atmosphere away from the actual sport. Equally important in creating potential tensions between sponsors' objectives and local interests is a sense of the target audience for the cultural events. The councils considered here all explicitly had a two-strand agenda for the events, to project the locality and its distinctiveness in a global economy, and to create a spirit of social inclusion. This latter objective has clear implications for the target audience, focusing attention on a variety of disadvantaged groups and maybe particular geographic areas within each city. It is more than likely that the community-based ethos of Nottingham's Euro96 programme (designed to reach the unemployed, disabled, women etc) and the community-centred agenda behind the Stanley Festival in Liverpool sat very uncomfortably with the commodified discourses of the family sponsors, which therefore explains their reluctance to fund such events. There is a serious and potentially irreconcilable clash of agenda and objectives that, if left unaddressed, can only result in a decline in the distinctiveness of events, a reduction of the genuine participation and involvement of the locality, and the predominance of the promotional needs of global capital. If the aim of the cultural events is to include all sections of the community in the tournament, then the systemic restrictions on these cities' ability to attract funding for such events does not bode well for future tournaments

It must, of course, be asked, why *should* global sponsors (or UEFA) be expected to take an interest in parochial, localised cultures of English regions? Obviously they are detached from them, benefit little from their events, and so should not be expected to ensure the expression of localisms, or provide cultural diversity. Such global interests have their own objectives, and there can be no obligation on them to focus on local events. It is thus not solely their attitude, but the system around them that needs to change, to offer local interests a full opportunity to become involved.

This suggests that the solution offered by officials in Nottingham and Liverpool could potentially create a new context in which sponsors' interests (profit), and council and community objectives (participation, projection of distinctiveness and community involvement and pride) can be reconciled to mutual satisfaction. The Nottingham event organiser suggested that 'the FA should look at separate sponsorship for local events', as 'many, if not all, of the local sponsors are in totally different businesses' from the global concerns. Such a tiered system would avoid the delays and competing demands on the global sponsors' limited funds (particularly once ISL's large fee was paid), and eliminate the difficulties in matching the global perspectives of family sponsors with local needs.

Larger tournaments than Euro96 have successfully used such systems and remained profitable: Schlossberg (1996) notes how the USA94 sponsorship system featured national and regional levels, each with a separate fee (from $20m downwards) and separate levels of sponsorship rights. There is no reason to believe that such a system would reduce the revenue that could be raised from the sponsorship programme for events like Euro96, since the exposure that global capital gets from local events does not compare with the enormous television audiences they can expect for fixtures and media campaigns. To this extent, ISL's scope to charge multi-million pound fees for sponsorship rights would not be damaged.

In any event, the family sponsors need not withdraw from local promotions:.Allowing diversity of funding is the key, and while there is no guarantee local capital will ensure the expression of local cultures, at least local organisers will have greater scope to raise funds and hence the possibility of creating a greater diversity of event, that genuinely involves the community, and expresses and celebrates diverse local histories and cultures.

Given the money made available to fund the Millennium celebrations, it can be argued that the Government should provide more funds (as Glen Kirton believed would have happened for the 2006 World Cup had England been awarded it), as could the FA. Their role was a problem throughout: apart from the fact that they refused to arrange meetings between the Association of Metropolitan Authorities (representing the host cities) and ISL sponsors, the Sports Council accused the FA of failing to help sponsors appreciate local opportunities, and of obstructing direct liaison between sponsor and city (a charge also made by some cities). They also concluded that 'the cultural programme ... was conceived too late and not adequately supported by either the FA or the Department of National Heritage in terms of funding and co-ordination' (Tourism Research and Marketing, 1996).

It was also suggested that 'in effect the cities were asked [by the FA] to produce cultural programmes but were not treated as partners'. While some cities (such as Liverpool) noted the contributions of individuals at the FA (Connor, 1996), their reluctance to act as genuine co-ordinators was cited by the Nottingham events organiser as an immediate problem. The FA could clearly take a more proactive role, liaising directly between cities and family sponsors, improving the flow of accurate information, or as Liepins and Connor suggest, guaranteeing each city a certain base sponsorship at an early stage. This would however require a sea-change in the FA's approach: instead of restricting themselves to an abstract, remote co-ordinating role, they would have to become directly involved and reassess their view of the tournament (which appeared very narrowly political, and financial, visible for instance from their total lack of concern at many low attendances and the high ticket prices). A much greater understanding of the social and cultural significance of sports tournaments would have to be injected into the FA's current conceptions of their role.

Conclusions

It would be wrong to suggest that all these problems were caused purely by the sponsorship system: obviously, councils have to provide the right framework for cultural programmes to proceed smoothly and so make the right impression on incoming trade delegations and sports tourists alike. But even those cities, such as Liverpool and Nottingham, that did plan strategically, created the necessary context, sought private sector involvement and put scarce resources into the cultural programme, could still not solve the problems created by a sponsorship system geared first and last to the needs of global capital, and not to local interests or organisers. While this analysis does not address in full the strategies of 'successful' cities like Sheffield and Newcastle, there is enough evidence from the cities analysed here, and from general debriefing reports about this aspect of Euro96, to suggest that the sponsorship system is fundamentally not attuned to the needs of host cities or local organisers, that it requires reform in order to meet those needs, and that the events that family sponsors are prepared to fund do not reflect local identities or genuinely involve local communities, and instead contribute to a predominance of global capitalism and commodified commercialism. This question comes down to our understanding of what sports events are essentially for, and what a tournament (in all its elements) should offer cities. It is the answers to such ultimately political debates that should inform the development of sponsorship and funding systems. Until central bodies like the FA and Government depart-ments move beyond current ideological constructs and private finance models to more pluralist, inclusive and pro-active agenda, cities and regions will be unable to benefit from sports tournaments as they could, particularly to use them to project their individual identity, history and culture, or indeed any sort of cultural diversity in the face of globalised sports consumer culture.

References

Birmingham City Council (1996), Euro96 Summary Report, Birmingham Marketing Partnership, July.

Brunet, F. (1996) 'An Economic Analysis of the Barcelona '92 Olympic Games: Resources, Financing and Impact' in Moragas and Botella (eds), *The Keys to Success*, Universitat Autonoma de Barcelona.

Connor, R. (1996) 'Staging the European Football Championships in Liverpool', Liverpool City Council.

Critcher, C. (1992) 'Sporting Civic Pride: Sheffield and the World Student Games of 1991' in Sugden and Knox (eds), *Leisure in the 1990s*, LEisure Studies Association publication No. 46, Eastbourne.

Cunningham, D. and Taylor, R. (1996) Euro96 Liverpool Visitor Survey, Liverpool City Council.

Dobson, N., Holliday, S. and Gratton, C. (1997) 'Football Came Home', Leisure Industries Research Centre, Sheffield Hallam University.

Football Supporters Association (1997) 'From Euro96 to World Cup 2006', Liverpool, May

Guardian (1995) 'Britain warned of invasion by soccer thugs', September 7th.

Liverpool City Council (1995a) Euro96 Working Party, minutes of the meeting held on January 17th.

Liverpool City Council (1995b) Euro96 Working Party, minutes of the meeting held on May 15th.

Liverpool City Council (1996a) Management Team Report on Euro96 Arrangements, Report no DLS/5/96, May.

Liverpool City Council (1996b) Euro96 Representatives Forum, minutes of the meeting held on February 16th.

Moragas Spa, M. and Botella, M. (1996) (eds), *The Keys to Success*, Universitat Autonoma de Barcelona.

Moragas Spa, M., Rivenburgh, N. and Garcia, N. (1996) 'Television and the Construction of Identity: Barcelona, Olympic Host' in Moragas and Botella (eds), *The Keys to Success*, Universitat Autonoma de Barcelona.

Nash, R. and Johnstone, S. (1997) 'Euro96: the Liverpool Experience', paper given to the British Sociological Association annual conference, York.

Nottingham City Council (1996) Original Euro96 Strategy.

Parkinson, M. and Bianchini, F. (1993) 'Liverpool: a Tale of Missed Opportunities?' in Bianchini and Parkinson (eds), *Cultural Policy and Urban Regeneration*, Manchester UP.

Schlossberg, H. (1996) *Sports Marketing*, Blackwell, Oxford.

Sugden, J. and Knox, C. (1992) (eds), *Leisure in the 1990s*, proceedings of the Leisure Studies Association conference, LSA publication No. 46, Eastbourne.

Sugden, J. and Tomlinson, A. (1996) 'What's Left When the Circus Leaves Town: an Evaluation of World Cup USA94' in *Sociology of Sport*, Vol. 13(3), pp 238–259.

Tourism Research and Marketing (1996) European Championships 1996: Review of Arrangements, Vols 1–3, produced for UK Sports Council.

Whitson, D. and Macintosh, D. (1993) 'Becoming a World-Class City: Hallmark Events and Sports Franchises in the Growth Strategies of Western Canadian Cities', *Sociology of Sport*, Vol. 10(3), pp 221–240.

Part IV

Urban sports tourism

9   Sporting a new image?

Sport-based regeneration strategies as a means of enhancing the image of the city tourist destination

Andrew Smith

Introduction

Over the past decade, several cities in the UK, including Birmingham, Manchester and Sheffield, have made determined efforts and devoted considerable resources to bidding for, and staging major sporting events and constructing prestige sport facilities. Despite other proposed benefits, including urban regeneration and local economic development, an important justification for the implementation of these schemes is the supposed resultant enhancement of the city's image. Indeed, the use of sporting initiatives as a means of city image enhancement is explicitly recognised by the authorities involved, as well as by several academic commentators. As Loftman and Spirou (1996: 28) state, rather than concentrating on the detailed financial implications of sport stadia, civic leaders tend to focus on the city's image and the future direction of the city. Therefore, recent sporting developments in cities are often motivated by, and justified by, the desire to forge a new image for a city.

The use of sport as a means of enhancing place-image is, however, by no means an exclusively contemporary phenomenon. Reiss (1981) identifies Los Angeles as a city that implemented a sport-based image enhancement strategy in the early part of the twentieth century.

> After World War I a handful of visionary movers and shakers decided to advance their city's reputation for the purpose of encouraging the expression of tourism, commerce and migration. The key to their plan was the construction of a huge outdoor sports facility where great sport spectacles and festivals would be staged.
>
> (Reiss 1981:50)

Despite such historical precedents, it could be argued that since the mid-1980s, the concept of sport reimaging has been embraced by a large number of developed cities with a new intensity and purpose. These cities, many of which have been severely affected by the restructuring of the international division of labour and the resultant collapse of their manufacturing sectors, have been forced into competition with one another as centres of consumption (Harvey 1989). This has significantly intensified the need to project a positive image of the city to an external audience of potential visitors and consumers. As a result, many cities have indulged in what has become known as place marketing (Madsen 1992), which involves striving to sell the image of a place so as to make it more attractive to economic enterprises, tourists and inhabitants (Philo and Kearns 1993: 3). Due to the contemporary dominance of the media and the popularity and exposure devoted to sport, it has become common for cities in the US, and increasingly in the UK, to use sport as a vehicle for city image enhancement.

Although there are notable exceptions (e.g. Edinburgh's staging of the 1986 Commonwealth Games) it would appear that the strategy of using sport events and prestige sport facilities as a means of image reorientation has primarily been implemented by 'industrial' cities. These cities are the product of industrial development and as Law (1996) affirms, their industrial character and image is a barrier for the evolution of their tourist industry (Law 1996: 2). The problem as Tim Hall notes, is that the word 'industry' and the identities and images that it evokes are highly problematic for the promotion of cities within the context of the post-industrial urban economy (Hall 1997: 216). According to Hall it evokes 'a whole series of negative, unfashionable images' (Hall 1997: 216). These 'industrial' cities have therefore attempted to develop associations with more positive concepts, in order to attract capital and people in the present period of intensified urban competition (Harvey 1989: 92). The media coverage devoted to sport, its intrinsic popularity in contemporary culture and its supposed positive connotations have therefore resulted in the adoption of sporting initiatives by industrial cities as a means of image enhancement.

As many commentators have recognised (Thorns 1997, Harvey 1989, C.M. Hall 1997), the explicit aim of a large proportion of city-imaging work is to enhance the way in which the city is perceived by prospective urban tourists. The focus in this chapter is on this tourism element of reimaging, and it is the intention to analyse exactly how the formation and structure of cities' images as urban tourist destinations may be affected by the adoption of sport reimaging strategies. After relating strategy of 'sport reimaging' to the contemporary cultural context, we will go on to examine the qualities of these initiatives which may enable them to influence city images. An attempt to conceptualise city images will then be made, which will seek to illustrate the way in which sport may be able to enhance the image of the city as a tourist destination. Finally, the implications of this conceptualisation will be discussed.

Sport, tourism and image enhancement

To compensate for the decline in manufacturing employment experienced by many cities, municipal authorities have begun to compete with one another for a share of urban tourism. In this new urban economic climate, where the attraction of large numbers of consumers into a city becomes imperative, it is unsurprising that cities have attempted to develop an impressive sporting infrastructure and event schedules in order to capitalise on the growing sport tourism market. As well as attracting people into a city to watch specific events, the potential for sport stadia to be developed as all year round visitor attractions has also been increasingly acknowledged. This is mainly a US phenomenon with regard to the development of 'Halls of Fame', but there are examples of successful European models, including tours and museums at prominent football stadia, most notably the case of the Nou Camp stadium in Barcelona, which attracts 500,000 visitors per year (Stevens and Wootton 1997). However, there is evidence to suggest that the development of sporting products within the city has taken on a much wider significance than simply attracting more sport spectators and sport tourists into urban areas. As Law (1993: 94) states, there is a tendency to see sport as more than simply a local amenity or visitor attraction. For many municipal authorities, sport epitomises a new era and a new direction for cities suffering a post-industrial identity crisis. Therefore, in the UK, cities such as Birmingham, Manchester and Sheffield have implemented sport initiatives to present a more attractive image to potential urban tourists. These sporting initiatives have typically involved bidding for and staging major sporting events and constructing major sporting arenas within which to stage them (Loftman and Spirou 1996). These two main facets of urban sport reimaging are examined in more detail below, starting with the use of sport events as a means of image enhancement.

Sport events

Sport events are typical of what have been termed special or hallmark events by tourism researchers. These events are defined by Ritchie as major one-time or recurring events of limited duration, developed primarily to enhance the awareness, appeal and profitability of the host location (Ritchie 1984: 2). As this definition implies, special events are deemed important promotional tools which can be used to boost the image of a city as tourism destination. Indeed C.M. Hall (1992), describes events as the image builders of modern tourism. Sport events are viewed by many cities as particularly effective for this purpose, as they generate substantial media exposure. The ultimate example is the Olympic Games, an event so intrinsic-ally associated with place promotion that Philo and Kearns (1993) have described it as the ultimate expression of place marketing. Cities have therefore attempted to stage major one-off and/or regular programmes of sport events as a means of presenting an attractive image to an exterior audience. Examples include Sheffield, which hosted the 1991 World Student Games and has since hosted over 300 national and international sport events (Kronos 1997).

The importance of sport events in the contemporary city may be placed in a wider urban context where it has been observed that cities have sought to become centres of consumption through the 'organisation of spectacle and theatricality' (Harvey 1989: 92). The importance of sport to this emerging 'spectacular city' is outlined by Bourdieu (1978) who states that 'it cannot be ignored that the so called popular sports also function as spectacles' (Bourdieu 1978: 340). It has been recognised that cities, rather than relying on the consumption of goods, have emphasised the consumption of experiences and pleasure, or what Harvey terms 'very ephemeral services in consumption' (Harvey 1989: 285). Staging major sport events is seen not only as a means of generating such consumption, but as an important way of symbolising the transition of the industrial city towards this envisaged role. In this contemporary urban context, popular and mass culture are regarded as more legitimate sources of prestige and cultural and symbolic capital. Accordingly, popular forms of culture such as sport are also being viewed as a more legitimate means of representing the city to an external audience. Therefore, the use of sport events may be a perfect example of the way in which traditional forms of cultural consumption are being revamped to cater for wider audiences, 'with the emphasis upon the spectacular, the popular, the pleasurable and the immediately accessible' (Featherstone 1991: 96).

Sport facilities

It is important to recognise that alongside promotional campaigns and the staging of special events, the process of reimaging frequently involves the construction of new spaces of consumption, often centred on spectacular 'flagship' or 'prestige' projects (Smyth 1994, Loftman and Nevin 1996). These flagship developments are innovative, large-scale projects which provide a focal point and catalyst for tourists and media coverage (Barke and Harrop 1994). According to Harvey (1989) the production of these spectacular urban spaces provides cities with symbols of urban dynamism, enabling the city to exploit conspicuous consumption in a sea of spreading recession. Sharon Zukin concurs and views this process as a means of producing a vibrant symbolic economy from which a legible image can be abstracted, connecting the city to consumption rather than production (Zukin 1993: 45). Several cities in the UK have developed sporting arenas as flagship or prestige projects. Examples include the National Indoor Arena constructed in Birmingham, Manchester's Nynex (now M.E.N) Arena and Velodrome and Sheffield's Don Valley Stadium, Arena and Pond's Forge swimming complex. Like the staging of special events, these developments attract sport tourists into the city, but are ultimately seen to have a more fundamental impact in terms of projecting an image of transformation, enabling cities traditionally associated with industrial production to shake off 'the last traces of its 19th century self' (Westwood and Williams 1997). Indeed, as Schimmel (1995) states, sporting arenas are perceived to be symbols of success, of urban machismo and vibrancy as well as providing multi-functional leisure facilities. This distinction between the functional use and perception of sport tourist products and their role as symbols is very important in terms of image impact and will be expanded upon later in this chapter.

The cultural context

In analysing the specific nature of sporting initiatives and their proposed impact upon city images above, it becomes apparent that the use of such strategies can be seen to be both an example of, and a vehicle for, certain cultural shifts which commentators have observed in the post-industrial urban arena. In terms of examining the concept of consumer images of the city, it is particularly useful to link urban sport reimaging to literature and debates concerning shifts in consumption patterns in contemporary society. David Harvey notes two major shifts in the arena of consumption. The first of these involves the mobilisation of fashion in mass markets as a means of accelerating the pace of consumption across a wide swathe of lifestyle and recreational activities, including new leisure and sporting habits (Harvey 1989: 285). A second trend is the shift away from the consumption of goods and towards the consumption of services. In effect this means the consumption of entertainment, events, happenings and distractions. As Harvey (1989) argues, if there is a limit to the accumulation and turnover of physical goods then it makes sense for cities to turn to the provision of ephemeral services in consumption. This is the process by which the city becomes a 'spectacle'. The role of sport in this process should not be underestimated, since sport events form a crucial part of the spectacular city and because of their popularity and exposure, can transmit a positive image of the city to wide and receptive audience of consumers.

The contention is that post-industrial cities have moved towards becoming centres of consumption, play and entertainment which are 'saturated with signs and images to the extent that anything can become represented, thematised and made an object of interest' (Featherstone 1991: 101). As Featherstone implies in his use of the term 'anything', the means by which spectacular cities have utilised imagery to generate symbolic or cultural capital has become increasingly diversified. Post-industrial cities have become regarded as centres of cultural production, not simply because of their association with the high arts, but also associations with the mass cultures. Therefore popular cultures, of which sport is an important part, have become regarded as 'more legitimate and the source of prestige and further up the symbolic hierarchy' (Featherstone 1991: 106). Cities, traditionally associated with industrial production are therefore able to transcend perceptions of low cultural capital by utilising sport and other more popular cultural forms as a means of transmitting positive imagery to potential tourists.

An important point to recognise when considering city marketing strategies or the deliberate manipulation of a city's image is that much of the imaging is aimed at the 'better off' (Bramwell and Rawding 1996) or 'the right sort of people' (Harvey 1989). Without a full appreciation of contemporary shifts in consumption trends and in the increasingly commodified sport 'industry', this would appear to lessen the appropriateness of sport as an urban reimaging tool. Traditionally, sport in cities has been associated with the urban working classes, hardly the image that would be deemed to attract 'right sort of people' to cities which already possess enduringly strong working-class reputations. However, the increasing gentrification of sport and the corresponding confusion of hierarchical consumer tastes and interests may mean that in the contemporary era, sport may be regarded as a more effective means of attracting the affluent sectors of the tourist market. Whereas it would be inherently contradictory in previous cultural eras to promote a city's sporting pedigree alongside more traditional forms of cultural capital, the contention here is that not only is this now an appropriate partnership, but one that can be effectively sold to a new market of more eclectic, rounded tourists whose tastes aren't necessarily confined to the different ends of an orthodox cultural spectrum.

Alongside the enhanced legitimacy of sport as a means of representation in an era in which the distinction between high and mass culture has become increasingly confused, there are other related indications which may point to the suitability of sport as an imaging 'tool'. Sport reimaging is an attractive compromise for cities which are seeking to attract the affluent consumer, but which are also attempting to avoid the comprehensive desertion and suppression of local tradition and history. Sport has long been an important part of the British city. This means that an emphasis on this urban feature as a vehicle for image enhancement may be a less controversial means of representation than other initiatives, which similarly attempt to reorientate the city towards being a site of pleasure and play. For instance, it may avoid the sort of controversy highlighted by Glasgow's imaging scheme earlier this decade, which revolved around the city's designation as the European City of Culture 1990. This imaging campaign was criticised by some people who clearly felt that the image presented was 'not one sedimented down the years in Glaswegian consciousness, but one which encourages thinking about Glasgow in new terms, i.e. without having reference back to external reality' (Boyle and Hughes 1991: 221). Although sport reimaging can also be accused of being selective in terms of its representation of a city, 'sanitising the real working class culture and cultural history' of cities such as Manchester and Sheffield (Boyle and Hughes 1991: 225), there is little doubt that sport has played a fundamental role in the development and daily life of these cities throughout the twentieth century. This may mean that sport is accepted as a more 'realistic' representation of these cities, not only placating sensitive residents, but as will be discussed later, presenting a more 'realistic' and therefore believable image to a critical external audience.

Whatever the status of sport in relation to culture and cultural capital, sport has clearly flourished in the post-industrial economy (Rowe 1995). Within this arena, sport has become an important part of the way in which cities have attempted to create, espouse and transmit images of the city as a reinvigorated centre of spectacle, pleasure and play. As has been touched upon, the proliferation and circulation of images is now an integral part of the way in which contemporary city can be understood. The city is at the very centre of this phenomenon. Cities are where social images are most prominently on display, where advertising and promotion are most intense and where the conspicuous act of consumption is most significant (Lyon 1994). However, cities have also invested in images themselves in an attempt to turn themselves into centres of consumption. The links between image and cities are therefore inextricable. In fact some would argue that there is no such thing as the city, only an imagined environment, an image which represents a series of practices, relationships and institutions. This is the city that concerns us here. The city of the mind. However, despite the influence and appropriateness of sport as a means of capitalising on the contemporary importance of urban imagery noted above, it still remains unclear as to what this concept of city image is, and more specifically how sporting initiatives may be able to influence the way in which potential consumers (i.e. prospective tourists) construct an image of the city in their minds. These concerns are addressed below.

Deconstructing the tourist image

In the development of tourism within a city, image is perceived as crucial. As Fakeye and Crompton state, tourist images are particularly important because they transpose a representation of an area into the potential tourist's mind and give him/her a pre-taste of the destination (Fakeye and Crompton 1991: 10). Within tourism research it has been recognised that the images which exist in individuals' minds may have as much to do with an area's tourist development success as material and more tangible tourist products and resources (Hunt 1975). Therefore, in emerging urban destinations such as Birmingham, Manchester and Sheffield, alongside developing attractive tourist products and infrastructure, a primary consideration must be to project a positive destination image. The value of sporting initiatives may be that they have the potential to fulfil both of these objectives.

Despite the protestations of academic commentators and municipal authorities concerning the fundamental role of sporting strategies in enabling city image enhancement, it remains unclear whether and how sport reimaging may be able to achieve this objective. Despite research relating to the impact of sporting initiatives on the external awareness of cities as visitor destinations (Ritchie and Smith 1991), there exists little or no research concerning the exact impact of those initiatives on tourist images. More specifically, the author is unaware of any investigations which attempt to explain these impacts. The purpose of the rest of this chapter is therefore to outline how sport reimaging may be able to influence city image enhancement and to make suggestions for the effective measurement of these proposed impacts.

The concept of destination image

To enable the evaluation of the influence of sport-led strategies on city image, it is first necessary to discuss what is meant by the term 'image' and exactly how and why sport may be influencing this vague concept. Traditionally, image relates to the reconstruction of a scene or object in literature, art or film. This application of the term is utilised in some academic fields (for instance the sub-disciplines of behavioural geography and environmental psychology), where it is conventional to refer to image as consisting of a mental reconstruction of a place, in this context the city, in a person's mind. However, as Raymond Williams (1976) points out, this traditional use of the term has been overtaken by the conception of image as perceived reputation or character. In effect image has become a jargon term of commercial advertising and public relations. It is argued here that it is perhaps most valuable and prevalent to use an amalgam of the different usages, in order to investigate comprehensively the concept of place image, as the two definitions are by no means mutually exclusive. As Echtner and Ritchie state, image should be regarded as the perceptions of individual attributes as well as more holistic impressions or mental pictures of a place (Echtner and Ritchie 1993: 3).

Sport and the formation of destination images

As has already been outlined, sport allegedly envelops a symbolic function in supposedly promoting an impression of transition and prestige. This theme is developed below, where it is proposed that sport reimaging strategies involve symbolic and other specific qualities that may enable them to successfully influence the way in which destination images are formed.

Place images are formed from a variety of sources, most notably direct experience of the destination and important secondary sources such as the press, promotional material, television, radio, film and literature (Gunn 1998, Gartner 1993). One of the most important categories of secondary agents noted by Gartner is that of autonomous image formation agents, which consist of independently produced reports, documentaries, movies and news articles (Gartner 1993: 201). Gartner states that because of their perceived high credibility and market penetration, these agents may be the only image formation agents capable of significantly enhancing an area's image in a short period of time (Gartner 1993). The relevance of this observation for sport reimaging is that sporting initiatives generate and encompass autonomous image formation agents. The transmission of sporting links is predominantly through factual reporting and 'unbiased' news transmissions. Although deliberate promotional campaigns involving sport are used by cities, the majority of information received by potential tourists about sport in the city is via what Gartner would regard as very credible and unbiased sources. Staging major sport events and constructing prestige sport facilities generates publicity and news coverage as well as resulting in media exposure from the coverage of the sporting events themselves. This may result in sport providing a credible, and therefore effective means of enhancing the image of the city tourist destination.

Gartner also asserts that 'effective image change depends on an assessment of presently held tourism images' (Gartner 1993: 207). In formulating an effective image enhancement strategy, it would seem valuable to know what images already exist of the destination, especially as people may tend to avoid contradictory information or what Gartner terms 'cognitive dissonance' (Gartner 1993: 205). Prospective tourists 'seek information that agrees with their beliefs and they try to ignore information that does not' (Mayo and Jarvis 1981: 35). This suggests that to be effective, it is important for imaging strategies to evolve from the current images held, rather than to instigate an instantaneous revolution of the destination image. This has important implications for emerging urban tourist destinations. It may be naive to think that potential tourists will accept hyperbolic imagery about industrial cities, proclaiming them to be attractive places to visit. In the UK, cities such as Birmingham, Manchester and Sheffield have had a long tradition of hosting regular and one-off sport events and have become intrinsically associated with high-profile teams and stadia. Therefore, there is nothing revolutionary about associating prestige sport with these urban areas. However, by strengthening, renewing and developing these associations, cities can use 'major sporting activities … to project a high status image of the city via media coverage which may help attract visitors' (Law 1993: 94).

It is also recognised that an individual's 'existing needs and desires' are an important factor affecting image formation (Ashworth and Voogd 1990: 81). Pocock and Hudson (1978: 19) cement this strong relationship between image and personal interests by defining image as 'the sum of direct sensory information as interpreted through the observer's value predispositions', implying that it is a person's own interests, motivations and values that help determine the form of their place images. The perception of cities is very selective, what people choose to perceive is very closely related to what they care about (Mayo and Jarvis 1981: 28). If this is indeed the case, then sport's popularity may mean sporting initiatives can be more easily accepted into potential tourist's image of the city. As Whitson and MacIntosh (1993: 236) state, the popularity of professional sport and of world events clearly extends beyond a small group of people. Figures from the General Household Survey show that in 1986, 11 per cent of adults had visited a spectator sport event in the previous four weeks and that in 1996 this figure would be 13 per cent, with a further 1 per cent rise by the year 2002 (LIRC 1998). The figures relating to armchair sport spectating are even more encouraging in terms of the amount of people who are interested in watching sport events. For example in 1996, 3.5 billion people watched the Atlanta Olympics – almost one third of the world's population (LIRC 1998). Furthermore, in the US the eight most watched television programmes are all sport events (LIRC 1998). The sheer scale of interest in sport and its obvious popularity may therefore add to the penetration of the sporting imagery. Mullin *et al.* (1993) also indicate the relationship between personal interest and image. As the authors identify, the marketer's goal is to create a balanced or consonant relationship between the image of the city and the consumer's self image so there is an overall consistency (Mullin *et al.* 1993). Therefore, if a person has an interest in sport, the promotion of a city through this medium may be particularly effective. This is not only because a person may want to visit the specific events/ facilities at first hand, but because the image of the city and the person's self image are consonant. Each image reinforces the other so that a very positive relationship builds up between prospective tourist and the city.

A final point about the specific qualities of sporting initiatives which may enable them to have a disproportionate influence on destination image formation, concerns 'imageability'. This concept was first explored by Kevin Lynch and refers to the quality in a physical object which gives it a high probability of evoking a strong image in any given observer (Lynch 1960). With reference to more recent debates, it is observed that authorities have encouraged strategies that aestheticise or focus on the visual consumption of public space (Zukin 1998: 825, also Lash and Urry 1990). In effect the contemporary trend is to capitalise on Lynch's notion of imageability and deliberately construct urban features and spaces which have the capacity to generate a significant reaction from the observer. It is proposed here that the sport stadia developed in local economic development strategies have the potential to be significantly 'imageable' elements of the urban environment and as such should be regarded as providing 'potent landscape features' (Stevens and Wootton 1997). As Raitz (1987: 5) states, sport stadia provide cities with buildings that are distinctive and which evoke a strong sense of place. This view is echoed by Bale (1993: 3) who observes that 'it is the floodlights of the stadium, not the spire of the cathedral that more often than not act as urban landmarks and points of reference'. As has already been mentioned, this visual element of destination image is very important and often neglected within tourism research (Echtner and Ritchie 1991,1993, MacKay and Fesenmaier 1997). Seen in context with the factors mentioned earlier concerning the penetrability, legitimacy and popularity of sporting strategies, the coverage of major events transmit 'images of large scale, dramatic, often aesthetically memorable stadia into our living rooms' (Stevens and Wootton 1997). This means that the development of sport facilities may be able to provide a city with important visual symbols which create a memorable and positive image in the mind of the tourist.

Conceptualising the city image and city product

Sporting initiatives may therefore provide a credible, realistic, popular and penetrative means of influencing the way in which destination images are formed. However, in order to enhance our understanding of the potential of sporting initiatives to influence the structure of city destination images, it is necessary to conceptualise the city and analyse how it is promoted and perceived by potential tourists. Therefore as well as examining the influence of sport in influencing the image formation process, it is also necessary to indicate how sporting initiatives may become a constituent of the form and nature of city image themselves.

As Shaw and Williams (1994) have argued, one way in which to consider the different dimensions of tourism in cities is to view the urban environment as a product (Shaw and Williams 1994: 202). The conceptualisation of the city product has been attempted by, among others, Jansen-Verbeke (1986) who states that cities contain primary elements (which incidentally incorporate sporting events and facilities), consisting of major tourist attractions, supported by secondary tourist elements involving retail and catering facilities. However, the term tourism product can be used at two distinct levels, one at the specific level and the other at the total level – the complete experience (Smith 1994). This argument is reaffirmed by Lash and Urry who observe that although tourists may consume various tangible products, they also consume the core product of a place (Lash and Urry 1994: 215). Therefore, when referring to the city as an urban tourism product, as well as involving the consumption of particular attributes or functions of the city, the city as a holistic entity can be consumed. It must therefore be recognised that the city as a tourist product is therefore bought, sold and imagined on different levels.

This multi-level conceptualisation of the city tourism product is important when examining the potential of sporting initiatives to enhance the image of the city tourist destination. The city destination includes specific products such as the provision of sport in general, and on an smaller scale still, individual attractions such as indoor sporting arenas. These products can be bought and sold separately from the holistic unit. It is important to recognise that these different product levels all promote and generate distinct images which are vitally important to the urban tourism system.

The importance of image in this multi-level city tourism product is therefore paramount. Indeed it could be argued that city tourism product only exists as an image. In terms of the holistic image of the city this argument is particularly prevalent. As Shields (1996) states, while we may speak of the reality of 'the city' as a thing or form, the notion of the city as a holistic unit is ultimately just a representation (Shields 1996: 226). The 'city' is a just a name we ascribe to give a series of diverse practices, relationships and spatial forms. The material reality of the product is therefore not as important as the way it is imagined. Hunt (1975) affirms this argument in asserting that 'whether or not an image is a true representation of what any given region has to offer the tourist, what is important is the image that exists in the mind of the vacationer' (Hunt 1975: 1).

The crucial point is that just as the city destination can be thought of as a multi-layered phenomenon, it should be recognised that potential tourist's images of the city also exist on different levels. In terms of destination image, the distinction between the city as a whole and specific products is just as relevant. An example may be a city with a poor overall image but which is still perceived as a place with excellent sport facilities and as an attractive venue for high-quality sport events. To appreciate the image of this city as a tourist destination, it must be considered on both levels. The city tourist product is therefore essentially a series of connected, bur stratified product images, and it is argued here that to be able to understand the impact of sporting initiatives, it is necessary to recognise this product image stratification.

The conception of the city destination as existing on different product image levels, concurs with Echtner and Ritchie's (1991, 1993) observations about destination image. Echtner and Ritchie assert that destinations are perceived both via individual attributes and holistic impressions. Using this conceptualisation, it can be proposed that sporting initiatives may be influencing tourist images of the city in two different, but related ways. First, through developing the attribute-based image component – by sporting initiatives developing perceptions of an important tourism product within the city. Second, sport reimaging may replace vague or negative images of the city as a whole with different holistic impressions and associations. The intention in the rest of this chapter is to develop this tentative observation in order to produce a framework which may explain how sporting initiatives are incorporated into the image of the city tourist destination. The conceptualisation outlined by Echtner and Ritchie (1991, 1993) explains the different components present in images of the tourism product. What it does not do is explain exactly how these components may be influenced by imaging strategies and other external factors. Suggestions will be made below to develop this important consideration.

Dissecting city images

As can be ascertained from the tentative conceptualisation that has been outlined, it is proposed that the image of the city exists on two main levels. This simplified representation of the form of city images is partly inspired by the Gestalt psychological tradition which dictates that with perception, the whole is greater than the sum of the related parts. Therefore, although it is relevant to consider city images as an amalgam of the perceptions of different aspects of the city, the human mind also tends to consider places with a unified wholeness that differentiates them from each other and the background from which they appear (Mayo and Jarvis 1981). Therefore although the city can be perceived through its individual attributes and functions, there also exists another level of perception which considers the city as a unified whole. These two different, though inextricably intertwined levels of city image are explained further below alongside the implications of this basic conceptualisation for the impact of sport reimaging strategies.

Functional/operational image enhancement of the attribute based image of the city

First let us consider what is termed here the attribute-based image component, where the city is perceived as offering a series of different functions and features. A tourist image of the city may mean that a city is imagined as a place which offers certain identifiable tourist products. This image level is very much a functional perception of the city in question, where the person imagines what features and aspects would be present in a city and how the individual may utilise these attributes for their own specific purposes. Appleyard calls this form of perception an operational processing of information, which consists of the perception of 'goals, barriers, noxiants and other elements related to purposeful action' (Appleyard 1973: 109). The implementation of sporting initiatives may have an impact on this city image level by enhancing the perception of a city's sport tourism product. The attribute based image of the city as a sporting destination may therefore be enhanced, which may influence a certain section of the tourist market. As a result of the construction of major sport facilities and the staging of sport events, urban sport tourists may be influenced by the imaging in a functional and operational sense.

Without wanting to devote to much attention to the subject, it should be stated that there are problems in defining the term 'sport tourist'. The most widely used definition is that provided by C.M. Hall (1992b), who sees sport tourism as travel for non-commercial reasons to participate in, or observe sporting activities away from the home range. However, care must be taken to avoid excluding viewing sporting infrastructure or sporting exhibitions, activities which despite there growing popularity, do not appear to be recognised in Hall's definition. For the purposes of the argument here, urban sport tourists can be loosely defined as those people who actively seek to use, view, visit, or spectate at, the sporting infrastructure of a city during their stay. The sporting element of their visit may be the primary reason and motivation for travelling, or part of a broader package of tourism products in the city which they wish to sample. Therefore, in this segment of the urban tourism market the links between sport and the city are taken much more literally. Sporting initiatives are perceived as a specific function and attraction of the city. The construction of major sport facilities and staging high profile events means that the city may develop an image as a sporting destination, where visitors can go and experience the urban sport tourism products at first hand. This obviously involves spectating at sport events, but may also include sport participation in competitive and non-competitive environments, sport based visitor attractions such as sporting museums and guided tours of certain stadia. Several cities in the UK have attempted to enhance their images in this manner. Stevens and Wootton (1997) see Sheffield as a city which has developed a successful sport tourism product based on its stadia infrastructure. This conception of sport as an 'experienceable' tourism product and therefore a means of promoting the city as a tourist destination is clearly discernible in the tourist literature produced by the cities of Birmingham, Manchester and Sheffield. This trend is perhaps most clearly exemplified by promotional literature produced by Marketing Manchester, who provide a hypothetical itinerary for the would-be sport tourist (Figure 9.1).

As can be seen from this example, the new prestige sport facilities developed in the city are being explicitly used as a means of enhancing the image of the city as a place within which to experience prestige sport events. The intended image impact therefore relates to an enhancement based on the operational or functional representation of the city. This image enhancement can be seen to be distinct from another means by which sport may enhance the image of the city destination.

Symbolic image enhancement of the holistic image of the city

The holistic image component differs from the attribute-based image in that it consists of overriding general perceptions of the city as a whole. Attempting to simplify the urban environment into a unified whole enables a tourist to organise information and derive meaning from the complex and diverse contemporary city, which otherwise is inaccessible to the imagination. The holistic image is therefore a very important facet of the tourist decision making process. As Law (1996) states, some people do travel to a city for a specific purpose, but if we return again to the doctrine of Gestalt school of psychology, it could be argued when considering the city tourism product that the sum is often greater than the parts. As Law argues, 'when visitors are asked why they went to London or Paris, many do not reply that it was because they wanted to visit the Tower of London or the Louvre, but rather that they just wanted to go there' (Law 1996: 19). When considering the potential influence of sport reimaging on this holistic manifestation of city image, it is

---

'Inspired Sport'

Morning – Visit Old Trafford and the Manchester United Museum, together with a behind-the-scenes tour of the world's greatest football club.

Afternoon – Lunch at the Kilhey Court Hotel or De Vere Mottram Hall followed by a round of golf on their championship golf courses.

Evening – A sporting choice of superb venues, experience Manchester's Velodrome, Britain's national cycling centre and the fastest cycle track in the world or Europe's largest events arena, the Nynex arena in Manchester with its resident, world renowned ice-hockey and basketball teams.

Figure 9.1 Extract exemplifying the promotion of sport as urban tourist attraction

Source: (Marketing Manchester Visitor and Convention Bureau 1998)

argued that rather than simply enhancing the way the city is viewed as a sporting destination, sport may have the potential to produce a more positive holistic image of the city. Where image enhancement concerns a city traditionally associated with industrial production, the level of city image can be influenced by a general enhancement replacing vague or negative images with more positive holistic impressions. What may result is an enhancement of the holistic image, based on abstract notions and symbolic representations, rather than any notion of sport as a function of the city.

This form of enhancement is a connotative means of image development, as it involves what is implied or suggested in addition to the sport tourism products, beyond their literal or explicit sense. The implication is that sport tourism products, like other consumer commodities, may have developed the capacity to take up a wide range of imagistic and symbolic associations which overlay their initial use-value (Featherstone 1991). Therefore, the city has begun to promote itself like other consumer goods, not just as a functional product that has certain attributes and qualities which may be experienced through its purchase, but through more abstract imagery associating it with positive concepts and emotions. It has been observed that in the contemporary era, surfaces and styles become more important, creating a 'designer' ideology. Jean Baudrillard argues that consumption should be understood as a process in which only the signs attached to the goods are actually consumed and hence commodities (in this case the city) are not valued for their use, but understood as possessing a certain meaning (Campbell 1998: 103). As Strinati (1992) states, when people shop in supermarkets, they are as interested, if not more interested, in the packaging and design of the goods on sale as the goods themselves. If this is indeed the case, then it could be said that we are increasingly consuming signs and images for their own sake. This may be of particular relevance to sport reimaging, for as Rowe (1995) argues, sport is inherently reliant on images and symbols rather on the production of use-valuable commodities per se. The implication here is that the use of sport as an imaging tool may provide a city with an attractive image, even though the recipients of the imagery may not view that element of the city in an operational sense. The image enhancement is based on a symbolic, abstract level of signs and symbols which influences the way in which people imagine the city, regardless of their interest in spectator sport. Sport provides the packaging, the image, rather than a specific function and feature of the city.

This argument is particularly relevant to sport reimaging because the proposed image enhancement is not necessarily explicit in nature, as it does not have to directly refer to the functional dimension of the city. It is the connotations attached to the sport events and the facilities that are as important as the facilities and events themselves. Prospective visitor images of the city may be enhanced by the staging of a major event or construction of a sporting arena despite the fact that they have no intention of sampling the sport tourism products within that city. As Hall (1997: 205) states the reimaging and representation of a city 'relies on both material and symbolic resources'. The development of sport facilities and the staging of events has a material outcome in terms of the provision of a specific tourism product, but the effects of the initiatives are not confined to this immediate impact. The city may become a more attractive destination because of the positive associations derived from the sporting initiatives, not the sporting initiatives per se, which may improve the way in which the city is viewed as a whole. According to Rowe (1995) these sporting connotations 'emerge out of the repetitive assertion of sporting values such as universalism, transcendence, heroism, competitiveness, individual motivation and teamship' (Rowe 1995: 138). Through this connotative process, the reimaging of the city through sport would appear to have the potential to influence the holistic element of destination image.

A good illustration of this symbolic image enhancement may be the sport reimaging implemented by the city of Manchester. This city in the North West of England made two unsuccessful bids for the Olympics (for the 1996 and 2000 Games), but despite this apparent failure, successfully used the bids as a focal point for the reorientation of the city's image. Although the mega-event never took place in the city and the majority of the proposed sport facilities were not built, it is generally regarded that the city's holistic image was improved greatly as a result. In effect the mere association with sport in general, and more specifically the Olympic Games themselves, replaced vague or negative perceptions of the city with more positive perceptions. Rowe's assessment of Manchester's Olympic bid concurs with this interpretation, perceiving that the city was keen to host the 2000 Olympics because of 'all its connotations of new era advancement' (Rowe 1995: 137). Manchester has used the legacy of the bid in the form of for example images of sports facilities in promotional literature, in an attempt to connote a new era for the city, illustrating the symbolic and abstract purpose of much sport reimaging. The image enhancement in this instance does not utilise the functional value of the bid in providing an improved sport tourism product, but on a more abstract, symbolic level which has enabled the holistic image of the city to receive a much needed boost. As Rowe (1995) asserts, such examples 'illustrate sports work as a metaphor and its articulation with other practices and values constitute an attractive capacity to popularise sometimes obscure notions of progress' (Rowe 1995: 138).

Two major ways in which sporting initiatives may influence the images of cities have therefore been identified. One relates to an operational image enhancement based on the improved perception of the city as a sport tourism destination and another to an impact on the holistic image resulting from a connotative interpretation of symbolic and abstract imagery. Recent debates in critical sociology would promote the importance of the symbolic over the functional, and the connotative over the denotative when considering the contemporary arena of consumption. However, it may be that the success of urban reimaging strategies depends on capturing and utilising both forms of image enhancement. The example of Manchester illustrates the fact that sport products can be utilised simultaneously as a means of enhancing both the functional and the holistic elements of destination image, applying both connotative and denotative imaging. Despite the obvious danger of over-simplification, the different means of image enhancement noted would appear to provide a useful means of conceptualising the proposed impact of sporting initiatives on city images. However, to understand the importance of this conceptualisation it is necessary to discuss the implications resulting from it. These will now be considered.

The importance of conceptualising destination image

Research implications

The identification and appreciation of holistic and operational image enhancement is important because it is only through such conceptualisation that it may be possible to measure the true impact of sport-led urban reimaging strategies. Research that attempts to evaluate image enhancement must consider the tourism product at a variety of scales in order to fully appreciate the possible impact of a sport-based strategy. City image research must acknowledge that the image of the city as a whole may be enhanced by a sport-led strategy, but that the initiatives implemented may also develop perceptions of improvements to a particular product (sport) within the city. This attribute-based image enhancement may take place even if holistic impressions remain largely unaffected. Therefore even if cities such as Sheffield and Manchester fail to develop desirable holistic city images, they may at least be able to develop images and reputations as sporting destinations offering an impressive sport tourism product. The use of examples from Manchester to exemplify both forms of image enhancement provides evidence that sport reimaging may have the potential to enhance both destination image components, thus developing the capacity to influence simultaneously different sectors of the tourist market. The key point is that image research must analyse these different strata of destination image in order to measure comprehensively any proposed image enhancement resulting from sporting initiatives.

Furthermore, the complex nature of any possible image enhancement the development of holistic images derived from symbolic imaging indicates that traditional image measurement techniques need to be made more flexible in order to allow the appreciation of such effects. While it may be acceptable to measure attribute-based images using conventional structured questionnaires and rating techniques, measuring holistic image enhancement requires the promotion of the use of less structured interviewing. As Echtner and Ritchie state 'to fully capture the components of destination image – attribute, holistic, functional, psychological, common and unique – a combination of structured and unstructured methodologies must be used' (Echtner and Ritchie 1993: 5). To understand the meanings attributed to certain initiatives and to explore the way in which sport reimaging is interpreted it is essential that the subjects of any research are allowed to express their perceptions on their own terms. Despite the acceptance and appreciation of such methodological implications in some contemporary geographical analysis, the relatively immature discipline of tourism has yet to embrace the methodological recommendations noted here. There is a recognition within the discipline that symbols, signs and holistic images are important parts of destination image, but as yet the methodologies used to examine the concept have not been modified accordingly.

A final note concerning methodological implications is that an attempt here has been made to analyse how image enhancement strategies may impact upon the images held by prospective urban tourists. It is vital that more research attempts to link strategies of urban representation with the effects of these initiatives on the way in which the city is imagined. Therefore, rather than simply analysing the ways in which cities are being represented, there should be more concentration on the way in which deliberately manipulated imagery is received and interpreted by consumers. Despite the burgeoning literature on the promotion of city images and associated changes in urban form, there has been little or no mention that the implications of these changes to external images of the city which exist in the minds of the prospective urban tourists would matter a great deal.

Marketing implications

The conceptualisation outlined above may also facilitate the future imaging of the city in targeting imaging strategies at specific segments of the tourism market. It is generally acknowledged within the tourism literature that place images must be designed to meet the needs of target markets (Kotler *et al.* 1993: 99). In sport reimaging, that obviously requires attracting the attention of sport tourists. However, it is necessary to realise that the most effective imaging may be that where 'the product is simultaneously sold to different customers with different needs and motives for visiting' (Page 1995: 216). This point is reaffirmed by Cunningham (of Proctor and Gamble) in analysing the marketing of Newcastle-Upon-Tyne. Cunningham asserts 'you are looking for a multi-faceted message that can appeal to different audiences with a different agenda' (Armstrong 1998). Although sport facilities and sport events may attract a significant amount of people into the city, the amount of money spent on such initiatives means that for image enhancement to be cost-effective they should ideally influence a more general audience. The success of sport-reimaging may therefore rely on the dual form of image enhancement noted above, where sport tourists and a more general audience can be influenced. This argument is recognised by Hughes (1993) in the case of Manchester. Hughes states that the city's desire to develop leisure tourism has been aided by the Olympic bid through enhancing the awareness and image of the city, which may directly stimulate sport tourism but which may also 'encourage a flow of tourists unconnected directly with the Olympics' (Hughes 1993: 160). By recognising the different levels on which city images exist, more effective marketing can be employed, directing sport tourists towards the sporting products that the city has to offer, while using the symbolic capital generated by the sporting initiatives to impact upon a wider audience – aiding the 'circulation of images that influence climates of opinion and mentalities' (Zukin 1996: 45). This connotative imagery may result in a more positive image of the city in the minds of urban tourists, or at the very least pave the way for the acceptance of more positive imagery in the future by negating negative and vague impressions of the city.

However, there is a danger that unless this 'multi-selling' of the city is properly managed, the positive impacts could be negated. For instance, it has been recognised that city marketing authorities tend to adopt a composite view of the city and its place product in selling the destination to potential visitors (Page 1993: 195). As Bramwell (1993) asserts, cities' marketing efforts are often disproportionately skewed towards the promotion of a city's overall image, rather than targeting specific visitor groups. The danger for cities implementing sporting initiatives may be that in aiming to enhance both the image of the city as a sporting destination and the holistic image of the city, they fail to do either to a significant degree. There are certainly indications from the cities of Birmingham Manchester and Sheffield that sport reimaging strategies have been implemented as a means of promoting the city to an ill-defined general audience, with less attention being paid to targeting specific imagery at the sport tourism market. This approach may mean that the cities are failing to capitalise on the market segment that may be most influenced by sport-based reimaging.

Sporting initiatives may therefore have the potential to enhance the way in which the city is viewed generally and as a sporting destination. However, in order to capitalise on this, marketing strategies must be formulated around the implementation of sporting initiatives which are targeted at specific market segments. This should include emphasising the attribute-based image of the city as somewhere to experience high quality sporting action in impressive arenas, as well as using sport to enhance the overall image of the destination. To maximise the benefits of this holistic image enhancement, cities may need to focus on the tourist market specifically, rather than presuming that imaging strategies will automatically and simultaneously project an attractive holistic image to investors, residents, governments and tourists alike.

A note of caution

The overriding tone of this chapter has been very positive, perhaps a little overly so. Essentially, this is because the arguments have centred on the *potential* of sport reimaging, rather than any objective assessment of a strategy's success. It is, however, necessary to identify briefly the limitations of sporting initiatives in achieving city image enhancement.

Concern has been expressed by Ritchie and Smith (1991) that any image enhancement may be short-lived once the initial impetus of the sporting initiatives has receded. This is a valid and important point. However, it could be stated that as long as the initial catalyst that is provided by sport is capitalised upon, either through further sporting initiatives or more diversified imaging strategies, then this inevitable image decay does not necessarily have to be a major problem. It should also be recognised that the very fact that so many cities are using sport as a means of image enhancement may result in a reduction in the intended impact. This may be part of a wider place marketing issue, where it has been observed that places seeking to differentiate themselves as marketable entities end up creating a serial reproduction of homogeneity (Harvey 1989). In implementing sporting initiatives, places may be failing to distinguish themselves from their competitors. This problem is further emphasised when related to the more general field of marketing. According to guidelines proposed by Kotler (1994), when attempting to develop a product image, companies should seek to identify sources of competitive advantage, choose an effective position in the market, identify the major differentiating attributes available to firms and consider the best means of communicating the firm's position in the market. The media exposure generated by sport means that this latter factor is a strong feature of a sport-led reimaging strategy. However, in terms of the other three recommendations it could be argued that the use of sport as an imaging tool means a city may fail to differentiate itself from its competitors and prevent it from occupying a distinct position in the market. As Whitson and MacIntosh (1993) argue, the implementation of a sport-led reimaging strategy may come more and more to mean simply reaching the standards of facilities and entertainments that are expected in any city by potential tourists. For the development of an attribute-based image, this may not necessarily be a major problem, as meeting these standards will attract sport tourists and sport events to the city. However, for promoting a distinct and memorable holistic image, the serial reproduction of images and associated developments may prove to be an obstacle to the successful reimaging of the city.

Conclusions

The media, municipal authorities and academic commentators often glibly refer to local economic development strategies as providing a means of enhancing the image of a city. Though this may indeed be the case, up to now few attempts have been made to suggest how and why this image enhancement may be produced. What this paper has tried to do is rectify this situation by looking at what city images may consist of and how their structure may be affected by sport-based reimaging strategies. This has been achieved through the conceptualisation of the city tourism product, the different components of destination images and the different effects that an imaging strategy may have. The city tourist destination exists as a series of product levels ranging from the holistic unit to the individual attractions, that all promote and generate images. It has been proposed that sport reimaging may have the potential to be a successful urban reimaging strategy because sport has the ability to influence both the holistic and attribute based image of the city through the transmission of connotative and denotative images respectively. The different effects on image generated by sporting initiatives mean that they have the potential to 'multi-sell' the city to both sport tourists and a more general audience. If this multidimensional image enhancement is implemented properly in cities such as Birmingham, Manchester and Sheffield, then the reimaging of the city as a tourist destination may prove to be successful in the long term. For tourism development in industrial cities, the real value of sport reimaging may be as a catalyst for image enhancement and tourism development. If this can be capitalised upon, it should provide the basis for the further diversification of the city tourist destination image. Already the indications are that Birmingham, Manchester and Sheffield have been able to utilise sport in this manner, generating a more positive image of the city as a holistic entity through sporting initiatives.

At the same time they have developed their images as sport tourism venues and have contributed to the critical mass of attractions that should help these cities to become significant leisure-tourist destinations (Hughes 1993: 161).

References

Appleyard, D. (1973) 'Notes on Urban Perception and Knowledge in Downs and Stea 1973', *Image and Environment*. Chicago: Aldine.

Armstrong, S. (1998) 'This Little City Went to Market', *The Guardian* 9 January 1998, p. 41.

Ashworth, G.J. and Voogd, H. (1994) *Selling the City*. London: Bellhaven.

Bale, J. (1993) *Sport, Space and the City*. London: Routledge.

Barke, M. and Harrop, K. (1994*)* 'Selling the Industrial Town: Identity , Image and Illusion', in Gold, R. and Ward, S.V. (eds), *Place Promotion: The Use of Publicity and Marketing to Sell Towns and Regions*. Chichester: Wiley.

Bourdieu, P. (1978) 'How Can One Be a Sports Fan?' First appeared in *Social Science Information*, Vol. 17(6) reprinted in During, S. (1993) (ed.), *Cultural Studies Reader.* London: Routledge.

Bramwell, B. (1993) 'Planning for Tourism in an Industrial City' *Town and Country Planning*, Vol. 62(1/2), 17–19.

Bramwell, B. and Rawding, L. (1996) 'Tourism Marketing Images of Industrial Cities' *Annals of Tourism Research*, Vol. 23(1), 201–221.

Boyle, M. and Hughes, G. (1991) 'The Politics of the Representation of "The Real": Discourses from the Left on Glasgow's Role as European City of Culture, 1990'. *Area* Vol. 23(3), 217–228.

Campbell, C. (1988) 'The Sociology of Consumption' in Miller, D. (1995) (ed.), *Acknowledging Consumption*. London: Routledge.

Echtner, C.M. and Brent Ritchie, J.R. (1991) 'The Meaning and Measurement of Destination Image'. *Journal of Tourism Studies*, Vol. 2(2), 2–12.

Echtner, C.M. and Brent Ritchie J.R. (1993) 'The Measurement of Destination Image: An Empirical Assessment'. *Journal of Travel Research*, Vol. 32(4), 3–14.

Fakeye, P.C. and Crompton, J.L. (1991) 'Image Differences between Prospective First-Time and Repeat Visitors to the Lower Rio Grande Valley'. *Journal of Travel Research 1991*, (Fall), 10–16.

Featherstone, M. (1991*)* *Consumer Culture and Postmodernism*. London: Sage.

Gartner, W. (1993*)* 'Image Formation Process' *Journal of Travel and Tourism Marketing*, Vol. 2(2/3), 191–215.

Gunn, C. (1988) *Vacationscape*. New York: Van Nostrand-Reinhold.

Hall, C.M. (1992) *Hallmark Tourist Events: Impact, Management and Planning*. London: Belhaven.

Hall, C.M. (1992b) 'Adventure, Sport and Health Tourism', in Weiler, B. and Hall, C.M. (eds), *Special Interest Tourism*. Halstead: Belhaven.

Hall, C.M. (1997) 'Geography, Marketing and The Selling of Places', *Journal of Marketing Management*, Vol. 97, 61–84.

Hall, T. (1997) '(Re)Placing the City: Cultural Relocation and the City as Centre', in Westwood, S. and Williams, J. (eds) *Imagining Cities: Scripts, Signs, Memory*. London: Routledge.

Harvey, D. (1989) *The Condition of Postmodernity*. Oxford: Blackwell.

Hughes, H.L. (1993) 'Olympic Tourism and Urban Regeneration'. *Festival Management and Event Tourism*, Vol. 1, 157–162.

Hunt, J.D. (1975) 'Image as a Factor in Tourism Development'. *Journal of Travel Research*, Vol. 13, 1–7

Jansen-Verbeke, M .(1986) Inner City Tourism; Resources, Tourists and Promoters *Annals of Tourism Research*, Vol. 13(1), 79–100.

Kotler, P. (1994) *Marketing Management: Analysis, Planning, Implementation and Control*, 8th edn. Englewood Cliffs: Prentice Hall.

Kotler, P., Haider, D. and Rein, I. (1993) *Marketing Places*. New York: Free Press.

Kronos (1997) 'The Economic Impact of Sports Events Staged in Sheffield 1990–1997'. *Final Report Dec 1997*, Report to Sheffield City Council (unpublished).

Lash, S. and Urry, J. (1994) *Economies of Sign and Space*. London: Sage.

Law, C.M. (1993) *Urban Tourism – Attracting visitors to Large Cities*. London: Mansell.

Law, C.M. (1996) *Tourism in Major Cities*. London: Routledge.

Lim, H. (1993) 'Cultural Strategies for Revitalising the City', *Regional Studies*, Vol. 27(6) 589–595.

Lipsitz, G. (1984) 'Sports Stadia and Urban Development: A Tale of Three Cities'. *Journal of Sport and Social Issues*, Vol. 8(2), 1–18.

LIRC (1998) *Leisure Forecasts – Leisure Away From Home 1998–2002*. Sheffield: Leisure Industries Research Centre/Leisure Consultants.

Loftman, P. and Spirou, C. (1996) 'Sports Stadiums and Urban Regeneration: The British and US Experience'. *Conference Paper Tourism and Culture*, 14–19/9/96, University of Northumbria.

Loftman, P. and Nevin, B. (1996) 'Going for Growth: Prestige Projects in Three British Cities'. *Urban Studies*, Vol.33(6), 991–1019.

Lynch, K. (1960) *The Image of the City*. Cambridge, MA: MIT.

Lyon, D. (1995) *Postmodernity*. Buckingham: Open University Press.

Mackay, K. and Fesenmaier, D.R. (1997) 'Pictorial Element of Destination in Image Formation'. *Annals of Tourism Research*, Vol. 24(3), 537–565.

Madsen, H. (1992) 'Place marketing in Liverpool: A Review'. *International Journal of Urban and Regional Research*, Vol. 16(4), 633–640.

Marketing Manchester (1998) *Manchester: Travel Industry Guide 1998*. Manchester: Marketing Manchester.

Mayo, E.J. and Jarvis, L.P. (1981) *The Psychology of Leisure Travel*. Boston: CBI Publishing.

Mullin, B.J., Hardy, S. and Sutton, W. (1993) *Sport Marketing*. London: Human Kinetics.

Page, S. (1995) *Urban Tourism*. London: Routledge.

Philo, C. and Kearns, G. (1993) *Selling Places*. New York: Pergamon.

Pocock, D. and Hudson, R. (1978) *Images of the Urban Environment*. London: Macmillan.

Raitz, K.B. (1987) 'Perception of Sport Landscapes and Gratification in the Sport Experience'. *Sport Place*, Winter 1987, 4–19.

Reiss, S. (1981) 'Power Without Authority: Los Angeles' Elites and the Construction of the Coliseum'. *Journal of Sport History*, Vol. 8(1) (Spring), 50–65.

Ritchie, J.R.B. (1984) 'Assessing the Impact of Hallmark Events: Conceptual and Research Issues'. *Journal of Travel Research*, Vol. 23(1), 2–11.

Ritchie, J.R.B. and Smith, B.H. (1991) 'The Impact of a Mega-Event on Host Region Awareness; A Longitudinal Study'. *Journal of Travel Research*, Summer 1991, 3–9.

Rowe, D. (1995) *Popular Cultures: Rock Music, Sport and the Politics of Pleasure*. London: Sage.

Schimmel, K.S. (1995) 'Growth Politics, Urban Development, and Sports Stadium Construction in the US: A Case Study', in Bale, J. and Moen, O. (eds), 1995 *The Stadium and the City.* Keele: Keele University Press.

Shaw, G. and Williams, A. (1994) *Critical Issues in Tourism: A Geographical Perspective.* Oxford: Blackwell.

Shields, R. (1996) 'A Guide to Urban Representation and What to Do About It', in Westwood, S. and Williams, J. (eds), *Imagining Cities.* London: Routledge.

Smith, S. (1994) 'The Tourism Product'. *Annals of Tourism Research*, Vol. 21(3), 582–595.

Smyth, H. (1994) *Marketing the City: The Role of Flagship Projects in Urban Regeneration.* London: Spon.

Stevens, T. and Wootton, G. (1997) 'Sports Stadia and Arena: Realising Their Full Potential'. *Tourism Recreation Research*, Vol. 22(2), 49–56.

Strinati, D. (1992) 'Postmodernism and Popular Culture'. *Sociology Review*, 2–7.

Thorns, D.C. (1997) 'The Global Meets the Local'. *Urban Affairs Review*, Vol. 33 (November), 189–208.

Westwood, S. and Williams, J. (1997) *Imagining Cities: Scripts, Signs, Memory.* London: Routledge.

Whitson, D. and MacIntosh, P. (1993) 'Becoming a World Class City'. *Sociology of Sports*, Vol. 10, 221–240.

Williams, R. (1976) *Keywords.* London: Croom Helm.

Zukin, S. (1996) Space and Symbols in an Age of Decline Chapter, in King, A.D. (ed.), *Re-Presenting the City: Ethnicity, Culture and Conflict in the Twentieth Century.* London: Macmillan.

Zukin, S. (1998) 'Urban Lifestyles: Diversity and Standardisation in Spaces of Consumption'. *Urban Studies*, Vol. 35(5–6), 825–839.

10 Sport in the port

Leisure and tourism in the maritime city

Jenny Anderson and Chris Edwards

Home of the BT Global Challenge, the Whitbread Round the World Yacht Race and the largest on the water Boat Show in the world, Southampton has an international maritime reputation. The city is located by the Solent which is one of the busiest stretches of water in Britain, and it is at the centre of the UK sailing and leisure craft industry which is seen as having a growing significance to the city. The port and waterfrontage provide an arena for water sports and water sporting events to take place. The city attracts visitors for its 'maritimeness' which is derived from its maritime heritage and current 'authentic' maritime activity. This is exhibited through amalgamation of industry, infrastructure, craft and participants.

This chapter will begin by reviewing changing shipping patterns which have lead to development in the docks and port. Further investment and the subsequent changing waterfront land use have lead to more attractive waterfront and dock areas, and changes in the way the city is marketed to visitors. There has been a move to a closer identification of the city's maritime strengths which reflects development towards niche markets in other areas of leisure and tourism. We will seek to explore the significance of the city's 'maritimeness' in marketing the city as a tourist destination, by profiling and estimating the economic impact of maritime visitors coming to Southampton. Maritime visitors in this study are defined as 'any visitor coming to Southampton whose main reasons for visiting are "the attraction of the boats/waterfront" or to attend a maritime event or show'.

What are the maritime factors which attract people? The maritime heritage factors are present in other great British ports – what is different about Southampton is the existence of the thriving small leisure craft industry with its own maritime sporting culture and heritage. This is packaged and marketed overtly through events, and a small maritime museum; and indirectly through the landscape. The chapter explores the success of this niche marketing through analysing the economic impact of maritime visitors compared to other visitors to the city. It also explores potential conflicts.

Southampton, a city of 197,000 people, has a large waterfrontage. It is a deep water port with a unique double high tide, a choice of safe anchorages for ships, easy access to the prosperous South East and close proximity to Europe. Southampton Water is three miles long and joins the Solent north of the Isle of Wight. The city lies between Bournmouth and Portsmouth and is less than one and half hours to London by train or car. This study focuses on the city but also includes the maritime hinterland to include the River Hamble. The city's unique location has been a major factor in its success as the UK's centre for sailing and other watersports.

Southampton as a maritime city and centre of UK sailing

The importance of the region as a maritime and sailing centre is illustrated by the fact that the International Sailing Federation is based in Southampton, and the Royal Yachting Association, the UK governing body for sailing, windsurfing and power boating, is located within five miles. Other national institutions such as the Southampton Oceanographic Centre (Europe's principal centre for Oceanographic studies), and the Maritime Safety Agency are also located in Southampton. There are a host of manufacturers and services supporting the small leisure craft industry. The Jubilee Sailing Trust, an organisation offering sail opportunities to disabled and non-disabled sailors, has chosen Southampton as the location for building a 65 ft square rigger.

Sailing, yachting and power boating generate income for the city. Sailing craft, essential elements of the sport, are designed, built, sold, repaired and maintained in the city. Support services such as sailing schools, tour operators, insurance brokers, maritime financiers, yacht charters, yacht brokers, marinas bring regular income to the city and hinterland. The sporting participants themselves bring money and other benefits into the local economy through direct and indirect spending driving a significant sector of the economy. Recent studies on the River Hamble and at Cowes indicated the considerable impact of a maritime honeypot has on the region. In 1996 it was estimated that 18,800 yachts visited the River Hamble bringing 78,000 yachtsmen who spent £3.5m in the region. This represents 9 per cent of the tourism spend for Eastleigh (Edwards 1996). A similar 1992 study on Cowes on the Isle of Wight indicated a spend by yachtsmen of £10m, which, together with spend from non-yachting visitors, supported 500 jobs (Edwards 1992).

The participants, maritime leisure infrastructure and craft themselves attract further visitors to Southampton. Watersports, with the possible exception of personal watercraft, are highly visible activities and on the whole pleasing to the eye. From the shore, leisure craft can contribute an additional dynamic to the land/sea scape with colour, speed and activity. On land, a distinctive ambiance is created through the dress codes and behaviour of participants.

Watersports, and yachting in particular, are seen by many as expensive and exclusive pastimes for an elite minority. They have an upmarket image, enhanced by portrayals in the press and on television, indeed 'Howards Way' boat trips (named after the television serial of that name based in Southampton) still operate from the city. Both power boating and sailing have had a close association with royalty and fashion since the seventeenth century, and Cowes Week is an event on the social calendar. Sailing, and other watersports are successful Olympic sports involving a high level of skills and ability. Participants tend to fall into the ABC1 male and over 45 profile. To some this very exclusivity can be attractive with marinas and waterfronts offering spectators an opportunity to gaze into the lifestyles of others at leisure and moored craft being seen as status symbols.

The growth of Southampton and the port

Southampton used to be one of England's mediaeval cities and one of Europe's greatest ports. The city has a checkered history and its development has always been closely associated with the sea. Many sailing ships were built in Southampton in the 1870s and 1880s. During the first world war Southampton was the number one embarkation point for troops with 7.5 million men passing through the port. It also paid a substantial role in the 1944 Normandy landings.

The city also had a pioneering role in the development of flying boats. However it is Southampton's association with passenger liners which has caught the public imagination especially with the recent release of the 'Titanic' film – a timely reminder that many of the crew who drowned came from Southampton. Travel by liner peaked in 1955 when almost 700,000 passengers went through the port, after which the jet aircraft took over in transporting people overseas. Today, Southampton is the home base for P&O and Cunard and their flagships Oriana, Queen Elizabeth II, and Arcadia. In addition Southampton is a ferry terminal for the Isle of Wight. Its role as a cross channel port was re-established when Sealink Stena was launched in June 1991 but was withdrawn in 1996. Visitors used Southampton as a transit port rather than a place to stay for more than one night.

Today Southampton handles 7 per cent of UK trade. On average there are 150 ship movements in the port area per day. Thirty four million tonnes of ship cargo are handled per year, this including 800,000 containers and 450,00 new cars (ABP 1997). 10,000 people are employed directly or indirectly in the docks and a further 30,000 are estimated to work in marine activities. Southampton is the UK's number one port for grain exports, cruise passengers, and the second busiest in terms of vehicles and container handling. In the last five years container ships have doubled in unit capacity requiring increasingly sophisticated port infrastructure especially cranes which dominate the skyline. In parts there is a decidedly industrial landscape.

Redevelopment of the dockland areas

Automation, containerisation and shorter ship turnround times have had a profound effect on world shipping and trade patterns. The construction of a new container port in Southampton meant that much of the older dockland became redundant. The City Council in conjunction with Associated British Ports drew up a strategy for redevelopment and marketed land as prime sites for leisure, retail, housing and employment developments. The city council maintained that the new growth must not be at the expense of traditional port activities such as ship building and repair industry (Southampton City Council 1990). Other priorities with this redevelopment were in securing activities which added to the city's image and identity, promoting tourism on newly released land, and integrating waterfront developments and port operation.

Table 10.1 Passengers throughflow in Southampton

Year	International	Cross Channel	Isle of Wight
1987	121,738		1,270,265
1988	126,815		1,312,150
1989	119,896		1,380,066
1990	132,574		1,526,700
1991	169,529	237,431	1,531,386
1992	164,833	508,142	1,627,819
1993	214,529	484,861	1,694,102
1994	210,572	580,963	1,839,179
1995	233,394	549,217	2,123,271
1996	224,175	464,915	2,132,657
1997(half year)	78,577	N/A	N/A

Source: The Port of Southampton 1997

Waterfrontage and docks as tourist attractions in the UK

The revival of city dockland areas first took place in America in the 1960s and 1970s. Bristol was the first UK city to develop the dock area with partial funding through the English Tourist Board (Yale 1997), and other British cities followed suit. In the 1980s government policies for inner city regeneration, decaying dock areas became targets for redevelopment as in London and Liverpool where Dock-land Development Corporations were set up. Imitations followed and by 1990 almost every town with docks or canal/riverside warehouses was striving to convert them into shops, offices, houses, and tourist attractions (Yale 1997). There is a 'sameness' about many of these schemes.

With the growth in water-based leisure there has been a dramatic increase in marinas all along the south coast. Outdoor recreation is on the increase nationally and has been throughout the twentieth century (Environment Agency 1997). Estimates of craft based watersports participants vary from 3–4 million (Anderson 1994), to 4.7 million (BMIF 1994).The popular types of watersports to be found on Southampton water are sailing, rowing, canoeing, water skiing, jet skiing, fishing and power boating. There are an estimated 30,000 recreational craft on the Solent (Solent Forum 1997) with an estimated 3,000 additional berths for visitors (Southern Council for Sport and Recreation, 1991). There are still 20-year waiting lists for prime moorings on the River Hamble, and the most popular and prestigious sailing clubs have lengthy waiting lists, however there are numerous creeks and rivers nearby for temporary shelter.

In the 1970s marinas were built in semi rural areas e.g. Lymington and Hamble, in the 1980s they were built in larger urban areas such as Hythe. Some of the surrounding coast is designated a heritage coast by Hampshire County Council. The better South coast harbour locations have now been used up, so city locations are being explored such as places where docks have been closed down. Marinas are becoming more sophisticated, with many now mixed in with retail development, housing, and some activity to encourage non-craft based visitors. Ocean Village in Southampton was one such development and alongside the retail, housing developments was a large marina adding to the mooring/berth base of the city. Marina developments have accounted for an additional 500 marina berths in Southampton.

Marina and docks – informal 'waterside' recreation

People have always enjoyed looking at the seascape. The development of marinas and waterfrontages has provided a venue for this informal activity. These informal recreationalists include walkers, sightseers and people simply enjoying the water. Although there are few local statistics (Thompson 1994), nationally 247 million day trips involved visits to water, either to rivers, still waters or coastal waters (OPCS/HMSO 1989). Of these 15 million were to take part in fishing, whilst 10 million trips were to take part in watersports. During 1994, 5,200 million day visits were estimated nationally, 4 per cent (180 million) of which were made to the coast, and 3 per cent to canals and rivers. Quite simply the presence of water attracts people.

A recent study of non-yachting visitors to the River Hamble (Edwards 1996) indicated that a significant spend was made by this group of people who came to see the river. This was also the case for similar visitors to Cowes who were estimated to bring in £3.25 m to the town (Edwards 1992).

In coastal and port locations it is the combination of commercial and leisure craft which provides the attraction. In Southampton harbour tours by boat are offered to casual visitors and more often pre-booked coach parties. Often it is the marina or dockside where the casual spectators come into contact with the watersports participants, dockside residents and commercial enterprise. This is where conflicts over privacy and space are most likely to arise.

The city as a tourist destination

Cities perform a variety of positive cultural, political and economic functions (Whitehead 1992). The increased awareness of the potential of cities as tourist destinations is a relatively recent phenomena (Mazanec and Wober 1997). Leiper (1990) has defined a tourist attraction as a system comprising three elements: a tourist, a sight and a marker. Leiper claims the tourist attraction comes into existence when the three elements are interconnected. He argues tourists are not simply pulled or attracted to an attraction, instead tourists are motivated to experience a nucleus and its markers (a marker being a system of information to highlight the tourist's appreciation). In the case of Southampton we argue that the marker is the event as it is difficult to put a signpost on a waterscape.

The benefits of employment creation, the stimulation of the economy and generation of wealth are as true for the leisure and sporting industries as they are for tourism. Southampton is not a traditional tourist destination. Prior to revitalising the docks and waterfront Southampton marketed itself as a short break destination with historic walls, access to New Forest and the Isle of Wight (Southampton City Council 1991). There was a proactive tourism unit encouraging visitors.

The maritime city as a tourist destination

Using the Jansen Verbeke's model (1986) this 'maritimeness' is further explored to evaluate the supply side of cities as tourist attractions (Table 10.2).

The model differentiates between primary elements such as the activity place and leisure setting, and secondary elements and additional elements. It is the primary elements which are of interest here in particular in the leisure setting which gives a city a distinct image and sense of place for visitors i.e. 'maritimeness' of the city. This includes the maritime history, the physical presence of the port, commercial and leisure craft, commercial and maritime infrastructure of the waterside industry and the newer maritime leisure industry in addition to the events.

In analysing the distribution of urban tourism in the city Page (1995) recognises cities can be identified through the 'tourism business district' and through 'tourism attraction research'. Page argues that, rather than produce inventories of all facilities used by tourists, it is more practicable to identify the areas used by the majority of visitors. This follows the ecological approach used by human geographers to identify regions within cities (Page 1993).

> The civic identity of most towns and cities grew out of buildings associated with public cultural provision – the great Victorian town halls, public libraries, municipal art galleries, parks, civic theatres and concert halls.
>
> (Bianchini and Montgomery 1991: p. 14)

In addition to civic buildings, historic walls and spaces in the centre of the city, the docks and now marinas have also supported the cultural identity of the city, and therefore become an important part of its heritage. Southampton waterfront and dock areas are about half a mile from the city centre – thus the 'tourist business centre' has relocated and stretched the critical mass of tourist activity. The importance of the 'tourist business district' is the identification of areas where tourists congregate. This clustering of tourist activity only brings problems when it comes into conflict with other city functions. In the case of Southampton it is on, and beside, the water where the conflict is most likely to happen, rather than within the city itself.

Many commercial docks in the UK operate alongside recreational activities in the UK (other examples are Medway, Harwich, Plymouth and Portsmouth). In fact there are growing concerns about conflicts of interest within ports, estuaries and waterfronts. 'Solent Forum' was established in 1992 and is a group of principal interests in the Solent with a membership of over 50 organisations. Its aim is to produce strategic guidelines and raise awareness of key issues. Recreation is regarded as one of the key issues. In addition a Coastal Recreation Officer is employed to implement the Southern Region Coastal Strategy – the priorities being communication and coordination, strategy development and future strategic issues

Table 10.2 Jansen Verbeke's model

Primary elements
An activity place – including all the overall supply features within the city, particularly the main tourist attractions

A leisure setting which includes both the physical elements in the built environment and the socio-cultural characteristics which give the city a distinct image and sense of place for visitors

Secondary elements
Supporting facilities and services which tourists consume during their visit (e.g hotel and catering outlets and shopping facilities) which shape the visitor's experience in the city

Additional elements
Tourism infrastructure which conditions the visit – such as availability of car parking, tourist transport provision accessibility and tourist type services

---

Source: Page, S. (1995: p. 63)

(Badman 1996). A possible issue is that the Solent may be nearing capacity at peak periods in the summer. Little research exists into issues of water carrying capacity in urban locations where recreational and commercial uses are combined, however the value of recreational sites adjacent to or lining urban areas are seen to be particularly important (Environment Agency 1997).

Southampton as a maritime tourist destination – role of events

Southampton's location at the heart of British sailing makes it a natural venue for racing. The Whitbread Round the World race left Southampton in September 1997 and returned in May 1998 after calling at Sydney, Capetown and Baltimore. Race assembly weeks are organised at start and finish with a range of entertainment catering for onlookers and spectators. Last year BT Global Challenge operated a fleet of fourteen identical yachts and spent ten months sailing the 'wrong way' around the world. The race start and finish together attracted 250,000 visitors to the city, injecting £7.5 million into the local economy (Elliot 1997).

Benefits of events include increasing sporting infrastructure as at Sheffield where seventeen new sports venues were generated. Events add to ambiance and sense of place for residents and workers. It can increase the sense of civic pride, and regional traditions and raise awareness of the city as a tourist destination (Ritchie 1988).

With over 500 local authorities in Great Britain, there is a growing proportion who are aggressively promoting the benefits of visiting their areas – whether as a leisure, tourism or sporting destination. Middleton (1996) estimates that between 1994 and 1995 there was a five-fold increase in local authorities buying and using visitor research in an attempt to develop the appropriate product and refine their marketing activity. Inevitably cities compete with other cities to hold major events. In the case of Southampton, the competition is with major ports and cities with waterfrontage and marina space, and there are over 400 ports and harbours along the coastline of the United Kingdom. Southampton competed with Bristol and Aberdeen to host the Tall Ships 2000 race. Nearby Portsmouth hosted the Festival of the Sea at the end of August 1998 with the largest expected gathering of warships seen for years.

Long distance sailing events are unique as spectator sports in that only the start that can be predicted; the finish is dependent on wind, weather and ocean currents. Nearly all of the race takes place out of sight – spectators are dependent on coverage through the media or the internet. The marina, dockland or waterfront becomes the stage to host the event. The interest is in seeing the preparation for the start, and seeing the participants or actors being welcomed home. As the drama and spectacle of sailing round the world is becoming more commonplace, so additional events are organised to coincide with starts and finishes. This wider programme from racing events has become more significant to the cities marketing in the last five years.

Another event with a long traditional association with the city is the International Boat Show. The Southampton International Boat Show has been run in the city for thirty years and is the largest floating boat show in the world. In 1996 it attracted over 120,000 visitors, produced almost £50 million worth of business and injected an estimated £3 million into the local economy (Elliot 1997). Much of the city changes during this week with the influx of thousands of high spending visitors and maritime entertainment.

Maritime City – segmenting the market

There are a number of well established ways of classifying visitors to maritime cities through market segmentation. This segmentation can take place through forward segmentation, factor and clustering techniques, demographic or socio-economic segmentation, product related segmentation, psychographic segmentation, geographic segmentation, purpose of trip, behavioural segmentation or channel of distribution segmentation (Page 1995). However because the focus of this chapter is maritime leisure, the relatively recent concept of sports tourism is used to segment the market.

The growth of sports tourism through the 1980s and 1990s has been reasonably well documented. A 1995 study estimated 22 per cent of all domestic holidays are activity based (Mintel 1995). Standeven (1997) suggests that as the number of participants and sports increases so do the destinations which experience them. With the increase of locations so there is an increase in the number of spectators, people who want to share the atmosphere or ambiance generated by a sport such as sailing.

Sport tourism encompasses three broad categories of tourist behaviour, those who travel to engage in their favourite sports, those who travel to watch sports events, and those who travel to visit sport related city infrastructure such as museums and stadiums (Gibson, Attle and Yiannakis 1997). The focus here is on the latter two groups.

Methodology

In 1997 a visitor survey was carried out to improve understanding of the origin, profile, spend, behaviour and opinions of visitors to Southampton, in particular those who took advantage of the city's maritime facilities (n = 908). Results are used to assess the economic impact of maritime tourism in the city using the 'Cambridge model'. Comparisons are made with findings of research in 1992.

Background

This survey formed part of a more general survey of visitors to Southampton carried out, on behalf of the City council, by the Southern Tourist Board and Southampton Institute's Maritime Faculty. A face-to-face questionnaire survey was carried out between 18 July and 27 September 1997. Strategic times were selected to take into consideration weekends/weekdays, major events – maritime and non-maritime and holiday periods.

Table 10.3 Definition of terms employed in the visitor survey

---

Definition of Terms
All visitors in the following definitions are non-residents of Southampton, not students at any academic institution in the city and not on day visits with their normal work or regular/household shopping.

'Maritime visitor' any visitor coming to Southampton whose main reason for visiting was 'The attraction of the boats/waterfront' or to attend a maritime event or show.

'Craft based maritime visitor' any visitor coming to Southampton whose main reason for visiting was 'the attraction of the boats/waterfront' or to attend a maritime event or show.

'Non-maritime visitor' visitors travelling to Southampton for any main reason other than the one given above (i.e. for maritime visitors). It is important to note that this category of visitor may have given 'The attraction of the boats/waterfront' as a secondary reason for visiting.

'Day visitors from home' visitors who had travelled from, and were returning to, homes outside Southampton City on the day of their visit.

'Day visitors from the city' visitors who had travelled from, and were returning to homes within the city on the day of their visit.

'Day visitors on holiday' visitors travelling to Southampton for the day from holiday bases outside the City.

'Staying visitors' visitors staying overnight in accommodation within Southampton City.

Adults were sampled on a random basis at eight locations within the City, consistent with those used in the 1992 Visitor Study carried out by PACEC Consultants and the Southern Tourist Board (Southampton Visitor Survey 1992). Locations were selected to cover the most significant parts of the City in an attempt to ensure a representative sample. Fifty nine interview sessions, each lasting 5 hours – typically between 11am and 4pm, were undertaken over the survey period

Filter questions were used to exclude residents of Southampton City, students at any academic institution in the city and those on day visits concerned with their normal work or regular/household shopping. A total of 3,300 people were stopped to be interviewed, of whom 25 per cent refused to participate, 40 per cent were residents of the City and 8 per cent were working/studying in the City or regular shoppers. Of those approached, 908, or 28 per cent, agreed to take part and were eligible to answer the main questionnaire.

Desk top research was carried out to provide indicative estimates of the volume of maritime and non-maritime visitors coming to Southampton and evaluate the economic impact of these trips, in terms of income generated and jobs sustained by visitor spending. This research involved an analysis of the application by the Southern Tourist Board of the Cambridge Tourism Economic Impact Model to SVS 1997. The Cambridge Model was developed jointly by PA Cambridge Economic Consultants Ltd, Geoff Broom Associates and the Regional Tourist Boards of England to generate local area estimates of the volume and value of tourism and the number of jobs sustained by visitor expenditure.

In its basic form, the Cambridge model uses a range of local data including details of accommodation stock, population, employment and visits to attractions. It applies this locally sourced information to regional estimates of tourism volume and expenditure derived from the following national surveys:

- United Kingdom Tourism Survey, 1996 (UKTS)
- International Passenger Survey, 1996 (IPS)
- The Day Visits Survey 1996
- Visits to Attractions 1996

However the model allows the estimates generated using the above data sources to be refined further using locally available survey data: Findings from the Southampton Visitor Survey (SVS) 1997 undertaken by Southampton Institute and the Southern Tourist Board have been used to adjust the Model to take account of the characteristics of local visitors.

To calculate the volume of maritime visitors, simple proportions were used from SVS 1997 of each maritime visitor type (i.e. staying, day visitors from home and day visitors on holiday). These proportions were applied to the overall numbers of visitors. In the case of staying visitors the overall number of visitors, to which the proportion was applied, excluded business visitors as these are under-represented in a street survey. The effect of this adjustment is a reduction in the estimate of maritime staying visitors.

To estimate value, average daily spend figures for each visitor type (i.e. day and staying) derived from SVS 1997, were applied to volume figures for maritime and non-maritime visitors. The average spend figures were for visitors on holiday or visiting friends and relatives and thus were not affected by business visitor spend. Average length of stay was also taken into consideration in the calculation of staying visitor spend. Information from SVS 1997 allowed spend to be calculated by industry sector.

The next stage of the analysis generates estimates of the employment impacts of visitor spending for each business sector affected by tourism in the City. The Cambridge Model uses national survey data and information from detailed local business surveys undertaken by PA Cambridge Economic Consultants to estimate the proportion of total turnover that is retained as wage costs. By applying regionally adjusted annual wage costs to these estimates, the number of Full Time Equivalent (FTE) jobs directly supported by tourist spending can be calculated i.e. accommodation, shops, catering, entertainment and travel.

With ratios of jobs created for a certain spend in each industry sector it is possible to calculate total jobs created by visitor spend in Southampton. To derive jobs created by maritime visitor spend, the proportions of spend in each industry sector for all holiday/VFR visitors are applied to the total maritime visitor spend. This gives maritime visitor spend in each industry sector to which job ratios can be applied.

To generate estimates of the numbers of FTE jobs indirectly sustained by tourist spending (linkage and multiplier jobs) and the number of resultant actual jobs (full/part-time and seasonal) the Model again applies ratios derived from past business surveys undertaken by PA Cambridge Economic Consultants.

Results – visitor profile

12 per cent (n = 112) of all respondents (n = 908) were maritime visitors. Of these 18 per cent were staying, 24 per cent day visitors on holiday and 58 per cent day visitors from home.

Maritime visitors are more likely to be either in the higher socio-economic grades and retired. Twenty-nine per cent of maritime visitors were in the A/B socio-economic category compared to 19 per cent for non-maritime visitors. A fifth of all maritime visitors were retired, representing twice the proportion for non-maritime visitors. The age findings suggest that visitors to Southampton during 1997 were, on average, more affluent than in 1992. However, the overall profile was similar to that of UK residents on all tourism trips to England during 1996 (UK Tourism Survey 1996).

Maritime visitors tended to be older than non-maritime visitors. A significant difference can be found in the 45–64 age category which accounted for 41 per cent of all maritime visitors and only 26 per cent of non-maritime visitors. Maritime visitor groups were less likely to contain children. Eighty per cent of maritime visitor groups contained adults only, as did 70 per cent of non-maritime visitor groups. No maritime visitor groups, staying in the City, contained children whereas 19 per cent of non-maritime groups taking up accommodation in the City, contained children.

The overall proportion of groups accompanied by children was 8 percentage points lower than in 1992 but comparable with the profile of visitors to the maritime venues of Portsmouth and Cowes and significantly higher than in historic cities such as Oxford and Salisbury (Southern Tourist Board 1996).

Research findings indicate an increase in day visitor activity around major events in the City – notably the finish of the BT Global Challenge in July, and the start of the Whitbread Round the World Race and International Boat Show in September, when the proportion of day visitors from home increased by 20 per cent points compared with 1992 (Southern Tourist Board 1992). Maritime day visitors from home represented 58 per cent of all maritime visitors compared to 45 per cent of non-maritime visitors in this category.

A smaller proportion of maritime visitors (11 per cent) came from overseas than did non-maritime visitors (18 per cent). This can partly be accounted for by the large number of overseas European visitors coming to shop in Southampton. Maritime visitors from overseas tended to come from further afield with significantly higher proportions coming from Australasia and North America.

The maritime heritage of Southampton exerts a stronger pulling power on day visitors from home who appear prepared to travel further than non-maritime visitors. The proportion of maritime day visitors coming from homes outside Hampshire (62 per cent) was nearly double that for non-maritime day visitor

Characteristics of the visit

All visitors were asked to give the main purpose of their visit and their main reason for choosing Southampton. It is acknowledged that there is a degree of overlap between these two questions however the second question was asked to illuminate the often broad response to the former question. For example, the main purpose of the visit could be 'a leisure day trip' and the reason for choosing Southampton 'plenty of things to see and do'.

Half of all maritime visitors gave their main purpose of visiting as a 'leisure day trip' compared to only a quarter of non-maritime visitors. A third of maritime visitors' main purpose of visiting was to attend an event/show. This indicates the importance of maritime-related functions in attracting visitors. Only 1 per cent of non-maritime visitors gave this as their main purpose of visit.

Shopping and visiting friends and relatives were given as the main purpose of visiting by 20 per cent and 17 per cent respectively of non-maritime visitors, yet were not mentioned at all by maritime visitors as a main purpose of visiting. As mentioned earlier in the methodology, the question concerning respondents' main reason for choosing to visit Southampton was used to determine maritime and non-maritime visitors for the purpose of this paper. Respondents answering 'attraction of boats/the waterfront' in the closed section and those giving maritime related events in the open ended 'other' part of the question were then classified as maritime visitors. Eighty-seven per cent of maritime visitors were in the former category.

It is important to note that when asked to give other (i.e. not main) reasons for choosing to visit Southampton, a significant proportion of non-maritime visitors (11 per cent) gave 'attraction of boats/the waterfront'. As explained above, these visitors were not taken into consideration when defining 'maritime visitors' and thus, for the purpose of this research, were classified as non-maritime visitors. If they had been taken into consideration then the proportion coming to Southampton as a result of the City's maritime influence would be almost doubled to nearly one quarter of all visitors.

The research indicates that, apart from the attraction of the boats and the water-front, there was little other reason for maritime visitors to visit. The only significant response given here was 'familiarity/been before/like area'. The maritime nature of the city seems to exert a continuous and irresistible appeal and results in loyal repeat visitors. Non-maritime visitors, on the other hand, gave a wide variety of reasons for choosing to visit Southampton. Shopping accounts for over half of these, with visiting friends and relatives a further quarter.

Maritime visitors tended to stay in Southampton for far less time than did non-maritime visitors. The average length of stay for maritime visitors was 3.2 nights compared to 6.5 nights for non-maritime visitors. This latter figure is influenced by the significant proportion of domestic and overseas visitors who were staying with friends or relatives and language students staying in the area for an average of three weeks with host families. Three-quarters of maritime visitors were on short breaks (1–3 nights) in the City as opposed to only 41 per cent of non-maritime visitors. Half of non-maritime visitors were staying for one week or more in the City. Maritime visitors tended to stay for longer days. Two thirds of maritime visitors stayed for over four hours whereas only half of non-maritime visitors did so.

Ocean Village and Town Quay were the most popular destinations for maritime visitors (mentioned by 64 per cent and 58 per cent per cent respectively compared to 39 per cent and 33 per cent respectively of non-maritime visitors). Three quarters of non-maritime visitors were visiting the town centre compared to less than half of maritime visitors. It is interesting to note that a far greater proportion of non-maritime visitors were visiting the maritime museum though a greater proportion of maritime visitors knew about this attraction.

Key differences between maritime visitors and non-maritime visitors' activities while in Southampton were in their shopping and eating out behaviour. Three quarters of non-maritime visitors shopped compared to only one third of maritime visitors. Though similar proportions were eating out, maritime visitors were more likely to patronise quality restaurants.

Two per cent of non-maritime visitors and 3 per cent of maritime visitors were participating in some type of sporting activity while in the City. Whilst the sample size is too small to draw any conclusions for maritime visitors, non-maritime visitors participated in eight activities.

Non-maritime visitors were far more likely to visit the Tourist Information Centre; very few maritime visitors did so. Maritime visitors were far more likely to have seen some form of promotion for Southampton with three quarters saying they had done so compared to less than half of non-maritime visitors. This was particularly the case for maritime related features and advertisements on television. Nearly half of maritime visitors had seen television promotion for the Whitbread and the Boat Show compared to only 12 per cent of non-maritime visitors. Television coverage of the BT Global Challenge reached the same proportions of maritime and non-maritime visitors (21 per cent). Local leaflets and guidebooks were more effective in reaching non-maritime visitors however local and national newspapers were a better medium for maritime visitors.

Maritime and non-maritime visitors had the same opinion of range and quality of places to visit and things to do during the day scoring this aspect at 3.1 (out of four). This is slightly below the regional average of 3.3. However maritime visitors had a significantly better opinion of range and quality of places to visit during the evening. Further research into the expectations of the two groups in this field would reveal causes for this difference in scores.

Visitors were asked to rate Southampton in terms of waterfront/maritime events. This received the highest score of any aspect covered by the survey. Scores of 3.77 and 3.5 (out of 4) were given by maritime and non-maritime visitors respectively. This is a significant finding as it illustrates how stimulating a waterfront is compared to other attractions. Maritime features were amongst those most frequently mentioned by visitors in response to the open-ended question: 'What do you particularly like about Southampton?' For this question two-thirds of maritime visitors mentioned boats and waterfront compared to 25 per cent of non-maritime visitors.

As mentioned earlier maritime visitors overwhelmingly liked Southampton's maritime characteristics. Non-maritime visitors particularly liked the shops (33 per cent). Parking (availability and price) was mentioned as a particular dislike by a significant proportion of both maritime and non-maritime visitors.

Approximately 7 per cent of all staying visitors (i.e. 47,595 trips) coming to Southampton are maritime visitors – they come specifically because of the attraction of the boats/waterfront. These visitors spend nearly £6m – approximately 6 per cent of the total staying visitor spend. Maritime day visitors from home number over half a million and account for 15 per cent of all visits of this type. This type of maritime visitor represents the greatest revenue for Southampton in total (£10.95m) however staying visitors spend more on a per head basis.

It is necessary to calculate this breakdown in order to estimate jobs generated as a result of visitor spend.

Maritime visitors to Southampton support 267 direct FTE jobs – 10 per cent of all jobs of this type in the City. 'Direct' employment is defined as those jobs within the City, including both working proprietors (self employed) and employees in businesses where visitors spend money. Indirect jobs are a combination of linkage and multiplier jobs. Linkage jobs are those which can be attributed to the spending of tourists, but which arise out of the purchase of supplies by the businesses in which visitors spend their money. Indirectly, linkage jobs in firms such as goods wholesalers and service providers are sustained by the spending of visitors.

Multiplier jobs result from the respending by employees of income earned, directly or indirectly, as a result of visitor spending in the city. The table above

Table 10.4 Economic impact – volume and value of tourism in Southampton for 1997

	All visitors		Maritime visitors	
	Trips	*Spend (£m.)*	*Trips*	*Spend (£m.)*
Staying visitors	669,000	92.8	7,595	5.97
Day from home	3,574,000	71.6	546,822	10.95
Day on hol	1,533,000	23.3	151,767	2.31*
Transit	2,496,000	1.0		
Total	8,272,000	165.0	746,184	16.92

Note: *Expenditure by day visitors on holiday is counterbalanced by expenditure outside Southampton by staying visitors and is therefore excluded from total expenditure.

Table 10.5 Spend by industry sector

	All visitors		Maritime visitors	
	Expenditure by those staying	*Expenditure by day visitors*	*Expenditure by those staying*	*Expenditure by day visitors*
Accommodation	30.17	–	2.05	–
Shops	25.55	52.26	2.24	8.00
Catering	18.84	13.61	1.25	2.08
Entertainment	3.86	1.43	0.15	0.22
Transport	13.67	4.30	0.27	0.66
Total	92.09	71.6	5.97	10.96

Note: Day visitors in this table refers to day visitors from home only. Spend is in £millions.

Table 10.6 Jobs created by visitor expenditure

	All visitors	Maritime visitors
Accommodation	64	51
Shops	911	120
Catering	710	74
Entertainment	149	9
Transport	150	13
Total FTE (direct)	2,683	267
Indirect FTE	1,344	134
Total FTE jobs (direct + indirect)	4,028	401
Actual jobs (full time + part time + seasonal)	5,516	549

Note: This table refers to direct Full Time Equivalent jobs (FTE)

shows the estimated number of indirect FTE jobs sustained by visitor spending in the City during 1997 – an additional total of 1,344 FTE jobs of which 134 can be accounted for by spend by maritime visitors. FTE jobs are only a theoretical guide and need to be converted into actual jobs which include full time, part time and seasonal work. Actual jobs supported by maritime visitor spend are estimated to be 549 – 10 per cent of all actual tourism related jobs in Southampton.

Conclusion

In the last twenty years Southampton like other ports has seen change. Investment has been made in the waterfront and through maritime events. Southampton has long attracted sportsmen and women through maritime leisure such as sailing and power boating, now other visitors are being attracted to watch and absorb this sport. There are several levels of attraction and interest – the port, the liners, the yachts, the dinghies, the small craft industry and participants.

The importance of the cities 'maritimeness' has been shown to be significant in terms of economic impact. Both maritime and non-maritime visitors rate this aspect above all other features in the city. It is this authentic 'maritimeness' factor which provides the sense of place, and distinct image so important to Southampton, and watersports and watersport events are a significant part of this. As yet there are few conflicts between visitors and normal city functions on or off the water. Southampton is now starting its modern career as a maritime tourist destination – it is a city at the start of the resort life cycle. A key issue is to ensure the sport is nurtured and protected, to ensure the future of the leisure and tourism around the port. It is about managing potential conflicts.

References

Anderson, J. (1994) 'Watersports Participation in Britain', *Insights.* English Tourist Board D-13–D-20.

Anderson, J. *et al.* (1996) *The National Youth Watersport Audit.* British Marine Industry Federation & Southampton Institute.

Association of British Ports (1997) *The Port of Southampton – Building on Success.* ABP booklet.

Badman, T. (1996) 'Regional Strategies for Coastal Recreation', in Goodhead, T. and Johnson, D. (eds), *Coastal Recreation Management The Sustainable Development of Maritime Leisure.* London: E&FN Spon.

Bianchini, F. and Montogomery, J. (1991) 'City Centres, City Cultures CLES', cited in Whitehead, A. (1992) *Politics and the Survival of Cities.* Inaugural Professorial Lecture. Southampton Institute.

British Marine Industries Federation (1994) *National Survey of Boating and Watersports Participation.* Market Research Solutions.

Edwards, C. (1996) *Hamble Visitor and Yachtsman Survey.* Unpublished consultancy report.

Edwards, C. (1996) *Cowes Visitor and Yachtsman Survey.* Unpublished consultancy report.

Elliot, T. (1997) *Southampton Home of Ocean Racing.* Southampton City Council.

Environment Agency (1997) *Water Related Recreation Strategy for the Southern Region.* Consultation Draft. English Sports Council & Environment Agency.

Goodhead, T. and Johnson, D. (1996) *Coastal Recreation Management The Sustainable Development of Maritime Leisure.* London: E&FN Spon.

Gibson, H., Attle, S.P. and Yiannakis, A. (1997) 'Segmenting the Active Sport Tourist Market: a Life Span Perspective'. *Journal of Vacation Marketing*, Vol. 4(1), pp. 52–63.

Grabler, K., and Mazanec, J.A. (1997) *International City Tourism: Analysis and Strategy*. London: Cassells.

Jansen-Verbeke, M. (1986) 'Inner City Tourism: Resources ,Tourists and Promoters'. *Annals of Tourism Research*, Vol. 13(1), pp. 79–100.

Laws, E. (1993) *Urban Tourism: Attracting Visitors to Large Cities*. London: Mansell

Leiper, N. (1990) 'Tourist Attraction Systems'. *Annals of Tourism Research*, Vol. 17(3), pp. 367–384.

Meethan, K. (1997) 'Consuming (in) the Civilized City'. *Annals of Tourism Research*, Vol. 23(2), pp. 322–340.

Middleton, V.T.C (1996) 'Measuring the Local Impact of Tourism'. *Insights*. Tourism Strategy Papers, September, A39–A46.

Mintel (1995) *Activity Holidays in the UK*. London: Mintel.

OPCS/HMSO (1988/89) *Leisure Day Visits in Great Britain*.

Page, S. (1995) *Urban Tourism*. London: Routlege.

Ritchie, J.R.B. (1988) 'Alternative Approaches to Teaching Tourism'. Paper presented at the Tourism Teaching into the 90s conference, Guildford, in Standeven, J. (1997) 'Sport Tourism: Joint Marketing – a Starting Point for Beneficial Synergies'. *Journal of Vacation Marketing*, Vol. 4(1), pp. 39–51.

Southampton City Council (1990) *Southampton City Official Handbook*. Southampton City Council.

Southern Council for Sport and Recreation (1991) *Coastal Recreation Strategy*. Subject Report no. 8, Sports Council.

Smith, B.H. (1993) 'The effect of ocean and lake coast amenities on cities'. *Journal of Urban Economics*, Vol. 33, pp. 115–132.

Stansfield, C.A. and Rickert, J.E. (1970) 'The Recreational Business District'. *Journal of Leisure Research*, Vol. 2(4), pp. 213–225.

Standeven, J. (1997) 'Sport Tourism: Joint Marketing – a Starting Point for Beneficial Synergies', *Journal of Vacation Marketing*, Vol. 4(1), p. 39–51.

Standeven, J. and Tomlinson, A. (1994) *Sport and Tourism in the South East England: A Preliminary Assessment*. London: SECSR.

Solent Forum (1997) *Strategic Guidance to the Solent*. Solent Forum (leaflet).

Southampton City Council (1992) *Southampton City Surevey*, Southampton: Southampton City Council.

Thompson, J.R. (1994) *Public Launch Points on the Hampshire Coast*. Hampshire County Council and Sports Council.

UKTS (1996) *United Kingdom Tourism Survey*, London: English Tourist Council, Northern Ireland Tourist Board, Scottish Tourist Board and Wales Tourist Board.

Weed, M.E. and Bull, C.J. (1997) 'Integrating Sport and Tourism: a Review of Regional Policies in England, in Cooper, C.P. and Lockwood, A. (eds), *Progress in Tourism and Hospitality Research*, Vol. 3. London: John Wiley.

Whitehead, A. (1992) *Politics and the Survival of Cities*. Inaugural Professorial Lecture, Southampton Institute.

Yale, P. (1997) *From Tourist Attraction to Heritage Tourism*. ELM Publications.

11 Imaging, tourism and sports event fever

The Sydney Olympics and the need for a social charter for mega-events

C. Michael Hall

Whether it is to attract a new car factory or the Olympic Games, they go as supplicants. And, even as supplicants, they go in competition with each other: cities and localities are now fiercely struggling against each other to attract footloose and predatory investors to their particular patch. Of course, some localities are able successfully to 'switch' themselves in to the global networks, but others will remain 'unswitched' or even 'plugged'. And, in a world characterised by the increasing mobility of capital and the rapid recycling of space, even those that manage to become connected in to the global system are always vulnerable to the abrupt withdrawal of investment and to [partial] disconnection from the global system.

(Robins 1991: 35–36)

Image

Image is a key concept of the late twentieth century. Whether one is restructuring, reimaging, deconstructing, reconstructing, promoting, advertising, or just being a dedicated follower of fashion, the role of image is highly important. Sports, tourism and urban development are three areas of human endeavour in which the image has assumed vital importance. With all three we are concerned with issues of commodification, identity and the development of products to be sold in the marketplace. All three are also intimately interrelated. This chapter will be examining the nature of these relationships and the implications for urban regeneration, communities and the hosting of sports events, with special reference to the hosting of large scale sports events such as the Olympic Games, especially the Sydney 2000 Games. However, the chapter will note that while mega sports events may be glamorous to cities and spectators, their hosting may not come without a price.

Urban centres and tourism

Although urban centres have long attracted visitors, it is only in recent years that cities have consciously sought to develop, image and promote themselves in order to increase the influx of tourists (Burns *et al.* 1986; Law 1993; Page 1995; Murphy 1997; Essex and Chalkey 1998). Following the economic restructuring of many regions and the subsequent loss of heavy industry in many industrial and waterfront areas in the 1970s and 1980s, tourism has been perceived as a mechanism to regenerate urban areas through the creation of leisure, retail and tourism space. This process appears almost universal in the developed world. Such a situation lead Harvey (1988, cited in Urry 1990: 128) to ask 'How many museums, cultural centres, convention and exhibition halls, hotels, marinas, shopping malls, waterfront developments can we stand?'.

One of the primary justifications for the redevelopment of inner city areas for sports and events is the perceived economic benefits of tourism (e.g. Hall 1992; Law 1993; Page 1995). For example, in Australia the 1986/87 America's Cup Defence was used to develop Fremantle, a Commonwealth Games bid from Victoria is being used as a justification for the further redevelopment of the Melbourne Docklands; while Sydney is utilising the 2000 Olympic Games to the same effect (Hall 1998a). However, such redevelopments are not without their social and economic costs (Olds 1998). As Essex and Chalkley (1998: 195) noted:

> As a result of the traffic congestion, administrative problems, security breaches and over-commercialisation, Atlanta did not receive the kind of media attention it would ideally have liked. Its experience highlights the dangers as well as the benefits of being under the international Olympic spotlight.

Urban imaging processes are clearly significant for sport and tourism planning and development. The ramifications of such an approach are far reaching, particularly in the way in which cities are now perceived as products to be sold with the focus on the supposed economic benefits of sport and tourism reinforcing 'the idea of the city as a kind of commodity to be marketed' (Mommaas and van der Poel 1989: 264). Contemporary urban imaging strategies are typically policy responses to the social and economic problems associated with deindustrialisation and associated economic restructuring, urban renewal, multi-culturalism, social integration and control (Roche 1992, 1994). The principal aims of urban imaging strategies are to

- attract tourism expenditure;
- generate employment in the tourist industry;
- foster positive images for potential investors in the region, often by 'reimaging' previous negative perceptions; and
- provide an urban environment which will attract and retain the interest of professionals and white-collar workers, particularly in 'clean' service industries such as tourism and communications (Hall 1992).

Urban imaging processes are characterised by some or all of the following:

- the development of a critical mass of visitor attractions and facilities, including new buildings/prestige/flagship centres (e.g. shopping centres, stadia, sports complexes and indoor arenas, convention centres, casino development);
- the hosting of hallmark events (e.g. Olympic Games, Commonwealth Games, the America's Cup and the hosting of Grand Prix) and/or hosting major league sports teams;
- development of urban tourism strategies and policies often associated with new or renewed organisation and development of city marketing (e.g. 'Absolutely, Positively Wellington', Sheffield City of Steel, Cutlery and Sport); and
- development of leisure and cultural services and projects to support the marketing and tourism effort (e.g., the creation and renewal of museums and art galleries and the hosting of art festivals, often as part of a comprehensive cultural tourism strategy for a region or city).

Reimaging is intimately connected to the competition between places in a time of intense global competition for capital. According to Kotler *et al.* (1993) we are living in a time of 'place wars' in which places are competing for their economic survival with other places and regions not only in their own country but throughout the world. 'All places are in trouble now, or will be in the near future. The globalisation of the world's economy and the accelerating pace of technological changes are two forces that require all places to learn how to compete. Places must learn how to think more like businesses, developing products, markets, and customers' (Kotler *et al.* 1993: 346). Tourism is intimately connected to the place marketing process because of the way in which it is often used as a focus by government for regional redevelopment, revitalisation and promotion strategies.

Place competition occurs at international, national and regional levels and may reinforce previous competition within existing political systems, particularly federal systems. For example, of considerable significance to urban tourism and reimaging strategies in Australia has been the degree of rivalry between the New South Wales and Victorian State Governments for investment and, hence, the generation of economic growth and employment. This rivalry is typically concentrated on attracting investment to the two state capitals of Sydney and Melbourne and is illustrated by the aggressive competition that exists for the hosting of events and the urban redevelopment and reimaging programs which have been established for both cities. For example, Melbourne's unsuccessful bid for the 1996 Olympic Games was followed by Sydney's successful bid for the 2000 Summer Olympics. In the case of Melbourne, the bid was tied to the redevelopment of the Melbourne Dockland area, while the key feature of the Sydney bid was the redevelopment of the former industrial site and waste dump at Homebush Bay on Sydney Harbour as the main Games stadium complex. In both cities the bidding for events by state governments has been integrated into the development of new cultural, leisure and tourism policies which focus on attracting visitors to the city and broader urban redevelopment programs which seek to develop cultural, housing, leisure and entertainment complexes in waterfront areas (Hall and Hamon 1996).

Event tourism

Short-term staged attractions or hallmark events have been a major component of the growth of tourism in Australia in the past decade. Hallmark tourist events, otherwise referred to as mega (Ritchie and Yangzhou 1987) or special events (Burns *et al.* 1986) are major festivals, expositions, cultural and sporting events which are held on either a regular or a one-off basis. Hallmark events have assumed a key role in international, national and regional tourism marketing strategies, their primary function being to provide the host community with an opportunity to secure high prominence in the tourism market place for a short, well defined, period of time (Ritchie 1984; Hall 1992).

The hallmark event is different in its appeal from the attractions normally promoted by the tourist industry as it is not a continuous or seasonal phenomenon. Indeed, in many cases the hallmark event is a strategic response to the problems that seasonal variations in demand pose for the tourist industry. Although the ability of an event 'to achieve this objective depends on the uniqueness of the event, the status of the event, and the extent to which it is successfully marketed within tourism generated regions' (Ritchie 1984: 2).

Events can help construct a positive image and help build commercial and public awareness of a destination through the media coverage which they generate (e.g. Tourism Victoria 1997a, b). For example, South Australia has for many years been known as 'The Festival State' to many Australians because of the success of the bi-annual Adelaide Festival of Arts, an image which has been reinforced by the hosting of the Adelaide Grand Prix and associated activities. More recently, Victoria has been aggressively promoting itself as the event state, with Tourism Victoria (1997b) reporting that its research indicates that it is now recognised as the Australian city which hosts major international sporting and cultural events, ahead of Sydney, Adelaide, Brisbane and Perth.

The positive image which events are able to portray to the public, and the media exposure they offer, probably explains the lengths to which governments and politicians will compete to host major national and international events. Australian examples include, the bidding process by which cities and State Governments competed for the right to host the 1996 and 2000 Olympic Games, the competition between Victoria and New South Wales to host the Australian Motorcycling Grand Prix, and the conflict between Victoria and South Australia over the hosting of the Australian Formula One Grand Prix. Such is the extent of interstate rivalry that nearly all State Governments have now established specific event units to assist in the bidding for major sporting and cultural events (e.g. Tourism Victoria 1997a, b). The extent to which imaging strategies influences the hosting of events is illustrated in the case of Eventscorp, the events unit of the Western Australian Tourism Commission, which uses the following criteria in assessing the viability of events:

- A targeted return of $7 economic impact generated by the event to each $1 of Eventscorp funding.
- A dollar-for-dollar private sector financial support to complement government funding.

- Significant identifiable national and international media exposure.
- The utilisation of existing infrastructure, tourism and sporting facilities, and the development of additional facilities when appropriate.

(Western Australian Tourism Commission 1992: 23)

Given the large sums of money involved and the potential for high media profile it is therefore not surprising that the analysis of the impact of events is also often highly political not only between government parties but between the government and public interest groups. For example, there has been substantial debate over the economic benefits of the Qantas Australian Formula One Grand Prix. According to Tourism Victoria (1997a: 24), the 1996 Grand Prix 'was watched by an estimated overseas audience of more than 300 million people. Total attendance at the race was 289,000 over the four days ... An independent assessment of the 1996... Grand Prix indicated that it provided a gross economic benefit to the Victorian economy of $95.6 million and created 2,270 full year equivalent jobs'. In contrast, a thorough evaluation of the 1996 Grand Prix by Economists at Large and Associates (1997) for the Save the Albert Park Group concluded that the claim of $95.6 million of extra expenditure was

1   ... a misrepresentation of the size of the economic benefit
2   claimed gross benefits are overstated or non-existent, and
3   ironically, compared to what might have been achieved, Victorians are poorer where they could have been wealthier, if the government had chosen a more 'boring' investment than the Grand Prix.

(Economists at Large and Associates 1997: 8)

The amount of local involvement and the actions of government in the planning of events would appear to be crucial to deriving the maximum benefit from hosting an event for the host community. The more an event is seen by the impacted public as emerging from the local community, rather than being imposed on them, the greater will be that community's acceptance of the event. However, the international dimension of many events will often mean that national and regional governments will assume responsibility for the event's planning. Because of the interests and stakeholders that impact upon upper levels of government, local concerns may well be lost in the search for the national or regional good with special legislation often being enacted to minimise disturbance to the hosting of an event. The short timeframe in which Governments and industry have to react to the hosting of events may lead to 'fast track planning', where proposals are pushed through the planning process without the normal economic, social and environmental assessment procedures being applied.

Hughes (1993: 157, 159) observed that 'the Olympics may be of particular significance in relation to the "inner city" problems that beset many urban areas of Europe and N[orth] America' and noted that Manchester's bid for the 2000 Summer Olympics was seen as a possible contribution to solving some of the city's 'inner city problems'. Indeed, it is the inherent belief that the Olympics or other mega events will attract tourism and investment because of the improved image and promotion of a place which serves to justify redevelopment, often with large investments of public funds and with the suspension of normal planning practice.

A classic example of the failure of governments to give adequate attention to the broad impacts of hallmark events is Sydney's hosting of the 2000 Summer Olympics. The bid for the Games had more to do with Sydney and state (New South Wales) politics than a rational assessment of the economic and tourism benefits of hosting the Games. As research on large scale events such as the Olympics or World Fairs has indicated, the net costs of the event often tend to far outweigh any net benefits, except in terms of potential political and economic benefits for urban élites (Hall 1992). The Sydney Games appears designed more to assist with urban redevelopment and imaging than it is with concern over the spread of social, economic and environmental impacts (Hall and Hodges 1996). Furthermore, there is a possibility that the hosting of the Olympic Games may actually serve to dissuade rather than encourage some visitor arrivals. As Leiper and Hall (1993: 2) observed in their submission to the House of Representatives' Standing Committee on Industry, Science and Technology Inquiry into Implications for Australian Industry Arising from the Year 2000 Olympics:

> A major outcome could be that the 'tourist boom' imagined by many commentators might be just that – imagination. The Olympics will attract certain types of tourists, but it will certainly repel other tourists who, in normal circumstances, would have visited Sydney and other regions of Australia. The net effect could be negative. Other Australian cities would not be more attractive as venues for the Olympics, but would certainly be less repulsive in this respect. Thus, in terms of tourism related benefits, Sydney is not the best place in Australia for the Olympics and Australian tourism is at risk because this city will be the host. Moreover, there is no certainty that publicity around the Olympics, broadcast internationally about Australia, will lead to any significant increase in inbound tourism in the months and years afterwards,

While these arguments were dismissed by the Australian Tourist Commission as being 'rather light' and 'unsubstantiated', it is interesting to note that Tony Thirlwell, Chief Executive Officer of Tourism New South Wales, confirmed that there was a need for some 'reality checks' to be brought home to New South Wales in the light of the Atlanta Olympics experience.

> The simple fact that people travel to Olympic Games for sports events cannot be overstated. … Zoo Atlanta, Six Flags Over Georgia and other attractions … suffered adversely because of the Olympic Games. Revenue losses were caused by Olympic distortion of attractions usual visitation patterns and by costs of their attempts to leverage off the Olympics.
>
> (Thirlwell 1997: 5)

Nevertheless, the expectations for the Olympics are high. According to Tourism New South Wales (1997a: 1), 'an extra 2.1 million overseas tourists are expected between 1994 and 2004 – A \$4 billion tourism boost', while the Games are also regarded as important in increasing the exposure of Sydney in the international media and contributing to the ability of the Sydney Convention and Visitors Bureau to win major international conferences. In addition, Tourism New South Wales (1997b: 9) reported the results of a survey which indicated that outside Sydney '39 per cent of respondents said they would definitely or probably travel to Sydney for the event' with the survey also finding 'that 73 per cent of Sydneysiders were interested in attending Games events'.

Despite both the overt and 'hidden' costs of hosting events substantial gains can be made through event tourism if strategies are carefully considered, appropriate strategies developed and there is meaningful consultation with affected stake-holders. However, unfortunately, this is rarely the case.

The Sydney 2000 Games

Until the recent confirmation of long alleged (Simson and Jennings 1992) corrup-tion and scandal within the International Olympic Committee (Evans 1999; Magnay 1999; Stevens and Lehmann 1999; Washington 1999), the success of the Sydney 2000 Olympic bid has been highly regarded by much of the Australian media and certain quarters of government and industry as having the potential to provide a major economic boost to the New South Wales and Sydney economy. The initial economic impact study undertaken for the New South Wales (NSW) Government by KPMG Peat Marwick suggested that the net economic impacts as a result of hosting the Games would be between \$4,093 million and \$4,790 million, and between \$3,221 million and \$3,747 million for Sydney (KPMG Peat Marwick 1993). More recently, a report by the accounting firm Arthur Andersen undertaken in conjunction with the Centre for Regional Economic Analysis at the University of Tasmania stated that the Olympics would generate a total of \$6.5 billion in extra economic activity in Australia from 1994–95 to 2005–06 with \$5.1 billion of this activity occurring in NSW. The report also indicated that the NSW government would collect about \$250 million in extra tax revenue against official government estimates of \$602 million. The State Treasurer, Mr. Egan, described the significance of the gap as 'an academic exercise' that would not affect the NSW budgetary position (Power 1999: 9). In addition, in January 1999 the NSW Auditor-General, Tony Harris, calculated the readily quantifiable cost to the state government of hosting the Olympics at \$2.3billion, which was approximately \$700 million above the \$1.6 billion figure included in the 1998 state budget. Presumably, the greatest benefit of the Olympics is seen in terms of employment with the Arthur Andersen report noted earlier, stating that the Olympics will create 5,300 jobs in NSW and 7,500 jobs Australia-wide over a 12-year period (Power 1999). However, the present author's calculations would suggest that this is still an expensive job creation exercise.

From its earliest stages the political nature of planning and decision-making associated with the Sydney Olympics was quite clear (political in the sense that politics is about who gets what, where, why and how). As with any mega-event, much, if not all, of these planning decisions will have substantial implications for the longer-term economic and social development of the city and the region. For example, the state government passed legislation in 1995 with respect to the Sydney Olympics to assist in the development and regeneration of projects associated with the Games. This was achieved at the cost of the people of Sydney losing their rights of appeal to initiate a court appeal under environment and planning legislation against the proposed Olympic projects. The location and dealings of the amendment were far from being open and honest. As Mr. Johnston of the Environmental Defenders' Office commented, 'this amendment is buried on page 163 of the threatened species legislation…. not a bill where you would find such a change, and you have to wonder why they put it there' (Totaro 1995: 1).

Further legislation passed under the New South Wales Government's *Olympic Co-ordination Authority Act* allows, somewhat ironically given the green image which was an integral part of the Games bid (Sydney Organising Committee for the Olympic Games (SOCOG) 1996), all projects linked with the Games to be suspended from the usual Environmental Impact Statements requirements. These changes are expected to affect all the areas involved with Olympic activities (Totaro 1995). Unfortunately, however, the same reasons which propel cities to stage large scale tourist events (i.e. redevelopment, dramatic urban development) and also to fast-track the planning process, 'are also the some of the very factors which result in an adverse affect on residents in cities in which they are held' (Wilkinson 1994: 28).

In the case of the Sydney Olympics at least the need to consider the environmental dimensions of the Games did receive attention. In contrast, the socio-cultural dimensions of the Games were not an issue in the bidding process, except to the extent in which the different cultures of Australia could be used to promote an image which might see the bid attempt succeed. According to the Sydney Olympics 2000 Bid Limited (SOB) (1992: 19):

> With the dawn of the new millennium, the peoples of the earth will look to the Olympic Movement for renewed inspiration. Sydney's cultural program for the 2000 Olympic Games will celebrate, above all, our shared humanity and the eternal goals of peace, harmony and understanding so sought amongst the peoples of the world.

Indeed, one of the objectives of the cultural program is to 'foster awareness and international understanding of the world's indigenous cultures, some of which have survived from earliest times, and to promote especially, a knowledge and appreciation of the unique culture of the Australian Aboriginal peoples' (SOB 1992: 19). It is therefore ironic that the Australian federal government has been trying to alter native title legislation in order to extinguish some Aboriginal claims to pastoral leases. This action is already leading to suggestions that some Australian Aboriginal groups may call on some African and South Pacific nations to boycott the Games in order to attempt to improve the human and land rights position of Aborigines (Sydney 2000 Olympic Games News 1997). While such a boycott is potentially significant, other social dimensions of the hosting of mega-events may have more immediate impacts on certain sections of the host community.

The housing and real estate dimensions of mega-events

Mega-events which involve substantial infrastructure development may have a considerable impact on housing and real estate values, particularly with respect to their 'tendency to displace groups of citizens located in the poorer sections of cities' (Wilkinson 1994: 29). The people who are often most impacted by hallmark events are typically those who are least able to form community groups and protect their interests. At worst, this tends to lead to a situation in which residents are forced to relocate because of their economic circumstances (Hall 1994; Olds 1998).

In a study of the potential impacts of the Sydney Olympics on low-income housing, Cox *et al.* (1994) concluded that previous mega-events often had a detrimental effect on low income people who are disadvantaged by a localised boom in rent and real estate prices, thereby creating dislocation in extreme cases. The same rise in prices is considered beneficial to home owners and developers. Past events have also shown that this has lead to public and private lower-cost housing developments being pushed out of preferred areas as a result of increased land and construction costs (e.g. Cox *et al.* 1994; Olds 1998). In the case of the Barcelona Games 'the market price of old and new housing rose between 1986 and 1992 by 240% and 287% respectively' (Brunet 1993 in Wilkinson 1994: 23). A further 59,000 residents left Barcelona to live elsewhere between the years of 1984 and 1992 (Brunet 1993 in Cox *et al.* 1994).

In relation to Australia, past mega-events have lead to:

- increased rentals;
- increased conversion of boarding houses to tourist accommodation;
- accelerating gentrification of certain suburbs near where major events are held; and
- a tendency for low income renters to be forced out of their homes (Hall and Hodges 1996).

Studies of previous events also indicate that an inadequate level of prevention policies and measure was developed to ameliorate the effects of hosting mega-events on the low-income and poor sectors of the community. The pattern that has occurred from past events therefore has very real and serious implications for the hosting of the 2000 Games. Nevertheless, despite the increasing concern and attention being given to resulting social impacts caused by hosting mega-events such as the Olympics (Olds 1988, 1989; 1998; Cox *et al.* 1994), and the undertaking of such a study with the previous Melbourne bid to host the 1996 Summer Games (Olympic Games Social Impact Assessment Steering Committee 1989), no social impact study was undertaken by the Sydney bid team during the bidding process. This may be considered as somewhat surprising given the potential impact of the Sydney 2000 Olympics and associated site development on housing and real estate values in the Sydney region. After the bid was won, a comprehensive housing and social impact study was carried out by Cox *et al.* (1994). The housing report also presented a number of recommendations that could be implemented as a positive strategy to ameliorate such impacts in relation to the preparation and hosting of the Sydney Games. However, this study was undertaken for low-income housing interests not the state Government or the Sydney Olympic organisation.

Since the announcement in September 1993 that Sydney would be the Olympic 2000 host city, an increasing number of developments have commenced in the traditional inner west industrial suburbs near the main Games site at Homebush Bay, while the Olympics has also assisted in giving new impetus to the Darling Harbour development. In the municipalities of Leichhardt, Ashfield, Drummoyne, Burwood, Concord and Strathfield an increasing number of apartment projects are being built in an area known as the 'Olympic corridor'. The increase of residential activity is having a significant effect on the housing areas located through the Olympic corridor with one of the main outcomes sought by real estate interests being to 'raise the profile of this area and create demand for residential accommodation' (Ujdur 1993: 1).

Recent housing developments have indicated a movement towards the 'gentrification' of many of the inner western suburbs of Sydney by white-collar professionals and a move away by lower income earners from the traditional low income areas as higher income households are targeted. The Olympics is therefore greatly accelerating existing socio-economic processes. As a result, the cost of private housing is increasing in the inner west region in particular and throughout the metropolitan area in general. The potential for problems to occur is heightened by the fact that many of the tenants in these areas are on Commonwealth (federal government) benefits for unemployment, sickness, disability and aged persons, and, more often than not, are single people (Coles 1994). It is these people who will suffer as the prices of houses and rentals increase in their 'traditional' cheaper housing areas forcing them to relocate in extreme cases.

Approximately 20 per cent of Sydney residents rent accommodation, yet Sydney is already facing a 'rental squeeze' as the shortage of rental properties continues to increase along with a rise in rentals. The situation worsened significantly throughout 1995, and church leaders and welfare groups expect the situation to get more desperate as the Olympics approaches (Russel 1995). Although the Sydney Olympics were four years away, by early 1996 housing impacts, such as increasing rental and real estate prices, had clearly begun to emerge in specific areas of Sydney. Indeed, as has been stated in the Sydney media: 'As the revitalisation of the inner city continues and is hastened by the Olympics, it is expected that the problem of homelessness will be exacerbated' (Coles 1994: 15). As the redevelopment for the Games continues, the Homeless Centre predicts that 'the greatest potential negative impact of the Sydney 2000 Olympics will be those living in low cost accommodation' (Coles 1994: 2).

A number of means are available for protecting and monitoring the effect of the Games on low-income residents (Hall 1992; Cox *et al.* 1994). The main options include:

- the establishment of a housing impact monitoring committee;
- development of an Olympics accommodation strategy;

- tougher legislation to protect tenants and prevent arbitrary evictions;
- provision of public housing and emergency accommodation for disabled people; and
- a form of rent control.

Despite intensive lobbying from housing, welfare and social groups the State and Commonwealth Governments have failed to act on the significant housing and community issues which have emerged. One likely reason for this is that the Olympic concerns of government have been concentrated more on the development of Olympic facilities and infrastructure and, more recently, the potential implications of the IOC scandal on both the image of the Games and any possible effect on the ability of the Sydney Games to raise commercial sponsorship (Riley 1999). Furthermore, a change in government at the federal level from the middle-ground Labor Party to the right-wing Liberal-National Party coalition, has meant that national financial assistance to the New South Wales Government for low-income housing and urban redevelopment and infrastructure projects has all but dried up (Hall and Hodges 1996). However, the political reality of the Olympics is that the social impacts of the Games are not an issue.

Share the spirit. And the winner is…? (SOCOG brochure, n.d.)

Despite claims to the contrary from the Olympic movement about the social value of the 'Olympic spirit', the Games are more about the spirit of corporatism than the spirit of a community. The Olympics are not symbolic of a public life or culture which is accessible to all local citizens (Hall 1999). The Sydney Olympics, along with the event and casino driven economy of the State of Victoria and the other Australian states, are representative of the growth of corporatist politics in Australia and the subsequent treatment of a city as a product to be packaged, marketed and sold, and in which opinion polls are a substitute for public participation in the decision-making process. Nevertheless, as Smyth (1984: 258) has recognised 'for sustenance of the urban economy and future livelihoods, it may also be necessary to first promote the project to the local population'. A tentative conclusion of this analysis is that local authorities and initiators fear local reactions, and so try to avoid them. This begins to induce two consequences:

- an inability to listen, understand and respond to local needs, in other words, reinforcing the move away from serving towards political and economic control and power; and
- an open invitation to move further towards governance and away from government, in other words, away from accountability and towards implicit secrecy.

In the case of the Sydney Olympic bid the former Premier and key member of the bid team, Nick Greiner, argued that 'The secret of the success was undoubtedly the creation of a community of interest, not only in Sydney, but across the nation, unprecedented in our peacetime history' (1994: 13). The description of a 'community of interest' is extremely apt, as such a phrase indicates the role of the interests of growth coalitions in mega-event proposals (Hall 1997). The Sydney media played a critical role in creating the climate for the bid. As Greiner stated:

> Early in 1991, I invited senior media representatives to the premier's office, told them frankly that a bid could not succeed if the media played their normal 'knocking role' and that I was not prepared to commit the taxpayers' money unless I had their support. Both News Ltd and Fairfax subsequently went out of their way to ensure the bid received fair, perhaps even favourable, treatment. The electronic media also joined in the sense of community purpose (1994: 13).

Greiner's statement begs the question of 'which community?'. Certainly, the lack of adequate social and housing impact assessment prior to the Games' bid and post 'winning' the Games, indicates the failure of growth coalitions to recognise that there may well be negative impacts on some sections of the community. Forever, in terms of the real estate constituency of growth coalitions such considerations are not in their economic interest. Those which are most impacted are clearly the ones least able to affect the policy making and planning processes surrounding the Games (Hall 1997). The perceived 'need' by some interests for the tourism and associated economic developments of hosting an Olympic Games, creates 'a political and economic context within which the hallmark event is used as an excuse to overrule planning legislation and participatory planning processes, and to sacrifice local places along the way' (Dovey 1989: 79–80). For example, it took the NSW Government and the Australian Olympic Committee eight years to release one of the major confidential documents outlining the terms and conditions under which NSW taxpayers through the government are responsible for funding Sydney's bid, building venues and meeting all costs associated with the Games (Moore 1999). It is only now that the IOC scandal has broken that the Australian commercial media is investigating the bidding process (e.g. Moore *et al.* 1999), but it is now too late. The recently released contract noted above states: 'The State and the city will not permit the [organising committee] to cancel the staging of the Games for any reason whatsoever, including *force majeure*' (Moore 1999: 7).

In focusing on one narrow set of commercial, economic and political interests in the pursuit of major sporting events such as the Olympics, other community and social interests, particularly those of inner-city residents, are increasingly neglected (Hall 1992, 1994). However, this is something which has been known for a relatively long time, but do we learn from it?

Toronto: 'the biggest and most costly mega-project in the history of Toronto'

Toronto is making a bid to host the 2008 Summer Olympic Games. Toronto's bid, as with its previously unsuccessful bid for the 1996 Games, is built on a waterfront redevelopment strategy which seeks to revitalise the harbour area through the development of an integrated sports, leisure, retail and housing complex. However, as in the case of Sydney, or in any other mega-event with substantial infrastructure requirements, substantial questions can be asked about the process by which the event has been developed and as to who actually benefits from hosting the event.

One of the most striking features of the new Toronto bid is the extent to which information on the bid is either unavailable or provides only limited detail on the costs associated with hosting the event. However, unlike the Sydney Olympic bid, Toronto has been fortunate to have a non-profit public interest coalition, Bread Not Circuses (BNC), actively campaigning for more information on the bid proposal and for government to address social concerns.

BNC argue that given the cost of both bidding for and hosting the Olympics, the bidding process must be subject to public scrutiny. 'Any Olympic bid worth its salt will not only withstand public scrutiny, but will be improved by a rigorous and open public process' (Bread Not Circuses 1998a), and also argued that Toronto City Council should make its support for an Olympic bid conditional on:

- the development and execution of a suitable process that addresses financial, social and environmental concerns, ensures an effective public participation process (including intervenor funding), and includes a commitment to the development of a detailed series of Olympic standards. A time-frame of one year from the date of the vote to support the bid should be set to ensure that the plans for the participation process are taken seriously;
- a full and open independent accounting of the financial costs of bidding and staging the Games;
- a full and open independent social impact assessment of the Games.

The other key elements of a public participation process include:

- a full, fair and democratic process to involve all of the people of Toronto in the development and review of the Olympic bid;
- an Olympic Intervenor Fund, similar to the fund established by the City of Toronto in 1989, to allow interested groups to participate effectively in the public scrutiny of the Toronto bid;
- an independent environmental assessment of the 2008 Games, and strategies should be developed to resolve specific concerns;
- the development of a series of financial, social and environmental standards governing the 2008 Games, similar to the Toronto Olympic Commitment adopted by City Council in September of 1989 (Bread Not Circuses, 1998a).

In addition to the factors identified by BNC, it should also be noted that the city's previous experiences with stadia and events raise substantial questions about the public liability for any development. For example, in 1982, the then Metropolitan Toronto Chairman Paul Godfrey promised that Toronto's Sky Dome, a multipurpose sports complex used for baseball and Canadian football, could be built for CAN$75 million with no public debt. However, the final price of the development was over

CAN$600 million, with taxpayers having to pay more than half. BNC also noted that even the previous Toronto bid costs were 60 per cent over budget, 'with a great deal of spending coming in the final, overheated days of the bidding war leading up to the International Olympic Committee (IOC) Congress. There was no public control, and little public accountability, over the '96 bid', while 'There was virtually no assessment of the social, environmental and financial impact of the Games until Bread Not Circuses began to raise critical questions. By then, it was too late to influence the bid' (Bread Not Circuses 1998c).

BNC lobbied various city councillors about their decision of whether or not to support a bid. However, only one councillor out of 55 voted against the Olympic bid proposal even though they only had a 20 page background document to the proposal in terms of information. When city councillors voted on the project, they did not have:

- an estimate of the cost of bidding for the Games;
- a list of the names of the backers of 'BidCo', the private corporation that is heading up the Olympic bid;
- a reliable estimate of the cost of staging the Games;
- a plan for the public participation process, the environmental review process or the social impact assessment process;
- a detailed financial strategy for the Games.

Such a situation clearly has public interest organisations, such has BNC, very worried as to the economic, environmental and social costs of a successful bid. Clearly, the history of mega events such as the Olympic Games indicates that such a situation is not new (Olds 1998). In the case of the International Olympic Committee (IOC) they have already sought to ensure that the Games are environmentally friendly, perhaps it is now time to see that they are socially and economically friendly and build wider assessment of the social impacts of the Games into the planning process as a mandatory component of the bidding process. In this vein BNC, in a letter to the IOC President has requested 'that the IOC, which sets the rules for the bidding process, take an active responsibility in ensuring that the local processes in the bidding stage are effective and democratic' and specifically addresses concerns regarding the 'financial and social costs of the Olympic Games' and proposed:

1 an international network be created that includes COHRE, the HIC Housing Rights Subcommittee, academics, NGOs (including local groups in cities that have bid for and/or hosted the Games);
2 a set of standards regarding forced evictions, etc., would be developed and adopted by the network;
3 a plan to build international support for the standards, including identification of sympathetic IOC, NOC and other sports officials, would be developed and implemented;

> 4 the IOC would be approached with the request that the standards be incorpo-
> rated into the Olympic Charter, Host City Contracts and other documents
> of the IOC (Bread Not Circuses 1998b).

Such a social charter for the Olympics would undoubtedly greatly assist in making
the Games more place friendly and perhaps even improve the image of the IOC.
However, as at the time of concluding this paper, the books of the Toronto bid
have still not been opened for public scrutiny. Nor has there been any response to
the proposal for creation of a set of social standards for the Olympics.

A new basis for mega-events and imaging strategies

Undoubtedly, there will be some positive benefits arising from the hosting of the
Olympics. Any event of an Olympic size with its associated spending on infrastructure must have some trickle-down and flow-on effects. However, broader
issues over the most appropriate long-term economic, social, environmental, and
tourism strategies have not been adequately considered, while the most effective
distribution of costs and benefits through the community is all but ignored. Indeed,
a substantial case could be put forward that the Olympics has in fact deflected
Sydney's planners and developers away from the longer term to concentrate on
the target year 2000 (Hall 1997). The irony is that government, which is meant to
be serving the public interest, is instead concentrating its interests on entrepreneurial and corporate rather than broader social goals.

The revitalisation of place requires more than just the development of product
and image. The recreation of a sense of place is a process which involves the
formulation of urban design strategies based on conceptual models of the city
which are, in turn, founded on notions of civic life and the public realm and the
idea of planning as debate and argument (Bianchini and Schwengel 1991). As
Smyth (1994: 254) has recognised:

> This needs to be undertaken in a frank way and in a forum where different
> understandings can be shared, inducing mutual respect, leading to developing
> trust, and finally conceiving a development which meets mutual needs as
> well as stewarding resources for future generations... This proposes a serious
> challenge to the public sector as well as to the private sector, for authorities
> have undermined the well-being of their local populations by transferring
> money away from services to pay for flagship developments ...

Unfortunately, such models have only limited visibility within the place marketing
and tourism realms as tourism and place planning is often poorly conceptualised
with respect to participatory procedures, while the institutional arrangements for
many of the public-private partnerships for urban redevelopment actually exclude
community participation in decision-making procedures (Hall 1999).

Policy visions, whether they be for places, sport or for tourism, typically fail to
be developed in the light of oppositional or critical viewpoints. Place visions tend

to be developed through the activities of industry experts rather than the broad populace. Perhaps because the vision of the wider public for a place may not be the same as some segments of business. Community involvement is undertaken through opinion polls, surveys or SWOT analyses rather than through participatory measures. Unfortunately, it is likely that the same mistakes will be made again.

References

Bianchini, F. and Schwengel, H. (1991) 'Re-imagining the City', in J. Corner and S. Harvey (eds), *Enterprise and Heritage: Crosscurrents of National Culture*, pp. 212–234. London: Routledge.

Bread Not Circuses (1998a) *Bread Alert!* (E-mail edition) 2(2) February 20.

Bread Not Circuses (1998b) *Bread Alert!* (E-mail edition) 2(3) February 26.

Bread Not Circuses (1998c) *Bread Alert!* (E-mail edition) 2(8) April 8.

Bread Not Circuses (1999) *The REAL Olympic Scandal: The Financial and Social Costs of the Games*. Media Advisory March 17.

Burns, J.P.A., Hatch, J.H. and Mules, F.J. (1986) (eds), *The Adelaide Grand Prix: The Impact of a Special Event*. Adelaide: The Centre for South Australian Economic Studies.

Coles, S. (1994) *Submission to the Preliminary Social Impact Assessment of The Sydney Olympics*. Sydney: The Homeless Persons Information Centre.

Cox, G., Darcy, M. and Bounds, M. (1994) *The Olympics and Housing: A Study of Six International Events and Analysis of Potential Impacts*. Sydney: University of Western Sydney

Dovey, K. (1989) 'Old Scabs/New Scares: the Hallmark Event and the Everyday Environment', in G.J. Syme, B.J. Shaw, D.M. Fenton and W.S. Mueller (eds), *The Planning and Evaluation of Hallmark Events*, pp. 73–88. Aldershot: Avebury.

Economists At Large (1997) *Grand Prixtensions: The Economics of the Magic Pudding*, prepared for the Save Albert Park Group. Melbourne: Economists At Large.

Essex, S. and Chalkey, B. (1998) 'Olympic Games: Catalyst of Urban Change'. *Leisure Studies*, Vol. 17(3): pp. 187–206.

Evans, M. (1999) 'Sydney Linked to IOC Crisis'. *Sydney Morning Herald*, 22 January, pp. 1, 9.

Greiner, N. (1994) 'Inside Running on Olympic bid'. *The Australian*, 19 September, p. 13.

Hall, C.M. (1992) *Hallmark Tourist Events: Impacts, Management and Planning*, Chichester: John Wiley.

Hall, C.M. (1994) *Tourism and Politics: Policy, Power and Place*. Chichester: John Wiley.

Hall, C.M. (1997) 'Mega-Events and Their Legacies', in P. Murphy (ed.), *Quality Management in Urban Tourism*, pp. 75–87. Chichester: John Wiley and Sons.

Hall, C.M. (1998a) *Introduction to Tourism: Development, Dimensions and Issues*. South Melbourne: Addison Wesley Longman.

Hall, C.M. (1998b) 'The Politics of Decision Making and Top-Down Planning: Darling Harbour, Sydney', in D. Tyler, M. Robertson and Y. Guerrier (eds), *Tourism Management in Cities: Policy, Process and Practice*. Chichester: John Wiley and Sons.

Hall, C.M. (1999) *Tourism Planning*. Harlow: Addison-Wesley Longman.

Hall, C.M. and Hamon, C. (1996) 'Casinos and Urban Redevelopment in Australia'. *Journal of Travel Research*, Vol. 34(3), pp. 30–36.

Hall, C.M. and Hodges, J. (1996) 'The Party's Great, but What About the Hangover? The Housing and Social Impacts of Mega-Events with Special Reference to the Sydney 2000 Olympics'. *Festival Management and Event Tourism*, Vol. 4(1/2), pp. 13–20.

Harvey, D. (1989a) *The Condition of Postmodernity*. Oxford: Blackwell.

Harvey, D. (1989b) 'From Managerialism to Entrepreneurialism: the Transformation of Urban Governance in Late Capitalism'. *Geografiska Annaler*, Vol. 71(B/1): pp. 3–17.

Hughes, H.L. (1993) 'Olympic Tourism and Urban Regeneration'. *Festival Management and Event Tourism*, Vol. 1(4): pp. 157–159.

Kotler, P., Haider, D.H. and Rein, I. (1993) *Marketing Places: Attracting Investment, Industry, and Tourism to Cities, States, and Nations*. New York: The Free Press.

KMPG Peat Marwick (1993) *Sydney Olympics 2000 Economic Impact Study*, 2 vols. Sydney Olympics 2000 Bid Ltd, Sydney, NSW, in association with Centre for South Australian Economic Studies. Sydney: Sydney Olympics 2000 Bid.

Law, C.M. (1993) *Urban Tourism: Attracting Visitors to Large Cities*. London: Mansell.

Leiper, N. and Hall, C.M. (1993) *The 2000 Olympics and Australia's Tourism Industries*, submission to House of Representatives' Standing Committee on Industry, Science and Technology Inquiry into Implications for Australian Industry Arising from the Year 2000 Olympics, Southern Cross University/University of Canberra, Lismore/Canberra.

Magnay, J. (1999) 'Games Scandals Hit Melbourne 2006 bid'. *The Age*, 21 January, pp. 1, 2.

Mommaas, H. and van der Poel, H. (1989) 'Changes in Economy, Politics and Lifestyles: an essay on the Restructuring of Urban Leisure', in P. Bramham, I. Henry, H. Mommaas and H. van der Poel (eds), *Leisure and Urban Processes: Critical Studies of Leisure Policy in Western European Cities*, pp. 254–276. London: Routledge.

Moore, M. (1999) 'Contract puts burden on taxpayers'. *Sydney Morning Herald*, 23 January, p. 7.

Moore, M., Evans, M. and Korporall, G. (1999) 'Sydney 2000 chiefs told: Lift the lid'. *Sydney Morning Herald*, 6 February: pp. 1, 7.

Murphy, P.E. (1997) (ed.), *Quality Management in Urban Tourism*. International Western Geographical Series. Chichester: John Wiley and Sons.

Olds, K. (1988) 'Planning for the Housing Impacts of a Hallmark Event: a Case Study of Expo 1986', unpublished MA thesis. Vancouver: School of Community and Regional Planning, University of British Columbia.

Olds, K. (1989) 'Mass Evictions in Vancouver: the Human Toll of Expo '86'. *Canadian Housing*, Vol. 6(1), pp. 49–53.

Olds, K. (1998) 'The Housing Impacts of Mega-Events'. *Current Issues in Tourism* 1(1):??

Olympic Games Social Impact Assessment Steering Committee (1989) *Social Impact Assessment Olympic Games Bid Melbourne 1996*, report to the Victorian Government an the City of Melbourne. Melbourne: Olympic Games Social Impact Assessment Steering Committee.

Page, S. (1995) *Urban Tourism*. Routledge, London.

Patterson, E. and Hagan, J. (1988) *First Australian Masters Games: Analysis Appraisal*. Hobart: Tasmanian Department of Sport and Recreation.

Power, B. (1999) '$350m tax jolt just "academic" says Egan'. *Sydney Morning Herald*, 22 January, p. 9.

Riley, M. (1999) 'Scandal a costly blow to funding for Games'. *Sydney Morning Herald*, 23 January, p. 7.

Ritchie, J.B.R. and Yangzhou, H. (1987) 'The Role and Impact of Mega-Events and Attractions on National and Regional Tourism: a Conceptual and Methodological Overview', Paper prepared for presentation at the 37th Annual Congress of the International Association of Scientific Experts in Tourism (AIEST), Calgary, Canada.

Ritchie, J.B.R. (1984) 'Assessing the Impact of Hallmark Events: Conceptual and Research Issues'. *Journal of Travel Research*, Vol. 23(1), pp. 2–11.

Robins, K. (1991) 'Tradition and Translation: National Culture in its Global Context', in J. Corner and S. Harvey (eds), *Enterprise and Heritage: Crosscurrents of National Culture*, pp. 21–44. London: Routledge.

Roche, M. (1992) 'Mega-Events and Micro-Modernization: on the Sociology of the New Urban Tourism'. *British Journal of Sociology*, Vol. 43(4), pp. 563–600.

Roche, M. (1994) Mega-Events and Urban Policy. *Annals of Tourism Research*, Vol. 21(1), pp. 1–19.

Russel, M. (1995) 'Plea for action as rent squeeze tightens'. *Sydney Morning Herald*, 20 September, p. 2.

Simson, V. and Jennings, A. (1992) *The Lords of the Rings: Power, Money and Drugs in the Modern Olympics*. London: Simon and Schuster.

Smyth, H. (1994) *Marketing the City: The Role of Flagship Developments in Urban Regeneration*. London: E&FN Spon.

Stevens, M. and Lehmann, J. (1999) 'IOC purge starts race for reform'. *The Australian*, 26 December: p. 1.

Sydney 2000 Olympic Games News (1997) 'Aboriginal activist Michael Mansell suggests that some nations could boycott the games'. *Sydney 2000 Olympic Games News*, 8 February, http://www.gwb.au/gwb/news/olympic/080927.html

Sydney Olympics 2000 Bid Limited (1992) *Fact Sheets: a Presentation of the Bid by the City of Sydney to Host the Games of the XXVII Olympiad in the Year 2000*. Sydney: Sydney Olympics 2000 Bid Limited.

Sydney Organising Committee for the Olympic Games (SOCOG) (1996) *Environmental Guidelines*. Sydney: SOCOG.

Thirlwell, T. (1997) 'Atlanta Revisited'. *Tourism Now*, Vol. 25 (April), p. 5.

Totaro, P. (1995) 'Olympic opponents denied sporting chance'. *Sydney Morning Herald*, December 16, p. 1.

Tourism New South Wales (1997a) *Sydney 2000: Tourism and the 2000 Games Fact Sheet*. Sydney: Tourism New South Wales.

Tourism New South Wales (1997b) 'Olympic Visitor Boost'. *News*, Spring, p. 9.

Tourism Victoria (1997a) *Annual Report 1996–97*. Melbourne: Tourism Victoria.

Tourism Victoria (1997b) *Strategic Business Plan 1997–2001: Building Partnerships*. Melbourne: Tourism Victoria.

Ujdur, G. (1993) *Sydney: Olympics 2000 : Impact on Property*. Sydney: Hooker Research Limited.

Urry, J. (1990) *The Tourist Gaze: Leisure and Travel in Contemporary Societies*. London: Sage Publications.

Washington, S. (1999) 'IOC allegations may affect funding'. *Australian Financial Review*, 19 January, p. 5.

Western Australian Tourism Commission (1992) *Annual Report*. Perth: Western Australian Tourism Commission.

Wilkinson, J. (1994) *The Olympic Games : Past History and Present Expectations*. Sydney: NSW Parliamentary Library.

Part V

Sport and the development of urban communities

12 The social benefits of sport

Where's the proof?

Jonathan Long and Ian Sanderson

Introduction

Most of us are familiar with the argument that sport is good for us; indeed such a belief underlies not only some of our personal decision making but also public policy. We know that that there are disputes about the value systems instilled by sport, that we may suffer injury or abuse and that one individual or group may unnecessarily be set at odds with another, but in general the balance is seen to be substantially in favour of sport. Beyond that there is also a related belief that benefits accrue at a level beyond the individual in ways that support community development and regeneration.

The significance of such arguments may fluctuate in the policy arena, but they continue to recur. At the moment they are of interest in the context of the government's agenda on social exclusion and have lain behind much of the spending on sport and leisure through government schemes such as City Challenge and the Single Regeneration Budget. Indeed, Simmonds (1994: 9) indicates that some £67 million was secured for sport, leisure and related projects by twenty authorities in the first round of City Challenge. However, we have previously seen such arguments in the context of the Minister for Sport's Review Group (DoE, 1989) and the Commonwealth Heads of Government who noted that 'sport not only lies at the heart of the Commonwealth association, but is also an integral part of individual growth and community development (McMurtry, 1993).

The authors of such statements were doing no more than taking their lead from Sports Council strategies (e.g. Sports Council, 1982), the Scarman Report, government concern for inner city deprivation (Willis, 1977; Lawless, 1978), the quality of life initiatives (Department of the Environment, 1977a, b), the House of Lords Select Committee (1973) and on back to the Albemarle and Wolfendon reports in 1960. The resilience of these arguments may be because the general principles can be accommodated within positions that vary from the social democratic intent to guarantee participation through a desire for social integration to concerns for regulation and social control (Coalter, Long and Duffield, 1987).

Nonetheless, our concern in the current exercise is to review existing material and attempt to gather our own data to assess whether there is in fact any evidence of the social benefits that accrue from sport and leisure initiatives in pursuit of 'community development' (or indeed any conviction that they exist). To that end we have undertaken small scale survey work among Directors of Leisure Services, Sports Development Officers and Leisure Centre Managers (Long and Sanderson, 1996); circulated members of the Chief Leisure Officers Association inviting responses; published an open invitation in the *Leisure Manager* seeking responses from members of the Institute of Leisure and Amenity Management (ILAM); and conducted in-depth interviews with people who have been active in the field.

We recognise that this exercise, based as it is upon the informed opinion and judgement of experienced practitioners, addresses only part of the task of evaluating the impact of sport and leisure initiatives although we would argue that local case study material of this kind can play in important role in such evaluation. Undoubtedly there will be calls for a comprehensive and 'rigorous' approach to derive quantitative measures of impact. However, it is likely that the difficulty of allowing for the influence of other factors in order to assess the 'net impact' attributable to initiatives will remain.

In the next section of this chapter we review briefly the community-based approach to sport, the nature of the benefits claimed for it and the current evidence for such benefits. We then present the findings of our research among practitioners in local government, indicating how sport is understood as contributing to confidence-building and empowerment, to social integration and cohesion and to the reduction of crime and vandalism. Finally, we highlight some of the implications for practice from these findings and draw brief conclusions.

Background

A community-based approach to sport and leisure has developed as local authorities have sought to address the economic and social problems of deprived inner city areas on the assumption that sport and leisure activities can have a real impact on such problems. For example, in Bradford:

> One of the Council's overall priorities is rebuilding communities. The Council has stated that in reshaping the strategy for leisure and culture its primary aim is to 'provide excluded groups with opportunities for participation and inclusion'.
>
> (Bradford MDC, 1997: 5)

Hence, one of two central aims of the Recreation Division is 'to contribute substantially to the development and improvement of the district's economic, social, cultural and environmental well-being' (p. 3).

Working from the approach developed in Leicester, Haywood and Kew (1989: 176–7) identified what they considered to be the key characteristics of the community sport approach: the identification of inner-city problems, such as unemployment, poverty, industrial decline, housing and racial disadvantage; the identification of specific (disadvantaged) target groups in need of special treatment; a shift in management styles from facility-orientation to client group-orientation;

the devolution of responsibility down the management structure; and an emphasis on outreach work and consultation with target groups about their perceived needs. Haywood (1992) maintains that this approach involves harnessing 'community resources' in the development and operation of leisure and recreation services and recognising the contribution of leisure and recreation participation to community development and change.

From our reading of the literature it seems that the most commonly claimed community benefits are:

- enhanced confidence and self-esteem;
- empowering disadvantaged groups;
- improving the capacity of the community to take initiatives;
- reduction in crime, vandalism and 'delinquency';
- increased social integration and co-operation, promoting a collective identity and increasing cohesion;
- encouraging pride in the community;
- improving employment prospects;
- generating employment and income;
- increasing productivity with a fit and healthy workforce;
- improving health;
- environmental improvements.

Although we shall be alluding to each of these, for the sake of developing our argument here we take as the major aim of community development the enhancement of skills and confidence of groups of people such that they are empowered to take control of their lives and act collectively to address social and economic deprivation. In the context of Kirklees, Craig (1997: 94) refers to this as:

> ... the recognition that the community has to have the necessary skills (coaching, leadership and organisational skills) to make community regeneration and empowerment an achievable and sustainable reality.

Unfortunately, although often-promoted, arguments about the beneficial consequences of sport such as those listed above are rarely substantiated. While still sparse, it is perhaps in the area of reducing crime that most effort has been made to gather evidence of the success of projects (see, for example, Witt and Crompton, 1997; Nichols and Taylor, 1996). But there too it has been noted that 'purely quantitative and pseudo-scientific models of evaluation are rarely appropriate for community-based initiatives' (Lightfoot, 1994).

In the context of the contribution made by community leisure to 'target groups', particularly the unemployed, Glyptis (1989a: 153) argued that 'virtually all provision had been made on the basis of assumed need and assumed benefit' and concluded that as such claims were rarely backed up by evidence there was a need for more rigorous evaluation of the impact of community sport initiatives (1989b:

172–3). More recently Allison and Coalter (1996) also concluded that it is difficult to find evidence to substantiate the claims made for community development and observed that:

> The lesson from Action Sport is that the shift from attempting to provide sporting opportunities at a local level for disadvantaged groups to the instrumental use of sport within community development programmes is fraught with dangers.
>
> (Allison and Coalter, 1996: 8)

Perhaps rightly then, the various Sports Councils' more common response to 'the community issue' is providing 'local' facilities, to which people can have ready access, or identifying particular sectors of the population currently under-represented among those taking part in sport and then trying to encourage greater participation on their part. For example, in one initiative, the Sports Council for Wales, has been concerned with how 'communities' might find a voice to express their wants for sports provision – a policy response to messages from communities. In this case it is the expression of interest that represents the community development. But the realisation of the plan was dependent on keeping 'the population of Narberth interested and involved in the project' (SCW, 1994:18), and it was noted that

> The Narberth Action Group ... were somewhat fortunate in that within its membership there were people with experience, confidence and skills to set up the organisation and develop long term aims and objectives for the benefit of the ... community.
>
> (SCW, 1994: 11)

But the only measure of this 'virtually unparalleled' success story is the rising number of 'visits' to the completed centre. We have no reason to doubt the assessment of the Sports Council for Wales (1995) that five out of six of the projects examined in a related initiative have been successful (or 'relatively successful'), but there is no demonstration of what the community development benefits have been.

In our search for constituent evidence, we thought it appropriate to return to perhaps the biggest attempt to address this set of issues in the UK, the Quality of Life experiments of the 1970s which had action research as an integral part of their rationale (Department of the Environment, 1977b). However, despite the community development philosophy of much of the work, the aims and objectives (and hence monitoring and evaluation) were most commonly expressed in terms of generating opportunity and increasing participation through involvement and creating events. Some 16 projects are reported by the evaluators, who identified a number of issues to which we shall return later.

For example, a community theatre project (Thompson, 1977) was concerned mainly with using community arts/arts in the community to engage more people in the arts. It had some limited success in this, but was rather less successful in 'helping the community to realise and mobilise its own creative resources'. There was insufficient time to gain what had been hoped for, and although some continuation was recorded involvement gradually fell away. Similarly, the objectives of a community festival project were to: 'foster and develop a sense of community and belonging among the population'; and 'encourage social contact, fraternisation and the formation of local groups' (Macbeath, 1977: 223/4). However, these elusive goals were not addressed by any of the evaluation, though they were deemed to have happened in part because further programmes were planned without subsidy, and there were 'many indications of greater community involvement'. Again it was noted that it takes a considerable period of time to develop a community spirit even in the most ideal conditions. For the adults involved in another project, 'the playschemes were far from being an end in themselves' (Horn and Harrop, 1977: 395). They provided an important social role through opportunities to meet new people in the community and members of other committees, some went on to register for formal educational qualifications and others to provide other facilities. As had been hoped some of the community workers were able to retreat as an increasing number of committee members and playgroup leaders came from the local community. It was also noted that the experiments helped to familiarise people with the ways of bureaucracies:

> ... one of the most valuable services that the Experiments performed was to introduce many small voluntary organisations to possible sources of funds and to ways of applying for them.
>
> (Perry and Batty, 1977: 171)

Trying to make sense of the policy documents that we have examined is complicated by what seems to be a common eliding of arguments such that, for example:

- it is good for the individual means it is good for the community;
- community development means increased participation in sport, which implies increased attendance at sports centres;
- community development means making good the shortfall of facilities in disadvantaged areas.

Considering the first of these, what might it be that makes them community benefits rather than benefits simply accruing to an individual?

1 *Summative* – there may be multiple individual benefits accruing from public goods – e.g. improved health, better education.
2 *Reinvestment* – an individual acquires skills that may then be put to use to benefit others (e.g. gets involved in basketball, gets hooked, gains a coaching qualification, starts a youth team).
3 *Shared benefits* – e.g. my neighbourhood is enhanced if your house is improved, or local pride in a successful team.

4 *Consequential benefits* – if, because of your involvement in sport, your health improves or your criminal activity decreases, it costs me less (also, I'm less likely to catch something if you're not ill).
5 *Communality* – as human beings we benefit from interaction, being together and sharing experiences.
6 *For us by us* – empowerment is associated with control.
7 *Sum plus* – there may be some activities/actions where the whole is greater than the sum of the parts listed under (1).

We are concerned here not with the inherent goodness (or otherwise) of sport, rights of citizenship or principles of equity (natural justice arguments alone may demand provision), but with the instrumental role that sport might play in securing community development.

In search of evidence

Our first foray in seeking evidence was a postal survey addressed to a sample of Directors of Leisure Services to elicit their views on the potential role of sports development programmes and activities in community-based approaches (Long and Sanderson, 1996). We also obtained the views of sports development officers and leisure centre managers. The potential benefits in making the case for community-based sports development (shown in descending order of perceived importance in Table 12.1) were in four groups:

1 benefits to personal development in terms of improved self-esteem and self-confidence which most regard as very important;
2 a group of factors relating largely to 'community-level' benefits – identity and cohesion, health and crime;
3 factors relating to empowerment and 'community capacity'; and finally,
4 economic benefits – employment prospects and enterprise development – which were seen as very important by less than a quarter of respondents.

The sport and leisure officers within the metropolitan authority were clearly persuaded that there are benefits an individual can gain from being involved in sport. However, they were less persuaded of the contribution of community-based approaches to regeneration, and had a more pessimistic view of the potential for empowerment of disadvantaged groups and building community capacity. There were also some who counselled that sport should not be seen as the answer to all society's problems. Notably, these workers closer to the 'front-line' showed a greater degree of scepticism about purported benefits which are difficult to identify and measure. The responses relating to community development clustered strongly around interaction/cohesion/community spirit, whereas those relating to urban regeneration tended to focus on civic pride and improving the profile of the city.

When asked what evidence they had to support these claims our respondents had no more definitive evidence than the inconclusive material in the literature.

Table 12.1 Perceived importance of potential benefits from community-based sports development (% rating 'very important')

Potential benefits		LAs[1]	MB[2]
Personal development	< Improving self-esteem and self-confidence	96	91
Cohesion and 'social benefits'	< Improving the sense of community identity and cohesion	66	53
	< Improving the health of the community	66	59
	< Diverting young people from crime and vandalism	57	53
Empowerment and capacity:	< Empowering disadvantaged groups	51	19
	< Improving the capacity of the community to take initiatives	40	16
Economic benefits:	< Improving the prospects of young people to achieve employment	23	16
	< Developing local enterprise around sports activities	17	13

Source: Long and Sanderson, 1996

Notes
1 Responses from local authority leisure services departments
2 Responses from sports development officers and leisure centre managers

The fact that they thought the Sports Council vouchsafed them was proof enough for some. However, many referred to experiential evidence arising from their own participation in sport or direct observation in their work. Given the problematic nature of any research designed to produce 'hard' indicators in this area, we thought that a more formal documentation of such experiential evidence might help to clarify the situation and identify the kinds of process that 'work'.

In the next stage of our research some sport and leisure officers took offence that we were questioning these claimed benefits. Nonetheless, when we approached people specifically because we understood that they had personal experience of successful projects they were happy to be interviewed. However, it was disconcertingly easy to dissuade respondents – when pressed they frequently retreated, not willing to set great store by their experience and unwilling to press the claim of a link between sport and leisure activities and community development. In this they were like the 'front line' workers in our earlier survey (see above). It was as if, cowed by the scientific method, they recognised that the brave claims made in political documents, or that underpin funding applications, are difficult to sustain. Only with further questioning did they identify the relationships they did feel happy to stand by in the light of their own experience.

Respondents often found it difficult to identify whether there were any consequential benefits beyond the project. Indeed, for one respondent an indication of the project's success was that people they work with 'behave in a more responsible and mature way' than they do when they are elsewhere. Similarly:

> In the last 18 months we've been relatively problem free, but I don't think the estate is any better. It's not like there's been a general improvement in the area in the attitude and behaviour of the children, that's as bad as it ever has been (Respondent 02).

> For 2 hours they play 5 a side, get them off the streets, shower and then back up the road and they're 'on the corner' again... When you shepherd them onto the minibus and take them to the astro-turf they will be good, but when you're not with them, their peers are a bigger influence (Respondent 17).

Perceptions of these limitations were sometimes compounded by a concern about the small scale of respondents' endeavours: out of 500 kids you might get 100 involved – that leaves a lot of kids out there to commit crime.

Confidence, esteem and empowerment

Those familiar with community work practices took it as given that they should be working towards enhancing confidence and esteem to help to empower the community. Although respondents may have been diffident about some of the other benefits we discussed, they *knew* that in good projects they had seen this at work and had feedback to that effect from participants.

> I'm not sure if empower is the right word, but maybe equipping people with the skills to act on their own behalf and if that means they somehow get more control over what they do then I suppose that's what people mean by empowerment. It comes through sports administration as opposed to sport (Respondent 17).

> We supported a local tenants/residents association in holding a public meeting in their area to look at what were the particular problems in that area. So we provided training for some of the group to facilitate that meeting... From that came a big list of problems and needs and that list was prioritised at the meeting (Respondent 14).

In the latter case the success of equipping people with the skills was seen immediately in a meeting that set an agenda councillors and officials were persuaded to support and the establishment of a steering group that has continued to meet. Less than half of those who got involved had previously been community activists; they became involved because they had been able to identify their own priorities and could see benefits for themselves and the rest of the community (improving access from the estate for informal leisure activities on land running down to the river). With the help of the community worker they were able to work out which organisations could assist them, what funding they needed and where they could get it from, raised money for British Conservation Trust Volunteers to put in steps and benches and worked with BCTV and the school on a community clean-up of the area. That respondent saw the whole project as an exercise in community learning whereby people learnt from each other, supporting each other in acquiring skills and knowledge that they are now communicating to a neighbouring group.

Because of the sport and leisure projects reported by respondents, people had become able to make presentations, run meetings, write applications, set-up events and run clubs. The evidence that skills and confidence have been enhanced often lies in the very existence of those community benefits; our respondents were undoubtedly persuaded that thus armed people could move on to new initiatives to the benefit of the community. Almost all referred to local residents who had started new initiatives or were now running things which had previously been dependent on local authority staff. There is a down side to this in that the sports project may lose their services when they move on to new ventures.

Social integration, cohesion and collective identity

> I think they have experienced it collectively. They won't have set out expecting to change, but they have changed. Rubbing shoulders together they have got used to living together (Respondent 11).

Respondents indicated that in their experience acts of collective creation were most likely to enhance community identity, coming together to work together. While they were in no doubt that sport had the ability to encourage a collective togetherness, they were not persuaded that it was a necessary consequence.

> I can give plenty of examples [of social integration], but then there are plenty of examples when they just go home afterwards. I don't think there's any categoric evidence of sport turning people into this Pepsi generation, the Coca Cola thing going on… When you meet people at matches and just talk there is that coming together of people. But I can also give examples like at East End Park where a predominantly black team has been run off the pitch by the losing team and its supporters. I suppose sport can be really good just as sport can be really nasty, in the words of Blackadder (Respondent 17).

Equally, if some in the community are seen to be 'getting their own way' others are likely to be aggravated. The challenge for the development worker is to engage those who 'don't want to know', and sport and leisure frequently offer an attractive vehicle to that end. The criticism is that the benefits of integration in these circumstances are more about social control than empowerment.

Some of the community cohesion comes through changing attitudes (towards the young/old, between minority ethnic groups, etc.) as a result of sharing an interest in sport or facilitating participation. In confirming that the apparently nebulous benefits of community identity did accrue one respondent established the conditions in which the potential was most likely to be realised:

> I'm in no doubt that where community groups have responsibility for the planning and management of their patch it creates a sense of identity through having a stake, particularly where it can be separated from council provision (Respondent 16).

Processes and benefits are closely intertwined. Part of the agenda for some of the projects described involved changing relationships. Enticing local authority officers and councillors out of city hall (or its equivalent) for meetings with local groups changed the nature of relationships. As one insider observed, 'council officers are very skilled at doing nothing, but they were shamed into action by the Forum in the presence of councillors'. Equally, meeting the challenge of some of these projects had allowed police to make links that would otherwise have been rejected.

Reduction in crime, vandalism and delinquency

Clearly sports provision can act as an additional target for vandals, and handled badly projects may serve to alienate local residents: most people aren't stupid they can work out why you're going into that area and there can be a backlash if you're not careful.

Focusing on the contribution to crime reduction the Chief Leisure Officers' Association had identified scores of projects that were thought to demonstrate the contribution made by sport and leisure. However, they were able to offer very little by way of evidence; some did refer to police reports of less crime and vandalism, sometimes in the shape of formally gathered statistics, sometimes comments from the local bobby. Another piece of evidence cited was more complex, but perhaps ultimately more persuasive. When a youth drop in centre was opened in the centre of town local people complained about young people congregating there and got the centre closed, but then crime rose and local people exerted pressure to get the centre opened again. This kind of community recognition may speak louder than police statistics.

Although our respondents were prepared to make use of favourable crime statistics there was some scepticism about what they might mean. One jaundiced respondent suggested that 'maybe nicking stuff from the project they don't feature in the police crime figures'. In the context of an arts project another respondent was somewhat ambivalent about what the data might indicate:

> Police documented 'a small but significant drop in the level of crime'. They examined figures for recorded crime that they attributed to those under 25 in the area before, during and after the project. There was a drop, but it may have been because of summer holidays or because they'd been shoplifting in the town centre. I wasn't convinced it was entirely our project. In the short term I'd be very dubious there had been a great change (some were quite

openly having a spliff outside the door), but in the longer term I had the feeling they were looking at things and rejecting the harder drugs (Respondent 12).

One of our respondents worked in a local authority that had examined the impacts by:

a) comparing insurance claims from their own properties (later broadened to other properties) before, during and after projects, compared with the same period the year before; and

b) a survey of local residents.

The first indicated that there had been very real savings during the period of the project (working with young people on sports leadership programmes). The worst response from the second was that the project had made no difference, but the rest were much more enthusiastic. This was seen to be quite remarkable as the projects had introduced onto the site ten times the number of young people that could normally be expected there. If nothing else, recognition that something was being done reduced the perception of deviant behaviour.

Although arguing vehemently in favour of community projects, some of our respondents were openly sceptical:

So in terms of reducing crime…It's a great way of getting resources if you're a sports administrator, but I don't see how they can make that causal link between sport and reduced crime (Respondent 17).

At the end of the day you can't prove anything through crime statistics. This is what we found. You can bang someone away and it reduces crime statistics drastically, but by looking at crime statistics you can't prove whether working with young people around their needs does reduce crime. The police are aware of this (Respondent 14).

That same respondent though did argue that far from leisure and recreation being just an end in itself it could be a means to the end of building-up a relationship with young people in order to challenge their behaviour and get them to think about its consequences. At the same time it is important to work with people who live in that community and shift their perceptions of the young people:

You'll never stop young people smoking gange. The main problem is adults' perceptions of young people – mistrust and mutual misunderstanding. Young people congregate in a shop doorway because it gives light, adults worry, make comments and upset the young people who respond. It's more than crime its the perception of crime. There was a marked change in perceptions of young people because of a change in attitude on both sides. We worked with young people over 18 months and got them to work with the local community association and also got them to go and work in the local youth club as volunteer helpers, which changed people's perception of them (Respondent 14).

One respondent drew on his personal experience of a process of inclusion/exclusion to demonstrate why he thought that criminal activity had been reduced.

> Because it gave them something the project allowed the group to ostracise someone who had previously had quite a bit of power over them – from that point of view she'd lost a lot of Fagan's boys as it were. There was a long term effect on crime because they were able to reject the power of the one person – for at least that time they'd formed some sort of cohesive group – 'ten of us and one of you – we're in, you're out because you've blotted your copy book'. In the past they could be excluded, now they had something they could exclude the other from and were able to fight against the influence of one person (Respondent 12).

If there is nothing 'given' (preferably something tangible as well as the experience) there is nothing to exclude 'Fagan' from. Respondents were pleased that their projects had offered people alternatives even though they were aware that what they do with those alternatives is a different matter all together.

Best practice

Our respondents were keen to share what they considered to represent good practice and discuss the important features of the development process.

Comparative merits

Does it matter then if a project involves sport, the arts, recreation, exercise or some other aspect of leisure? To the individual concerned, quite possibly; to our argument, probably not.

Clearly an ability to identify with what is on offer is vital, but beyond that, time after time our respondents argued that it was the process that counted, a process that needed to include involvement in the decision making. Interestingly the process was thought to be more successful if there was a tangible product at the end. On that basis a play or an exhibition was seen to be superior to playing sport (better still if there was some artefact from the exhibition that could be kept by the participants). Best of all though is if a permanent physical reminder is left in the community (e.g., a park project or public art).

People working in other areas of policy might be prepared to concede that sport and leisure initiatives could bring such benefits, but question how effective they are compared with other initiatives based around housing, education, training or employment. However, just as projects have to work with people where they are physically (through outreach rather than relying on attracting people to centralised facilities) they also have to be prepared to work with them where they are psychologically. As one centre manager observed, if it is sport that interests them, that makes the best starting point.

> It's part of the education process. We eventually get through to the kids that when they're here there's a certain way in which they're expected to behave. You can't expect them to be quiet but you don't want them to be swearing. You can explain and after a while they'll accept that and understand that. 99 per cent are highly intelligent children and by being with them you can get through to them. You're using the sport as a vehicle to get to that basis. In the teams, competing with each other, and you're able to talk with them. Sports participation involves a certain amount of self-discipline in any case. It teaches them a lot more self control although they don't realise that's going on. If you told them today we're going to have a lesson in self-discipline and self-control…. whoah! (Respondent 2).

Self-determination

Writing about the contribution to community development, Freeman (1998) noted that 'benefits are often greater when the provision itself arises from community involvement, through needs assessment, planning, funding and construction' (hence the significance of the Narberth project mentioned above). Consequently, a better response is likely to be achieved if the local people concerned have had a chance to decide what sport or other leisure activity they wish to develop rather than 'selling' them the development officer's current favourite.

Following this approach also necessitates recognition of the different resources and skills available in an area.

Control over resources

Alien though the idea may be to public bodies, giving local people a meaningful say or direct control over the use of resources changes the dynamics involved and ensures far greater commitment to the project. Respondents advocating this argued that being alert to the potential problems had allowed good community workers and good management structures to avoid abuses or domination by cliques. Of course there are almost certain to be dissenting voices among neighbours never mind the councillors and officials, but it helps to establish alternative processes that challenge the idea of 'delivering a service' to people in need.

Continuity and sustainability

Respondents took as one indicator of community benefits the fact that the project was sustained beyond their initial input: 'two out of the three groups are still running 7½ years later'. Equally they were concerned about the transience of many initiatives: 'when you leave the problem starts again'. The latter, of course, does not mean that the benefits gained during the project were not worth having.

However, one of the major frustrations for fieldworkers is that they feel they rarely have the time necessary to effect any real change. Referring to the Kirklees approach, Craig (1997: 95) notes a timescale of '15 to 20 years or even more', and observes that this:

> ... is considerably longer than most Action Sport or sports development initiatives. It recognises the real timescale for community development and the reality that enablement must be a long term vision.

There is little doubt that where such benefits do occur they are normally small scale, which is not good for making funding applications. Moreover, initiatives/ schemes may take a long time to bear fruit and need to be sustained if the benefits are to be anything other than transitory. Unfortunately the current funding models are not sympathetic to such timescales – even if the project is not designed to be wound-up in three years' time, the scheme (if it is still there) is likely to have moved into a new funding round with different priorities.

Conclusions

We know from our own investigations that there are plenty involved in sports development who think that claims for community development benefits are an unnecessary bridge too far and that efforts should be narrowly directed to spotting talent and developing appropriate levels of excellence. However, one of our respondents maintained that sport for sport's sake is no longer sufficient to persuade councillors or funding agencies who want to know the community benefits.

Although cautious about some of the claims made for sports initiatives, our respondents were quite happy to substantiate these types of development with multiple examples as long as there was no naive assumption that it would apply to all those involved in the initiative or to all initiatives: 'They don't all succeed because they never will all succeed'.

As Maxwell (1998: 5) observed recently:

> ... poverty reduction is not just about income, but also about autonomy and self-respect. Social participation is an objective in its own right. This means helping the poor to challenge the institutions of exclusion, and take control at local level. The analogy often used is of a 'participation ladder'.

Whereas the sports development continuum from foundation to excellence is essentially about the individual, this kind of participation ladder can benefit the community and assist sustainability. If we are moving towards a society increasingly dominated by consumption, in which people do not really want the commitment and responsibility implied by community development, such contributions may be harder to elicit. The community benefits are then likely to be depressed towards a minimal version of the summative model identified above.

Some of our respondents insisted that a programme had produced real benefits, but because of the interrelatedness of people's lives they could not be sure that it was their particular project that had produced the benefits they observed. The organisational challenges of working across departmental and organisational divides are daunting, but in trying to address something as complex as community development the efforts of the Local Government Association (1998) to argue for sport and leisure as part of an integrated public service delivery seem entirely appropriate, though ideally the emphasis might shift from delivery to response.

It is easy to be dismissive of experiential evidence, after all 'they would say that wouldn't they'. However, some of the propaganda can be guarded against by the natural cynicism of the worker. On the basis of our research we are persuaded that there is sufficient cause to believe that community benefits can be obtained from sport and leisure initiatives. However, these may appear small scale, many or most of the population or target group are still likely to be left out, and there are plenty of reasons why individual projects may not deliver the benefits associated with the trumpeted successes. Changes may be considerable to the individual, even appreciable to small communities, but perhaps only tiny in the greater scheme of things (but then they do normally exist on a shoestring), though there is also plenty of experience to believe that beyond those immediately involved in community sport/recreation/leisure initiatives there is a ripple effect inducing wider benefits. However, it is entirely appropriate that largely intangible benefits, which cannot be guaranteed and which are for relatively small numbers to boot, should be subject to intensive political debate.

Clearly we are some way from a comprehensive and 'rigorous' evaluation design. Continuing the initiative we are embarked upon here will help to lay bear the interstices of the complex processes involved and the potential benefits for particular client groups in particular circumstances. But decision makers will almost certainly demand precise (however inaccurate) evidence of the scale of different impacts and the (cost) effectiveness of different forms of initiatives in achieving such impacts. There may after all be better ways of achieving these social and community benefits than through sport and leisure initiatives, and projects cannot be approved simply because they are tagged with the 'community' label. An appreciation of the complexity of such a challenge can be gained from even a cursory consideration of key issues to be addressed:

- the extent to which social and community impacts can be 'captured' in measurable terms;
- the need to address the 'time profile' of impacts and their 'sustainability';
- how to capture 'capacity-building' impacts;
- the need to capture any 'negative side effects';
- explaining how observed effects are attributable (causally) to initiatives;
- estimating 'net additional benefits', excluding effects which would have occurred without the initiative.

Methodologically we find ourselves in an ambivalent position. More precise evidence of this nature might provide the basis for more effective arguments in support of sport and leisure policies and programmes at the local level. It would help to clarify realistic objectives and priorities; and it would help in the design of effective local initiatives which can play an appropriate role in community development in the context of broader strategies and programmes. Nevertheless, scarred by experience of community initiatives that are justified on the basis that they process people at a lower per capita cost we are wary of the siren call of quantitative measures, any of which are likely to be criticised by those who did not design them and which must almost inevitably place consideration of service delivery and social control above those of elusive social dynamics. While we try to resolve such dilemmas, it is vital that in the meantime we do not detract from the proactive efforts of those willing to argue their case and instigate community initiatives.

References

Albemarle Report (1960) *The Youth Services in England and Wales*. London: HMSO, Cmnd 929.

Allison, M. and Coalter, F. (1996) *Sport and Community Development*. Edinburgh: Scottish Sports Council.

Bradford Metropolitan District Council, Recreation Division (1997) *A Strategy for Sport and Recreation: a Framework and Guiding Principles*. Bradford: the Council.

Coalter, F., Long, J. and Duffield, B. (1988) *Recreational Welfare*. Aldershot, Avebury.

Craig, S. (1997) *Working Towards Racial Equality in Sport: a Good Practice Guide for Local Authorities*. London: Sports Council.

Department of the Environment (1977a) Leisure and the Quality of Life: a Report on Four Local Experiments. Volume 1. London: HMSO.

Department of the Environment (1977b) Leisure and the Quality of Life: a Report on Four Local Experiments. Volume 2, Research Papers. London, HMSO.

Department of the Environment (1989) *Sport and Active Recreation Provision in the Inner Cities*, Report of the Minister for Sport's Review Group 1988/89. London, HMSO.

Freeman, A. (1998) *National Issues: Leisure and the Wider Social Objectives*. ILAM Discussion Paper.

Glyptis, S. (1989a) *Leisure and Unemployment*. Milton Keynes, Open University Press.

Glyptis, S. (1989b) 'Public Sector Sport and Recreation Initiatives for the Unemployed in Britain's Inner Cities', in Bramham, P., Henry I., Mommaas, H. and van der Poel, H. (eds), *Leisure and Urban Processes: Critical Studies of Leisure Policy in Western European Cities*. London: Routledge.

Horn, C. and Harrop, K. (1977) Sunderland Neighbourhood Playschemes, in Department of the Environment (1977b) *op cit*, pp. 385–405.

House of Lords Select Committee on Sport and Leisure (1973) *Second Report. The Cobham Report*. London: HMSO.

Lawless, P. (1978) *Urban Deprivation and Government Initiative*. London: Faber and Faber.

Lightfoot, J. (1994) (ed), *Towards Safer Communities: Community Development Approaches to Crime*. London: Community Development Foundation.

Local Government Association (1998) 'Enriching People's Lives: an Advocacy Paper for Leisure and Tourism'. London, LGA Publications.

Long J. and Sanderson I. (1996) 'Sport and Social Integration: The Potential for Community-Based Approaches to Regeneration', in S. Hardy, B. Malbon and C.

Taverner (eds), *The Role of Art and Sport in Local and Regional Economic Development*. London: Regional Studies Association, pp. 28–33.

Macbeath, A. (1977) 'Mynydd Isa Community Festival, Clwyd (Deeside)', in Department of the Environment (1977b) *op cit*, pp. 223–230.

MacDonald, D. and Tungatt, M. (1992) *Community Development and Sport* (CDF Briefing Paper No. 3). London: Community Development Foundation.

McMurtry, R. (1993) *Sport and the Heads of Government Round Table* (London) No. 328, pp. 419–426.

Maxwell, S. (1998) 'The Same Difference'. *Guardian* 25/2/98 (Society Supplement) pp. 4–5.

Nichols, G. and Taylor, P. (1996) *West Yorkshire Sports Counselling: Final Evaluation*. Sheffield: Leisure Management Unit, University of Sheffield.

Perry, N. and Batty, A. (1977) 'Themes in the Best Use of Leisure Facilities', in Department of the Environment (1977b) *op cit*, pp. 159–201.

Simmonds, B. (1994) *Developing Partnerships in Sport and Leisure: A Practical Guide*. Harlow: Longman.

Sports Council (1982) *Sport and the Community: the Next Ten Years*. London, Sports Council.

Sports Council for Wales (1994) Communities in Action: a Case Study of Bloomfield House Community Centre, Narberth. Cardiff: SCW.

Sports Council for Wales (1995) Active Communities: Local Initiatives for Leisure. Cardiff: SCW.

Thompson, A. (1977) Community Theatre Project, Stoke on Trent, in Department of the Environment (1977b) *op cit*, pp. 315–331.

Willis, A. (1977) *Recreation and Deprivation in Inner Urban Areas*. London: HMSO.

Witt, P. and Crompton, J. (1997) 'The At-Risk Youth Recreation Project'. *Parks and Recreation*, Vol. 32(1), pp. 54–61.

Lord Wolfenden (1960) *Sport and the Community*. London: Central Council of Physical Recreation.

13 Sport and cultural diversity

Why are women being left out?

Tracy Taylor and Kristine Toohey

Introduction

According to 1991 Australian Bureau of Statistics census data, females born in non-English speaking countries comprised nearly 15 per cent of Australia's population. However, as a group they are significantly under-represented in national sport participation figures (Australian Bureau of Statistics, 1994) and virtually invisible in the literature on sport in Australia (Taylor and Toohey, 1995). By listening to the voices of women from Chinese, Croatian, Greek, Italian, Lebanese, Serbian and Vietnamese backgrounds in the research project reported here, we aimed to delve into the nexus of women, ethnicity and sport.

Most research exploring ethnicity and sport has focused on the experiences of males, while investigations of gender and sport have based their discourses primarily on the practices of Anglo-Australian women. By excluding women from non-English speaking backgrounds the conceptualisation of sport as a site of cultural and identity formation in Australia is problematic. Involvement or non-involvement in sport by all sections of the population must be explored in order to develop a more inclusive and richer understanding of the real place and space of sport in the Australian context. This research explores this largely uncharted territory and contributes to our understanding of women, ethnicity and sport within Australia.

While overseas research on sport and ethnicity has been gaining momentum, research in Australia has been much slower to emerge. Work examining Australian Football and Rugby League, two popular mainstream male sports, has highlighted a substantial level of participation by migrant group members. Cultural adaptation, social acceptance, and in some cases, economic security have been sought by male participants from non-English speaking backgrounds through these sports (Stoddart, 1986). However, there is no evidence to suggest that sport has had the same significance in the acculturation and assimilation process for women from non-English speaking backgrounds.

The role of sport in the acculturalisation and assimilation of first generation male migrants has been well documented. As Richard Cashman (1995: 163) has commented, 'Sport played a crucial role in community formation because it provided a largely accepted way for immigrant communities to organise themselves

… it was also a bridge between such a community and the wider Australian society'. However, sport has also been instrumental in assisting ethnic groups to maintain their distinctive cultural identities.

Thus sport has taken on a number of divergent roles in relation to ethnic minority participation. It has been used to promote assimilation, integration, cultural diversity, and ethnic identity. However, the documented cases of ethnic minority participation have almost exclusively focused on male experiences (see Mosely *et al.*, 1997 as an exception). What about female sport participation, are the same issues and conclusions applicable? The research outlined in this chapter has sought to answer these questions by listening to the voices, experiences and perceptions of women from non-English speaking backgrounds.

Methodology

The framework for researching the nexus of sport, gender and ethnicity that we used in this study drew from overseas research on ethnicity and sport (Floyd, Gramann and Sanchez, 1993) but also attempted to move beyond explanations of otherness and difference to incorporate theoretical analyses of gender, acculturation and identity.

Individual interviews were conducted with eleven women and nineteen focus groups. These interviews canvassed the opinions, experiences and comments of first and second-generation women from Chinese, Croatian, Greek, Italian, Lebanese, Serbian and Vietnamese backgrounds. Discussion of a range of issues related to sport was pursued. This included getting the women to talk about their own sporting involvement, their general perceptions of sport and women in sport, constraints to participation and cultural aspects of sport participation. Throughout this paper we have incorporated the women's own words to best illustrate their perceptions and interpretations of sport.

Selection of interview participants for the focus groups was via contacts provided by the Ethnic Affairs Commission of New South Wales, Area Health Services, and sporting organisations. The convenor consulted the group about their involvement in the process and upon receiving group approval the interview was arranged. In the majority of cases a translator was present during the focus group interview. All interviews were taped and transcribed verbatim for analysis.

Every focus group interview began with an introduction to the research, explaining the aims and objectives of the project. All participants were given the option to withdraw from the discussion at any point during the proceedings. Participants were assured of confidentially of responses and their permission to tape each interview was obtained. The focus group interviews had some logistical limitations. There were times when many women spoke at once and the loudest voice was recorded. Also, precise meanings and words were sometimes lost in the translation process.

Further to the focus groups, individual interviews were conducted with eleven women from the seven selected groups.

Table 13.1 Focus groups conducted for the study

Group	Group type	Number of focus groups (total number of people involved)
Chinese	Women's support groups	2 (28)
Croatian	Pensioner group. Welfare Assoc. group	2 (17)
Greek	Community group. Older women's group	2 (18)
Italian	Youth group. Women's support group	2 (21)
Lebanese	Neighbourhood Centre group. Welfare Assoc. group. Women's support groups	4 (45)
Serbian	Pensioner group. Neighbourhood Centre group. Welfare Assoc. group	3 (23)
Vietnamese	Martial Arts group. Neighbourhood Centre group. Women's group. Work experience group	4 (34)
Total		19 (186)

Listening to the voices of women

The women interviewed in both the focus groups and individually expressed a broad range of opinions about sport. Their general feelings about sport and attitudes to participation are summarised in this section. The women's perceptions about sport were clearly influenced by their experiences and opportunities, both here in Australia and in their country of origin. This distinction is further articulated in the following remark:

> It's culturally unacceptable for women who migrated here and didn't follow the changes because they were alienated. They worked two jobs, three jobs. The change in the environment, and being scared and not trusting. Whereas back home, women don't work and didn't work (outside the home). Whereas women worked then walked and walked, they came out here and didn't walk. So their health has naturally deteriorated in this country now. They would have been naturally active back home. Not sport as such but in their daily lives. Whereas in this country, the lifestyle was to work (first generation Greek woman).

As one interviewee observed: 'it was different for my parents, they had to struggle to earn a living, struggle to learn English and work hard to get established, they didn't have time to play or think about sport, they were driven by basic survival needs' (Greek woman).

Numerous remarks were made about the influence of generational and cultural expectations regarding acceptability of women participating in sport. The pressure of conforming to role expectations was a recurrent feature in many women's comments, as one first generation Serbian woman observed: 'the family comes first, only when everything is done around the house then can you think about yourself'. When the following comment was made at a Lebanese focus group there were women nodding their heads in agreement all around the circle: 'After school the girls would go home and the boys would play sport. The girls would work at home, cooking, sewing, knitting'. Women in the focus groups and individually repeatedly remarked that they often had wanted to engage in sporting activities but were not allowed to pursue this interest as it was not seen as feminine and therefore was not acceptable behaviour:

> I like karate and I want[ed] to learn but my mother didn't want me to learn because maybe if I do maybe the muscle (Vietnamese focus group member).

While very few women indicated that they had experienced overt racial discrimination while playing sport, it is still a problematic area. In commenting about her unease and hesitation in going into a local sports venue, a Vietnamese focus group participant said 'I would like to go but the comments that have been made are not nice'. Racial tension was quite commonly experienced in the school yard, as these woman recalled in their interviews:

> At school we were singled out from the rest because we spoke differently. We weren't asked to join the teams, we were seen as poor at sports (Croatian woman).

Lack of appropriate information, facilities and programs were also raised in the interviews as concerns. The issue of privacy for participants in changing rooms and sports facilities was a primary issue of anxiety for a significant number of the women interviewed. 'There were no curtains in the change room. You feel uncomfortable about your body at that age' (Arabic focus group member). This was exacerbated by feelings of frustration at not knowing how to 'work the system' or having the right contacts … 'We seemed to be going around in circles, nobody could help us start the club. It's knowing who to speak to, and we didn't know' (Greek woman).

The problem of organising transport to sporting venues is a correlate to lack of local facilities and is also linked to issues of prohibitive cost of participation and safety considerations. Several women indicated that they did not have access to private transport … 'If I have to drive there, with one car for all the family, my husband takes the car, what can I do?' (Chinese focus group member). For others, the thought of driving in a large new city and new country is quite frightening. 'Just scared, scared of driving. If it's not close to our place, you know you won't go there' (Chinese focus group member).

For many migrant women sport was not seen as a high priority in their lives, there were many other important issues associated with settling into a new country which took precedence. Refugees found it particularly difficult to afford to partake in sport, 'For refugees it is very expensive with no money left for membership, clothing' (Croatian woman) or to even think about it:

> Most women are coming as refugees, they are so stressed. Sport is not yet a thing for them to think about. How to look after the family, how to get to school, how to get the food is more important for them now (Serbian woman).

Other recently arrived families clearly identified that their priority was to achieve success in school and business, 'We were pushed into other things, certainly not sport' (Italian focus group member). Success in sport was not highly valued, 'We find difficulties in language and finding job so most of the parents here really encourage their children to ... learn. To pass their HSC, to do well academically rather than to do well at swimming or to do other sports' (Chinese/Vietnamese woman).

The lack of female sporting role models within ethnic communities who could encourage others was another common discussion point. 'If the woman doesn't have any role model or active parents, it's less likely they will enjoy sports' (Chinese focus group member).

For most of the women interviewed social aspects of sport were identified as more important than competitive ones.

> The social element is really important ... spot some key informants, sort of like, key people who don't mind to spend a bit of time to ring up people or to catch up with people and also to spread the information around (Chinese focus group member).

Programs with a social emphasis have been successful in allowing women to combine exercise within their established ethnic community organisations and networks, as outlined in the example below:

> We started a walking group out of the church women's group. As everyone was already together it was relatively easy (Lebanese woman).

In summary, many of the women interviewed indicated that they were not encouraged to participate in sport while growing up. Family attitudes to participation ranged from viewing sport as unimportant and thus a low priority for time or resources, to outright disapproval of females involvement in sporting pursuits. Women who did want to participate indicated that they often faced barriers such as lack of sport skills, minimal information, limited access, inappropriate programs/facilities, racism, and prohibitive cost, and were often frustrated by their need to overcome these obstacles.

Discussion of results

This research does not aim to present a conclusive or definitive theory on women, sport and ethnicity. What it does offer, however, is a commentary from women, in their own voices, relating their personal experiences with sport. As such it provides information which both supports and indeed contradicts some other ethnicity-based research.

The women interviewed for this project who were from Chinese, Greek, Italian, Lebanese, Serbian and Vietnamese backgrounds articulated different and diverse value systems, and stated that these values have had an impact on their participation in sport. Participation differences between groups were identified in the course of the study (i.e. Chinese-born women were ten times as likely to engage in cycling than women from Italian backgrounds), complementing other research findings (see Phillip, 1995; Carrington *et al.*, 1987; Bhandari, 1991). However, we also found that there were many similarities between groups (i.e. role expectations had a major impact on participation levels across all the ethnic groupings interviewed) and variations within a group.

The similarities can be extended to universal issues that have been found to contribute to low levels of female involvement in sport. The experiences of the women interviewed clearly demonstrate that the discriminatory practices of access and equity which have prevented many females in Australia from participating in sport (see Bryson, 1990; McKay, 1991; and Darlison, 1985) are further exacerbated for many women from culturally and linguistically diverse backgrounds. Safety concerns (Shaw, 1996), low self-efficacy, limited access to facilities, lack of time, feelings of entitlement, (Hargreaves, 1994) gender roles and ethic of care (Henderson and Bialeschki, 1993) also exist for women from non-English speaking backgrounds. These factors combined with socio-cultural dimensions, such as gender bias and gender role stereotyping, can produce conditions that prohibit or severely restrict sport participation. Such role conflicts are often presented as psychological rather than social (Theberge and Birrell, 1994). This is problematic as it then assumes that women's low involvement in sports is the fault of the women themselves and does not suggest that a challenge of the organisation or provision of sport is required.

From our research is it clearly evident that steps must be taken to change current sport provision if the needs of women from non-English speaking backgrounds are to be met. To date we have not heard much about the circumstances or experiences of this section of the population and as such have not involved them or included their needs in planning sport provision in this country and have made assumptions about their sporting interests. As Seymour (1995: 158) has observed: 'if ethnic minorities have an unheard voice in most records and sources, then female members of such minorities come close to being silenced'.

However, making generalisations about any one ethnic group or even women from non-English speaking backgrounds is inherently problematic. Explanations that attempt to measure everyone else in comparison to the majority culture's norms should be viewed with reticence. While many overseas studies appear to have an ultimate goal of sporting assimilation (Floyd, Gramann and Saenz, 1993) the extent to which Australia should be aiming for this same end is questionable, especially given this country's stated commitment to multicultural expression.

As demonstrated in the comments of the women interviewed for this study, the sporting needs of many women from non-English speaking backgrounds are not being adequately met. Reasons for this relate to personal, community and structural dimensions. The latter can be begin to be addressed by recognising the necessity to make changes in the structure and delivery of sport in this country. How any given sport organisation proceeds with addressing these concerns will depend on the nature of the service, its staff, its location and its resources. However, it is essential to remember that the first stage in designing and implementing any strategies should involve consultation with women from the target groups.

Recommendations

There are many ways in which sports providers can better meet the needs of women and girls from culturally and linguistically diverse backgrounds. The strategies employed will vary from organisation to organisation and from region to region. Listed below are just some suggestions that may assist providers in this process.

- Determine the size and composition (e.g. age, income) of the ethnic community in the region that your service covers.
- Determine needs and preferences through consultation – this may highlight the need to modify or adapt how programs are designed or implemented.
- Implement strategies which value, encourage and empower cultural diversity both within the organisation and with clients.
- Create operating structures and practices should not assume that one cultural perspective is more valid than other perspectives.
- Set specific goals and objectives that relate to culturally and linguistically diverse women and girl.
- Identify specific language and cultural skills required to service clients.
- Challenge stereotypical perceptions held by staff about ethnic groups.
- Develop positive role models of women and girls from culturally and linguistically diverse backgrounds.
- Establish a local sport network for women and girls from culturally and linguistically diverse backgrounds.
- Establish pro-active policies that address equity and access issues, thereby encouraging women and girls from culturally and linguistically diverse backgrounds to participate in sport.
- Provide appropriate facilities which are suitable, hygienic and safe for women.
- Develop and document model/pilot programmes.
- Consider special training and accreditation initiatives for women from culturally diverse backgrounds in relevant sports.
- Develop promotional material about sport, emphasising the social aspects of such involvement and using women from culturally diverse backgrounds as role models.
- Include an anti-racism policy in your code of conduct.
- Develop documentation and training material for staff regarding sport for women from culturally diverse backgrounds actively seek nominations for appointments to advisory committees, boards, task forces and other bodies

associated with sport and physical activity from ethnic women 's groups or representatives.

- Pursue proactive hiring practices - expand your job advertising beyond traditional outlets, use ethnic newspapers and networks. Understand the cultural expectations of the communities you are targeting.
- Redefine job qualifications - expand the definition of education and experience for a position, e.g. many women re-entering the workforce argue that their experience in the home and with their children's school shilling in organising, fundraising, and budgeting.
- Provide for career development information and advice given about the opportunities for jobs in sport and recreation from traineeships to management positions. Special training programs may be needed to meet specific requirements such as improving english language skills. Mentoring schemes can be used to facilitate professional development of an employee.
- Translate rules and regulations of a particular sport or activity into the main community languages.
- Use non language based communication symbols.
- Utilise cross-cultural communications-strategies.
- Incorporate cultural diversity issues in advertising and promotion.
- Try women only classes/groups – these may be required for cultural or religious reasons, participant preference, safety and comfort.
- Emphasise social and fun aspects.
- Timing considerations – consider the target group's daily life and avoid overlap e.g. significant religious holidays, child care requirements.
- Provide appropriate child care.
- Create family friendly environments.

Conclusion

The literature suggests that sport has been one avenue through which people from culturally and linguistically diverse backgrounds have been able to maintain their distinct cultural identity, and also acculturate into wider Australian society. However, what is not pointed out in previous studies is that the use of sport for these ends has primarily been a male experience. In listening to the voices of the women interviewed for this study it is strikingly clear that much of the existing literature on ethnicity and sport is male-generated, male-oriented and therefore largely irrelevant to the lived experiences of women from non-English speaking backgrounds.

Facing a number of constraints and restrictions to sport participation, women from non-English speaking backgrounds have not been able to access sport to the same degree as their male counterparts. These women have therefore been denied the benefits associated with participation in sport, which range from social inclusion to minimising health risks.

In Australia, cultural diversity is both a goal and a reality. We live in a nation of many cultures, yet there are numerous institutions that do not fully recognise or support the independent and co-dependent existence of these diverse cultures.

Sport is a prime example. If cultural diversity is the goal of this nation, then a shift must occur in the way in which sport is currently structured. Sport providers need to open their doors to all members of the community and actively engage in inclusive practices, rather than just acting as passive purveyors of sport. The right to quality of life, which includes opportunities to participate in sport, should be available to everyone, regardless of gender or ethnicity. To this end, assimilationist modes of operation must be discouraged and re-oriented to encompass, encourage and embrace the rich and diverse range of cultures that are found in this country.

References

Australian Bureau of Statistics (1994) *Involvement in Sport Australia March 1993.* Canberra: Australian Bureau of Statistics, Catalogue No. 6285.0.

Bhandari, R. (1991) 'Asian Action'. *Sport and Leisure*, Vol. 25.

Bauman, A., Bellew, B., Booth, M., Hahn, A., Stoker, L. and Thomas, M. (1996) *NSW Health Promotion Survey 1994.* Sydney: NSW Health.

Bryson, L. (1990) 'Challenges to Male Hegemony in Sport', in M. Messner and D. Sabo (eds), *Sport, Men, and the Gender Order: Critical Feminist Perspectives.* Champaign: Human Kinetics Books, pp. 173–184.

Carrington, B. Chilvers, T. and Williams, T. (1987) 'Gender, Leisure and Sport: A Case Study of Young People of South African Descent'. *Leisure Studies*, Vol. 6(3), pp. 265–279.

Cashman, R. (1995) *Paradise of Sport: The Rise of Organised Sport in Australia.* Melbourne: Oxford University Press.

Darlison, L. (1985) Equality. Department of Sport, Recreation and Tourism, Australian Sports Commission. *Australian Sport: A Profile.* Canberra: AGPS, pp. 98–118.

Dew, S. (1992) *Ethnic Involvement in Sport in Geelong 1945–1990.* MA Thesis, Melbourne, Deakin University.

Duda, J. and Allison, M. (1990) 'Cross-cultural Analysis in Exercise and Sport Psychology: A Void in the Field'. *Journal of Sport and Exercise Psychology*, Vol. 12(2), pp. 114–131.

Fleming, S. (1994) 'Sport and South Asian Youth: the Perils of "False Universalism" and Stereotyping'. *Leisure Studies*, Vol. 13(3), pp. 159–177.

Floyd, M. Gramann, J. and Saenz, R. (1993) 'Ethnic Factors and the Use of Public Outdoor Recreation Areas: the Case of Mexican Americans'. *Leisure Sciences*, Vol. 15, 83–98.

Grey, M. (1992) 'Sports and Immigrant, Minority and Anglo Relations in Garden City (Kansas) High School'. *Sociology of Sport Journal*, Vol. 9, pp. 255–270.

Hargreaves, J. (1994) *Sporting Females: Critical Issues in the History and Sociology of Women's Sports.* London: Routledge.

Henderson, K.A. and Bialeschki, M.D. (1993) 'Exploring an Expanded Model of Women's Leisure Constraints'. *Journal of Applied Recreation Research*, Vol. 18, pp. 229–252.

Hallinan, C. and Krotee, M. (1993) 'Conceptions of Nationalism and Citizenship among non-Anglo-Celtic Soccer Clubs in an Australian City'. *Journal of Sport and Social Issues*, Vol. 17(2), pp. 125–133.

Hughson, J. (1992) 'Australian soccer: "Ethnic" or "Aussie"? The search for an image'. *Current Affairs Bulletin*, Vol. 68(10), pp. 12–16.

Kondos, S. (1994) *Recreation for Health: Recreation for Non-English Speaking Background Women.* Melbourne: North East Women's Health Service.

Lawrence, G. and Rowe, D. (1986) (eds), *Power Play: The Commercialisation of Australian Sport*. Sydney: Hale and Iremonger.

McKay, J. (1991) *No Pain, No Gain? Sport and the Australian Culture*. Sydney: Harcourt Brace Jovanovich.

Mosley, P. (1992) 'Soccer', in W. Vamplew, K. Moore, J. O'Hara, R. Cashman, and I. Jobling (eds), *The Oxford Companion to Australian Sport*, (2nd edn). Melbourne: Oxford University Press, pp. 316–323.

Mosely, P., Cashman, R., O'Hara, J. and Weatherburn, H. (1997) (eds), *Sporting Immigrants*. Crows Nest: Walla Walla Press.

Murphy, B. (1993) *The Other Australia: Experiences of Migration*. Melbourne: Cambridge University Press.

Phillip, S. (1995) 'Race and Leisure Constraints'. *Leisure Sciences*, Vol. 17(2), pp. 109–120.

Seymour, M. (1995) 'Writing Minority History: Sources for the Italians', in S. Fitzgerald and G. Wotherspoon (eds), *Minorities: Cultural Diversity in Sydney*. Sydney: State Library of NSW Press, pp. 157–173.

Shaw, S. (1996) 'The Gendered Nature of Fun: Individual and Societal Outcomes of Leisure Practice'. *FreeTime and Quality of Life For the 21st Century*, Cardiff: WLRA, p. 54.

Stoddart, B. (1986) *Saturday Afternoon Fever: Sport in the Australian Culture*. Sydney: Angus and Robertson.

Stoddart, B. (1988) 'The Hidden influence of Sport', in V. Burgmann and J. Lee (eds), *Constructing a Culture*, Melbourne: McPhee Gribble/Penguin, pp. 124–135.

Tatz, C. (1995) *Obstacle Race*. Sydney: NSW University Press.

Toohey, K. and Taylor, T. (1997) *Strategies to Increase the Sport Participation of Ethnic Females in New South Wales*. Canberra: Report to the Australian Sports Commission, unpublished.

Taylor, T. and Toohey, K. (1995) 'Ethnic Barriers to Sports Participation'. *Australian Parks and Recreation*, Vol. 31(2), pp. 32–36.

Theberge, N. and Birrell, S. (1994) 'The Sociological Study of Women and Sport', in D.M. Costa and S. Gutherie (eds), *Women and Sport: Interdisciplinary Perspectives*. Champaign: Human Kinetics, pp. 323–330.

Washburn, R. (1978) 'Black Under-participation in Wildland Recreation: Alternative Explanations'. *Leisure Sciences*, Vol. 1(3), pp. 175–189.

14 Sports facility development and the role of forecasting

A retrospective on swimming in Sheffield

Peter Taylor

In the late 1980s forecasts were made of the number of admissions for swimming in Sheffield to the year 2001, under assumptions which reflected the building of the World Student Games facilities and the closure of the four older swimming pools. This chapter examines what happened subsequently to swimming participation in Sheffield and analyses the relationship between the reality and the forecasts. In doing so the chapter addresses the following issues:

- the problems of forecasting sports participation;
- the impact of new facilities on swimming participation;
- the relationship between a city-wide initiative and an important, constituent, sports activity;
- the role of forecasting and rational planning in decisions to build new facilities.

The value of forecasting

Standard texts typically portray the model process for the planning of new recreational facilities as consisting of assembling the right management information to service key decisions such as facility type, size and location. Illustrative of such an approach is the following:

> For investment decisions, demand forecasting is of critical importance. Investing in an expansion of production facilities, or relocation or starting up a new facility, requires detailed information about the long-term trends in the demand for the product, or the characteristics of demand in alternative locations' catchment areas. Without such information the decision is quite simply more of a gamble.
>
> (Gratton and Taylor, 1992, p. 84)

Implicit in the rationality of such textbook advice is a belief that demand forecasting can yield sufficiently credible predictions (i.e. with sufficiently low error margins), to be a reliable basis for other important estimates. In particular, demand forecasts provide a basis for estimates of direct income, at assumed price levels, and consequently the cash flow, profit and loss and, if appropriate, the subsidy requirements of the facility. In addition, demand forecasts can help to identify peak usage and therefore required capacity levels. The sustained belief in demand forecasting techniques is explicit in the feasibility studies constructed for all new major sports facilities, most recently and conspicuously as part of applications to the Sports Lottery Fund in the UK.

Counter to the rationalist views prevalent in new facility planning, there is a long history of scepticism in the value of demand forecasting. In recreation, these sceptical views were expressed more than two decades ago:

> leisure forecasting at the quantitative level flounders in a morass of uncertainty because it lacks an adequate database ...
>
> ... techniques depend utterly on both the statistical strength and stability through time of the observed associations between socio-economic attributes and the propensity to recreate in specific ways.
>
> (Rodgers, 1977)

> we can be sure that the one future situation that will not occur is an exact extrapolation of the past.
>
> (Elson, 1977)

In Sheffield the use of sport as an important part of an urban regeneration strategy has been subject to evaluations which tend to concentrate on the financial impact of the building of facilities and the economic impact of major events hosted in these facilities (Critcher, 1992; Dobson and Gratton, 1996; Foley, 1991; Roche, 1992a, 1992b; Williams, 1997). This has been mirrored in the local press by a debate on the merits of the strategy which continues to this day.

Whereas 'hindsight is blessed with 20:20 vision', little of the appraisal of Sheffield's sport for regeneration initiative has attempted to re-live the decision-making environment of the 1980s. To the author's knowledge, no retrospective examination has been made of demand forecasts for new sports facilities, such as those in Sheffield, to test the rationalist belief in the forecasts. This paper does so by returning to one important aspect of the new facility construction of the late 1980s in Sheffield – the construction of two new, 'wet and dry' leisure centres.

The paper assesses the accuracy of demand forecasts estimated in advance of this change in provision of swimming facilities, and in doing so it also identifies and assesses the impact of the facility changes on swimming participation in the city. Underpinning this appraisal, and an explicit consideration later in the paper, is the issue of the rationality of using demand forecasts as part of the decision-making process. The conclusions, however, are specific to the Sheffield swimming case and are not necessarily transferable even to other sports in Sheffield, let alone other cities.

Swimming's role in Sheffield's sports initiative

Swimming facilities have played an important role in the public investment in sport by Sheffield City Council. Two major new facilities, Ponds Forge International

Sports Centre and Hillsborough Leisure Centre, have swimming pools at their core. Together they consumed 43 per cent of the £147 million capital spend in preparation for hosting the World Student Games in 1991.

The change in provision for swimming in Sheffield in the early 1990s consisted of not only building two new facilities but also closing four older pools. This resulted in a stock of 11 facilities which subsequently have provided swimming for the public, although one soon went into the ownership of a private charitable trust and two have reverted to ownership by schools.

Two aspects of the change in swimming provision in the early 1990s are particularly worth emphasising. First, it represented a reduction in the stock of local, neighbourhood pools and, to a degree, a substitution by the two new, larger pools – both with a catchment which was anticipated to be city-wide and beyond. Second, it represented a change from concentration almost entirely on participation to a much greater role for spectator events, particularly at Ponds Forge.

The demand forecasts for swimming in Sheffield

In 1988, Leisure Research Services (a team including the current author) were commissioned to produce demand forecasts for swimming in Sheffield for the City Council. An important part of many forecasting exercises is to appreciate the past as an important determinant of the future. The recent past for indoor swimming by Sheffield's population was a vital contextual consideration in this particular forecasting exercise. Swimming in Sheffield had fallen from a level which mirrored the national average participation rate and frequency in 1980, to a level which was substantially below the national average by 1986 (the latest General Household Survey (GHS), data available at the time of the forecasts).

The 1980s saw a surge in swimming attendances nationally. By 1986 it was estimated that the 'attendance factor' – the total number of swims per year divided by the population of Great Britain (GHS was a GB survey) – was 9.8 swims per individual nationally, having risen from 2.9 in 1980. Both participation rates and the frequency of swimming had more than doubled in this period. We assumed a ratio of junior to adult swims of 2:1, taken from the little evidence available at the time of junior participation (GHS is only a survey of adults).

In Sheffield we estimated the attendance factor to have declined from 3.05 in 1980 to 2.87 in 1987. The contrast with the national growth in swimming could hardly have been more dramatic. If Sheffield's swimming attendances had kept pace with the national growth rates of the 1980s, by 1987 they would have been more than three times higher than the figure they actually reached for that year. Clearly the plans to build new swimming facilities were not only part of the grander plan to help regenerate the city, but also compatible with an effort to reverse this disastrous performance of swimming in the city.

There was no reason at the time of the forecasts to suspect that Sheffield's population was radically different from the national average in respect of potential for swimming. It was therefore an important root to the forecasts to assume that there was a large latent demand for swimming in Sheffield by the late 1980s.

Four projections were made in the demand forecasts, shown in Figure 14.1.

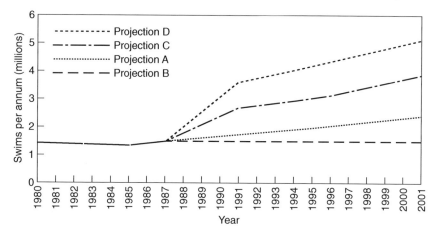

Figure 14.1 Summary of forecasts to 2001

Projections A and B

These assumed no change in facility mix, i.e. no building of Ponds Forge and Hillsborough, and continuation of all the older pools. Projection A assumed a mild growth in the attendance factor, echoing to a lesser extent the assumed, continuing growth nationally in swimming. Projection B assumed an attendance factor constrained to that experienced by Sheffield in the mid-1980s.

Projections C and D

These projections assumed the intended re-investment, i.e. building the two new facilities and closing the four older pools, with the new pools having a wider catchment than the old pools and annual visits per square metre of water area in line with other urban leisure pools. Projection C demonstrates only the facility change, with no improvement in the management, particularly the marketing of the existing or the new facilities. The strongest growth projection D, however, was predicated on the additional assumptions of a strong marketing initiative for the two new facilities and improvement in marketing of the older pools, helping to inspire a sustained recovery in the swimming attendance factor for Sheffield's population, to the 1986 national average of 9.8 swims per year per head of population.

In the most optimistic of these four forecasts, Projection D, the attendance factor for Sheffield swimming was not taken above the national figure for 1986, even by the year 2001. It was likely that the growth in swimming nationally would continue beyond the 1986 attendance factor but this was not built into the more optimistic estimates for Sheffield. In this sense the exercise concluded with the statement that:

... we regard the projection D growth forecast as a conservative estimate of the extent of additional swimming demand in Sheffield post 1991.

(Leisure Research Services, 1988, p. 21)

The conclusion of the demand forecasts was that the main hope of Sheffield getting anywhere near the national average levels of swimming participation lay in the proposed change in facilities, although some growth prospect also depended on improvement in the marketing of swimming in the city.

In an additional exercise conducted for Sheffield City Council, Leisure Research Services (1989) employed the Scottish Sports Council's Facilities Planning Model to predict the spatial distribution of demand in relation to the facilities anticipated in Sheffield after the building of two new facilities and closure of four older pools. This planning model, since adopted and further developed by the English Sports Council, does not predict actual demand but rather the demand that would pertain if an area had a well distributed supply of good quality facilities that are well promoted; i.e. the model predicts the level of potential demand. Nevertheless, such an estimate provides a useful benchmark for planning facility provision. Furthermore, the model uses local population data to predict the distribution of potential demand in an area, compared with the geographical impact of existing (and planned) facilities. The difference between the two can reveal a position somewhere between at one extreme a surplus demand uncatered for by the existing (and planned) facilities, to at the other extreme a surplus capacity underutilised by demand.

The results of the facilities planning model for Sheffield's swimming market are summarised in Figure 14.2. It reveals a potential market demand which is almost entirely capable of being satisfied by the proposed facility mix. This is despite a very high level of potential demand estimated under the positive assumptions identified above. The planning model's estimate of potential demand is higher than Projection D in the demand forecasts of Figure 14.1. This endorses the conservative nature of the demand forecasts estimated in the first exercise.

What has happened to swimming in Sheffield?

The experience of swimming attendances in Sheffield after the facility changes of 1991 offers, on first inspection, little comfort to those wishing to maintain the rationalist line that demand forecasting has a vital purpose in the planning of new facilities. Figure 14.3 represents the two forecasts made under the assumption of the 1991 facility changes (projections C and D in Figure 1) and adds the actual attendances of the 1990s. It is clear that swimming attendances have not come near to reaching the most pessimistic forecast. Indeed they do not even approach the forecasts made in respect of no new facilities in 1991 (projections A and B in Figure 14.1).

The actual attendance factor nationally has risen slightly to 10.5 for the latest date available, 1996. By comparison the attendance factor in Sheffield for 1996 was 2.2. New facility provision has therefore not narrowed the gap between

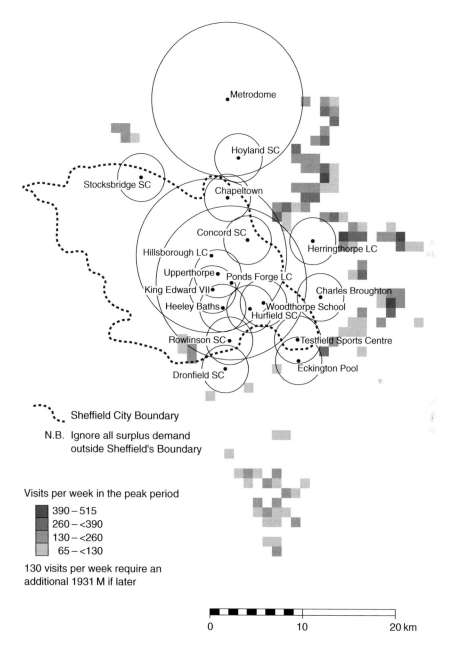

Visits per week in the peak period

  390 – 515
  260 – <390
  130 – <260
   65 – <130

130 visits per week require an
additional 1931 M if later

0   10   20 km

Figure 14.2 SSC supply demand model: Sheffield analysis surplus demand for swimming
in 1 km squares

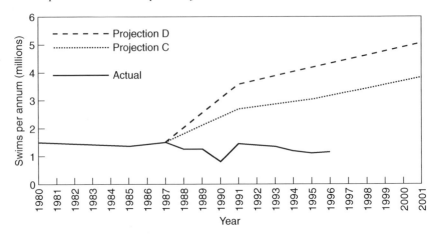

Figure 14.3 Actual attendances against forecast

Sheffield's swimming behaviour and national participation. In fact the gap has continued to widen. The total number of swims in Sheffield in 1996, 1.16 million visits, was two million below the conservative demand forecast for the new facility mix, and more than three million visits below the more optimistic forecast.

In the period since the investment in the two new pools, total swimming attendances in local authority pools in Sheffield have never climbed above their norm for the early- to mid-1980s, and have only matched this norm briefly in the immediate 'afterglow' of the World Student Games. Since 1991/2 total attendances fell steadily for four years, then rose slightly in 1996/7. Only two out of Sheffield's 11 public swimming pools had higher attendances in 1996/7 than they had in 1991/2.

In addressing the mismatch between the forecasts and reality, two key questions can be identified:

- what prevented swimming attendances in Sheffield from 'taking off' after the 1991 initiative of two major new facilities?
- did the demand forecasts for swimming have any value, given their inaccuracy?

Constraints to growth in swimming

There has been national concern over swimming attendances in the 1990s, reflected in two national surveys of local authorities' swimming attendances conducted for the Institute of Sport and Recreation Management (ISRM) (Taylor and Kearney, 1995; Taylor and Kwok, 1998). The first of these surveys suggested a rise in overall swimming attendances in local authority pools of 1 per cent in the year 1991 to 1992, followed by a 4 per cent fall in the year 1992 to 1993. The second survey suggested constant aggregate attendance figures for the period 1994 to 1996, but this was the net result of half the responding authorities suffering a further decline in swimming attendances, whilst the other half enjoyed increasing swimming attendances.

Both ISRM surveys revealed considerable variation between local authorities in swimming attendances. In the first survey, 51 authorities reported a greater than 10 per cent fall in attendances between 1991 and 1993 while 39 authorities reported a greater than 10 per cent rise in attendances. Sheffield's experience was not out of line with many local authorities which suffered decline in swimming attendances. However, given the major new build in 1991 it might have expected to be among those authorities with increasing attendances.

By comparison, evidence from the General Household Survey suggests a stable level of national swimming participation in the 1990s, with the adult four-week participation rate more or less constant at 13 per cent and the average frequency of participation also constant at four occasions per four weeks during the period 1990 to 1996.

The aggregate picture of swimming attendances in Britain, however, conceals some more dramatic changes in the constituent elements. According to the ISRM evidence, nationally there has been a significant fall in casual swimming attendances by juniors, and in educational attendances. There is, however, evidence of a sustained, strong growth in attendances for private swimming lessons, typically for juniors. Anecdotally these national patterns are reflected in Sheffield's swimming attendances, with a fall in educational use and junior casual swims, and a rise in private swimming lessons' attendances. A puzzle both nationally and locally is why young people show such a strong demand to learn to swim but a weakening demand to enjoy swimming.

A factor that may have prevented increasing attendances in swimming is increased entrance prices. Nichols and Taylor (1995), using CIPFA data, have demonstrated a rise in local authority swimming prices nationally in the early 1990s that exceeded the rate of inflation by over 30 per cent. In the mid-1990s, CIPFA data disclose a rise in local authority swimming prices only just higher than the rate of inflation. The same source reveals Sheffield's swimming prices to be, by 1995, well above the median for local authorities nationally, for both adult and junior casual swimming and junior private lessons.

Despite coincidental evidence of falling swimming attendances and swimming prices rising faster than the rate of inflation, there is as yet no conclusive evidence that price rises are an important cause of falling swimming attendances. The little evidence there is on price elasticity of demand for indoor sports facilities (Gratton and Taylor, 1995) suggests price inelastic demand is the norm. This may still explain the fall in swimming attendances in Sheffield, however, since a large rise in prices may have caused a less than proportionate, but still significant, fall in demand.

Taylor and Kwok (1998) report perceptions of local authority swimming pool managers and they rate rising prices very low in a list of factors they felt contributed to falling swimming attendances. Top of these managers' perceived reasons for falling attendances were growing competition from new attractions, deterioration in the quality of their facilities, and the growth of alternative health and fitness activities. The last of these reasons was not well supported by evidence of dry side attendances compared to swimming attendances at the centres investigated – there was little evidence of substitution of dry for wet side attendances.

Financial pressure on local authorities has been shown to increase markedly in the 1990s compared with the 1980s (Taylor and Page, 1994; CELTS, 1996). Sheffield has been conspicuous with its problems of financial readjustment in the face of declining Revenue Support Grant from central government. Two important negative consequences for attendances in sports facilities are likely to have been reduced maintenance budgets and reduced promotion budgets. The first of these consequences has been documented as a common threat to services in Taylor and Page's (1994) survey of local authority financing of sport and recreation. It is also endorsed by the second ISRM survey (Taylor and Kwok, 1998), not only by the perceptions of managers but also by evidence of a national decline in expenditure on improving the physical condition of local authority swimming pools, in the period 1994 to 1996.

A potentially important factor for the largest Sheffield facility, Ponds Forge, is the disruption of participatory swimming by major events, demonstrating a conflict between the economic impact of major events and the social impact of normal swimming participation. Of the 300 sports events staged in Sheffield in the period 1990 to 1997, 56 have utilised swimming facilities (typically the main pool in Ponds Forge), an average of eight a year (Kronos, 1997). Of these most will have occupied the facility for a weekend, but a few major ones such as the European Swimming Championships of 1993 and the World Masters Swimming Championships of 1996 will have disrupted normal swimming programmes for up to two weeks of the year. In addition, there are many regional and local events, which can disrupt normal programming on a regular but infrequent basis.

Both the cumulative impact of regular disruptions to normal programmes and the occasional long duration disruption may have had negative impacts on swimming attendances, not simply while the events were staged but also for a time afterwards. Normal swimming participants may, as a result of the disruption, stop swimming and be slow to return. This effect, if it exists, is largely confined to one swimming pool in Sheffield, Ponds Forge. However, this pool accounts for well over a third of swimming attendances in the city, so changes in its attendances do impact significantly on the total for the city.

Another factor inhibiting the growth of public sector swimming attendances is the growth of private swimming participation, particularly in hotels and commercial fitness clubs. In Sheffield there are five pools provided by the commercial sector, most built in the 1990s, three of which are quite small (12–15 metres long) but the two most recent are of reasonable size (20 and 25 metres long). The latter two developments are too recent to have impacted on the total attendances reported for the city above, however, so private competition is unlikely to have contributed to the decline of the 1990s.

In combination, private pools in Sheffield now have the capability of attracting considerable numbers of swimming participants. This effect is likely to increase in importance with the continuing development of large-scale fitness clubs, following the successful model of the Esporta club, which contains the 25 metre pool and opened in 1997. An unresolved empirical question, however, is whether private commercial pools divert demand from local authority pools or create a new market which is looking for a different product – i.e. better quality, especially in the changing and ancillary facilities. If commercial pools are creating a new market, then there is still a largely unresolved question concerning the 1990s decline in local authority swimming in Sheffield.

Another form of competition which may have diverted swimmers away from Sheffield is regional – Barnsley Metrodome, Doncaster Dome and Rotherham's Herringthorpe pools all have a regional presence. However, it is unlikely that these pools have taken a substantial demand from Sheffield. Evidence from market research at swimming pools generally suggests that a 15 minute drive time defines the catchment area for most facilities and even for large facilities it is unlikely to be extended much further.

A final consideration, which is of uncertain relevance to swimming attendances, is a shift from local authority management to charitable trust management. In Sheffield, Ponds Forge has been managed under a trust arrangement (in recent years, Sheffield International Venues) for most of its lifetime. Most of the other pools in Sheffield are, at the time of writing, in the process of transferring to a trust management arrangement. However, the forerunner to this was one pool, King Edwards, which moved from local authority ownership to a charitable trust in 1993 after being threatened with closure by the local authority. Interestingly, King Edwards Pool is one of the two pools in the city to have increased attendances since 1990.

Lessons for forecasting

Even with the blessing of hindsight, it is difficult to envisage constructing demand forecasts for swimming in Sheffield at the end of the 1980s in a different manner to the method and assumptions chosen at that time. Whilst there are some factors which would have been difficult to anticipate, their effects are not clearly to blame for the inaccuracy of the forecasts:

- The fact that a fifteen year strong growth trend in swimming nationally came to an end in the 1990s is not really significant, because national participation has stabilised, not fallen significantly. In any case even the most optimistic demand forecast for swimming in Sheffield was based on an attendance factor taken from 1986 and the current national attendance factor is still well above that figure.
- Radically higher entrance charges might have been predicted, given the increasing financial constraint being imposed on local authorities. Even so, it is not clear if the higher entrance charges have had a significant effect in causing declining swimming attendances, although this is distinctly possible.
- The conflict between hosting major swimming events and sustaining normal casual participation may be apparent in one facility only, albeit the main one, Ponds Forge, and this affects attendances sporadically.

- The rise in private sector competition in swimming has not been significant until the mid- to late-1990s and it is not yet clear if it substitutes for local authority swimming demand or creates a new market.

Other possible contributory factors to explaining the error in the demand forecasts for Sheffield were difficult to predict at the time of the forecasts. These variables include the decline in junior casual swimming; the reduced maintenance and deterioration in the quality of facilities; increased competition from new attractions; and reductions in schools' curricular swimming.

Data problems

In constructing the demand forecasts for Sheffield's swimming, one of the problems was the lack of accurate data, which echoes Rodgers' concerns quoted at the beginning of this paper. Facility attendance data was corrupted by absent or inaccurate recording of numbers attending block booking sessions, including educational use, club use and private lessons. Similar problems still exist. It is not uncommon for block-booking sessions' attendances to be inaccurately recorded or for simple assumptions to be used, such as 30 children per school session.

Such data problems extend to private, multi-facility, fitness complexes, with members paying for use of all the facilities and the numbers using the swimming pool are typically unrecorded. A different data collection problem is that the ownership of 'public' pools is becoming increasingly fragmented, so a holistic view of swimming attendances in the city is becoming more of a detective job than before. In Sheffield two dual-use facilities have returned to the management of schools. Furthermore, the continued shift in ownership and management of facilities from local authorities to charitable trusts may give rise to problems in acquiring information from the latter.

Conclusions

The answers to both the central questions of this paper – concerning the inaccuracy of forecasts and an explanation for swimming attendances in Sheffield in the 1990s – remain elusive. Both answers, of course, coincide since the reasons for the lack of growth in swimming are the reasons for the inaccuracy of the forecasts.

The use of sport for urban regeneration often highlights both social and economic benefits. The change in swimming provision in Sheffield in the early 1990s was proclaimed as one that would bring both kinds of benefits – it was for the community as well as for the city's economy. It would appear that one half of this aspiration, the social impact of increased swimming participation, has clearly not manifested itself in Sheffield as a result of the sports initiative. This brings into even sharper focus the economic impact from major swimming events in the city, i.e. the effects of events and associated spectators (see Chapter 3). It also draws attention to other sports development impacts, such as the development of elite squads in Sheffield, of which diving is a successful example.

Sheffield City Council decision-makers did attempt to inform themselves with appropriate information in the run up to their sports initiative of the early 1990s. However, although demand forecasting informed these decision-makers with the best information available at the time, it turned out in this case at this particular time to be unreliable.

To use the Sheffield case as a reason to abandon such demand forecasting in future facility planning, however, would be a serious mistake, as Veal (1994) points out:

> The whim of a powerful politician can achieve more in a few months than the most carefully researched plans ...
>
> ... However, every anecdote of such whims producing positive outcomes can be matched by stories of disasters, of 'white elephants', wasted resources and real needs neglected.
>
> (Veal 1994, p. 109)

References

CELTS (1996) 'Will the Money Go Round?'. *Recreation*. Institute of Sport and Recreation Management.

Critcher, C. (1992) 'Sporting Civic Pride: Sheffield and the World Student Games of 1991', in *Leisure in the 1990s: Rolling Back the Welfare State*. Leisure Studies Association.

Dobson, N. and Gratton, C. (1996) 'From City of Steel to City of Sport: an Evaluation of Sheffield's Attempt to Use Sport as a Vehicle for Urban Regeneration'. Paper presented to Tourism and Culture conference, Durham.

Elson, M. (1977) 'The Poverty of Leisure Forecasting', in Howarth J. and Parker S., *Forecasting Leisure Futures*. Leisure Studies Association.

Foley, P. (1991) 'The Impact of Major Events: a Case Study of the World Student Games and Sheffield'. *Environment and Planning*.

Gratton C., Dobson N. and Shibli, S. (2001) 'The Economic Impact of Major Sports Events: A Case Study of Six European and World Championships', in Henry, I. and Gratton, C. (eds), *Sport in the City*. Routledge.

Gratton, C. and Taylor, P.D. (1992) *Economics of Leisure Services Management*. Longman.

Gratton, C. and Taylor, P.D. (1995) 'From Economic Theory to Leisure Practice via Empirics: the Case of Demand and Price'. *Leisure Studies*, Vol. 14, p. 4.

Kronos (1997) 'The Economic Impact of Sports Events Staged in Sheffield 1990–97'. Kronos.

Leisure Research Services (1988) *Swimming Demand in Sheffield: post-1991 Forecasts*. Unpublished report to Sheffield City Council.

Leisure Research Services (1989) *Sports Facility Planning in Sheffield*. Unpublished report to Sheffield City Council.

Nichols, G. and Taylor, P. (1995) 'The impact on local authority leisure provision of compulsory competitive tendering, financial cuts and changing attitudes'. *Local Government Studies*, Vol. 21, p. 4.

Roche, M. (1992a) 'Mega-Events and Urban Policy'. *Annals of Tourism Research*, Vol. 21, p. 1.

Roche, M. (1992b) 'Mega-Event Planning and Citizenship: Problems of Rationality and Democracy in Sheffield's Universiade 1991'. *Vrijetijd en Samenleving*, Vol. 10, p. 4.

Rodgers, B. (1977) 'Forecasting: the Last of the Black Arts?', in Howarth J. and Parker S. (eds), *Forecasting Leisure Futures.* Leisure Studies Association.

Taylor, P. and Kearney, J. (1995) *Swimming in Decline?* Institute of Sport and Recreation Management.

Taylor, P. and Page, K. (1994) *The Financing of Local Authority Sport and Recreation: a Service Under Threat?* Institute of Sport and Recreation Management.

Taylor, P. and Kwok, K.C. (1998) *Swimming Participation: Down and Out or On The Up?* Institute of Sport and Recreation Management.

Veal, A.J. (1994) *Leisure policy and planning.* Longman.

Williams, C. (1997) *Consumer Services and Economic Development.* Routledge.

Part VI

Politics and sports policy

15 Sport, leisure and European Union regional policy

A case study of Merseyside (UK)

Nicola Matthews and Ian Henry

Introduction

The European Commission devoted 25 per cent of the European Union's budget (153.038 billion ECU for the period 1994–9) to addressing the disparities between the prosperous regions of the Union and those on the economic periphery. Funds supporting EU Cohesion policies are administered through the European Structural Funds, primarily the European Regional Development Fund (ERDF) and the European Social Fund (ESF). Grant aid is given to rural and urban communities seeking to come to terms with the loss of traditional industries and needing to retrain the local workforce for the demands of new industries. This chapter focuses on the use of regional development funds in sport and leisure for the purposes of social and economic regeneration. Sport, leisure and tourism are increasingly elements in strategies for local economic restructuring, however, their place in European level regional development programmes (Single Programming Documents) is becoming more evident. The chapter outlines the principles of EU regional policies and seeks to demonstrate, the ways in which leisure, and in particular sports-related projects, have become incorporated into European regional programmes in the UK. Merseyside, an Objective 1 area, is used as a case study region.

The study reported here is part of an on-going programme of work on European leisure policy. The focus of the research reported here is on evaluation of the impact of regional policy, in particular the role of the European Union's Structural Funds, on investment in urban sport and leisure.

The development of a European Union level regional policy

The European Community was founded on the vision of including the largest number of European states possible. The accession of Spain and Portugal, in 1981, following the UK and Republic of Ireland, who had joined in 1973, tested the feasibility of this goal, particularly in the sphere of economic policy. The membership of these states meant the inclusion of regions with a GDP substantially below the Community average. The issue was further reinforced with the accession of Greece. Enlargement of the Union exacerbated the difficulties of reconciling the differences between regions in the economic core and those on the periphery of the Community (Armstrong and de Kervenoael, 1997). The problem remains a concern, since per capita GDP in the ten richest regions is more than 3.5 times greater than the ten least affected regions; and unemployment in the 10 worst hit regions has been up to seven times greater than the ten least affected regions (EC, 1996). The difference between most of the UK regions in this position and those of Ireland, Greece, Portugal and Spain, is that the British regions which lagged behind European economic norms were predominantly urban and industrial.

The desire to reduce regional inequalities between Member States was articulated in the Treaty of Rome (EEC Treaty, 1957) but it was at the Paris Summit of the European Council in 1974 that the policy was formalised. This complemented the re-structuring of the Commission in 1968 which led to the creation of DGXVI (Directorate General for Regional Policy). The budget, for the newly formed Structural Funds, was set at 5 per cent of the Community's total expenditure and the grants were to be a maximum of 50 per cent of project costs. This allowed European programmes to be developed which acknowledged the importance of cohesion but which did not take responsibility away from Member State governments.

The Single European Act (1987) added to the EEC Treaty a clearer reference to the goal of regional equality. It established 'Cohesion' as a key Community policy, based on concerns the European institutions had for the effect the internal market would have on peripheral regions (EC, 1996). Following on at the Brussels Summit of the European Council in 1988 it was agreed, in principle, that there should be an increase to the Structural Fund budget, and it rose to 25 per cent of the total EC budget by 1993. This represented a sizeable increase in funds being channelled into cohesion policies.

The Single European Market was to be the foundation of Economic and Monetary Union (EMU). Central to the process is the introduction of a common currency, made possible through a degree of convergence between the economies of the Member States choosing to sign up to the currency (EC, 1996). The decision led to a further increase to the Structural Fund budget to 25000M ECU per annum, to off-set the 'feared disintegrative effects of EMU' (Halpin, 1998: 1). The criteria for EMU were set during the negotiation of the Maastricht Treaty in 1992 and these led to changes to the economic policies pursued by governments. In particular, the EMU criteria presented difficulties for the least prosperous Member States, since they had to invest to increase their potential for growth, yet reduce their public budget deficits to keep debt under control, to meet the criteria for joining EMU. The predicament increased the importance and necessity of Cohesion policies. Currently 25 per cent of Commission expenditure is channelled into the goal of reducing regional economic inequalities, approximately 153 billion MECU.

The structure of the regional programmes

Subsidiarity, the devolving of decisions to the lowest appropriate level of government, is the foundation of the Commission's approach to regional policy. However, the Structural Funds are managed through operating principles agreed in 1989. The Funds are governed by four principles: concentration (targeting); multi-annual programming; additionality; and partnership. The most fundamental principle is concentration. To ensure the efficient use of the budget, the Commission focuses on six Objectives areas, these ensure resources are directed towards those regions hardest hit by economic change (see Table 15.1). The programmes also encourage partnership between tiers of government and the different sectors.

> There is expected to be 'horizontal' interaction between many regional and local authorities, social partners such as trade unions and business and voluntary and environmental groups as well as engagement with 'vertical' partners in national government departments and sections of the European Commission.
>
> (Turok and Bachtler, 1997: 5)

The reform of regional policy in 1989 also gave funding a defined temporal structure: Programme One was 1989–93, and Programme Two 1994–9. The final characteristic is additionality. Community funding is not intended to replace government aid offered by the Member States. Each state must maintain 'its public structural or comparable expenditure at least at the same level as in previous programming period' (EC, 1992: 20).

EU regional programmes: objective areas and funding regimes

Grant aid is predominately given via the European Regional Development Fund (ERDF) (infrastructural works and business development) and the European Social Fund, (ESF) (occupational integration for long-term and young unemployed). The ERDF is the larger of the two funds contributing 49.5 per cent of European regional grant aid. The ESF provides 29.9 per cent of funding for the 1994–9 programme (EC, 1996). The six target areas which are the focus of the Commission's work are outlined in Table 15.1.

In our focus here on investment in urban sport and leisure, objectives 1 and 2 are the most significant of these. Objectives 1, 2 and 5b are primarily financed by the ERDF and objectives 3, 4 and 5a are financed by the ESF. Objective 6 is a specific programme in its own right. These objectives take up 90 per cent of the funds allocated to regional assistance. Community Initiatives take up a further 9 per cent of the grants available. These programmes, run at the European level, deal with sectoral rather than regional issues. In June 1994, 13 initiatives were approved, including: RECHAR II: conversion of coalmining areas; HORIZON: employment opportunities for people with disabilities; URBAN: regeneration of crisis areas in large towns.

The final 1 per cent of funding for regional development contributes towards a programme of innovative measures. It does not operate through predetermined priorities, rather it empowers 'the Commission to initiate pilot projects, networks for co-operation … with the aim of generating input for new policies through Community-wide experimentation' (EC, 1997). The system is beneficial to agencies operating in regions without objective status and is an additional source of funding for ESF projects, looking at new approaches to vocational training.

Table 15.1 The six objectives of the European Commission's regional policy

Objective	Priorities
Objective 1	Lagging regions[a]
Objective 2	Regions affected by industrial decline[b]
Objective 3	Long-term unemployed, youth unemployment and equal opportunities
Objective 4	Worker adaptation to technological and industrial change
Objective 5a	Reform and modernisation in the fisheries sector and in line with the CAP
Objective 5b	Structural adjustment of rural areas and communities[c]
Objective 6	Aid for regions of very low density of population

(a) GDP per capita less than 75% of the Community average in the preceeding three years
(b) Higher than Community average unemployment
(c) High agrarian employment or 'significant depopulation trend' (EC, 1992)

European structural funds in the UK

Over the last three decades there has been a period of re-structuring whereby the major industrial countries are deemed to be moving towards an economy based on services. An issue arising out of the shift is that the emerging service industries have not been directly replacing the jobs lost from manufacturing (Vanhove and Klaassen, 1987). This has been exacerbated by uneven geographical development of the tertiary sector. Expansion of the labour force in the South East, South West and East Anglia has run in parallel to the declining levels of employment in the North East and North West. The UK thus came to be seen as a 'dual' economy divided between a 'post-industrial' south and east and a 'deindustrialised' north and west (Allen and Massey, 1988).

The UK is a major beneficiary of the Union's regional policy (in phase 2, 1994–9, 3 regions had objective 1 status, 12 had objective 2 status and 7 objective 5b). In total the UK was receiving the equivalent of £1.07bn, from EU programmes (EC, 1997) and the contribution of European funding to UK regional policy budget more than doubled between the 1989–93 and 1994–9 programmes. Most EU finding came from the ERDF and the primary recipients were local authorities. During the period 1994–9, the ERDF was to contribute £1,250m to UK regions (Martin, 1997).

Structural funds in the UK: policy planning and execution

In the absence of a regional tier of government in the UK at the time of conducting this research, the system of grant aid was co-ordinated through central government departments and government agents located in the administrative regions of England and Wales. (The Labour Government elected in 1997 has since set up Regional Development Agencies, and indicated that Regional Political Assemblies may possibly follow.) The Government Offices for the Regions (GORs) were secretariats for the Structural Funds and worked in conjunction with the Department of the Environment, Transport and the Regions and local authorities. The single programming document (SPD), central to regional economic planning was thus negotiated by local partners, the appropriate GOR and central government. It was then approved, usually with amendments, by the Commission. The single programming document identifies areas of weakness in a region's economic profile and suggests priority policy 'measures', outlining key areas for investment, namely: investment in new technology, small or medium-size enterprises, and the retraining of workforces.

In the absence of a regional authority, the GOR was responsible for the evaluation of project bids and the distribution of payments to successful applicants. Project evaluation was undertaken by staff assigned to specific structural funds who compared bids to criteria set at the level of policy measures. Successful bidders then received grant payments from Government Offices for the Region, as long as the project continued to meet the objectives set in relation to the single planning document.

The research focus: sport and leisure in European regional development

The focus of the work presented here is on the impact the structural funds have on funding for sports projects. The difficulty is that structural funds deal specifically with issues regarding employment training and business investment, and sport projects as such are not eligible, in their own right, for EU investment (via DGXVI), they are only supported as vehicles for achieving economic objectives. Our study illustrates the use of structural funds in Merseyside, an objective 1 area. The study was based on semi-structured interviews conducted with representatives of local government and Government Offices (13 interviews) and documentary evidence collected, from project application forms and project evaluation forms.

The ERDF and ESF: the potential for leisure-related expenditure in the UK

Regional funding is about helping the peripheral regions within the Union. To this end, a single planning document will outline areas of local deficit and identify areas in which the region seeks to make economic gains. All projects must contribute *directly* to the rejuvenation of local economies. The key concern for the regions in receipt of European funding is economic diversification, the fostering of a business environment and the targeting of new industries. As an additional means of diversifying local economies, regions have also been proactive in promoting tourist and leisure ventures. It is under the latter that sports infrastructure and training in sport-related occupations are concentrated. Projects, however, fulfil economically-driven objectives. Thus one is led to ask whether, and in what ways, sports projects, normally associated with social rationales and community activity, can contribute to programmes designed to rejuvenate local economies.

Sports-related expenditure can *only* be justified when it relates back to the primary concerns of the European Union's regional policy, that is, to infrastructural improvement which will attract inward investment or employment training which relates directly to identified demands in the local labour market for new skills. The latter might relate, for example, to sports coaching development courses, the former encompasses a more broad range of objectives. Leisure expenditure (inclusive of spending on sport) can contribute to the redevelopment of an area in two ways: (a) the tourism focus: bringing tourists in or extending an existing tourist season; (b) the environmental focus: as a secondary, contributory factor to the attraction of new companies seeking to relocate. The area of sports tourism is of course a growing field. The case study outlined below demonstrates the significance of leisure to regeneration.

A case study of Merseyside: the Wirral

Large-scale investment in sport and leisure has been central to strategies employed by cities such as Sheffield, Leeds and Birmingham seeking to restructure local economies and rethink their respective images. The research for this chapter however, focuses on the potential for smaller projects to contribute to the redevelopment of local communities affected by changing economic forces. Merseyside is an objective 1 region (a lagging region with a GDP below 75 per cent of the Community average). The Wirral is a Metropolitan district within the region that has sought to maximise its share of European funding coming into the region.

> The Metropolitan Borough of Wirral has attracted over £40m of European Regional Development Funds … The assistance, managed through a targeted, co-ordinated strategy, is regenerating the local economy and has helped to:
>
> * create and safeguard jobs
> * encourage private sector investment
> * put Wirral on the international map
>
> (Wirral Metropolitan Borough Council, 1996: 2)

In the single planning document for Merseyside 1994–6, investment in the cultural, media and leisure industries was identified alongside a need to encourage investment in the knowledge-based and advanced technology industries. The programme of measures followed on from previous Merseyside Integrated Development Operations (MIDO) objectives designed to encourage leisure and tourism (the MIDO programmes were forerunners to the 1994–9 objective 1 single planning document). The range of projects supported through European funding is outlined in Table 15.2.

The projects exhibit similar objectives: contribution to the local economy and to *direct* employment. Projects are framed by anticipated gains to the Wirral area and not by the potential benefits of the projects to the Borough's current residents. The absence of social rationales is deliberate as few European programmes (outside some of the Commission's own initiatives) allow for community-based activities

Table 15.2 Details of the successful European funding bids submitted by Wirral Metropolitan Borough Council, all information taken from ERDF application forms

Project	Project background	Project objectives
West Kirby Marine Lake 1984	The lake once reconstructed and extended will form a considerable tourist attraction in the Dee estuary setting, which will stimulate fresh hotel accommodation development in the area ... The scheme must be seen in the context of the Council's objective of developing the tourism potential of the Wirral	Modernised sailing facilities among other structural improvements; anticipated usage figures, pa.: 1,200 licence holders 1,000 casual users 1,000 sailing school entrants 5,000 pleasure boat users.
Bebington Oval, International Athletics Track, 1989	The project is intended to attract ... athletic events with the attendant economic benefits. In 'Measures: Priorities for Action' of the NW Regional Plan one measure is the 'Provision of the new attractions and development of existing activities. Measures include – sports arenas'. The project will contribute economic benefit by the exploitation of Wirral's proven ability to attract national and international competitors to the area.	1 modernised facility; 10 temporary jobs; 1 permanent job; 100,000 more spectators and competitors.
Conway Park Swimming Centre, 1993	As a regional and local facility the project will have a key role in developing Wirral's tourism, serving strategic objective (iv) ... a key element of the wider redevelopment of Conway Park ... serving strategic objective (i) modernising major economic infrastructure and (ii) building a positive image ... encouraging investment.	1.2 hectares of land improved; 1 new visitor attraction; 85 temporary jobs; 50 permanent jobs; 75 indirectly created (1.5 multiplier used); 531,890 users per annum.
Wirral Sports Centre, 1993	The project facilities will attract participations and spectators from throughout the NW region and beyond and will be promoted as a major tournament venue within Wirral's marketing theme 'The Leisure Peninsula' ... The provision of modern leisure facilities helps attract new businesses to the area thus contributing to strategic objective 1.	1 new visitor attraction; 45 temporary jobs; 19 permanent jobs; 5 indirectly created jobs.

to be endorsed. The inability of project managers to declare 'social' intentions within a structural fund bid can be problematic. First, project managers are usually applying to a variety of funding agencies, each with their own objectives and criteria. This necessitates that bidders must revise rationales and 'sell' their projects in a variety of ways, often without declaring other overt rationales (for fear of prejudicing the individual claims). Second, with specific regard to European funding, the failure to acknowledge community benefit is invariably failure to acknowledge the main beneficiaries. Grant aid secured under tourism measures will naturally support projects with limited seasonal appeal, even where facilities are sought to extend the tourist season. The European Officer for the Wirral reflected on both these points:

> I wouldn't use the word leisure in terms of European funding because basically leisure reflects local use and European funding is definitely not for local use ... predominately you are going to be selling 'leisure' projects as tourism projects. Some of which are difficult to do because they are obviously local use. You can only have a certain number of international pools in your area! ... The European dimension has to be an economic impact, so although people would argue it is retaining the economy by causing people to spend in the area, rather than going outside the area to spend, they are rather looking for inward economic investment.
>
> (Wirral European Officer, interview March 1998)

Becoming attuned to European terminology and criteria is also essential to a successful bid. The Conway Park Swimming Pool was named 'the Europa Pool' and Bebington Oval became an 'international' athletics track, to aid the attraction of European support. The European Officer acknowledged 'We look at the project, we know the eligibility criteria, we know the right strings to pull and those words are put into the application' (op cit).

This brief look at the way leisure projects have been incorporated into the regional policies of Merseyside highlights a number of issues. First, direct economic impact in terms of inward investment must take priority over community rationales or the retaining of money in the local economy. Second, where other rationales are the dominant force behind the bid, project managers must maintain an overt appreciation of the economic significance of their bids. The potential for utilising European sources of grant aid is a function of project managers having a good understanding of the principles behind the Structural Funds and an ability to 'sell' their product accordingly. Clearly, support for many projects is motivated by the impact they will have on the local economy but there are also many others seeking to fulfil community-oriented goals.

Leisure and the revitalisation of local economies

European funding is designed to aid the process of economic regeneration. This has invariably implied the use of funds to help with the transition from the secondary to tertiary sector. These 'drivers for change' come in the form of incentive funding for small or medium-size enterprises and the new technology industries but, in addition, there has been an interest a pursuit of the service sector through tourism. Leisure attractions and sports facilities can and do contribute to strategies which seek to enhance either the environment (use of derelict sites) and/or the 'market-ability' of a location. Vanhove and Klaasen (1987) identified the main benefits of tourism expenditure.

> Five major benefits might result from the development of tourism: (a) income generation, (b) employment generation, (c) improvement of the economic structure, (d) encouragement of entrepreneurial activity, and (e) an improve-ment of population distribution.
>
> (Vanhove and Klaassen, 1987: 297)

It is important to consider the economic-orientation of these benefits when reflecting on the use of the Structural Funds for sports-related projects. European funding is designed to address specific issues. Projects must lead to *direct* employ-ment opportunities, increase the potential for inward investment and contribute to the sustainable development of a location. Infrastructural work, in particular, must be of long-term benefit, for example, lead to the development of a permanent hosting venue (e.g. Bebington Oval Athletics Track). The difficulty of these criteria for sports projects is that most are associated with community activity and social benefit (e.g. encouraging participation by under-represented groups such as women and people with disabilities). This perception of the role of sport for local communi-ties can lead to questions being raised about the appropiateness of the European structural funds supporting sporting expenditure.

Is there a genuine role for sport and leisure-related regional expenditure?

Evidence collected from the wider study of European funding suggests that leisure, in all its manifested forms (the arts, cultural heritage, tourism and sport), has become increasingly common place in single planning documents. Many county councils and local authorities seek to incorporate leisure strategies into regeneration plans. Difficulties arise, however, when such groups seek to capitalise on European funds. The opportunities to exploit this source of funding are limited but as local authorities become more comfortable with European regulation, so their ability to focus on European priorities is increased.

How are the projects expected to contribute to single programming document objectives?

Merseyside in particular (but also other British regions in which this research was conducted), specified the development of the leisure, tourist and sporting industries as a priority areas within their respective single planning documents. What is of interest is to establish the ways in which leisure and sports-related projects have contributed to the economic regeneration programmes. The concern is to consider what the projects have sought to achieve and the significance of their presence in regeneration plans. Economic rationales, be they of investment or employment value, must be emphasised in this ERDF application, over and above social gains for the local community. Invariably the projects complement schemes designed more specifically to attract inward investment. Single programming documents contain a range of policy priorities, most of which seek to support the development of local small or medium-size enterprises and to encourage companies to relocate through re-training workforces previously dependent on traditional industries. For urban locations, sport and leisure projects tend to perform complementary rather than primary roles in regeneration.

Were expectations of leisure and sports-related projects being met?

The frequency with which leisure appears in regional strategies would suggest that local authorities and government offices perceive such projects to be of economic value. The reality, however, is that regions have not faired equally under such policies. The North West region had dropped investment in media and sports training for the 1994–9 programmes, and the Government Office for Yorkshire and Humberside (GOYH) had to negotiate with the Commission to retain tourism in its single planning document for 1994–9. The previous programme's tourism measure had failed to yield more than 12 per cent of the jobs anticipated (interview with GOYH official, May 1997). The inability to fully quantify gains from tourism and leisure-related expenditure could be one of the reasons why the Commission is hesitant to encourage investment in these areas.

Conclusions: issues arising from the structure of regional policy in the UK

This chapter has primarily concerned itself with technical issues regarding the rationales for, and the roles of, sport and leisure-related expenditure in the UK's use of European structural funds. Merseyside provides an example of a region which has linked local regeneration plans to the aims of the European Union's own regional policy. Policy at the European level is a complex process of negotiation and communication between three tiers of governance. Each tier has specific responsibilities regarding the shape and interpretation of policy, the distribution of information and the allocation of resources. The British case provides an example of the complexity of policy networks, and of the way in which, within such contexts, rationales for policy have to be negotiated and renegotiated to gain funding through the European structural funds.

In Britain local administrators have worked within the context of a strong involvement of central government in regional development decisions. Unlike Spain, France, or Germany, for example, there has not been a strong regional presence in the policy system, and Government Offices for the Regions are the conduit through which applications to Brussels have had to be routed. These GORs are, however, representative of the interests of central government. Up until 1997 (thus, given the lead time required for planning and submitting projects, for virtually all planned projects for the period 1994–9) local administrators were faced with negotiating single planning documents through a Conservative administration's regional governmental wing (GORs). This was a government ideologically opposed to increasing local expenditure (European funding of projects is only partial and has to be matched in some degree by local funding), and one which in its own regeneration packages had from the mid-1980s onwards downplayed social aspects of urban regeneration in favour of projects with an economic rationale (Henry, 1993). The single planning documents also had to be negotiated via a European Commission charged with fostering economic growth regionally. In this context local administrators have had to become particularly inventive in justifying projects which they themselves may promote for social benefits, by reference to the potential economic impacts to be generated. The economic benefits rationale is not, however, without dangers since projects of considerable social value may be negatively evaluated if they fail to achieve the promised gains in employment or inward investment.

References

Allen, J. and Massey, D. (1988) *The Economy in Question*. London: Sage.

Armstrong, H. and de Kervenoael, R. (1997) 'Regional Economic Change in the European Union', in Bachtler, J. and Turok, I. (eds), *The Coherence of EU Regional Policy: contrasting perspectives on the Structural Funds*. London: Regional Studies Association, pp. 29–47.

DETR (1997) *Building Partnerships for Prosperity: Sustainable Growth, Competitiveness and Employment in the English Region*. London: Department of the Environment, Transport and the Regions.

European Commission (1992) *The Usage of European Funding Initiatives: Capital Projects*. Brussels: Office of Official Publications for the European Commission (OOPEC).

European Commission (1996) *European at the Service of Regional Development*, 2nd edn, Brussels: Office of Official Publications for the European Commission (OOPEC).

European Commission (1997) *Which regions are covered?* http://europa.eu.int/en/comm/dg05/esf/

European Commission (1998) *What does the European Social Fund do?* http://europa.eu.int/en/comm/dg05/esf/hwesf.htm

Halpin, C. (1998) *Structural Funds: Success or Failure?* http://www.economics.tcd.i.e/ser/1996/cormac.htm

Henry, I. (1993) *The Politics of Leisure Policy*. London: Macmillan.

Martin, S. (1997) *European Union Capital Funding and Local Authorities in England and Wales*. Warwick: Warwick Business School.

Turok, I. and Bachtler, J. (1997) 'Introduction' in Bachtler, J. and Turok, I. (eds) (1997) *The Coherence of EU Regional Policy: contrasting perspectives on the Structural Funds*. London: Regional Studies Association.

Rhodes, R.A.W. and Marsh, D. (1992) *Policy Networks in British Government*. Oxford: Clarendon Press.

Vanhoven, N. and Klaassen, L.H. (1987) *Regional Policy: A European Approach*, 2nd edn. Aldershot: Avebury.

Wirral Metropolitan Borough Council (1996) *A Decade of European Funded Projects in Wirral*. Birkenhead: EuroWirral.

16 The making of the UK Sports Institute

Eleni Theodoraki

Introduction

In 1995 the government published *Sport: Raising the Game*, its most significant policy statement on sport since the 1975 White Paper *Sport and Recreation* (Department of Environment, 1975). Core to this statement was the declared intention to establish a UK Sports Institute (UKSI), (originally referred to in the document as a 'National Academy of Sport'), a proposal which was broadly inspired by the Australian Institute of Sport (Pickup, 1996). Subsequently, a number of decision and policymaking processes could be observed, relating to decisions over the establishment of the UKSI, including the selection of priority sports; choice of partners in the process of the construction of bids by cities or consortia to host the UKSI; the selection of best bid proposal and others which are presented in detail in the first part of the results' section below. The aim of this chapter is to outline features of these processes from a managerialist perspective and to explain how such policy proposals are implemented in what became a key battle between competing cities (or urban consortia) to attract this prestigious initiative.

Setting out to investigate decision making related to the making of the UKSI the underpinning rationale is founded on the notion that decisions are important parameters of organisational life. It is argued that the dynamics of organising in structured societies created a need for decision-making (Miller *et al.*, 1996). Indeed, as earlier studies have suggested (Mintzberg, 1973; Stewart, 1983) managers spend a large proportion of their time making decisions. In the context of the making of the UKSI, a further reason for investigating decision-making concerns the significance of the new Institute to British sport, performers and administrators. Decisions can be viewed as being fundamentally concerned with the allocation and exercise of power in organisations and as Miller *et al.* (1996: 293) suggest:

> The making of decisions, especially the larger, consequential ones which govern what things are done and shape the future direction of the organisation and the lives of people within it, are of vital significance to organisational stakeholders. The study of decision-making is crucial to the comprehension of how and why organisations come to be what they are and to control whom they do.

Ministerial statements have emphasised the importance of the creation of the UKSI in improving prospects for British élite performers. As the Minister for Sport argued (Banks, 1997: 7) in a world where sport seems to be replacing war as a measure of national ascendancy, the pressure on governments to promote sporting success is irresistible.

> But the demand for sporting success is incessant and the government is bound to respond. Unfortunately, ministers are rarely in a position to take direct action when it comes to sport. In their past wisdom, politicians have removed themselves from the central role by an arm's-length policy operating through quangos.
>
> The tendency then, for ministers to put their friends on such bodies naturally attracted accusations of hypocrisy and evasion of responsibilities. In the intensely competitive atmosphere of the sports' world, we must think and organise ourselves professionally. Otherwise we will fail.
>
> (Banks, 1997: 7)

The original name of British Academy of Sport was changed to UKSI after the general election in May 1997, with the incoming Labour government changing the name created by the outgoing Conservative government in order to place its own stamp on the project.

The decision-making processes undertaken by the government and quasi-autonomous non-governmental organisations (quangos) like the UK Sports Council (UKSC) has been reported by the press, which sought to highlight the inadequacy of the existing policy system to respond swiftly, and of the decision-makers to reach decisions. Indeed the history of delays on the UKSI project and the manifold complications involved in the decision-making process made one wonder if the various deadlines for an announcement could ever be met. At the heart of the selection problem was the in-built conflict over the UKSI's function. Was it to be primarily a powerhouse to lead a sporting revolution (major administrative head-quarters with on-site accommodation and élite training facilities) or the central offices of an agency to co-ordinate the country's existing regional facilities and develop new ones? It is argued that it was this conflict which was the prime cause of the delay. Iain Sproat, the ex-Minister for Sport, wanted the former, a showcase like the Australian Institute while the governing bodies of sport and their associations thought the latter would best meet the country's real needs (Trelford, 1997: 30).

The debate over the function of the UKSI is just one of a number that arose as a result of the policy initiative to foster and promote elite sporting performance. These are presented in further detail in the results' section.

The theoretical context: a review of the literature

In reviewing organisation decision theory, attention is given to approaches that investigate how decisions actually happen in organisations and how decision processes are affected by the broader context within which they take place. It is argued that the study of how decisions happen provides a setting for a cluster of contested issues about human action: do decisions stem from actors' choices or do they pursue the logic of rules? Is decision-making clear and consistent or ambiguous and inconsistent? Are decision processes outcomes attributable to actions of autonomous actors or an interacting epistemic community (March, 1994)? Arguably decision processes can be characterised by all of the above and the relevance of any analysis would depend on the extent to which the above extremes are used to illuminate the phenomena under investigation.

In seeking to highlight the nature of decisions made in organisations one identifies a number of characteristics of organisational decision-making. First, that ambiguity is pervasive in organisations (stemming from ambiguity in information, preferences and the history of decisions). Second, decision-making in and by organisations is embedded in a longitudinal context. That is, participants in organisational decision-making are part of ongoing processes even if they do not take active roles in all phases of decision-making. Third, incentives, penalties and their ramifications are real and may have long lasting effects. Fourth, conflict is pervasive in organisational decision-making as often power considerations and agenda setting determine decisions (Shapira, 1997).

Neo-classical economic assumptions suggest that individuals normally act as maximising entrepreneurs, with decisions aimed at a step-by-step process which is both logical and linear. Often commentators of the neo-classical persuasion left out or assumed the implementation stage and this has received criticism (Miller *et al.*, 1996). Other writers, such as Pettigrew (1973) and Pfeffer and Salancik (1978), have pointed out that decision-making may be seen more accurately as a game of power in which competing interest groups vie with each other for the control of scarce resources. This acknowledges the increased political complexity of decisions made in organisational settings. Indeed the rational mode begins to break down when faced with a pluralist vision of multiple competing interest groups vying for supremacy.

Hinings and Greenwood (1988) urge researchers to also consider the macro level where organisations can be seen to be imitative and management follow leads taken by other organisations in the sector and sometimes outside it. For example, the concept of the UKSI deriving from the Australian Institute of Sport in Canberra. Similarly, Abercrombie *et al.*, (1994) imply that the study of individual decisions in an organisation needs to consider the effects of socio-political factors. A relevant example would be the enterprise culture in Britain whereby particular strategic decisions are framed by interventionist government policies such as privatisation, reduction of dependencies and increased emphasis on the customer as a major influence in product and service decisions. Similarly, had funding from the National Lottery not been available for expenditure on sport, the UKSI project would certainly have been smaller with a more marginal impact.

The research project on which this chapter draws, has employed the aforementioned conceptual frameworks to understanding decision-making and utilised the proposed techniques for interrogating the phenomena under investigation. These aided in the operationalisation of variables employed in order to study and identify major decisions taken during the process of the making of the UKSI by looking at both government decisions and those of bidding consortia.

The research strategy

The first stage of the research included secondary data collection (government documents, ministerial announcements, press releases, newspaper articles) and analysis. These provided an insight into the context of the making of the UKSI be it political interest and rhetoric, snapshots of government decision processes as graphically presented in the press, national public perception or local criticisms in relation to particular bids. Due to the fact that different methods of translation of incidents may have been used in the various cases reviewed, documents were subjected to analytical reading and caution was exercised since the accuracy of the material (e.g. press coverage) is sometimes subject to question (Bedeian, 1980; Hakim, 1987).

The identification of themes appearing in texts of various kinds was organised into a taxonomy of issues and major events occurring in the making of the UKSI. It is argued that events punctuate the decision-making process and offer landmarks for guidance in research. To this effect a chronology of events surrounding the UKSI was created covering the period from July 1995 to December 1997 (summarised in Table 16.1).

Organisational documents relating to the bidding institutions under investigation were also reviewed and provided information on: a) the vision of what the function of the UKSI would be for each bidder; and b) the extent of consultation undertaken, the use of outside expertise, and nature of negotiations (e.g. over land development).

Participant observation was also employed at the early formative stages through participation in the consultation process undertaken by the government via its arm's length quango organisations. This allowed the observation of meetings when sport organisations were invited to express their views and declare their interests in the concept of the UKSI.

Interviews with key respondents from three shortlisted bidding consortia (De Montfort University, Sheffield and the Loughborough-based Central Consortium) and UKSC representatives were carried out and gave insightful accounts of the process of bidding and decision-making respectively. Their accounts were elicited of what went on, what issues confronted them in the process of decision-making, and how such issues were dealt with.

The broader context of the UKSI proposal

The sequence of events presented in Table 16.1 provides landmarks for our guidance in the unfolding of the story of the making of the UKSI, a project, which involved political parties, sports organisations and the press during 1995–7. It provides a chronological reference to the main events that took place and outlines the

Table 16.1 Chronological review

July 1995	John Major's announcement of the Sport: Raising the Game Programme. Publication of the respective document (which included the British Academy of Sport) from the Department of National Heritage.
Autumn 1995	Publication of 'The British Academy of Sport: a Consultation Document' by the Department of National Heritage. Commencement of the consultation process with meetings across the UK.
January 1996	End of consultation process. Deadline for written responses.
July 1996	Publication of 'The British Academy of Sport Prospectus' by the Department of National Heritage. Bidders are invited to submit plans by 31st October 1996. Publication of 'Sport Raising the Game: The First Year Report' by the Department of National Heritage.
October 1996	Twenty-six bids are received for the British Academy of Sport.
December 1996	Thirteen bids are short-listed.
January 1997	Creation of the UK Sports Council and the English Sport Council out of the old (GB) Sports Council.
February 1997	Three bids are short-listed.
May 1997	General elections in the UK.
June 1997	New Labour Minister for Sport is Tony Banks. Renaming of the Department of National Heritage to Department of Culture, Media and Sport. Labour Secretary of the Department of Culture, Media and Sport is Chris Smith. Renaming of the British Academy of Sport to UK Sports Institute.
December 1997	Announcement of the winning bid.

progression through stages such as the announcement of the project, the invitations to bidders and the final selection of the successful bid.

One of the first questions posed during the earlier stages of data collection was: why did the government propose the creation of the UKSI? Sproat (1996: 3), argues that the then government embarked on this revolution because there were problems such as low participation in sport, low performance indicators (medal scores) and alarming reports on the health of British youth, that had to be addressed.

> Problems, which were apparent to those who were working in sport and in education – to people in organisations like the CCPR – but perhaps problems which had been less apparent to the Departments, which were responsible for the policy and resources that could make things happen.

The successor to Iain Sproat, the Labour Minister for Sport, Tony Banks, agreed:

> Having inherited the concept from the previous administration, we set about designing a structure, which, hopefully, will meet the needs of our athletes, their coaches, and governing bodies. Although the term might grate, the institute should be viewed as a medals factory.
>
> (Banks, 1997)

The newly formed UK Sports Council joined forces with the Department of Culture Media and Sport (DCMS) to promote the idea of the UKSI and was centrally involved in the decision-making process. As the Chief Executive at the time declared, British sport was in urgent need of support and co-ordination in order to improve sports performance at the élite level.

> We need the British Academy of Sport to create a WOW!!! effect in British sport ... We will not create this by cobbling together a load of old tired and dilapidated facilities. We need a sharp focus for sporting excellence, which a new site will provide. It doesn't need to be colossal, but it does need to be state of the art. It needs to provide a constant and obvious reminder that we are in the business of sporting excellence. That central site needs to drive forward the network cohesively. If we leave it to the sports councils or governing bodies to do this it will not work. I am amazed, not appalled at the negativity surrounding the Academy. I am surprised at the lack of vision from within the sporting community about this project – the lack of appreciation of what this might do for British sport – and the amount of time it has taken us to grasp that fact. We need also to be selective in our decision-making. Which sports have the ability to be world class? Which governing bodies have the leadership and desire to be up with the world's best? This cannot be done on gut feeling. This must be 'a partnership to excellence' involving the British Olympic Association, UK Sports Council, Home Country Sports Councils, governing bodies, schools etc.
>
> (Wells, 1997)

The events that followed the initial announcement of the Sport: Raising the Game proposals created hope as well as tension in the sports organisations. Hope as the proposals presented the blueprint as a panacea to aforementioned problems and promised results (Department of National Heritage, 1995; Department of National Heritage, 1996; UK Sports Council, 1997; UK Sports Council, 1998). Tension as announcements were not forthcoming and the results of the extensive consultation process (to establish the needs and aspirations of sports people and organisations) did not seem to be considered (Fretwell, 1998; MacKay, 1998; Trelford, 1997; Wilson, 1998).

Interviewees also reflected upon a rather disappointing picture of the state of British sport. As the De Montfort University respondent argued:

> Sport organisations at elite level suffer from duplication of effort, rivalry ... jealously guarded secrets. There is no national policy for effective communication. There are people out there setting up different systems to do the same job. Furthermore we see suspicion and National Governing Bodies of sport unwilling to share good practice as some feel in competition with each other for the young athlete. We are not consistently bringing in success in the Olympics or world championships and yet we see fragmentation in national policy for elite sports people.

The Loughborough interviewee compared how sport is run in this country in relation to other industries. He argued that the principle of having the delivery of the mission of the organisation as a sole responsibility, without advocates and hidden agendas, is not very well understood in sport.

All respondents agreed that sport organisations operate in an arena were hugely varied interested parties exercise their power; and disentangling their interests for the benefit of sport is probably very difficult. In addition to concern expressed about the state of management of British sport, respondents commented on funding arrangements, which at the time of the interview were still unclear and appeared problematic.

Given that lottery funding was distributed by the Home Country Sports Councils (HCSCs) (i.e. the Sports Councils for England, Scotland, Wales, and Northern Ireland) and that the UKSC did not have any direct say over the allocation of Lottery funds, it appeared that whoever was to host the UKSI would have to apply to HCSCs and not the UKSC for funding. Considering the high profile that government wanted to give to the UKSC it appeared odd that this organisation did not have such powers. In addition private sector money was to be sought with the UKSI being envisaged to be run on commercial principles whereby sports organisations and individuals would spend their lottery money for services sold by the UKSI. Respondents' views on this issue reflect the uneasiness about the arrangements. The De Montfort University respondent found it unethical for the government to depend on private funding; for athletes and research programmes to be dependent upon the whims of the commercial sector. Her request was for the government to subsidise with the commercial sector providing an additional support only. The Sheffield respondent agreed that funding posed an embedded problem.

> I agree that the funding is a problem. It all comes back to short termism versus long termism. I trust that sense will prevail at the end of the day. It all comes back to the concept of getting this Institute right versus petty power politics. I mean it is the inevitable tensions, which exist in all of these things. The home nation Sports Councils, as lottery distributors, want to hang on to what they are paying for. They want to control what they are paying for.

Early in 1998 the Secretary of State announced the strengthening of the UKSC's remit, which for the first time would include direct control over Lottery funding which it would exercise independently (Press Office DCMS, 1998). Despite such reassurances funding from the Lottery remains insecure given its volatile nature. As the following response from the UKSC interviewee suggests, this particular source of funding could one day be withdrawn.

> Put it in context … both political and public. We need some success in the Sydney 2000 Olympics, so it is important to focus on a few sports up to Sydney and help government to justify investment. As for reliance on lottery funding the fact is that we need massive amounts of money. The 2001 government review of lottery funding will reconsider good causes. We are very much aware that money could go. Another good cause may be added if the public

decide otherwise. This poses a long-term threat ... we are like any business in that respect. Not being over reliant on one source of funding (e.g. Lottery or sponsorship) is therefore very significant.

Resource dependence of sports organisations is documented in both the Canadian and British contexts (Slack and Hinings, 1992; Kikulis, Slack, and Hinings, 1995; Kikulis, 1992; Theodoraki, 1996). Relationships with funding agencies provide interesting insights into the power interplay between providers and recipients and the financial crisis of British Athletics presents a vivid example of such a case where systems failed to intercept the use of public money for unaccountable practices (Chadband, 1997).

The Sheffield respondent perceived that the revenue for the UKSI would be coming from the National Governing Bodies (NGBs) who have received broadcast performance programme money and can therefore come and buy services from the UKSI.

So then what you are saying is 'all right, we'll build the swimming training tank for the swimmers at a cost of six million pounds or whatever, which is going to cost an arm and a leg to run. Will you please come and use it and pay us?' 'Well what are you going to charge, well we've got this money'. So in two year's time if they decide they will go and spend their money somewhere else, so what do we do with this six million-pound pool that we've built.

The money has got to go through the Institute; otherwise these things are not viable. The UKSC understand this point full well and with the eight sports that are coming to Sheffield we're already talking about developing the performance plan jointly so the Institute staff and the NGB performance staff talk to one another in the development of the programme, so then we know which money is coming our way and can plan accordingly. But clearly the implication of that is that it's got to keep coming that way.

It is argued that while British sport is richer than ever, its management and financial structures were in many cases, established more than a century ago. The 'Blazerati', enthusiastic amateurs promoted for long service more than their ability, often hold key positions. While the English Sports Council claim to have increased the number of checks and balances they impose on recipients of National Lottery funding, athletics is an example of what can happen if a sport does not move to keep pace with its expenditure growth. 'Governing bodies are effectively businesses now, they have to move out of the back bedroom and into the office. And remember to lock up the valuables!' (MacKay, 1998).

The parties/agents involved and their decisions

Prior to the investigation of decisions related to the UKSI it was important to identify the key players and significant agents involved with it at various stages. These emerged from the secondary data analysis and were confirmed during discussion with parties who had bid to host the Academy. They are listed below in

Table 16.2 and include: a) the nature of the composition of consortia which were involved with bidding; and b) the government and related agents/agencies that initiated the UKSI and ultimately decided on the successful bid.

Having identified the groups of interests and types of organisations who were key players the next stage of the analysis involved the identification of major decisions which in essence outline the process of the establishment of the UKSI (see Table 16.3). Again these surfaced through discussions with the various key respondents and included decisions taken by: a) bidding institutions; and b) public sector agents and quangos like the UKSC and HCSCs.

The next stage of analysis of data included the mapping of the terrain of the decisions mentioned above. The analysis takes them all in turn and presents respondents' perceptions of the decision process. These present some differences across respondents and as some of the decisions were more political and/or complex than others the variation of the views forms a tapestry of multiple perceptions of reality.

Bidders' decision to become involved

The decision to become involved with the bid was presented as strategic and rational in all of the investigated cases. As the example of the Loughborough respondent's rationale illustrates, the links of such a development with the University's strategy were obvious.

> If you take Loughborough-sporting excellence, from student participation through to research, excellence has been a characteristic of the institution for twenty years or longer and therefore it seemed to me to be absolutely right that we should be contributing to the UK Sports Institute.

It seemed logical that Sheffield with all its extensive facilities and infrastructure should bid; that Loughborough with its reputation as the Sports University should contribute to such an initiative and that DMU a fast growing University with regional centres and a strong sports tradition should invest in exploring a unique opportunity.

Bidders' decision on selection of partners

For all respondents from the bidding institutions this decision posed little complexity or ambiguity. In most cases there was an attempt to build on existing partnerships and select the most 'presentable' team which would contribute vital elements in the partnership. For Sheffield, the key partners arose naturally and they were the obvious partners to involve.

> There were issues that arose from previous processes where we realised that it was really very important to get the quality business consultants on board early in the process and so we made sure we did that quite early on.

Table 16.2 Types of organisations found in bidding consortia and organisations/agents involved with decision-making (DM); from the inception of the UKSI to the evaluation of bids

Types of organisations found in bidding consortia	Universities (e.g. Loughborough University)	Local authorities (e.g. Harnwood Borough Council)	Medical Institutions (e.g. Queens Medical Centre, Nottingham)	Consultants (e.g. KPMG, Westminster Strategy)	Sports Organisations (e.g. Lawn Tennis Association)	National Centres of Excellence (e.g. Lilleshal)
Organisations/ agents involved with DM from the inception of the UKSI to the evaluation of bids	Department of Culture Media and Sport	Ministers for Sport	Prime Ministers	UK Sports Council	Home Country Sports Councils	Consultants

Table 16.3 Main decisions made during the UKSI project

Bidders' decision to become involved	Decision on creation of the UKSI
Bidder's decision on selection of partners	Decision on function of UKSI (e.g. centralised headquarters with facilities or network) expected from bidders
Bidders' decision on function of UKSI presented in bid	Decision on successful bid

De Montfort University chose partners on the basis of their national and international repute. Most of them were people they had worked with before and had expertise that they did not have.

> The strengthening of existing partnerships was an additional motivation in some cases. The benefits of the contacts are immeasurable. They now know: a) DMU better; and b) that Bedford Physical Education is now DMU.

In all investigated cases practical considerations more than political came into play when selecting partners, and personal links were fostered and built upon.

Bidders' decisions on the function of the UKSI

When proposals where first invited by the Department of National Heritage to submit bids for the Academy, bidders presented a variety of different proposals. Some envisaged a headquarters site with adjacent facilities, others a smaller site with links to a network. Similarly the financial packages varied significantly. The short listing procedure that followed eliminated the number of alternatives to thirteen and then three, all of which could be viable options. As the Sheffield respondent claimed, all of the three finally shortlisted bids were equally workable alternatives.

> We had this evaluation panel that were involved all the way through the process to get us down to the last three and at that point it was obviously considered that in principal, any of these three bids shaped up, in terms of a site and a suite of facilities and provisions, in principal, any of these three were acceptable.

Until that stage in the process, bidding consortia were presenting a particular type of proposal but guidelines were to change and Loughborough found it more difficult than Sheffield to adapt. The Sheffield respondent referred to the Secretary of State's request in November 1997 to amend bids to deal with eight specific sports. Before that the three bidders were all bidding for different sports and so the scale of business was varied and it was difficult to make straight comparisons. The correspondence that bidders received from the Secretary of State in the middle of November made it quite clear that he expected to see how well bidders tuned the bids to a new set of requirements. The new term 'cohesive' was introduced. This had a clear impact on the Central Consortium bid, the Loughborough respondent argued, but not upon anyone else because they were effectively single sites.

> ... it was decided upon by lawyers, I was told and it has no legal definition. So it was very difficult for us to address it. We did our very best and in some quite difficult discussions in which a lot of maturity was shown around the table actually by others, I don't claim it! But Lilleshall agreed that if we would back them for part of the UKSI related network then they would step off from being formally part of the Consortium. We enquired and enquired, did cohesive mean single site and all of the feedback that we had was no, it did not mean single site. We had this privately through No.10 advisers, and right at the end we had a meeting with someone from the Department of Culture Media and Sport, we asked them directly, did it mean single site. The answer was 'No' it did not. So we agreed to go forward, Loughborough with Nottingham access.

For the Central Consortium, the decision over the function of the UKSI to propose in the bid presents a case of little choice. Following the move of the goal posts in the eleventh hour, a compromise of their initial bid was inevitable.

Government's decision on the creation of UKSI

As regards the origin of the idea the literature suggests that plans for an Academy of Sport were existent as early as 1975. Goodbody (1997) reports that the ex shadow minister for sport Tom Pendry claimed that there were no original ideas in the whole of the *Sport: Raising the Game* document. When asked if Labour would support the location and role of the Academy, Pendry in a way pre-empted the developments that were to follow:

> We are certainly in favour of the Academy in principal. However, we don't know if we would run with the location and role because we don't know whether we want to continue with something on which we have not been consulted. Unlike the Tories, if we come to power we will involve the opposition in talks about this. We have a different view from this Government. We see the Academy as being smaller than it has been planned and concentrating on generic services, such as sports medicine and research. It would be at the centre of a network of other sites, like Bath, Loughborough, etc.

It was argued that Iain Sproat led the Conservative's initiative of the Academy following his visit to the Australian equivalent where he saw a solution to the problems of elite performers in the UK. The Atlanta 1996 Olympics placed added emphasis on the need for the Academy as low medal scores worsened public perception and morale was low. John Major's announcements in 1995 (Department of National Heritage, 1995) spoke of a unique opportunity to develop the UKSI to mirror the Australian model with money which the availability of Lottery funding provided.

Government's decision on the function of the UKSI

Following the 1995 Sports Council publication *The British Academy of Sport: A Consultation Paper* (Sports Council, 1995) written responses were invited and twelve open meetings were held in different parts of the United Kingdom. This process attracted 1,600 people who attended the meetings and approximately 600 written responses were received (Department of National Heritage and The Sports Council, 1996). According to the analysis of the responses the concept of UKSI as the pinnacle of a network of regional institutes and sports specific academies received wide support. Sixty per cent of the written responses argued that the UKSI should be established as a combination of a central site aligned to a network of institutions. Seven per cent thought there should be a network only while three per cent thought there should be a central site with no network.

Respondents from the UKSC commented on the effect of the general election in May 1997 and subsequently the new government on the decision over the function of the UKSI.

> The general election meant a big delay. We saw a change of administration and the Labour Government took time out to look at the ideas. There was support from the beginning but they wanted to see the details. The government came back in September–October with a new view of smaller headquarters and a network. The change of the name came forward as UK encompasses Northern Ireland. John Major wanted the decision before the election but the consultation process was very thorough and not at all rushed. The selection process evolved through the open bidding. Then the short listing was done and we had consultants at every stage. They offered good value for money and their advice was sound. We were able to compare bids equally on financial terms as regards the budget, the design and the support services. Obviously there were senior people from the DCMS and the UKSC involved. We had an evaluation committee and consultants were also involved. The UKSC finally made recommendations to the Government and the Secretary of State.

Respondents from the bidding consortia presented similar views on what was needed but the Loughborough respondent argued that the government did not seem to listen:

> Whatever the government of that day might say it (the UKSI) came over very much as being a big centralised thing, preferably on a greenfield site, and I chaired a review for a sports panel for the Committee of Vice Chancellors and Principals and a Standing Committee of Principals, these are all the higher education heads, and we argued for a lean hub towards a distributed regional delivery, drawing on the best that there is. This is what we argued for. That

was in the consultation period. That is a possible vision. This was certainly somewhat different from the big, huge criticised mass greenfield site which the government was envisaging, and I think at that time wrongly envisaging because the model of Australia itself has moved on since then, and so what we are putting in place may or may not be as good. It shouldn't model Australia because it is for us and we are a smallish country but I would just like to see something happening.

The Sheffield respondent claimed that what the government proposed was what their bid was delivering and what sports organisations were asking for.

> The sporting world said that they wanted a network of sites. The sites must be accessible and it helps if sites could facilitate a wide range of service delivery so that if you come into the Institute it's all there for you. Everything you need is there, you don't have to go two miles down the road to this University for that service and three miles over there for that facility, time is precious. The exception is the freshwater training for the triathlon and the cycle track. But in essence it's all there.
>
> When they did the consultation they asked everybody to say if a HQ site was developed, would you move your sport work there? Would you relocate and develop a national league-training centre there? And the eight sports that were listed either said definitely yes or probably yes.

Both respondents seem to agree that the big bold centralised site was not what the sports world called for. As the Labour Government came back in September–October 1997, after the general election, with a new name and a view of smaller headquarters facilitated by a network, the function of the proposed UKSI was redefined.

Government decision on successful bid

The Labour Government revised the guidelines and invited short-listed bidders to respond to the new criteria. It might appear that Government power was not absolute (given the inclusion of independent advisors on the panel) when the decision was taken. This needs to be investigated not merely against criteria of quality of the bids but also in light of both the underlying political considerations and priorities of national regeneration policy. As the Loughborough respondent described:

> In the end the decision was made after three rigidly hour-long presentations and discussions and everyone was going to be locked in a room. It was a huge meeting of people that came to the presentations at the DCMS on the 17th December. My personal reaction to that is that it is hard to believe the government wasn't going into that without having a pretty preconceived idea of what it wanted, in fact an outcome, and we have had it from a number of sources who are extremely well placed and understand it that the issue of the

regeneration of Sheffield was strongly on the table on December 17th. So that was a significant fact. I would say that it wasn't so much our dealing with the government as our prejudice about some of the criteria that they might tactically have adopted.

I don't know whose decision it was in reality, although I am sure it was the Government, because on that final day we presented to a grouping which consisted of members of the UK Sports Council, the Chairmen and Chief Executives of the Home Country Sports Councils and five Ministers, which were Chris Smith, Tony Banks and the three ministers responsible for sport in Wales, Scotland and Northern Ireland. Now whose decision was it? It was a decision that emerged from that group around half past two or whenever it was, that afternoon. There were clearly within that grouping some figures who are more influential than others and who might have had a leaning one way or another.

The interplay of party political considerations and power issues figures prominently in the above statement while the rationale of the decision is left unresolved for the Sheffield respondent to defend.

Frankly I just think we blew them away on the 16th December. We went in there, and we'd done everything we'd been asked to do: We illustrated our methodology allowed us to make these changes without it being a big deal, our philosophy didn't have to move because it was the right philosophy in the first place. Also, we were able to give the value added dimension that we were already a network, we were already centralised on one site, this coherent argument that the Secretary of State's letter had made a big deal of was well illustrated. Also, we were cheapest and we demonstrated that we could fine-tune our requirements quickly in the light of what had been required and present a coherent set of financial and usage data and frankly I just don't think the other Consortia were at that level of sophistication at all.

Originally ranked as an outsider, Sheffield appeared to burst through on the home straight. When making their decision, the Government and the UKSC stated that the city presented the best case for a number of reasons. Primarily, it provided a cohesive site with good transportation and infrastructure; it had responded well to the revised vision set out by the government and the bid built on existing investment in sport. Ironically in 1989, the city proposed that the facilities built for the Games should be used afterwards as an Academy of Sport. Clearly at the time the idea was too radical for sport in the UK and funding was not forthcoming (Sutcliffe, 1998). It may be ironic that the UKSI project had to wait for nine years for the financial conditions to be right (or for crisis to be felt) but it is sad that 26 organis-ations or consortia had to spend hundreds of thousands of pounds in bidding to host UKSI. Despite the resource-intensive nature of the UKSI project a select few have benefited: a) Sheffield's leadership as it won the bid; b) the government, since it enjoyed free consultancy by inviting open bids; and c) the unsuccessful short-listed bidders as they have generally maintained a good fall back position. Sport, however, the intended recipient of any benefit, seems to suffer. At the time of writing, two premier Olympic sports (athletics and swimming) had refused to move to Sheffield, and others, including, in particular, cycling were still considering their decision, the implementation of the investment in the UKSI, given its declared rationale, remains elusive.

Conclusions

The central results of this research project relate to: a) the context within which decisions related to the UKSI were taken; and b) respondents' perceptions of the decision process. Government intervention in sport has been seen as an extremely cheap method of raising national morale, strengthening a sense of national unity, and enhancing British prestige abroad (Hargreaves, 1986). Given this assertion one can suggest that the government chose to create the UKSI in order to enhance sporting performance which would in turn strengthen morale and improve the electorate's views on government performance. John Major genuinely felt that the *Sport: Raising the Game* proposals presented a solution to the problems elite sport was facing. The availability of Lottery funding at a time when so much was needed by so many in British sports, came as a blessing. The urge to do something and spend while the money was available and the Conservatives were still in power created added momentum for the UKSI operation. The prospectus came out and an open bidding process commenced which, given the loosely defined government specifications, involved bidders carrying out their own extensive consultation process and market review. Against this background the Sports Council was undergoing its own transition with the creation of the UKSC and the clarification of the complicated funding distribution arrangements.

During the whole process of the UKSI project, aspects of political rationality, as well as the enactment of power, feature clearly. Evidently, the decision to create the UKSI was the product of a rationale. The need was clearly felt – in principle – by sports organisations, the timing was right, the funding was available and the political benefits were considerable. Similarly, bidders' decision, to become involved with the project and form partnerships with established counterparts was in line with their institutional priorities and longstanding strategies.

As regards the decisions surrounding the function of the UKSI presented by bidders, issues were highly controversial and complex as bidders had to both produce viable proposals to benefit NGBs/other sport organisations and at the same time be able to adapt swiftly to changes in the government's criteria. The Government's decisions over the function of the UKSI appear to be the most contested issues in the history of the project. Here, rationality does not feature prominently. On the contrary, decision processes evidenced over this matter were often constricted around central agents/key organisations (UKSC and two governments) and repeatedly failed to consider the unanimous voice of sports organisations like the NGBs of sport.

It appears that there are two ways of explaining this attitude. Either that they were never truly clear on what they wanted the function to be, or that they had to keep altering the parameters depending on the power balances at various points in time. Although this research did not aim to reveal the exact nature of the power games, it provides alarming evidence to support the latter suggestion. These decisions were at the centre of machinations and intrigue, which the press was particularly critical of. Party political involvement and the power structure of the key players presented earlier posed a highly political and complex backdrop against which the function of the UKSI was debated and discussed.

Finally, the decision over the selection of the successful bid provides the climax of the decisions over the function of the UKSI. It is argued (Miller *et al.*, 1996) that the understanding of decisions in organisations is inseparable from the organisation of our understanding, the material available and the ways in which we choose to analyse it. Different respondents provided different accounts of the process of this decision and defended their position. While for Sheffield the decision was presented as expected as they had clearly met all criteria and done their home-work, Loughborough was disillusioned with the manoeuvring of the goalposts before the ultimate presentation of the revised short-listed bids in December 1997.

Although some of the decisions attracted less attention, were less controversial, or required work to be done by relatively fewer people, others were a whirl of interested activity. The amateur ethos, voluntarism and the cultural specificity of sports organisations might account for some of these findings. The visibility and popular nature of sport may account for the high levels of political 'interference' while the existence of numerous policy agencies may account for fragmentation and complexity.

Conceptual perspectives investigated and the results of the study suggest that: a) a multidimensional approach is needed for dealing adequately with the complex phenomena of decision-making; and b) the agents' accounts of decision processes alone are not sufficient for understanding the process of decision-making; interaction effects and environmental influences (macro and micro) must also be considered.

This chapter has sought to provide an account of the framework within which cities bidding against one another for hosting the UKSI had to operate, and to illustrate ways of understanding this. There is clearly a contrast between seeing decision-making as a functional prerequisite of effective organisation and seeing it as a maelstrom of political activity and sectional conflict, where power games are played out in an arena which is only partially open to view. While the former is often presented by some stakeholders (particularly those who hold most power, or who are most successful), the latter is clearly reinforced by the overall pattern of evidence emerging from this research project.

References

Abercrombie, N., Warde, A., Soothill, K., Urry, J. and Walby, S. (1994) *Contemporary British Society*, 2nd edn. Cambridge: Polity Press.

Banks, T. (1997) 'Time to pay the full price if you want top-quality goods: My resolution for New Year'. *The Observer*, December 28, p. 7.

Bedeian, A. (1980) *Organisations: Theory and Analyses.* Illinois: Dryden Press.

Chadband, I. (1997) 'Running on empty'. *The Sunday Times*, October 19, p. 8.

Department of Culture, Media and Sport, Press Office (1998) Reply to Parliamentary Question from Jim Cunningham MP. Department of Culture Media and Sport.

Department of Environment (1975) *Sport and Recreation.* London: HMSO.

Department of National Heritage (1995) *Sport: Raising the Game.* London: Department of National Heritage.

Department of National Heritage (1996) *Sport: Raising the Game. The First Year Report.* London: Department of National Heritage.

Department of National Heritage and The Sports Council (1996) *The British Academy of Sport: Prospectus.* London.

Fretwell, S. (1998) *Competition in a Political Arena: the Making of the United Kingdom Sports Institute.* Unpublished MSc., Loughborough University, Loughborough.

Goodbody, J. (1997) Labour's Day. *Ontrack*, pp. 15–17.

Hakim, C. (1987) *Research Design Strategies and Choices in the Design of Social Research.* London: Allen and Unwin.

Hargreaves, J. (1986) 'The State and Sport: Programmed and Non-Programmed Intervention in Britain', in L. Allison (ed.), *The Politics of Sport*, pp. 242–261. Manchester: Manchester University Press.

Hinings, C. R. and Greenwood, R. (1988) 'The Normative Prescriptions of Organizations', in Zucker, L.G. (ed.), *Institutional Patterns and Organizations: Culture and Environment.* Cambridge, MA: Ballinger.

Kikulis, L. (1992) *Strategic Change in Organizational Design of National Sport Organizations.* Unpublished Ph.D., University of Alberta, Edmonton, Alberta.

Kikulis, L.M., Slack, T. and Hinings, C.R. (1995) 'Toward an Understanding of the Role of Agency and Choice in the Changing Structure of Canada's National Sport Organisations'. *Journal of Sport Management*, Vol. 9(2), pp. 135–152.

Levin, P. (1996) *Making social policy: the mechanisms of government and politics, and how to investigate them.* Buckingham: Open University Press.

MacKay, D. (1998) 'Murky waters dredged up in Bland affair'. *Observer*, May 17.

March, J.G. (1994) *A Primer on Decision-Making: How Decisions Happen.* New York: Free Press.

Miller, S. J. *et al.* (1996) 'Decision-Making in Organizations'. In S.H. Clegg, C. Nord, W. (eds), *Handbook of Organization Studies*, pp. 293–312. London: Sage Publications.

Mintzberg, H. (1973) *The Nature of Managerial Work.* New York: Harper and Row.

Pettigrew, A.M. (1973) *The Politics of Organizational Decision-Making.* London: Tavistock.

Pickup, D. (1996) *Not Another Messiah: An Account of the Sports Council 1988–1993.* Edinburgh: Pentland Press

Pfeffer, J. and Salancik, G.R. (1978) *The External Control of Organizations: a Resource Dependence Perspective.* London: Harper and Row.

Shapira, Z. (1997) (ed.), *Organizational Decision Making.* Cambridge: Cambridge University Press.

Slack, T. and Hinings, B. (1992) 'Understanding Change in National Sport Organisations: An integration of Theoretical Perspectives'. *Journal of Sport Management*, Vol. 6(2), pp. 114–132.

Sports Council (1995) *The British Academy of Sport: A Consultation Paper* (Consultation Paper). London: Sports Council.

Sproat, I. (1996) Sport: Raising the Game. The Government's Strategy for Sport: Department of National Heritage.

Stewart, R. (1983) 'Managerial Behaviour: How Research has Changed the Traditional Picture'. In M. Earl (ed.) *Perspectives on Management: a Multidisciplinary Analysis*, pp. 82–98. Oxford: Oxford University Press.

Sutcliffe, M. (1998) 'John Alderson'. *Sports Management*, pp. 8–10.

Theodoraki, E. (1996) *An Organisational Analysis of the National Governing Bodies of Sport in Britain.* Unpublished Ph.D., Loughborough University, Loughborough.

Trelford, D. (1997) 'Academy process set to run and run'. *Daily Telegraph*, January 28, p. 30.

UK Sports Council (1997) *Doorstep Delivery for Britain's Brightest Sports Stars.* London: UK Sports Council.

UK Sports Council (1998) *UK Sports Institute (HQ and Network) Menu of Technical Services* (Draft). London: UK Sports Council.

Wells, H. (1997) The Future of British Sport and the British Sports Councils. Speech to British Olympic Academy, Loughborough.

Wilson, N. (1998) 'Olympic big guns turn their backs on Academy'. *Daily Mail*, Friday November 6, p. 71.

17 Sport matters

Urban regime theory and urban regeneration in the late-capitalist era

Kimberly S. Schimmel

> Sports! … With their galvanizing effect on the human spirit, sports offered an attractive way to draw people's attention and enlist their cooperation in a partnership across the lines that so easily divide them … Sports could motivate people to rally round. They have an energizing effect that other causes – such as building a steel mill or making us the insurance capital of the country or improving city housing – just do not posses.
>
> (William H. Hudnut III, Mayor of Indianapolis 1976–1991, cited in Hudnut, 1995, p. 97)

I will return to Mayor Hudnut's comments at the conclusion of this chapter. Whether or not one embraces the romanticised view of this former Indianapolis Mayor, it is difficult to ignore the notion that sport matters. From Manchester to Melbourne and Calgary to Cleveland, civic leaders tell us that sport is good for the city-as-a-whole. So while the research examples presented in this chapter are embedded within the US context, the themes will be relevant to a number of urban contexts. Like John Crompton, C. Michael Hall and others in this volume, I will seek in this chapter to present a critical view of sport in the city.

At the outset, I would like to make the following assertions. First, there is no city-as-a-whole that benefits uniformly from sport-related economic initiatives. Urban development strategies produce winner and loser social groups. The fact that urban policy connected to sport 'motivates people to rally round' (in Mayor Hudnut's words) is cause for concern, not celebration. Second, our analyses of sport events, or stadium development impact, or sport as 'wise investment', must include an examination of the broader urban context in which sport is located. In other words, while micro-analyses might be useful in separating economic myth from reality; they are usually studies of projects, not the urban policies that legitimate them. Policies are not made by 'cities', they are made by people who have various material interests in and differing understandings of the decisions that are made (Stone, 1987). In addition to the fact that sport matters, is the fact that politics matters.

Investing in sport in the US: stadium boom, or boondoggle?

In the US context, privately owned professional sport franchises receive huge public subsidies. Within the last two decades, public investment in professional sport has escalated mostly in the provision of supplying tax-supported stadiums to team owners. It is fair to say that currently the US is undergoing a stadium boom – publicly funded stadium construction has recently been completed or is underway in Baltimore, Jacksonville, Nashville, St. Louis, Columbus, Cleveland and Cincinnati. The events that have taken place in the two Ohio cities of Cleveland and Cincinnati illustrate the extent to which the American public is literally 'buying into' professional sport and the stadiums that house them.

Located on the banks of Lake Erie, Cleveland, Ohio's second largest city has for years been the target of taunts from outsiders. Known to most of the US only as 'The Mistake on the Lake', its image problems are rooted in its rustbelt past. In the mid-1980s city officials and private entrepreneurs collaborated to construct a strategy for economic and civic image enhancement. Included on the agenda were a new $180 million baseball stadium (Jacobs Field) and $150 million basketball arena (Gund Arena) – collectively called Gateway Complex – and a planned $175 million football stadium renovation. The baseball franchise's participation in the 1995 World Series provided a national stage for both civic leaders and local sports fans to display the city's new 'successes'. Sending a retort to the national television audience, a handmade banner flew from the upper deck of Jacobs Field during game three of the Series that read: 'NOW do you believe in Cleveland?"

Whatever national envy existed during the October Series certainly came to an end in November when professional football franchise owner Art Modell announced plans to relocate his Cleveland Browns to Baltimore. The conflicts and turmoil included in the months to follow threatened not only the 'comeback' image of the city, but also the very existence of the civic leadership group that constructed the economic development policy. Despite the fact that the Gateway project was on the verge of bankruptcy, 'officials' in Cleveland 'made a deal' with the National Football League requiring the city to construct a new lakefront stadium in order to 'save the Browns'. In Cleveland, construction has begun on a new $280 million, tax-supported football stadium. This, despite the fact that Gateway Complex is $20 million in debt, has an annual operating deficit of more than $1 million, and owes $600,000 in unpaid Cuyahoga County property taxes. In essence, Cuyahoga County voters approved a plan that equated the building of tax supported, deficit-ridden stadium construction with community development.

Located on the banks of the Ohio River, Cincinnati, Ohio's third largest city relishes its image as a 'major league' town and staunch defender of conservative family values. It is a city seemingly more at ease clinging to an idealised past than fashioning a strategy to meet the future. The professional baseball franchise – the first in the major leagues – has for decades enforced an edict forbidding its players to wear facial hair. In 1990, Cincinnati caught the nation's attention by suing its own Contemporary Arts Center for 'pandering obscenity' in hosting a Robert Mapplethorpe exhibition. In the words of Mike McConnell, a midday-talk-show host of the city's radio station: 'Cincinnati would be happy if the river changed course and made the place an island and it wouldn't be Cincinnati, Ohio. It'd be Cincinnati, Nowhere'.

However, in the early 1990s Cincinnati's inability (or unwillingness) to plan for the future reached a crisis-point. The downtown was in severe decline: major department stores were moving out, the 887-room Clarion Hotel was bankrupt, office vacancies were at 20 per cent, and the city's $50 million attempt to build a new skyscraper existed as nothing more than a parking lot. Further, owners of both professional sports franchises voiced growing concerns about the conditions of outdated Riverfront Stadium. In 1993, the President of the Greater Cincinnati Chamber of Commerce broke with the city's isolationist tradition and led a contingent of business leaders to Cleveland – the butt of a generation of jokes – to see how that city had managed to 'transform itself'. In 1994, pro-growth leaders in Cincinnati launched a $20 million advertising campaign supporting an increase in the local sales tax to finance the construction of two downtown, state-of-the-art sports facilities. In 1995, Hamilton County voters approved the tax-supported, $544 million stadium construction plan – the largest in North American history.

Brookings Institute Economist, Roger Noll stated in 1974 that the history of stadium development in the United States has been written in red ink. Given the number and location of American cites that are currently developing or planning new stadiums, it is reasonable to predict at the time of writing that by the year 2000, not one major league sport franchise will have to share a facility with another tenant. Has anything changed in the 24 years since Noll's statement? Evidence, some of which will be presented in this volume, suggests not. Yet despite their weak economic justification, questionable grounds of social good, and dubious distribution of burdens and benefits among community residents, a stadium has come to symbolise civic health. Given this context, one might be compelled to ask: If stadium development is an urban solution; what must have been the problem? And who was empowered to define the 'problem' in the first place?

One of the more troubling peculiarities of the US urban context, says urban sociologist Harvey Molotch (1993), is the perception that overarching social problems should be handled at local levels and that 'more development' is the solution. The US urban scene is contoured by a doctrine of home rule that implies that cities and communities can best handle 'their own' problems, even though realistically they are only tangentially place-related. Local level politicians are expected to 'do something about' the cumulative effects of various broad-scale social ills (violent crime and structural unemployment for example) that manifest themselves in local areas. Coupled with this expectation, is the fact that locally elected officials are held accountable for problems (such as fiscal shortfalls and decaying infrastructure) that are authentically place-connected. The solution for many politicians is to 'do something' by manipulating the use and regulation of urban land, one of the few autonomous realms of local-level governance. The result is the ideological hegemony of pro-growth politics and the use of public subsidies for convention centres, urban shopping malls, retail anchors – and I would add (because Molotch does not mention) sports stadiums and arenas. In many cities, these projects are trumpeted as 'successful' not because of any objective assessment about their benefits to local residents, asserts Molotch, but rather because of the symbolic power attached to the edifices themselves. What they point to is a 'something' that can be done, and their mere presence colours local perceptions and builds political careers. As Susan Zukin (1991) has demonstrated in her book *Landscapes of Power*, because these urban centres contain the types of glamorous landscapes – a concept she uses to embrace material practices as well as aesthetic forms – that now symbolises revival, they are read as urban triumph. Neither Molotch nor Zukin include specific analysis of sport in their work. This seems to me curious; especially given the fact that stadium development is steeped in political/symbolic power, requires more public money, more urban space, more infrastructural support, and can alter the urban landscape more than any other urban project.

In the 1970s and 1980s, nearly every professional sports franchise in the US demanded a new stadium and other benefits. Threats, either implicit or explicit, to relocate their teams to another community accompanied each demand. These types of tactics are not unique to the professional sports industry. 'Playing the field' – encouraging inter-city bidding wars – is a standard feature of US capitalist system. In a confrontation between a firm and a city, says Charles Euchner (1993), 'the city is like a boxer with his shoes nailed to the ground' (p. 167).

The quest for capital accumulation and the mobility of firms vis-à-vis cities and communities means that cities must compete with one another for capital investment. Firms are mobile, cities are not. Capital that promises investment and growth can also threaten disinvestment and decline. The tensions and conflicts caused by mobile capital has been a defining characteristic of urban politics in the late-capitalist era.

Studying the urban context: the critical perspective

The critical urban studies paradigm emerged in the US in the 1970s as a challenge to mainstream urban social science. Readers of Marx, Weber, and more recent European sociologists Henri Lefebvre, David Harvey, and Manuel Castells criticised the dominant perspective which was heavily influenced by the ideas of Herbert Spencer and was ultimately linked to Social Darwinism. Lefebvre's book *La révolution urbaine* (1970), Harvey's critical articles published in *Social Justice and the City* (1973), and Castells' book *The Urban Question* (1977) have been identified as landmarks in the incipient development of a paradigmatic alternative to traditional US urban sociology. Both Harvey and Castells moved to the United States from Europe in the 1970s and continued to publish in the area of urban development, thereby stimulating other scholars who joined them in producing new urban work (Feagin, 1988).

In the late 1970s and early 1980s, critical urban scholarship flourished in the US as investigators influenced by the work of Lefebvre, Harvey, and Castells began to develop a new perspective of the urban condition. Emphasised in this new perspective was the importance of analysing particular features of capitalism in any assessment of urban life. The dynamics of urban structures and space were seen to be contoured by state involvement in capital investment patterns, class conflict, and unequal resource distribution (Feagin, 1988). Michael Peter Smith's book *The City and Social Theory* (1979), for example, critiques mainstream urban sociology by providing an analysis of an activist state and corporate capital in shaping urban form. Urban planning is a 'value-laden' activity, says Smith, and urban planners serve a political function which is to 'cloak the major private bene-ficiaries of land-use and investment decisions that have shaped contemporary American society, justifying profit seeking behaviour as beneficial to the larger public interest' (p. 253). Through a case study of Houston's economic development policies, Smith provides evidence that the state 'contributed directly to the tragedy of desperate poverty amidst opulence' (p. 248). Subsequent critical scholarship focused on the capitalist state has resulted in a variety of theoretical approaches to the analysis of the state's role in urban development.

In the mid-1980s, David Harvey and Manuel Castells were again at the forefront of critical urban analysis. Both published ground breaking books that sought to place urban political phenomena within the context of the universal tendencies of contemporary capitalism. For example, the problematic explored in Harvey's books *The Urbanization of Capital* (1985) and *Consciousness and the Urban Experience* (1985) is, 'Can we derive a theoretical and historical understanding of the urban process under capitalism out of a study of the supposed laws of motion of a capit-alist mode of production?' (Feagin, 1988, p. 22). For Harvey, the answer is yes. Similarly, Castell's book, *The City and the Grassroots* (1983), generalises to a capitalist system in searching across cultures and through history for the common-alty of urban social movements. In five lengthy case studies, Castells' concern is to demonstrate that urban social movements are 'collective actions aimed at the transformation of the social interests and values embedded in the forms and functions of the historically given city' (Castells, 1983, p. xvi). Throughout the 1980s many leftist scholars in the US including Stephen Elkin, Susan and Norman Fainstein, Joe R. Feagin, Mark Gottdiener, Richard Child Hill, Clarence Stone, and Alan Whitt among others, continued to contribute to a growing body of critical urban literature that included sophisticated theoretical discourse and empirical case study research.

As this body of knowledge grew, so too did the diversity of the specific perspec-tives taken by adherents to the broader critical urban paradigm. Because of the fecundity of Marxist thought and the variety of its interpretations, a number of different approaches to urban analysis developed. Paradigmatic refinement has lead to wide variation over the relative weight of the economy, the social production of space, the significance of political processes, and the role of the state in urban development.

Throughout the 1990s critical urban studies scholars have continued the challenging task of disentangling political aspects from urban processes. According to Molotch (1993) the single most useful concept in this endeavour is the 'growth machine'. Whether labelled as 'growth machines' (Logan and Molotch, 1987; Molotch, 1986), 'growth coalitions" (Mollenkopf, 1983; Swanstrom, 1985), 'governing coalitions' (Stone, 1987), or 'urban regimes' (Elkin, 1985; Fainstein and Fainstein, 1983), the basic premise is the same: local level urban policy is produced through the proximate actions of interested actors. I will refer to these groups as 'urban regimes' – they are interest groups with common stakes in urban development who use their political and cultural resources to intensify land use for profit. This perspective on urban inquiry emphasises the diverse politics of local situations and recognises that urban regimes not only develop different agendas, but they also have differing abilities to implement them (Horan, 1991). Clarence Stone (1987), whose case study of Atlanta was seminal in the construction of the regime paradigm, points to three factors the shape the specifics of local urban growth:

- the composition of the community's coalition for growth;
- the relationships among the members; and
- the resources available to the coalition.

However, the interconnections between development policy and political arrangements remain under explored territory. Urban studies researchers in the 1990s, say the regime theorists, must intensify their efforts to more fully understand the ways in which political actors shape urban areas. Given this scenario, I suggest that the time is right for sport studies researchers to begin a broad-based agenda that explores the ways in which the sport industry is being used by local growth regimes in their plans for urban development and regeneration. As we have seen, sport facility construction is implicated in numerous cities' attempts to redevelop their cores and stimulate local economies. An important aspect of this research agenda should be to focus on who constructs and supports these policies and what the material consequences of these plans are – for example the effects of local shifts in employment opportunities and the isolation of certain segments of the population from 'important' (i.e. the new city centre) parts of the city. This focus may be especially fruitful now given the current state urban distress and the current stadium boom. More and more cities are building sport facilities that require larger capital investments, more urban space, more skilled political manoeuvrings, are supported by more growth advocates, and garner more media attention than any other time in urban history. Is it possible that these policies also bear deeper distinctions between burdens and benefits among local populations? We await systematic investigations, but even brief excursions into these issues can be revealing.

With this in mind, I will highlight aspects of a larger case study I completed on the City of Indianapolis, Indiana – a city that has been called the 'Cinderella of the Rustbelt' by urban growth advocates. It is the site of one of the most intensive and successful growth coalitions in the US. Parts of this research are reported elsewhere (see Schimmel, 1995). Data for this project included formal interviews with Indianapolis civic leaders, public and private memos, media reports, local government policy statements, and census and employment data (see reference list).

Indianapolis: a showcase for growth

Indianapolis is a mid-western US city that, like many others, was facing in the mid-1970s a complex set of social and economic challenges. Prior to its new growth strategy, the backbone of the local economy was heavy manufacturing. Especially prominent were factories connected to the automobile industry. This made the city vulnerable to capital disinvestment and firm mobility spurred by national economic downturns and foreign competition. In order to regenerate 'Naptown' civic leaders argued, it would be necessary to build and promote a new image of the city. The problem, according to local leaders, was not that the city had a bad image, but rather that the city had no image at all. Local growth advocates decided to attempt to transform Indianapolis from a sleepy mid-western town into a white-collar tourist and corporate headquarters centre and to target the nation's expanding service sector economy in an attempt to redevelop the city's downtown. Perhaps realising the city's aesthetic limitations, public officials and local entrepreneurs collaborated to use sport as a foundation on which to build an amenity infrastructure. Leveraging the sport industry as a tool with which to build a national image and buttress large-scale brick-and-mortar projects, from 1974 to 1984 a total of $1.8 billion in public and private resources was invested in inner-city construction. The 'sports strategy' would, argued growth advocates, bring national reputation, capital investments, and jobs. In many ways, Indianapolis may be viewed as a counterpart to Sheffield in the UK. In fact it has been widely reported that Sheffield city leaders used Indianapolis as a model for designing and implementing a strategy for growth anchored by sport.

Although lacking in 'natural' attractions, Indianapolis is not without geographical assets. First, it is located near the geographical centre of the nation and quickly accessible from both coasts. Second, five US highways and four interstate highways converge on the city, making it within one day's drive for 60 per cent of the US population. Millions of potential tourist either drove through (or flew over) the city annually. Third, because it has no natural boundaries such as mountains, coastlines or large neighbouring cities Indianapolis has plenty of room for development. For example, the downtown area covers seven square miles and the central county (Marion) in the statistical metropolitan area covers about four hundred square miles. With these factors in mind, regeneration efforts were aimed at enticing private capital and luring large conventions and affluent tourists and residents to the downtown area. City leaders entered the 1980s with a determination to put their city 'on the map'.

Completion of this goal would be no small feat. In the 1980s the core of the city was dirty and filled with vacant dilapidated buildings. Businesses and residents were fleeing from the central business district. When city officials reviewed development patterns they discovered an almost total mismatch between areas targeted for development and areas where development was occurring. According to the city's 1980 growth policy review, residents were moving away from places where capital investments in schools, thoroughfare and shopping existed. In areas where services, facilities, jobs, and tax bases were limited, the resident population was increasing. This lead the city's Department of Metropolitan Development to state: 'The result is the underutilization of developed areas of the county leading to abandonment, isolation of low-income groups, and a reduced tax base'. Reflecting on this time, the Director of the Indianapolis Department of Metropolitan Development in the early 1980s recounted to the *Indianapolis News* (November 13, 1989):

> We had nothing downtown, If our goal was to create a city nobody wanted to live in, we'd done it. I just make the comment that the mayor would mortgage his mother-in-law to get jobs in downtown Indianapolis. We couldn't get anything down there (p. A7).

The Director's comments are reflective of city leaders concerns about the 'empty' downtown. However, overlooked is the fact that people did live there. In fact, in 1980, 208,624 residents lived in the city's centre most township (aptly named Center Township). The community know as Midtown was a vibrant centre for African-American residents. The Midtown Jazz festival, held each summer, was one of the city's largest cultural attractions. However, not only were these residents overlooked in discourse about the emptiness of the downtown, this sub-community's needs were seemingly not counted among the problems that the 'city-as-a-whole' faced and that growth strategy aimed to solve. I suggest this is a result of the composition of the urban regime that constructed the agenda for Indianapolis' regeneration.

The composition of the growth regime

With respect to planning and implementation of Indianapolis' growth agenda, the influence of the Eli Lilly Company cannot be over emphasised. In August 1972, Indianapolis Mayor Jim Lugar met with Eli Lilly (at Lilly's invitation) to discuss the city's future. Lilly, who was 87 at the time, was the son of J.K. Lilly, Sr, co-founder of Eli Lilly & Company, one of the largest pharmaceutical concerns in the world. The company was founded in 1876 in Indianapolis (where it remains). Eli Lilly, his father, and his brother (J.K. Lilly, Jr) established a private family endowment in 1937. According to James H. Madison, an Indiana University historian who wrote Eli Lilly's biography:

> The Lilly brothers knew their father was not going to live forever, and they knew that upon his death, they would pay large inheritance taxes. Putting stock in the foundation was a way for many families to keep outsiders from controlling the business.
>
> (Quoted in *Indianapolis News*, November 13, 1989, p. A7)

The Lilly Endowment, Inc. was founded with $280,000 worth of stock, and by the early 1970s would contain assets of $1.2 billion, making it the second largest (behind the Ford Foundation) charitable foundation in the United States (Nielsen,

1985). Eli Lilly was still president of the Lilly Endowment, Inc. in 1972 when he met with Mayor Lugar.

The Lilly family had always been active in philanthropy, making frequent and generous contributions to Indianapolis charities. However, the Tax Reform Act of 1969 requiring that foundations pay out at least 5 per cent of their assets meant that the Lilly Endowment, Inc. would have to begin making much larger contributions (up to $50 million per year). Lilly family donors believed strongly that the endowment should focus on Indianapolis and Indiana. Recalling his meeting with Lilly, Lugar told the *Indianapolis News*: 'He told me that he was prepared to recommend a sizeable benefaction to the city of Indianapolis and looked forward to my counsel on what it might be' (November 13, 1989, A1). Lugar suggested the restoration of the city market to which the endowment eventually donated $5 million. According to the *Indianapolis News*, Lugar and Lilly did not meet again after this first meeting. However, in 1973, Jim Morris, who had been Mayor Lugar's top aide since 1967, left Lugar's administration to become an officer in the endowment's community development division.

In 1977 Thomas H. Lake, former president of Eli Lilly & Co., was named president and chairman of the Lilly Endowment, Inc. Although the two organisations are legally separate, there have always been close connections between them. For example, the company's chairman has always been on the endowment's board of directors. Over the years former company employees, like Lake, have joined the endowment. According to Waldmar Nielsen (1985), a member of the endowment's board once questioned former Eli Lilly & Co. CEO Eugene Beesley about the propriety of exchanging members back and forth between the company and the foundation. Beesley is reported to have replied, 'I know its questionable and can't last but we will keep on doing it as long as it is legal' (p. 289). During his years with the company Lake's known enthusiasm for sports balanced his reputation as a staunch buttoned-down executive.

At the same time as Lake assumed his new position with the endowment, Mayor Lugar's former aide, Jim Morris, was promoted to vice president with increased responsibility for community development projects. Morris had witnessed the political machinations of urban development from the inside and had forged important corporate community connections through his experiences with the eminently skilled Lugar. Morris, too, had earned a reputation as quite a sports enthusiast. Through his travels with Lugar, he had the occasion to see the role that sports played in other cities. Morris would continue to rise in the ranks at the foundation, eventually becoming president in 1984, replacing Lake who became chair. Jim Morris would become the single most influential member of the city's growth coalition.

In the late 1970s board members of the Eli Lilly & Co. had become increasingly concerned over the condition of Indianapolis. As one of the city's largest employers (7,442 in 1989) and a Fortune 500 company, Eli Lilly & Company's interests in the community were quite keen. As expressed by Harris Ulman, runner-up in the 1984 Indiana gubernatorial election, and publisher and editor of the *Indiana Letter*:

There was a concern by the Lilly company about the quality of life and the ability to attract people to Indianapolis. Executives, scientists, technicians, are highly mobile and can go anywhere.

(Personal communication, September 24, 1992)

Ulman's comments appear accurate. The Fantus Study, commissioned by the Chamber of Commerce in 1972 with a Lilly Endowment, Inc. grant, read in part:

Living conditions are a factor of increasing importance in corporate location decisions ... A company located in a community offering superior living conditions enjoys a significant advantage in recruiting and retaining executive talent ... Executives may refuse to transfer to a location where it is likely that their standard of living or style of life will undergo a change for the worse.

Apparently, Lilly's interest in the Fantus study's conclusions was well known among civic insiders. Sidney Weedman offered the following details:

Eli Lilly Company was recruiting some of the best minds to work for them and there was a high number of them that said 'no' ... in the exiting they would ask them why [the recruits] turned them down ... the city did not have the quality of life these people were looking for. So Lilly had a vested interest in the city having a quality of life, altruism aside ... The company and the endowment are two separate entities but there are conversations I'm sure. The endowment was on a mission to revitalise downtown.

(Personal communication, October 20, 1992)

Weedman served as director of a small group of corporate élites whose organisation became a tool through which the endowment channelled capital resources.

Being well-versed in the style of Indianapolis politics, Morris met informally with public officials and corporate élites who would be likely to have an interest in and who could be of assistance in planning and implementing a strategy designed to enhance the city's 'quality of life' for middle- and upper-class populations. According to the *Indianapolis News*, one important meeting occurred in the late 1970s. Morris and Robert Kennedy, director of the Department of Metropolitan Development, met privately to discuss the city's direction. During the meeting, Morris handed Kennedy a one-page list of 'big ticket' projects that Morris said the endowment would consider funding. He offered Kennedy the advice to 'think bigger' on projects than the city had in the past. Morris told the *Indianapolis News* that he did not recall handing anybody a list of projects, but he recalled talking to a number of people about ideas. According to Kennedy, the list provided,

the scope and breadth of things they [the endowment] would like to see happen in the town. It shed a whole new light on how you think about the possibility of getting some things done. Things that you never thought possible before. All of a sudden ... you think 'My God, we can really get some things done'.

(Quoted in *Indianapolis News*, November 13, 1989, p. A8)

With the realisation that the Endowment's considerable financial resources were available to 'get things done', discussions concerning a growth strategy became more enlivened and more frequent. Representatives from the Greater Indianapolis Progress Commission, the Corporate Community Council, the Mayor's office the Department of Metropolitan Development and the Lilly Endowment, Inc. met formally and informally throughout the 1980s to devise and implement the city's agenda for development. In addition to these institutional groups, an informal but exclusive group of young executives began meeting regularly with Jim Morris to discuss the way in which downtown revitalisation and economic development should proceed. The group, active throughout the 1980s, called themselves the 'city committee'.

Whereas the city committee represented the young establishment, the Corporate Community Council (CCC) was the group with the real power. When a recommend-ation for a project was developed, 'if the Mayor liked it and Lilly liked it, the business community would get involved' (T. Binford, personal communication, October 8, 1992). As explained in the *Wall Street Journal*, CCC was composed at 'the chief decision-makers' of the largest firms in Indianapolis and was founded to place corporate resources behind 'selected projects' (July 14, 1982, p. A1).

Though in large part it was comprised of second-tier executives, the most powerful local corporations were represented on the city committee. Not surpris-ingly, that included local banks, insurance companies, law and architectural firms, and Eli Lilly & Co. Also represented were the mayor's office, the Department of Metropolitan Development, and the state legislature. No members of the locally elected 29-seat city-county council were ever extended invitations to the exclusive club. Democratic state representative, William A. Crawford was the committee's only African-American member. Crawford told the *Indianapolis News* that his inclusion on the committee put him in the position of making sure issues important to African-Americans 'hit the table'. Nevertheless, the urban development strategies that were devised for Indianapolis, in part by the city committee, evidence clear class and race bias. The ways in which the 'city's problems' were defined and the solutions aimed at solving them were shaped by the interests represented in the coalition. Improving the 'quality of life' in the downtown was clearly seen by the coalition to be of great concern. The question begged is, improvement for whom? In reference to the city committee, Louis J. Mahern, Jr, Democratic state represent-ative and early city committee member said:

> These were by and large white middle-class males who view the world a bit differently. If you say, 'What are the problems in downtown Indianapolis?' inadequate housing might not be the first thing that occurs to them. The need to ensure that we have good public schools might not be the first thing that occurs to them, because their kids may be at Park Tudor or they're at North Central or they're at Carmel [suburban schools]....
>
> (*Indianapolis News*, November 14, 1989, p. A5)

The city committee existed, said many of its members, to 'dream' about what Indianapolis might become. The city resident identified as being the most visionary was Jim Morris, of the Lilly Endowment, Inc. Not insignificant is the fact that Jim Morris sat on the city committee. He was joined by the vice president of finance and chief financial officer (James M. Cornelius) and the Director of financial development (Ronald D. Henriksen) of Eli Lilly & Company. Referring to his activities with the city committee, Morris stated:

> One of the central themes of my work there was the importance of downtown. Indianapolis is a city of about 300 neighborhoods, but the downtown is one neighborhood that belongs to everybody.
>   The idea of the endowment's involvement was to be supportive and helpful to *good* [emphasis added] ideas that would cause Indianapolis to become that special community.
>   (*Indianapolis News*, November 13, 1989, p. A8)

Between 1978 and 1988, when the city committee was most active, the endowment spent $140 million on 'good' downtown construction project ideas. I would like to suggest that not only did these gifts hasten the implementation of development projects (e.g. constructing sport facilities), they also served as a 'foot-in-a-door' technique for legitimising these projects. In other words, large philanthropic gifts to (what is presented as) state-proposed development may help to construct consensus by implicitly suggesting that the projects are 'worthy' or will be good for the 'community-as-a-whole'. The public may therefore be more compelled to support such projects, especially when they feel they have the opportunity to obtain them at a discount price (i.e. minus the sum of the gift).

This does not mean, however, that the other members of the city committee or their corporate bosses determined the way the endowment spent its money. Thomas Lake (of Lilly Endowment, Inc.) expressed this point quite clearly:

> It may be that this was a group of people that communicated easily together and talked about things and it may be that, yes, we funded some of the things that came out of the ideas of the city committee. But as far as the city committee setting our agenda, no way.
>   (*Indianapolis News*, November 14, 1989, p. A3)

In fact, more evidence suggests that the city committee was one vehicle by which the endowment implemented its agenda. Although local public relations campaigns were successful in attributing the city's growth strategy to Mayor Hudnut, growth coalition insiders say that it was Jim Morris who determined that sports should be used as an urban growth vehicle. His vision got fleshed out through the city committee and public (i.e. visible) organisations – some of which were born out of city committee meetings.

In his 1995, semi-autobiographical account of the 'Indianapolis story, ' former Mayor Hudnut underscored the importance of the Lilly Endowment:

> Supplying the glue that held it all together was the Lilly Endowment. Across the country, as I tell the Indianapolis story, people ask whether we could have

accomplished what we did without Lilly Endowment. I always say no. Indianapolis would not be what it is today without the tremendous support for these initiatives – and many others – from the endowment. Its generosity during the past 20 years has been a blessing (p. 98).

Critics of the Indianapolis story do not agree with Mayor Hudnut. One of those critics is Waldmar A. Neilsen, who in 1985 published *The Golden Donors,* an historical analysis of American philanthropy. In his analysis of the Lilly Endowment, Inc., he makes the following statement about the Lilly/sport strategy connection (specifically in reference to the funding of the Hoosier Dome):

> In the history of American philanthropy, there has never been a foundation expenditure of equivalent size given on weaker economic justification, more questionable grounds of social benefit, and more dubious distribution of benefits among local politicians, profit-seeking entrepreneurs, and the needier elements of the population (p. 295).

Implementing a growth agenda

In 1980 a document (Regional Center Plan), prepared for the Department of Metropolitan Development by Hammer, Siler, George Associates outlined to the year 2000 the city's revitalisation objectives. The 300-page report focuses exclusively on the downtown.

> The image of the downtown area serves as constraint to some market groups. Crime is perceived to be a major problem, as is security of private personal property. Also, the predominance of lower income households in the central area creates an overall *image* [emphasis added] of poverty households living in substandard and overcrowded housing. Most downtown neighborhoods are not safe, pleasant, and attractive neighborhoods that most *new* [emphasis added] homeseekers would consider (p. 165).

This segment of the Regional Center Plan suggests that problems related to Indianapolis' downtown had to do with the perceptions that outsiders have of it, rather than the reality of life for its residents. According to Jim Morris, 'the sports strategy was a part of community development, of helping to build an infrastructure for a community' (*Indianapolis News,* 15 November, 1989, p. A12). This type of legitimating argument was not well received by large segments of the city's racial and ethnic minority populations. According to Sam Jones, president of Indianapolis' Urban League:

> Infrastructure for us means sewers, transportation … I'm not sure that we in the black and minority communities had very much input into the sports strategy …
>
> (Personal communication, 30 October, 1992)

Nevertheless, between 1974 and 1991 over $168.05 million (in 1991 dollars) was invested in downtown state-of-the-art sports facilities. Among the most expensive were: (a) a $21.5 million, 5,000-seat swimming and diving complex; (b) a $6 million, 20,000-seat track and field stadium; and (c) a $2.5 million, 5,000-seat velodrome. Funding for these projects was provided by public and private sources. The local state provided grants, tax abatements, and industrial revenue bonds. As illustrated in Table 17.1, the Lilly Endowment contributed $60.6 million to sport facilities.

Interestingly, the Hoosier Dome, the city's and Lilly's largest the largest investment (in terms of physical size and financial cost) was something of a Trojan Horse sports facility. David Carley, former Director of the Indianapolis Department of Metropolitan Development explained:

> You see we wanted to [build] a stadium and it met with resounding negativism everywhere. So, about that time we were looking to expand the Convention Center. So we said OK, we're going to expand the Convention Center, we're going to add 200,000 square feet of meeting space on, and oh, by the way, it's going to have this multi-purpose room attached, which has this inflatable ceiling, seats 60,000 – but the floor can be used for exhibits. And honest to God, we sat around the table at the Mayor's office and took a vow that we would never call it anything but the Convention Center Expansion.
>
> (Personal communication, 20 October, 1992)

The 'Convention Center Expansion' is a 60,300-seat structure and one of only six air-supported domed stadiums in the United States. It contains 99 luxury suites that each accommodate up to 16 guests and a projection screen with instant replay capabilities. Six weeks after Mayor Hudnut announced the philanthropic community's investment in the stadium, the Indiana legislature passed a bill authorising the city-county council to enact a 1 per cent food and liquor tax on all restaurants and taverns in Marion County to back revenue bonds. Announcement of the new tax prompted law suits from local citizens who opposed the stadium project. Their sentiments were likely expressed by Julia Carson, Center Township trustee:

> I had difficulty supporting a stadium [the Hoosier Dome] when our schools are woefully underfinanced and other city services are inadequate. The mayor and the Lilly Foundation wanted the stadium, so it was built. That's the way things get done here.
>
> (Personal communication, 14 September, 1992)

Not surprisingly, the Hoosier Dome was promoted by Mayor Hudnut as a wise investment for 'the community'. The growth ideology that justified such a conclusion was clearly articulated by him:

> In Indianapolis, we are trying to leverage amenity infrastructure for economic advantage. Our commitment to sports facilities, for example, is not an end in itself. The Hoosier Dome is a job generator. It creates new business

Table 17.1 Cost breakdown of Indianapolis' sport facilities 1974–91

Facility	Year of completion	Cost in millions/ Lilly contribution
Market Square Arena	1974	$23.5/6.0
Tennis Complex	1979	$7.0/3.6
Natatorium	1982	$21.5/10.7
Track & Field Stadium	1982	$5.9/4.1
Velodrome	1982	$2.5/0.72
BMX Track	1985	$0.05/0
Hoosier Dome	1984	$77.5/25
National Institute for Fitness and Sport	1988	$12/6.0
Soccer Complex	1987	$1.3/1.0
Regatta Course at Eagle Creek	1987	$0.07/
Archery Range at Eagle Creek	1987	$0.05/
Renovation of Golf Courses at Eagle Creek	1988	$2.6/2.3 (combined for Eagle Creek Facilities)
World Skating Academy	1987	$7.0/na
Renovation of Sports Centre	1988	$1.0/0
	1990	$2.0/0
Little League Regional Headquarters	1990–91	$3.0/1.2
Total		**$168.5/60.6**

opportunities. As a result of its construction, new convention business is coming to town, new restaurants and hotels are opening up, new national organizations are moving to Indianapolis, and new people are interested in investing in our city.

(Hudnut, 1987, p. 22)

According to Hudnut and other civic boosters, the 'Indiana Convention Center and Hoosier Dome' (its official name at the time) symbolised the rebirth of downtown. Whether or not it and the other downtown amenities would serve as a magnet to 'new people' did not seem much solace to some of the city's established residents. Shadeland Avenue, on the city's east side, where working-class communities once thrived on manufacturing jobs, began to be referred to as 'Memory Lane'. When Chrysler and RCA announced they would be closing Indianapolis branches, 800 people lost their jobs. When Western Electric closed in 1985, 8,000 people were left jobless. On the west side of the city, 2,000 employees at General Motor's Detroit Diesel plant were victims of a 1982 cutback. A former Chrysler employee, who lost his $28,000 per year forklift job, told Levathes and Felsenthal (1987) that after 24 years with the company, 'it's alarming to think about having to scratch at this point in my life. But I'll think of something' (p. 24). This worker's optimism was not shared by all. Quoting from Levathes and Felsenthal (1987):

'I don't know what I'll do', said Tim Fout, 33 'The only thing I know is that I don't want my son working here'.

> To many workers the downtown development is like a mirage in the desert. 'Who are they bringing the city back for? Not for us', said Ted French, 42, a job setter, 'I pay tax on restaurant food and beverages in the city to help finance the Hoosier Dome, but I've never been in it' (p. 241).

Presumably, the Hoosier Dome/job generator, would in some way ease these residents' burdens. Perhaps this was the intention of the Lilly Endowment's $25 million cheque to 'the community'. Perhaps belief that the convention centre's 'expansion' would benefit people in need somehow justified the actions of a philanthropic institution whose traditional concerns had been related to education, science, health, religion and social services.

If this was the case, the belief was not shared by many leaders in the African-American community. In fact, one of the main criticisms of the city's growth strategy voiced by community leaders was that growth advocates were so consumed with efforts to construct facilities that the needs of downtown residents (particularly African-Americans) had been neglected. To quote Sam Jones, the executive director of the Indianapolis Urban League:

> I'm not knocking the growth, I can show you relative progress here for blacks. But we have not really been financial recipients from the massive development that has occurred, and the feeling in the black community is that while we're building a city with bricks and mortar, the inclination is to forget the human side.
>
> (Personal communication, 30 October, 1992)

Conclusion

Growth politics in Indianapolis emerged and evolved from a long tradition of alliance-building between corporate élites and eminently skilled mayors who were able to combine their financial, bureaucratic, and political resources behind 'big ticket' development projects. Designed to enhance the city's quality of life for middle and upper-class residents, sport projects were presented to the community as a way to solve local urban problems. These public and private élites, fuelled by a desire to shed their small-town image, mobilised behind a banner of pro-growth that not only sought to promote the interests of the dominant class, but also sought to legitimise political solutions by symbolically constructing consensus (i.e. by blurring conflict in the redevelopment process). What I am suggesting is a critical interpretation of Mayor Hudnut's sentiment (cited at the beginning of this chapter) regarding the 'galvanising effect' of sport and the power of sport to 'draw people's attention *and enlist their cooperation* [emphasis added] in a partnership that so easily divides them'.

Concerned that Indianapolis' 'Naptown' image put them at a competitive disadvantage for specially skilled labour and capital investment local élites fashioned a growth agenda that propagandised their visions of a good business climate and 'quality of life' throughout the population. Thus, the power of the local state and the influence of private capital merged to define and solve 'the city's' problems. The building of new sport facilities, the attempt to lure professional and amateur sports organisations, and the hosting of sports events articulated with these broader strategies of pro-growth and urban development. Given these circumstances, perhaps we can understand the cynicism of Indianapolis' Judson F. Haggerty, former Marion County Democratic Party Chairman:

> If the point is to make a city appear to be beautiful, prosperous, functioning, no matter what the real underlying problems are, then of course the Hoosier Dome and all the other things have been a success.
>
> (*Indianapolis News*, 15 November, 1989, p. A1)

In addressing issues related to sport in the city, we should the temptation to embrace the city-as-a-whole assumptions that dominate much of the discourse related to hosting professional and élite-level sport events. Though well intended, the following questions reveal much about our underlying assumptions regarding cities: Are professional sports good for 'a city"? Is a new stadium complex a wise use of 'the city's' resources? And does a sport-related development policy serve 'the public interest"? These questions are at best conceptually flawed and politically naive: at worst they lead to regressive social policy. A city is simply not a unitary entity that benefits uniformly from development policy. Further, as Gregory Stone has argued the 'public interest' that is supposedly addressed in development policy cannot be determined objectively. Public need gets defined through political arrangements of urban élites who have similar interests and concerns. People whose needs differ from those within these élite coalitions are often excluded from the planning process (see also Euchner, 1994). Sport matters. As Mayor Hudnut instructs, a sport strategy for urban development may serve as a vehicle to symbolic-ally construct consensus. However, we should also be cognisant of the fact that such a powerful symbol of common interest may also obscure other less dramatic concerns such as improving city housing, or health care, or schools, or job training.

References

Bamberger, R.J. and Parham, D.M. (1984, November) 'Indianapolis's Economic Develop-ment Strategy'. *Urban Land*, 12–18.

Castles, M. (1977) *The Urban Question*. Cambridge, MA: MIT

Castells, M. (1978) *City, Class, and Power*. New York: St. Marten's.

Castells, M. (1983) *The City and the Grassroots*. London: New Left Books.

Department of Metropolitan Development (1980) *A Growth Policy for Indianapolis*. Indianapolis, IN: Author.

Department of Metropolitan Development (1981) *Demographic Trends in the Indianapolis SMSA from 1970–1980*. Indianapolis, IN: Author.

Department of Metropolitan Development (Producer) (1984a) *Indianapolis a City in Concert* [video]. Indianapolis, IN: Indianapolis Economic Development Corporation.

Department of Metropolitan Development (1984b, August) *A Decennial Statistical Profile of Indianapolis–Marion County/1960–1970–1980*. Indianapolis, IN: Author.

Downtown Development Research Committee (1980) *Indianapolis: Downtown Development for Whom?* (Research Report). Indianapolis, IN: Author and Indiana Christian Leadership Conference.

Elkin, S.L. (1985) 'Twentieth Century Urban Regimes'. *Journal of Urban Affairs*, Vol. 7(2), pp. 11–28.

Elkin, S.L. (1987) *City and Regime in the American Republic*. Chicago and London: University of Chicago.

Euchner, C. (1993) *Playing the Field: Why Sports Teams Move and Cities Fight to Keep Them*. Baltimore and London: Johns Hopkins University Press.

Fainstein, N.I. and Fainstein, S.S. (1983) 'Regime Strategies, Communal Resistance, and Economic Forces', in S.S. Fainstein, N.I. Fainstein, R.C. Hill, D.R. Judd and M.P. Smith (eds), *Restructuring the City: The Political Economy of Urban Development*, pp. 245–281. New York: Longman Press.

Feagin, J.R. (1988) *Free Enterprise City: Houston in Political-Economic Perspective*. New Brunswick: Rutgers University.

Hammer, Siler, George Associates (1980) *Downtown Indianapolis: Economic Analysis and Development Strategy*. Indianapolis, IN: Department of Metropolitan Development.

Harvey, D. (1973) *Social Justice and the City*. Berkeley, CA: University of California.

Harvey, D. (1975) 'Class Monopoly Rent, Finance Capital and the Urban Revolution', in S. Gale and E. Moore (eds), *The Manipulated City: Perspectives on Spatial Structures and Social Issues in Urban America*. Chicago, IL: Maaroufa.

Harvey, D. (1978) 'The Urban Process Under Capitalism'. *Urban Regional Research*, Vol. 2, pp. 101–131.

Harvey, D. (1982) *The Limits to Capital*. Chicago, IL: The University of Chicago.

Harvey, D. (1985) *The Urbanization of Capital*. Baltimore, MD: Johns Hopkins.

Horan, C. (1991) 'Beyond Governing Coalitions: Analyzing Urban Regimes in the 1990s'. *Journal of Urban Affairs*, Vol. 13(2), pp. 119–135.

Hudnut, W.H. III and Keene, J. (1987) *Minister/Mayor*. Philadelphia, PA: Westminster.

Hudnut, W.H. III (1995) *The Hudnut Years in Indianapolis 1976–1991*. Bloomington, IN: Indiana University Press.

Kirch, R.V. (1980) 'Unigov Stratagem Revisited: 1979 Indianapolis Election', in A.O. Edmonds (ed.) *Indiana Academy of the Social Sciences Proceedings*, pp. 103–106. North Manchester, IN: Manchester College.

Kriplen, N. (1993) *Beyond the Games: A History*. Indianapolis, IN: Indianapolis Chamber of Commerce.

Levathes, L.E. and Felsenthal, S. (1987) 'Indianapolis: City on the Rebound'. *National Geographic*, August, pp. 230–259.

Logan, J.R. and Molotch, H. (1987) *Urban Fortunes, the Political Economy of Place*. Berkeley, CA: University of California Press.

Mollenkopf, J. (1983) *The Contested City*. Princeton: Princeton University.

Molotch, H. (1976) 'The City as Growth Machine'. *American Journal of Sociology*, Vol. 82, pp. 309–332.

Molotch, H. (1993) 'The Political Economy of Growth Machines'. *Journal of Urban Affairs*, Vol. 15(1), pp. 29–53.

Neilsen, W.A. (1985) *The Golden Donors*. New York: Truman Talley.

Owen, C.J. and Wilbern, Y. (1985) *Governing Metropolitan Indianapolis: The Politics of Unigov*. Berkeley, CA: University of California.

Peirce, N.R. (1991) *Remarks by Neal R. Pierce*. Address to the Indianapolis Corporate Community Council, Indianapolis, IN, April.

Policinski, G. (1978) 'Indianapolis Outgrows its Small-Town Image'. *Planning*, Vol. 44(4), pp. 13–15.

Schimmel, K. (1995) 'Growth Politics, Urban Development, and Sports Stadium Construction in the United States: A Case Study', in J. Bale and O. Moen (eds), *The Stadium and the City.* Keele, Staffordshire: Keele University.

Schimmel, K.S., Ingham, A.G. and Howell, J.W. (1993) 'Professional Team Sport and the American City: Urban Politics and Franchise Relocations', in A.G. Ingham and J.W. Loy (eds), *Sport in Social Development: Traditions, Transitions, and Transformations*, pp. 211–244. Champaign, IL: Human Kinetics.

Smith, M.P. (1979) *The City and Social Theory.* New York: St. Marten's Press.

Smith, M.P. (1980) 'Critical Theory and Urban Political Theory'. *Comparative Urban Research*, Vol. 7(3), pp. 5–23.

Smith, M.P. (1984) *Cities in Transformation.* Beverly Hills: Sage.

Smith, M.P. (1988) *City, State, and Market: The Political Economy of Urban Society.* New York: Basil Blackwell.

Southern Christian Leadership Conference (1973) *Wealth, Power, and Poverty in Indianapolis.* (Research Report). Indianapolis, IN: Author.

Stone, H.T. (1987) 'The Study of the Politics of Urban Development', in C.N. Stone and H.T. Sanders (eds), *The politics of Urban Development*, pp. 3–24. Lawrence, KA: University of Kansas.

Swanstrom, T. (1985) *The Crisis of Growth Politics.* Philadelphia, PA: Temple University Press.

Walls, J.W. (1978) 'Indianapolis – An Analysis of Indiana's Urban Laboratory Since World War II'. In L.F. Schmidt (Ed.) *Indiana Academy of the Social Sciences Proceedings 1978*, pp. 21–27. Indianapolis, IN: Indiana Central University.

Whitt, A. (1984) 'Structural Fetishism in the New Urban Theory', in M.P. Smith (ed.), *Cities in Transformation.* Beverly Hills: Sage.

Zukin, S. (1991) *Landscapes of Power.* Berkeley, CA: University of California Press.

18 Sports policy research in the city of Antwerp

Marc Theeboom and Paul De Knop

Introduction

Antwerp, with a population of almost half a million inhabitants, is the largest city of Flanders, the northern Dutch-speaking part of Belgium. It is one of the largest port-towns and the most important diamond centre in the world. Antwerp has a typical demographic profile of a large Western European city of today. For example, it is characterised by a clear ageing of its inhabitants. Over the last 15 years, there has been an increase of almost 14 per cent in the ratio of senior citizens (over 65 years of age) to young people (under 15 years), resulting in a ratio of 1.21:1 in 1996. These data indicate that there is an overrepresentation of the elderly and that it is increasing over time. Also, Antwerp has a large group of Moroccan and Turkish immigrants, who are mainly situated in specific old inner city areas. Almost 50 per cent of this population consists of youngsters under the age of 20. Furthermore, there is a distinct decrease in the average size of households. Almost half of all households in Antwerp consist of only one person, considerably exceeding the national average.

Sport in Antwerp

The municipality of Antwerp has a long sporting tradition. For example, in 1920, Antwerp hosted the 7th Olympic games. Since 1937 the municipality has developed a unique leisure organisation through its education system, called 'Children's Joy' (*Kindervreugd*). This has been engaged, among other things, in offering a large variety of sports to school children aged 3 to 18 years (Corijn and Theeboom, 1989).

In 1983, Antwerp underwent a merger operation of seven former municipalities into 'greater Antwerp'. This centralisation, which had a considerable number of consequences on the structural and organisational level in general, also affected the situation of the municipal sports structures. For example, the Municipal Department of Sport and Recreation (*Stedelijke Dienst voor Sport en Recreatie*) was created in replacement of the various local sports services. By 1998, it employed around 320 people. Its major tasks included the management of the municipal sports infrastructure; the organisation of promotional activities; informing the public about sports matters; supporting the organisation of various national and international sports events; and linking different sports structures. There is also a 'Municipal Sports Council' (*Stedelijke Sportraad*), which is composed of representatives of the various district sports councils. The latter are formed by representatives of every interested sports club in Antwerp. The municipal sports council is the most important advisory body regarding sports matters to the city council. However, the Sports Council has always been very active in organising activities itself or supporting events set up by its affiliate organisations. Consequently, in 1997, the association 'Antwerp Sport City' (*Antwerpen Sportstad*), was founded to better institutionalise the sports council's active organisational role. The association is composed of representatives of the Sports Service and the Sports Council.

In the mid-1990s, a large reorganisation process was initiated at the general municipal level which resulted in an administrative structure with nine organisational units and one staff unit, thereby replacing the former 60 municipal services. The purpose is to increase the efficiency of the municipal administration and to enhance the quality of the service the city provides to its population. The sports service, which will be located in the same organisational unit as cultural affairs (e.g. cultural centres, museums and libraries), will undergo distinct structural changes with more personnel on the central and local (district) level. The aim is to enlarge the autonomy of the districts (former municipalities) and bringing the municipal sports service closer to the public (again). In a sense, this can be considered as a return to a more decentralised approach. This decentralisation process, which can also be witnessed in the reactivation of the local sports councils, is only one of the objectives that have been put forward in the policy statement that was agreed by the city political coalition for the period 1995–2000. Other objectives of the statement were:

- to use sport more as a means of social integration for its population as a whole;
- to emphasise the renovation and actualisation of the existing sports infrastructure;
- to provide more and better information to the public about the use of swimming pools;
- to attract élite sports events to Antwerp;
- to support the self-activation of sports clubs by providing them with infrastructural opportunities;
- to stimulate specific target groups to become more involved in sport (youth, senior citizens, and so on);
- to provide opportunities for non-organised sports practice;
- to stimulate the use of well-trained personnel in both managerial and guidance aspects of sport.

Municipal sports policies

According to Bramham *et al.* (1989), six categories of municipal leisure and sports policies can be distinguished. These are:

- *the minimalistic model*: authorities do not take any initiatives and leave this to the private or voluntary sector;
- *the welfare-oriented model*: authorities complement provision organised by the private sector by providing facilities to ensure equal opportunities for all citizens;
- *the profit model*: authorities stimulate and support the private initiatives. They accept an entrepreneurial style of leisure and sports policy;
- *the therapeutic model*: authorities regard leisure and sport as a means of social integration of specific target groups (e.g. ethnic minorities, unemployed);
- *the marketing model*: authorities make use of the existing (or new) sports facilities to create an attractive place for investors and tourists;
- *the cultural model*: authorities consider all forms of leisure and culture as equal and therefore support forms of popular, mass or particularistic culture.

As indicated by the authors, this classification is not exhaustive and there is often an overlap of different models in particular cases. De Graaff (1996) has described the evolution of municipal sports policies in the Netherlands and concluded that three periods can be distinguished. The first period (1975 to 1980) was characterised by the welfare-oriented model. The emphasis in most municipalities was on the provision of sports facilities. During the eighties, a second period could be distinguished as municipal sports policies were characterised by the stimulation of sports participation of target groups and a partial withdrawal of municipal tax in sport (the latter was primarily a result of financial restrictions). This period can be regarded as a kind of transfer between the welfare-oriented model and the profit model. According to de Graaff, the municipal sports policies after 1990 can be described in terms of the welfare-oriented model as well as by the profit model. De Graaff describes a number of developments which characterise the municipal sports policies during the nineties in the Netherlands:

- The use of sport as a means of social renewal which implies that sports policy is no longer only aimed at providing sports opportunities for the population, but also for other purposes such as integration and social participation of specific target groups. This policy involves also an increasing responsibility of the so called 'social centre' (including structures such as sports clubs, community centres, schools, social welfare work, etc.). This evolution is based on the fact that a municipal sports policy is no longer legitimated solely from a health-improvement perspective during a period that municipalities are confronted with budgetary problems. As a result, sports policy is revalidated because of its relevance to a more general social welfare policy.
- The increasing use of a 'directive' style of sports policy by putting more tasks in the hands of the private and voluntary sector: there is however a 'safety net' for those groups that might be left out involuntarily.
- The change from a separate to an integral policy approach in which sports policy is developed in relation to other domains such as welfare, education, urban renovation, etc.

- The shift from central policy making to a community level approach ('territorial' strategy) in order to better respond to specific local problems.
- A change from 'a provision-oriented' strategy towards a 'demand-oriented' approach in order to reduce the discrepancies between the facilities that are provided and the actual demands that exist. To determine these discrepancies, it is necessary to document and analyse the needs and situation of the population through regular research (e.g. demographic and socio-economic changes, sports demand, existing sports activity and facility provision). This approach implies a shift from facility planning based on general ideas to planning based on actual needs.
- Changes in the policy regarding subsidy to sports clubs as a result of financial restrictions. These changes include more follow-up evaluations, higher user tariffs for accommodation ('the user pays'), and lower subsidies.
- A growing emphasis on efficiency as well as an evolution from formulating vague towards more measurable and exact aims (e.g. strategic plans) and the regular use of policy and effect evaluation.
- A shift from an executive towards a more advisory and guiding role for the municipal sports structures, thereby rearranging the responsibilities between local authorities and private sector.
- Stimulating the responsibility of citizens themselves for the development of sports activities and stimulating new social groups within sport (sport on the community level). This process can be facilitated among other things by the provision of opportunities and support of community sports practice, as well as by supporting organised sports in such a way that they can better respond to demographic and cultural changes. For the traditional clubs are characterised by self-organisation, involvement and shared responsibility. These social values of sports practice are not used by developments such as the trend towards spots consumption, or passive sports practice, the increasing commercialisation and the trend towards larger entities in sports (e.g. bigger clubs). These social values, which are important within the traditional sports club structures, need to be strengthened and restored.

However, with regard to the latter, de Graaff indicated that, to date, most sports clubs are not interested in responding to these social changes (e.g. through actively attracting specific target groups). They primarily regard sport as a end to itself, not as a tool. Furthermore, this approach often requires a more professional staff, which clubs cannot afford.

Although the above-mentioned developments describe the situation in the Netherlands, several aspects are comparable to the Flemish situation. In the 1970s, municipal sports policies in Flanders could be described as 'passive' as they were characterised only by the provision of sports facilities and a specific policy on subsidy. Later on, as a result of a number of national campaigns, municipalities became more dynamic in their sports policy. This more active involvement was undoubtedly also influenced by the introduction of specific municipal sports structures (such as sports services, functionaries and councils).

Several of the above-described developments in Dutch municipal sports policies are similar to the policy measures that have been formulated by the Flemish Minister of Sport in his recent strategic plan for sport in Flanders (Martens, 1997). Among other things, this plan stresses:

- a sports policy which is part of a more general cultural and welfare policy;
- more decentralisation, which, among other things, refers to an increasing responsibility of the municipalities in the Flemish sports policy;
- more quality (of sports provision as well of the sports organisations) and a better way of controlling this quality;
- an approach where stimulation of the private and voluntary sector is preferred rather than organisation by the authorities themselves;
- more efficiency;
- an impact evaluation on all levels.

Sports policy research

Similarities can also be found between the developments in the Dutch municipal sports policies and the earlier described Antwerp policy statement (e.g. the use of sport as a means of social integration; the stimulation of the voluntary sector; the increasing decentralisation process). Here too, a shift is noticed from a 'provision-oriented' strategy towards a 'demand-oriented' approach in which more attention is paid to providing adequate responses to the sporting needs and interests of the public. Such a policy is based on a thorough insight into the demands with regard to sport among the population. At the end of 1997, a one-year study by order of the 'Alderman for Sport' was started with the intention of preparing a new sports policy for the city of Antwerp. The study (which is on-going at the time of writing) is composed of the following phases.

An analysis of sporting demand

Various groups of sports consumers are included in this part of the study and asked about their sports participation in general, their experiences with sport in Antwerp and their sporting needs:

- Participants in several activities organised by the municipal sports service or council are interviewed immediately after their activities.
- Non-organised sports participants (who practice sport frequently at least one hour per week) are interviewed at a variety of locations (e.g. swimming pools, sports halls and centres, parks). Specific questions include their experiences with the existing sports facilities (accessibility, service, prices, etc.), municipal sports provision (providing information, stimulating participation) and their acquaintance with the municipal sports service and council.
- 'Potential' sports participants (who practice sport less than one hour per week or not frequently) are also interviewed at various locations (e.g. shopping

centres, supermarkets, libraries, cinemas, railway stations, sports events, etc.). Specific questions include reasons for their low sports participation, their attitude about starting (again) with regular sports participation and their acquaintance with the municipal sports service and council.

- Representatives of organised sports (recreational, competitive and élite sport) receive a questionnaire. Specific questions refer to their own structural and organisational aspects as well as their experiences with the existing sports facilities (accessibility, service, prices, etc.), the municipal sports provision (information, participation) and their acquaintance with the municipal sports service and council.
- Representatives from specific target groups (elderly, ethnic minorities, handicapped, underprivileged youth) are interviewed.

An evaluation of the actual sports situation

Different aspects are analysed here. These include, among other things, a complete census of the sports infrastructure, sports clubs, municipal sports activities and an analysis of the financial aspects of municipal sports.

A Delphi study with expert witnesses

Policy measures can be formulated based on the data which are collected through the two previous phases of the study. In order to do this, the Delphi method is used. This social-scientific method is developed to systematically correct predictions by including experts in a scientifically guided process both as providers and processors of information. It creates an interactive process where the participants are confronted with future oriented policy innovations. The experts are chosen based on their involvement with the specific topic. Consequently, it can be expected that every member of the Delphi group has a distinct opinion on different aspects regarding this topic. Also, Delphi members are often selected based on their involvement in pursuing the actual policy as it might influence the feasibility of the suggested measures. The members of the group for the Antwerp study consist of people coming from:

- the general municipal level (e.g. education, youth service);
- the municipal sports service;
- the sports sector (recreational, competitive, élite sport);
- target groups (elderly, ethnic minorities, handicapped);
- Antwerp branches of external sports structures (Flemish sports administration; provincial sports service; Olympic Committee; Physical Education Board; etc.).

The Delphi study is done anonymously and in writing, thereby eliminating personal and psychological dominance during the discussions. Via three rounds, the experts are confronted with each others' statements and opinions. They are asked to respond to them in order to detect possible explanations, agreements and conflicts. Finally, they are asked to formulate what policy measures need to be taken. During the first round, the panel is asked to respond to the data that are collected through the two previous stages of the study (i.e. an analysis of sporting demands of sports consumers and an analysis of the existing situation in Antwerp). They are asked to indicate if, and to what extent, they feel that specific data (e.g. experiences of sports consumers, demographic changes) should be taken into account when preparing a new sports policy. In the second round they are asked to respond to each others' opinions and are provided with other data (e.g. results from other studies; existing policies in other comparable cities in Flanders and abroad). Finally, the third round is used to come to a consensus (if possible) and to suggest a strategic plan. It is important to indicate that, in case no consensus can be found (which is very likely to happen considering the composition of the Delphi panel), different scenarios will emerge. It will then be up to the authorities to decide which scenario they prefer.

A feasibility study on the suggested policy measures

The final stage of the research includes a feasibility study to determine to what extent the municipal sports service is capable of implementing the suggested policy measures. The study involves interviews with several staff members. It is important to mention here again that the sports service staff members are also involved in the Delphi study.

Conclusion

Municipal sports policies in Flanders and the Netherlands in the 1990s can be characterised by a welfare-oriented model as well as by a profit model. During times of financial cut-backs, municipalities can no longer afford to promote sport merely for its health improvement effects. Instead, sport is viewed as an important element in a more general welfare policy. For example, sport can be regarded as a useful instrument for social integration of specific target groups. Other character-istics of municipal sports policies today include, among other things, a more efficient use of resources, a decentralisation process, more stimulation of the private and voluntary sector and a trend towards a demand-oriented approach. Similar trends can be noticed in the municipal sports policy in Antwerp, Flanders' largest city. As a result of the demand-oriented approach, there is a increasing need to analyse the demands of sports consumers. Consequently, a study consisting of four phases, was set up by order of the Alderman for Sport to determine these needs and to use them as a basis for formulating future sports policy measures. The methodology of the ongoing study enables a clear involvement of a variety of people who can be regarded as interested parties (e.g. organised, non-organised and potential sports consumers; representatives of specific target groups; sports service staff members; external sports structures). It can be expected that this approach, where planning is based on actual needs and with the active involvement of those parties that are concerned, will result in a relevant as well as a feasible sports policy.

References

Bramham, P., Henry, I., Mommaas, H. and van der Poel, H. (1989) (eds), *Leisure and Urban Processes. Critical Studies of Leisure Policies in Western European Cities*. London: Routledge.

Corijn, E. and Theeboom, M. (1989) 'Leisure Education and the Antwerp School System', in P. Bramham, I. Henry, H. Mommaas, and H. van der Poel (eds), *Leisure and Urban Processes. Critical Studies of Leisure Policies in Western European Cities*, pp.102–122. London: Routledge.

de Graaff, D. (1996) *Ontwikkelingen in het Gemeentelijk Sportbeleid in de Jaren Negentig: een Verkennende Studie in Drie Gemeenten* [Developments in Municipal Sports Policy in the Nineties: an Exploratory Study in Three Municipalities] Doctoral Dissertation. University of Amsterdam, the Netherlands.

Martens, L. (1997) *Strategisch Plan voor Sportend Vlaanderen* [Strategic Plan for Sporting Flanders]. Brussels, Belgium: Ministerie van Cultuur, Gezin en Welzijn.

19 Sports policy in the city

A case study of Leeds

Peter Bramham

The direction of local government leisure policies within the UK offers an interesting insight into current claims of seismic postmodern change. The growing influence of transnational economic processes on local policy decisions demands explanation. While some commentators have traced the political centralisation of the policy agenda under the direction of New Right ideology, others in contrast, continue to provide detailed maps setting out the autonomy and complexities of decision-making in local government. What is undeniable is that local government has witnessed substantial changes with diverse cultural, social, economic and political consequences. De-industrialised cities in the UK have been at the forefront of change, as documented by the work of Taylor *et al.* (1996) on the post-Fordist cities of Manchester and Sheffield.

These studies have been paralleled by recent work on the changing focus of leisure policies in Leeds in its attempts to reimage itself as a European city (see Bramham and Spink, 1996) and more recently as a 24-hour city (Spink and Bramham, 1998). The first section of this paper provides a brief contextual intro-duction to the local politics of Leeds, while the second traces the development of a city Schools Sports Strategy and the final section provides data from a city-wide survey in 1996 of school sports provision, facilities and development.

Changing Leeds and changing policies

Local policy direction in Leeds can be presented as one of Right-Post-Fordism, following Henry's (1993) threefold typology of Fordism, Right-Post-Fordism and Left-Post-Fordism. Leeds' local policy system has complemented New Right central government policies, particularly with respect to economic redevelopment, national and local partnerships with both commercial and voluntary sectors, and by tuning policies to be in sympathy with new urban managerialism in its emphasis on compulsory competitive tendering, value for money, customer care and quality assurance. The *leitmotiv* of Leeds policies is one of local pragmatism, embedded within a ratepayer ideology and a 'contract' culture (see Bramham *et al.*, 1994). The local economy of Leeds has proved to be exceptionally buoyant even during recessions; in marked contrast to (and often at the expense of) other northern industrial cities. This sustained vitality has left Leeds well placed to cope with the vicissitudes of economic change in global, national and regional markets (see Leeds Economic Handbook, May 1997), and responding positively to new initiatives around sport and leisure.

Flexibility has meant reshaping and restructuring traditional policy systems, policy networks and processes. Under 'old Labour' during the 1960s and 1970s there was a plethora of independent departments, with distinctive chairs and officer alliances, committed to public service development within a generic welfarist policy rationale. In sports policies, there was a strong local commitment to sport for all. The city embarked upon substantial capital investment in sports facilities with the building of an international-sized swimming pool, in conjunction with the refurbishment or replacement of the Victorian legacy of swimming pools and bath houses. During the 1970s there was sustained city-wide provision of local leisure centres. Their precise location in the city was primarily a function of ward or turf politics, as councillors ensured that their ward would not be denied access to libraries, swimming pools and sports facilities. It is therefore no coincidence that 'state-of-the-art' community swimming pools and leisure centres were developed first in the wards of successive chairs of leisure services. Despite the partisan mechanisms of 'old Labour', the primary aim of departments, each with separate and distinctive policy empires, was to plan and develop services on ill-defined measures of need, particularly in relation to the disadvantaged communities in Labour-controlled wards in South and East Leeds. There was no real corporate vision of Leeds as a city, and ward politics dominated policy and planning processes.

By the 1990s there was growing pressure from the Labour-controlled city administration to organise and centralise policy around a few expanded committees. The leader of the Labour group dominated the powerful Policy and Resources Committee and disparate policy functions and practices were drawn into three major 'super-committees' – Technical Services, Community Services and Economic Development.

This internal reorganisation of committee structures produced considerable insecurity and organisational change for local politicians and officers. Traditional service functions had to be refocused in relation to the new structure and to the civic fathers' developing vision of Leeds as a European 24-hour city, as well as in response to the assault on local government by the New Right central government. During the mid 1990s there was evidence of an emergent, more flexible local state. Local politicians and planners adopted the dominant pro-business ethos and realigned themselves more comfortably with the Leeds Urban Development Corporation, the Leeds Chamber of Commerce in the Leeds Initiative, as well as with mushrooming interdepartmental task forces, chasing European and central government funding.

Destabilising and centripetal processes of internal reorganisation in Leeds local government found expression in leisure policy and leisure services during this period. Given their broad remit, it was first assumed that leisure services would report to Community Services – pursuing a welfare function alongside health, education and social services. However, it was finally decided by the central Policy and Resources Committee that leisure services would promote its tourist function and consequently, report to the Economic Development super committee. Whatever the professional discourse, this represented a significant shift from a social to an economic rationale, and from a welfare discourse to a postmodern business one.

Exacerbated by organisational change, Leisure Services were weakened by a wave of early retirement by principal officers whose careers had developed within a technical remit – in sports, parks management, museums, art galleries and so on. Introduction of a new Chief Leisure Services Officer recruited from outside traditional local policy networks, temporarily confused the picture even more. Within this kaleidoscope of changes, leisure services were encouraged to develop a new mission statement. This resulted in internal staff development as members and officers of the separate constituent parts of Leisure Services – sport/sports development, open spaces and countryside, arts and cultural services attended 'away days' to clarify rationales and objectives. These had to 'test the water' of the new policy agenda by articulating what contribution their sections could and would make to the emerging policies for the city.

Officers and members were compelled to reposition and restate their policy priorities in the light of the new policy agenda for Leeds as a 'postmodern' 24-hour European city. Policy direction was far from clear and officers sought to second guess what direction the leader's office was taking, with such slogans as 'Leeds – City of Sport', 'Leeds – City of Drama', 'Leeds – City of Heritage' and so on. These slogans took visible expression both in local authority promotional literature as well as more tangibly expressed in lights on key buildings within the city-centre core.

Squeezed by the dual centralising pressures of a New Right government in Westminster and a modernising local Labour party in Leeds, both challenging the legitimacy of traditional service delivery, one sure and safe response to policy changes was to renew databases to take accurate stock of current policies and provision and thereby reliably inform future policy directions. There followed a flurry of decisions to collect objective statistical data within the local authority. Some performance indicators were already available or research projects well underway, because of CCT contract specifications and auditing demands.

Leeds City Council also used the Policy Research Unit at Leeds Metropolitan University to develop strategic research around such topics as local labour markets, training needs, cultural industries, social auditing and local service provision within particular neighbourhoods (see Policy Research Unit publications: Piercy-Smith and Sanderson, 1992). These waves of data collection were usually driven by new inter-agency teams in order to evaluate (and legitimate) the impact of contemporary policy initiatives.

The growth of social auditing within policy communities in health and social services was a response to growing criticisms from central government and from local communities as to the relevance and efficiencies of a whole range of local government services. These criticisms of public sector provision and accountability in local government have been repeated recently by the Blair administration. Such democratic concerns, and the need to legitimate policy, drove a large-scale research initiative into young people's experience and perceptions of a range of public services in Leeds. The publication of *Finding a Voice* in 1997 signalled that Leeds politicians were trying to do something about young people in the city. Other aspects of urban policies, like that of the 24-hour city, were having a significant impact on young people's use of the city (see Spink and Bramham, 1998).

School sports strategy

It is within this changed policy context of local government that visions of policy become both attractive and pervasive. Particular visions or versions of urban policies gain momentum, achieve clarity and provide coherence and direction in the face of diversity and change. By the early 1990s the star of sport and sports policy was in the ascendancy in urban politics. The growing globalisation of sport did not bypass Leeds which now represented itself as a City of Sport by promoting the World Cyclo-Cross Championships in Roundhay Park, televised city centre Leeds Classic cycle races, in addition to international test cricket matches at Headingley. Leeds City Council traditionally had substantial involvement with Elland Road football ground which rapidly developed into an important venue for international Rugby League matches and Euro 96, as well as hosting the first soccer international played outside Wembley. Conscious of both international and Olympic aspirations in neighbouring Sheffield and Manchester, Leeds City Council invested heavily in partnerships to build a major sports stadium complex in South Leeds. Sport was felt to have not only a crucial role in city promotion and urban regeneration but also carried a plethora of positive externalities in dealing with youth and urban problems.

Growing confidence in sport in the city was shared in equal measure by central government. National Lottery funding offered a new source of capital to local authorities who had experienced cuts in capital expenditure over the past ten years. John Major's *Sport: Raising the Game* focused political debate on the vitality of the sports continuum from its foundation in schools, to participation levels within local clubs up to international standards of excellence with the establishment of a National Sports Academy. Changes in the national curriculum challenged the local authority to re-evaluate its schools sports policies and particularly sports development work. All dimensions of sports policy came under the local microscope from its foundation in schools, participation levels in local communities, performance levels in sports clubs, as well as strategies for developing regional and national excellence.

Such diverse interests and supportive visions of sport in the city gained greater focus and momentum when the city fathers commissioned consultants Knight, Kavanagh and Page in 1995 to complete a review of sport in Leeds with the intention of promoting and improving city-wide provision and access. Leeds was already adopting a Right-Post-Fordist response to change with the development of flexible inter-agency policy teams and sport proved to be no exception to this general policy shift. Indeed, one part of the consultants' report focused on the need for the council's Department of Education and Leisure Services to work closely together to deliver the sports programme for schools. Given the stimulus of *Sport in Leeds* and the configurations of local politics, there was much to be gained from a joint policy venture between Education and Leisure Services. Both departments had a shared interest in detailed city mapping of the national curriculum, schools sports provision, and sports facilities. As a result, the Schools Sports Strategy was set up with the aim of

> contributing to the development of the City Council's sports strategy by establishing a framework of sports provision in schools through curricular physical education and extra curricular based activities.
>
> (Drever, 1996: 4)

Members of the steering group included representatives from the Education and Leisure Departments. The LEA seconded a Head of PE in a secondary school to work closely with the Sports Development Unit, Advisory Inspection Service, Policy and Administration, and with schools and elected members to produce a city-wide physical education survey. Leisure Services also took responsibility to complete a detailed leisure audit of all community-based facilities within the city.

The City Council had already completed a survey of sports provision in 1992 undertaken by the Project Management Group and Leisure Services which had focused on sport in schools, sport in local authority sports centres and the work of the Sports Development Unit. The response rate to the 1992 survey was on average about 29 per cent although it was assumed that this constituted a representative sample of all schools. (The actual response rate was Secondary Schools, 37 per cent, Middle Schools, 29 per cent and primary schools 23 per cent producing an overall average of 29 per cent.) The main conclusion of the survey suggested that there was a wide and extensive provision for sport in schools, with increasing choice as children progressed through school. However, concern was expressed that excellence in sport at a senior level could only be achieved by high levels of primary school participation in curricular and extra-curricular sport, particularly through the development of clubs and sports. The survey indicated that high levels of sports participation were not being realised at a primary level and only a third of schools used the Sports Development Unit, with many schools not knowing of its existence or the services available.

The 1996 sports strategy survey

The main aim of the School Sports Strategy Steering Group 1996 was to gain an accurate picture of current physical education and sports provision in all schools, within constraints of time and staff resources. Nevertheless, it was hoped that the survey would provide a detailed local audit which could be used in similar fashion as the Sports Council's national data on *Young People and Sport* 1994, in providing a baseline from which developments in physical education and sports provision could be monitored.

The School Sports Survey set out with the following research aims:

- to measure the range of activities offered to boys and girls in the school curriculum at Key Stages 1, 2, 3 and 4;
- to collect information on how schools are addressing the National Curriculum and enable the Advisory Service to identify areas of need and to plan accordingly;
- to provide a city-wide view on sporting provision and on the opportunities for team sports participation at each stage of the curriculum;
- to collect data on the perceived in-service training needs of staff responsible for developing the PE curriculum;
- to assess the knowledge and use of Sports Development Unit services;
- to document the extent and nature of the links with sports clubs, voluntary bodies and with local Further and Higher Education institutions.

As was clear from the 1992 survey, it is one thing for the Local Education Authority to decide to survey its schools and another to achieve a high response rate from them. It was therefore essential for headteachers to become aware of and committed to the questionnaire and thereby delegate staff to complete the survey. It is common knowledge that schools are inundated with paperwork and indeed twenty of the Leeds schools were approached at the same time to complete a questionnaire for the Department for Education and Employment, *Survey of Physical Education and Sport in Schools* (1996). (Despite the generic title, the primary focus of this national questionnaire was the measurement of time devoted to 'traditional team sports' taught in the school curricula, following the government's initiative *Sport: Raising the Game*, 1995.) Information about the nature and rationale behind the School Sports Strategy was circulated through the Education Forum so as to secure headteachers' consent. The secondment of a Head of PE who had been actively involved in running PE in-service training courses locally, ensured a clear under-standing of local issues involved and some knowledge of staff who were responsible for PE teaching in Leeds. However, the Head of PE had little experience of research methodologies, questionnaire design and analysis, having to develop knowledge and skills, with consultancy support, during the research period. Pressing issues about the scope and validity of the data collected, the categories deployed and their relevance to policy makers fade under the pressure to produce a report for the council. How politicians and professionals interpret and use data to shape is another matter. (The attractions of quantitative data to inform policy are well known – such data appear scientific, neutral, objective and detached but tell us little of the *process* of delivering PE, or of the experiences of different children in different schools.)

A high response rate from all the schools depended upon several factors in the research process. These included consultation at the Education Forum, a relevant survey rationale; headteachers informed by letter that the survey was going to the school. The survey was then sent to heads of department and physical education coordinators for completion, ensuring a suitable timing of delivery into schools. Perhaps most important was the adherence to a strict 'follow up' regime. This consisted of initial phone calls to schools, letters of reminder to the headteacher, then further follow up calls to individual subject leaders. In addition, the preamble to the questionnaire argued that the survey would feed back directly into the Education Forum and, most importantly, would provide the basis for the Family School Credit Scheme. It did, however, signal to respondents that the survey was part of local authority education planning strategy and that resources would be made available, informed by the data collected.

Policy makers were keen to encourage schools to make more use of city-wide sports development services. Since legislation introducing the Local Management of Schools in the late 1980s, they lacked any direct control over school budgets and priorities. In this respect, the LEA was attempting to encourage a more integrated, responsive and coherent approach to education policy by grouping feeder schools, secondary schools and colleges into four local 'families'. Partnerships and effective use of resources were policy keywords. This can be seen as one intriguing attempt to strengthen collective provision and planning in the face of fragmentation under the New Right ideas in the 1980s.

In Leeds, the 'family' aim is

> to develop in partnership with nurseries, schools, colleges and other community education providers a range of joint curriculum and resource initiatives which will lead to the raising of overall pupil and student achievement at the various National Curriculum Key Stages and in National Education and Training Targets.
>
> (*Family News Issue*, 1 July 1995)

Prior to the 1996 survey, it was felt that resource credits could be made available to families to enable them to plan collectively their use of the Sports Development Unit over the long term, which would be kick-started by an initial subsidy which would annually decrease. The precise data from the 1996 Survey would help to add flesh on to the bones of a policy initiative already formulated.

Because of the context of the school sports strategy and a strong commitment to follow-up, the 1996 survey team achieved a much higher response rate than the 29 per cent on average earlier (Table 19.1).

Table 19.2 summarises primary school sports provision in Leeds by counting the number of schools providing different sorts of activities at both Key Stages 1 and 2 (addressing ages 6/7 and 10/11 respectively), as well as noting the gender organisation of the teaching groups. (Five primary schools failed to respond to this question in the questionnaire, leaving a sample size of 170 schools.) Some categories such as gender are on the policy agenda and more open to unproblematic quantitative measurement by quantitative surveys. Other categories such as class, race/ethnicity or ability or skill levels, whilst central to classroom teaching, are more difficult to operationalise and measure, despite their crucial bearing upon policy development.

Table 19.2 emphasises the absence of gender segregation in the teaching of the school curriculum, with at least 90 per cent of primary schools sampled offering

Table 19.1 School sample and response rate in 1996

School type	Total population	Sample size	Percentage return
Primary	244	175	72
Secondary	45	40	89
Special	14	11	79

Table 19.2 Curricular provision in primary school (number of cases)

	Key Stage 1			Key Stage 2		
	Boys	Girls	Mixed	Boys	Girls	Mixed
Athletics	2	2	113	3	3	157
Swimming	1	2	16	3	2	158
Gymnastics	3	3	156	2	2	155
Dance	2	2	156	1	1	153
Outdoor adventurous activity	0	0	35	1	1	112

mixed gymnastics and dance at Key Stage 1. Athletics is provided in 66 per cent of the schools, whereas only 20 per cent of primary schools provide opportunities for outdoor adventurous activities, and only 9 per cent of the sample offer swimming at Key Stage 1. These percentages strengthen at Key Stage 2 with at least 90 per cent of the primary schools providing mixed groups in all four disciplines of athletics, swimming, gymnastics and dance at Key Stage 2, in addition, 66 per cent provide opportunities for outdoor adventurous activities at Key Stage 2. Over 20 per cent of primary schools indicated that they taught other activities within the curriculum in addition to the categories mentioned in the above table, but only rarely specified the Key Stage level or its organisation. Of the 157 primary schools in the sample responding to the questions on games teaching – the games in Table 19.3 were listed as part of the curriculum

In the survey of primary schools, 77 per cent replied that the school organised teams, the remaining 22 per cent did not organise team sports, with 1 per cent not responding. There is an important policy issue here concerning the reasons why nearly a quarter of primary schools chose not to organise team games. This may be a function of lack of facilities, or primary school teachers having less confidence, training or involvement in sport and games. Recent policy initiatives such as 'Top Play' have started to address such issues. Perhaps of equal importance is the finding that basketball and hockey have little presence in primary school games but are far more popular as team sports in the secondary school curriculum. School team activities were ranked in order of popularity of response (see Table 19.4).

All primary schools run an extra-curricular programme, 80 per cent of the activities were offered to mixed groups, 12 per cent to girls only groups and 8 per cent to boys only. Further data need to be collected about the precise numbers of teams organised for gender groups and their inclusive or exclusive nature in sporting

Table 19.3 Games taught in the primary school curriculum

Football	Mini rugby	Badminton
Netball	Rugby Union	Volleyball
Kwik cricket	Rugby League	Short tennis
Cricket	Basketball	Baseball
Rounders	Tennis	Uni Hoc

Table 19.4 Team activities in primary schools

1	Football
2	Netball
3	Cross country
4	Rugby
5	Cricket
6	Rounders
7	Swimming
8	Athletics
9	Table tennis
10	Gymnastics
11	Basketball
12	Hockey
13	Dance
14	Angling
15	Stool ball

skills. Recent government funding has started to develop after-school clubs. There is a complete absence of extra curricular activity in Leeds Schools at Key Stage 1, with practically all extra-curricular activities (95 per cent) offered at Key Stage 2. These covered the following broad range of activities shown in Table 19.5.

Physical education curriculum in secondary schools

Secondary schools throughout the city received a separate and comparable questionnaire to primary schools, but one designed to collect data concerning the diversity of the PE curriculum at Key Stages 3 and 4 (ages 13/14 and 15/16 respectively). The figures presented below represent the data collected from 40 secondary schools, which constitutes 89 per cent of the LEA schools in this sector. The questionnaire sought to measure the variety of activities provided in the schools and the gender divisions in pedagogy, over the wide range of PE activities offered.

In the city's secondary schools, 'traditional' invasion team games retain gender divisions, as boys play football and rugby and girls play hockey and netball. Although there is some evidence of girls' involvement in traditional male sports such as football and rugby, there is far less provision for boys playing 'female' sports – for example, netball or hockey. Despite its absence from the primary school, basketball remains the dominant form for mixed invasion games provision at all stages of the secondary school curriculum. Most PE teachers hold strongly

Table 19.5 Extra-curricular programmes offered in primary schools

Aerobics	Athletics	Badminton
Basketball	Cricket	Cross country
Cycling	Outdoor adventurous activities	Golf
Gymnastics	Health related fitness	Hockey
Dance	Rounders	Rugby
Skiing	Swimming	Table tennis
Tennis		

gendered views about games and their suitability for coeducation; basketball is viewed as the least gendered invasion game (Flintoff, 1995). What is also striking is the reduction of activities and provision for post 16 year olds.

Badminton, tennis and volleyball are the dominant forms of net/wall games, with little provision for squash and table tennis. Throughout Key Stage 3, 4 and particularly post 16, these games are usually provided for mixed groups.

Within striking/fielding games there is strong mixed provision in secondary schools of cricket, rounders and softball. In terms of segregated provision, more schools provide opportunities for boys to play cricket and softball, whereas schools provide more opportunities for girls to play rounders at Key Stage 3 and 4. Once again only a quarter of the schools surveyed provide striking/field games post 16 and practically the sole form of provision is taught in mixed groups.

Half the schools surveyed provided cross country and athletics for boys, girls and mixed groups, although provision completely disappears at post 16, with only two schools providing mixed athletics.

In contrast with other areas of the secondary curriculum there are far fewer opportunities for swimming and aquatics. The number of schools teaching swimming nearly doubles (7>13) when moving from Key Stage 3 to Key Stage 4 and yet the number falls back to 7 schools at post 16 for mixed swimming provision.

Figure 19.6 documents the city-wide dominance of gymnastics at Key Stage 3 and of trampolining at Key Stage 4 and post 16.

Although approximately one quarter of the schools surveyed provide dance for boys and girls and over half the schools provide a mixed dance curriculum at Key Stage 3, opportunities are severely reduced at Key Stage 4 and they disappear altogether post 16.

All secondary schools run school teams and Figure 19.7 documents the variety of activities that offer opportunities for inter-school competition. Figure 19.7 provides an interesting comparison with the vitality of school teams in sports in primary schools (see Table 19.3). Football, netball, cricket, and athletics occupy identical ranking positions in popularity in school team provision at both primary and secondary levels. Swimming, rugby, table tennis and cross country achieve relatively higher ranks for school team opportunities in primary schools. Hockey, Basketball and Rounders achieve higher school team rankings in the city's secondary school sports teams provision. Gymnastics, dance, angling and stool ball appear at primary school level only whereas tennis, badminton, volleyball,

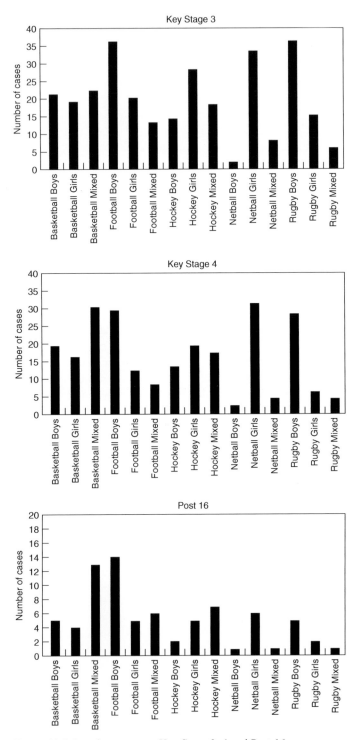

Figure 19.1 Invasion games at Key Stage 3, 4 and Post 16

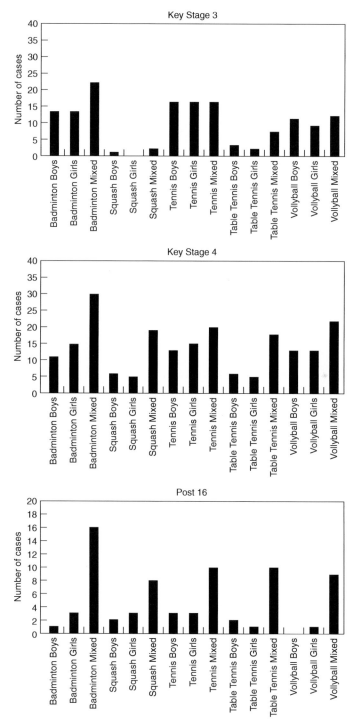

Figure 19.2 Net/wall games at Key Stage 3, 4 and Post 16

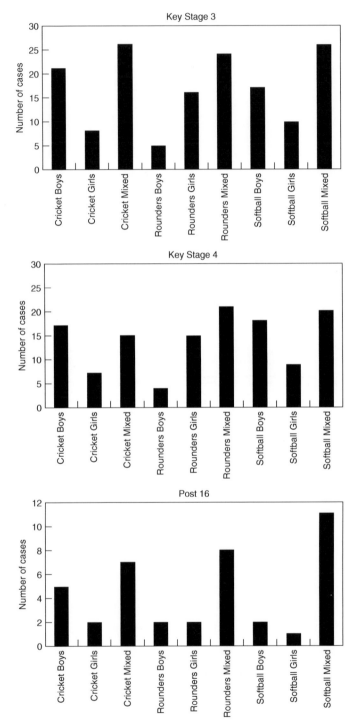

Figure 19.3 Striking /fielding games at Key Stage 3, 4 and Post 16

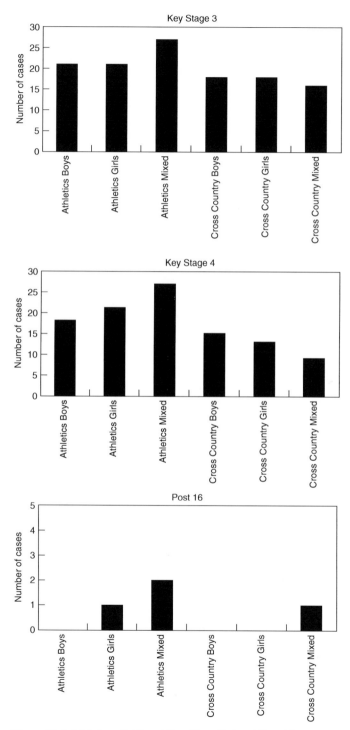

Figure 19.4 Athletic activities at Key Stage 3, 4 and Post 16

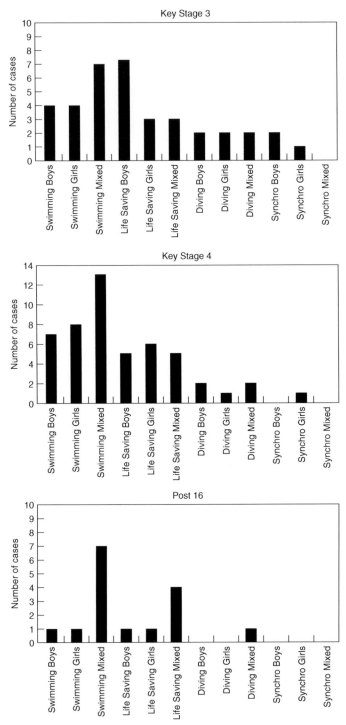

Figure 19.5 Swimming activities at Key Stages 3, 4 and Post 16

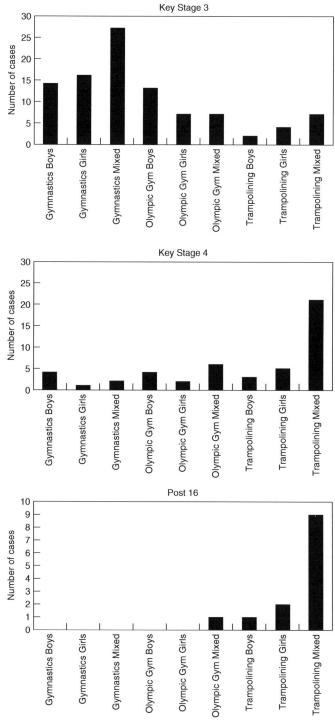

Figure 19.6 Gymnastic activities at Key Stage 3, 4 and Post 16

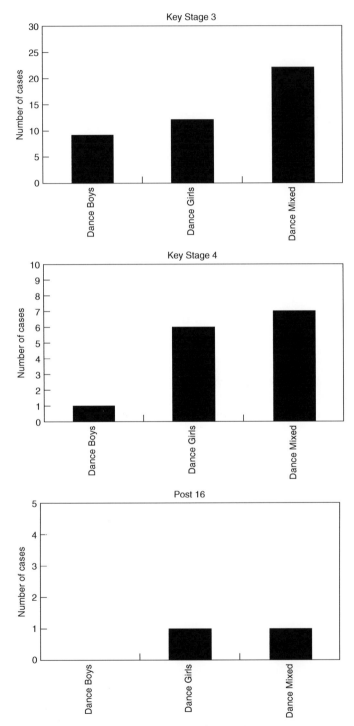

Figure 19.7 Dance at Key Stage 3, 4 and Post 16

Table 19.6 Team activities in secondary schools

1	Football
2	Netball
3	Rounders
4	Hockey
5	Cricket
6	Basketball
7	Cross country
8	Athletics
9	Rugby
10	Tennis
11	Badminton
12	Volleyball
13	Swimming
14	Table tennis
15	Softball
16	Golf
17	Ten pin bowling

softball, golf and ten pin bowling appear as school team sports only in secondary schools. The list for the secondary school sample is listed in order of popularity of response (see Table 19.6).

As with primary schools, all the secondary schools stated that they also ran an extra-curricular programme. Table 19.7 lists the diversity of programmes available within secondary schools in the city. Those activities that have an asterisk set against them are also provided in extra-curricular activities mentioned by primary schools, thereby providing continuity in extra-curricular programmes for some children (see Table 19.4). Those without an asterisk testify to the enhanced extra-curricular activities for secondary schools pupils in the city.

Extra-curricular opportunities offered to boys, girls and mixed groups were equally divided. The actual division for extra-curricular activities within secondary schools were boys, 33 per cent, girls, 32 per cent and mixed, 35 per cent. 47 per cent of activities were offered at Key Stage 3, 43 per cent were offered at Key Stage 4 and 10 per cent at post 16. This is an interesting finding given national trends, yet the data are not sufficiently detailed to measure the precise number of opportunities offered to different gender groups outside school hours.

It is clear from the primary and secondary school survey that the choice of curricular and extra curricular activities widens for pupils during Key Stages 2, 3 and 4 and that there is a marked absence of extra-curricular work at both Key Stage 1 and post 16. The precise diet of activities throughout the school curriculum follows traditional gender stereotypes in team games, whereas net/wall games, striking/fielding games and aquatics are dominated by mixed provision. However, the fact that sports are taught in mixed groups does not necessarily challenge gender stereotyping in physical activity and sport. It is abundantly clear that opportunities for physical education are drastically reduced for post 16 year olds – a situation which sits uncomfortably alongside national curriculum aims of developing active and healthy lifestyles amongst young adults. Conscious of the need to

Table 19.7 Extra-curricular programmes in secondary schools

The range of activities includes

Aerobics*	Athletics*	Badminton*
Basketball*	Baseball	Cricket*
Cross country*	Dance	Fencing
Football	Golf*	Gymnastics*
Health related fitness*	Hockey*	Judo
Netball	Outdoor adventurous activities*	Rugby league*
Rugby Union	Skipping	Softball
Squash	Swimming*	Table tennis*
Ten pin bowling	Tennis	Trampolining
Volleyball	Weight training	

encourage sports participation, the LEA has recently produced a *Directory of Sport for School Leavers* which includes a list of contacts, clubs and local addresses, as well as vouchers for free taster activity sessions at local leisure centres.

One important policy aim of the Sports Strategy was to assess the impact of the city's Sports Development Unit and school use of services. Table 19.8 presents the extent to which schools knew and used the Sports Development Unit.

The nature of the input of the Sports Development Unit is one of coaching, advice and use of facilities for Key Stage 2 and advice and facility use for Key Stages 3 and 4.

Developing an urban sports strategy

The growing interest in sport in Leeds has provided a propitious background for politicians and officers to develop new policy initiatives. Whether at the macro level of city imaging or at the micro level of school physical education, sports policy makers must be seen to be doing something within this policy domain. Indeed, the Schools Sports Strategy and the 1996 Physical Education Survey has to be contextualised within broader city visions of Leeds.

City policies are usually rooted in the past, hatched in the present, with an eye to the future. This chapter has summarised data from a city-wide audit of curricular and extra-curricular sports provision and facilities, completed in 1996. There are many ways in which empirical data can feed into policy processes. First, evidence can be deployed selectively to provide ammunition to push policy preferences already shaped in the minds of power holders. Second, surveys could be presented as a detached and technical exercise in data collection to monitor present provision and policy outcomes. Third, data could simply be ignored – as just another report, hastily constructed to meet internal contingencies and realignments in local power configurations. Finally, and perhaps more ambitiously, it could provide current informed data from which to introduce new urban sports policies. However, precise blends of traditional agendas, current practices and future innovations are contingent upon local and non-local politics. The precise flavour of sports policies and resource priorities in Leeds have yet to be determined. Whether a satisfactory

Table 19.8 School knowledge and use of sports development unit

Percentage of schools knowing of all the services of the sports development unit	
Primary	45%
Secondary	77%
Special	50%

Percentage of schools currently receiving input from the sports development unit	
Primary	23%
Secondary	25%
Special	80%

Table 19.9 Current usage of sports development unit/facilities

	Primary Key Stage 1	*No. of requests Key Stage 2*	
Advice	1	37	
Resource materials	1	17	
Use of facilities	0	21	
Coaching in curricular time	5	56	
Coaching in extra-curricular time	0	10	
	Secondary Key Stage 3	*No. of requests Key Stage 4*	*Post 16*
Advice	8	6	4
Resource materials	0	0	1
Use of facilities	6	8	5
Coaching in curricular time	3	1	0
Coaching in extra-curricular time	0	0	0

and coherent balance between school, community and elite sports can be struck is open to wider political debate. Nevertheless, city-wide audits may provide important sources for urban policy makers to deploy in the construction and legitimation of the urban sports policy mosaic.

References

Bramham, P., Butterfield, J., Long, J. and Wolsey, C. (1994) 'Changing Times, Changing Policies', in Henry, I. (ed.), *Leisure: Modernity, Postmodernity and Lifestyles.* Eastbourne: LSA Publications No. 48, pp. 125–134.

Bramham, P. and Spink, J. (1994) 'Leisure and the Postmodern City', in Henry, I. (ed.), *Leisure: Modernity, Postmodernity and Lifestyles.* Eastbourne: LSA Publications No. 48, pp. 83–103.

Bramham, P. and Spink, J. (1996) 'Reimaging the European City', in *Accelerating Leisure? Leisure Time Space in a Transitory Society,* joint conference of the British and Dutch Leisure Studies Associations, University of Wageningen, September 1996.

Drever, M. (1996) *School Sports Strategy: Physical Education Survey.* Leeds City Council.

Flintoff, A. (1995) 'Learning and teaching in PE: A lesson in gender?', in Tomlinson, A. (ed.), *Gender, Sport and Leisure: Continuities and Change.* Aachen: Meyer and Meyer Verlag.

Henry, I.P. (1993) *The Politics of Leisure Policy.* Macmillan.

Long, J., Bramham, P. and Spink, J. (1995) 'Changing Leisure Policies and the postmodern city'. BSA Conference, Leicester University.

Piercy-Smith, J. and Sanderson, I. (1992) *Understanding Local Needs.* Institute of Public Policy Research.

Spink, J. and Bramham, P. (1998) 'The Myth of the 24hr City', in Bramham, P. and Murphy, W. (eds), *Policy and Publics: leisure, culture and commerce.* Brighton: Leisure Studies Association Publications No. 65.

Taylor, I., Evans, K. and Fraser, P. (1996) *A Tale of Two Cities.* London: Routledge.

Part VII

Conclusion

20 Sport in the city

Where do we go from here?

Chris Gratton and Ian Henry

In the introduction to this book, we argued that there were strong theoretical arguments supporting the case that sport had an important role in the city both economically, in terms of being an industry around which cities could devise urban regeneration strategies and socially, through using sport for the development of urban communities, reducing social exclusion and through using sport to bring about a reduction in urban crime. Most of the chapters in this book have attempted to improve the evidence either in support of this theory or to critically challenge some aspect of the theory. This final chapter attempts to evaluate the role of sport in economic and social regeneration in the city.

A model of the relationship between sport and economic and social regeneration in the city

The economic and social benefits from sport are not independent. In achieving one, we partly achieve some of the others. These interdependencies are sufficiently important to make it essential to model all of them if we wish to estimate any one of these benefits. This naturally increases the complexity and difficulty of measuring the level of these benefits.

Gratton *et al.* (1997) suggested a possible model as shown in Figure 20.1. It links high level benefits – increased work productivity, increased health, increased self-esteem, increased quality of life, and increased employment in the local economy – through a series of intermediate outputs to some specified changes in sports activities or sports facilities. Each of these relationships (i.e. each of the links in this figure) is a hypothesis which requires to be tested. While this model attempts to demonstrate the main linkages that are conventionally suggested between sports activity and the broader benefits of sport, the strength and direction of the links in the model can only be established by empirical research. What many of the chapters of this book have shown is that, as far as the urban context is concerned, much of this empirical research still needs to be done. In general, there has been inadequate measurement of the final outputs of the model as well as the inputs and intermediate outputs. The benefits of sport for economic and social regeneration in cities therefore remains a theoretical proposition that still requires testing.

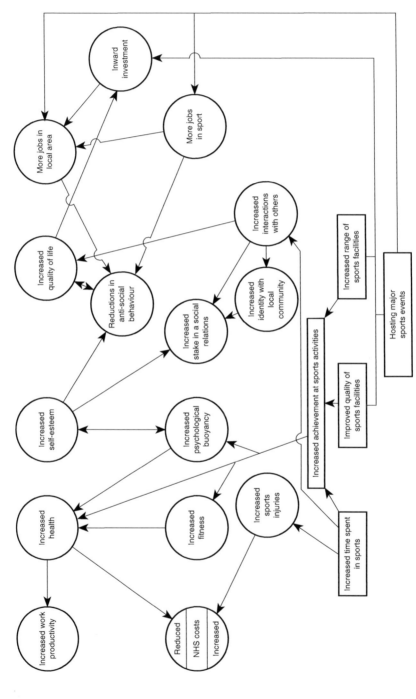

Figure 20.1 Model of relationship between sport and social and economic benefits

Sport and economic regeneration

We have seen a wide range of examples in this book of sport-led regeneration strategies employed in cities in North America, Australia, and Europe. In the USA, Cleveland and Indianapolis are prime examples where such a strategy has been employed. The main examples in Britain are Sheffield, Glasgow, Birmingham, and Manchester. These two countries are similar to the extent that the cities that have been most prominent in the use of sport for economic regeneration have employed such a strategy in response to economic decline. The Australian examples differ from the above in that cities such as Adelaide, Melbourne, Brisbane and Sydney, that have used sport as part of an economic development strategy, have been much more driven by inter-city and inter-state rivalry to establish a stronger tourism industry in that city/state.

There is a clear difference between the USA and the UK, in that the sports strategies of cities in the USA have largely been based on infrastructure (stadium) investment for professional team sports, in particular, American football, baseball, basketball, and ice-hockey. As several chapters of this book have revealed, over the last decade cities have offered greater and greater incentives for these profess-ional teams to move from their existing host cities by offering to build a new stadium to house them. The teams sit back and let the host and competing cities bid up the price. They either move to the city offering the best deal or they accept the counter offer invariably put to them by their existing hosts. This normally involves the host city building a brand new stadium to replace the existing one which may only be 10 or 15 years old. The result is that at the end of the 1990s there were 30 major stadium construction projects in progress, around one-third of the total professional sports infrastructure, but over half of all professional teams in the USA have expressed dissatisfaction with their current facilities. It is estimated that the total cost of stadium construction in the USA in the 1990s alone could exceed $9 billion (Baade, 1999).

The use of taxpayers money to subsidise profit-making professional sports teams is justified on the basis that such investment of public money is a worthwhile investment since it is clearly outweighed by the stream of economic activity that is generated by having a professional sports team resident in the city. Such justifica-tions are often backed up by economic impact studies that show that the spending of sports tourists in the host city more than justifies such a public subsidy. John Crompton's chapter illustrates that such studies have often been seriously method-ologically flawed, and the real economic benefit of such visitor spending is often well below that specified in such studies. There has probably been more empirical research investigating the nature of the link between investment in sports facilities and the creation of new jobs in the local economy than in any other part of the model shown in Figure 20.1. The problem is that the research has often been politically driven to justify the expenditure on new facilities and the validity of many of the results is questionable.

Crompton argues, however, that hosting professional teams, or major sports events, in cities may yield substantial economic benefits through increased community visibility, enhanced community image, the stimulation of other economic development and increases in psychic income. However, there has been little serious research into the evaluation of the size of these benefits and in many cases economists have not yet developed adequate methodologies for the measurement of such benefits. We are left then with a rather patchy and uneven collection of evidence consisting of a mixed bag of economic impact studies of dubious validity and case-study evidence of indicators of the potential importance of the other economic benefits. We can only conclude in the American context, the economic justification for sport-led economic regeneration strategies has not yet been proven.

The situation outside of the USA is quite different with sports events the major focus of the use of sport for economic regeneration. In the UK, following several failed bids in the 1980s and 1990s to host the Olympics, several cities followed a strategy of hosting major sports events as part of an economic regeneration strategy. Chapter 3 describes the changing policy focus in the UK towards hosting sports events with the economic success of Euro 96 leading to an increasing emphasis on raising the UK's international profile in sport by bringing world class events to the UK. Lottery funding for major international events was introduced in 1999 as a further incentive for governing bodies to bid to bring World and European Championships to the UK, and the World Class Events Programme is an attempt to coordinate policy towards international events on a national basis.

However, the economic benefits of hosting major sports events are not clear-cut. Hosting the Olympics, the soccer World Cup and European Championships generate substantial economic benefits to the host cities and as a result there is massive competition between nations and cities to host these events. Outside of these three, however, World or European Championships in some sports do not generate substantial economic benefits to host cities as Chapter 3 shows. There are other events, such as the Wimbledon Tennis Championships or the US Masters Golf Championship, that are clearly massive global events that generate significant economic impact, but always take place at the same venue and therefore are not 'on the market' for other cities that might want to bid to stage the event. Given our present state of knowledge of the economic importance of major sports events, it seems that the global demand of cities to host them exceeds the supply of economically significant events. Any single city therefore will struggle to devise an economic development strategy based on sport solely on the basis of sports events.

Australia adopted a similar strategic approach to hosting international sports events as the UK, but at State level rather than city or national level, and much earlier than the UK. The Western Australia Events Foundation was set up in 1985 to prepare an events strategy around the focus on the hosting of the America's Cup in Perth in 1987. The competition between states in Australia meant that other states quickly followed, with the Queensland Events Corporation being set up in 1989. The states provided the finance for cities to bid to bring a series of international sports events to Australia. Aitken (1999) argues that: the result of these policies is that events now are a key component of Australia's booming tourist industry and that 5 per cent of Australia's tourism income of around $16 billion is derived from major events.

In Chapter 4 of this book, Lynley Ingerson gives a positive account of how the strategy has operated in the state of Victoria. Michael Hall, however, in Chapter 11 argues that the staging of the 2000 Olympics in Sydney may generate substantial negative impacts, most notably on local residents and the environment, and this potential conflict between the generation of economic and social benefits is feature of many of the chapters of this book. If the ability of sport to generate economic regeneration in the city is still under question, what of the ability of sport to deliver in terms of social policy objectives?

Sport and social regeneration

Our conclusions regarding the role of sport in social regeneration in the city reflect those of Coalter *et al.* (2000):

> There is a general absence of systematic empirical evidence relating to the impact of sports-related projects (especially large-scale development initiatives). However, the strength of the theoretical arguments, with a range of indicative and associative information and anecdotal evidence, have led most commentators to agree that sports activities have a positive role to play as ingredients in wider ranging initiatives to address issues of health promotion, diversion from crime, education and employment initiatives and community development and social inclusion.
>
> However, there is a clear need for an improvement in the systems for monitoring and evaluation of the effectiveness of sports-centred initiatives. There is a need for clearer rationales for such programmes and greater clarity about the nature of the relationships between inputs, outputs, intermediate outcomes and strategic outcomes. Such an approach will permit the more precise identification of the role of sports, lead to more coherent design of integrated programmes, a better evaluation of their effectiveness and optimal allocation of resources.

A similar conclusion would follow from the evidence presented in Parts 5 and 6 of this book. In Chapter 12, Long and Sanderson indicate the difficulties of finding the evidence that clearly demonstrates the social benefits generated by sport and the increasing difficulties in finding funding for new initiatives simply because such evidence does not exist. In Chapter 13, Taylor and Toohey clearly demonstrate the failure of one aspect of sports policy, its lack of success in reducing social inclusion of women in Australia from non-English speaking backgrounds. Peter Taylor in Chapter 14, shows how heavy investment in swimming facilities in Sheffield in the 1990s failed to deliver the forecast growth in swimming participation in the city. Social benefits obviously cannot be generated if the initial policy intervention fails to increase the involvement in sport of targetted populations. Part 6 looks at the policy-making process in both Europe and the USA at supranational, national and local level and indicates reasons why the policy that emerges may often not be rational nor expressed in the terms of inputs, intermediate outputs, and final outputs as expressed in Figure 20.1. The case-studies also provide reasons why we do not often see rigorous evaluation of such policies.

Conclusion

The general theme of this concluding chapter is that the potential benefits to social and economic regeneration of sport in the city have not yet been clearly demonstrated, and that this is applies across the USA, Europe, and Australia. Our criticisms of poorly expressed sports policy, lack of adequate monitoring and evaluation of such policies, and lack of evidence of successful outcomes does not mean that sport does not have the potential to deliver such benefits. There is a need to target and solve the problem of output measurement and improve the level of monitoring of sports programmes whether aimed at economic or social regeneration, or both. The generally critical stance of many of the papers of this book are aimed at making sure we move to a situation where the benefits of sports programmes in cities will be able to be more clearly demonstrated to city residents than at present. If this is not achieved then obtaining funds for such programmes in the future will become increasingly difficult.

References

Aitken, M. (1999) *Major Sports Events: The Australian Experience*. Paper delivered to UK Sport's Major Events Conference, Lords Cricket Ground, London, 25th February.

Baade, R.A. (1999) 'An analysis of why and how the United States' Judiciary has interpreted the question of professional sport and economic development', in Jeanrenaud, C. (ed.), *The Economic Impact of Sports Events*. Neuchatel, Switzerland: International Centre for Sports Studies (CIES).

Coalter, F., Allison, M. and Taylor, J. (2000) *The Role of Sport in Regenerating Deprived Urban Areas*. Edinburgh: Scottish Executive Central Policy Unit.

Gratton, C., Taylor, P., Bovaird, A. and Kokolakakis, T. (1997) *A Review of the Economic Importance of Sport Studies*. Report to the Scottish Sports Council.

Index